Ed Folsom

SERIES EDITOR

Horace Traubel at about the time he was transcribing
his conversations with Whitman.
Courtesy Library of Congress.

Intimate with Walt

SELECTIONS FROM

Whitman's Conversations

WITH

Horace Traubel, 1888–1892

EDITED BY

Gary Schmidgall

University of Iowa Press
IOWA CITY

University of Iowa Press,
Iowa City 52242
Copyright © 2001
by the University of Iowa Press
All rights reserved
Printed in the United States of America

Design by Cameron Poulter

http://www.uiowa.edu/~uipress

The publication of this book
was generously supported by
the University of Iowa Foundation.

Printed on acid-free paper

Library of Congress Cataloging-in-Publication Data
Traubel, Horace, 1858–1919
[With Walt Whitman in Camden. Selections]
Intimate with Walt: selections from Whitman's conversations
with Horace Traubel, 1888–1892 / edited by Gary Schmidgall.
        p.   cm. — (The Iowa Whitman series)
Includes bibliographical references and index.
ISBN 0-87745-766-2 (cloth), ISBN 0-87745-767-0 (pbk.)
1. Whitman, Walt, 1819–1892—Interviews.   2. Poets, American—
19th century—Interviews.   3. United States—Intellectual life—19th century.
4. Poetry—Authorship.   I. Schmidgall, Gary, 1945–   II. Title.   III. Series.
PS3231.T68   2001
811'.3—dc21
[B]   2001018116

01 02 03 04 05 C 5 4 3 2 1
01 02 03 04 05 P 5 4 3 2 1

Contents

IV

V

Introduction

I am disposed to trust myself more and more to your younger body and spirit, knowing, as I do, that you love me, that you will not betray me—more than that (and in a way better than that), that you understand me and can be depended upon to represent me not only vehemently but with authority.

—Walt Whitman to Horace Traubel

On a "rainy & dark & raw" March day in 1888, Walt Whitman wrote somewhat forlornly to his journalist friend William Sloane Kennedy from Camden, the rather gritty New Jersey town across the Delaware River from Philadelphia: "Nothing new in particular with me—more or less evidences of gradual physical deterioration—but spirits good—appetite &c fair—& you know I begin my 70th year now in ab't two months—thank God indeed that things are as well as they are."

Little could Whitman have imagined that, two days later, something new and remarkable would happen to change the four remaining years of his life—and cause him many times to thank God that "things are as well as they are"—for on March 28 commenced the most astonishing oral history project in all of American letters. On that day twenty-nine-year-old Horace Traubel began to record, in a personal form of shorthand, what he thought were the salient portions of his almost daily conversations with the most famous resident of Camden—and, one might venture, of America. Traubel, indeed, tells us that one day a letter arrived from Great Britain at 328 Mickle Street addressed simply "Walt Whitman, America," and the old poet was delighted at how smartly it had reached him.

The very first of the more than 1.9 million words transcribed were a simple "At Walt's this evening." Titled *With Walt Whitman in Camden*, the first volume of these conversations was published under Traubel's supervision in 1906. He brought out two more volumes before he died in 1919; only in 1996 did the final eighth and ninth volumes appear.

Inevitably, much in these nearly 5,000 pages is mundane and ephemeral: Horace's daily eyeball on Walt's look and mood, housekeeping affairs, and the inconsequential comings and goings of friends and strangers. The intrepid reader can be forgiven for thinking certain topics become beaten like the proverbial dead horse. Several in Walt's circle (though not Walt himself), for instance, were keen on the debate over authorship of the plays of Shakespeare; this subject frequently surfaces at Mickle Street. Then one thinks of the extended lucubrations over the goodness or badness of photographic, painterly, and sculptural images of the poet, not to mention page upon page of jawboning about the design and printing of Whitman's books that only a bibliographical scholar could dote on. And many of the hot political and cultural issues of Whitman's day, chewed over at length, are of small interest now.

That said, *With Walt Whitman in Camden* must still be accounted a uniquely rich resource, for running through it are veins of pure gold. It is laced with so many passages crucial for a full, rounded, and, finally, humane understanding of America's first great national poet. Whitman made much of the charisma of the individual human voice, and nothing on the wide shelf of Whitman's own writings and all the commentary on him gives a more vivid sense of the poet's actual, personal voice than Traubel's nine volumes. They also give us much of more specific import, that is, observations and assertions that Whitman (being America's "Good Gray Poet") would never have dared to voice in public or in print: candid views about himself; revealing retrospects on his purposes and methods in composing his poems; superbly philosophical or trenchant squelches of his critics; poignant memories of his past life and friendships; provocative, often coruscating comments on American society; and rousing views, both hostile and honeyed, on literary celebrities and public figures.

Perhaps most valuable are the many remarks Whitman threw off en passant that resonate as credos fundamental to our understanding of *Leaves of Grass*. Nor of small price is the wonderful window provided here on Whitman's sense of humor (there was a theory abroad in his day that he had none) and on just how the "critter" Whitman actually existed in the America he so enthusiastically celebrated. There is much serendipitous hilarity in these pages but also, at the other extreme, many a wrenching, deeply moving, or epiphanic passage. These veins of critical gold are mined in the following pages—but not exhaustively, for there is no substitute for the experience of reading all from beginning to end.

Young Traubel had first met Whitman in 1873, when he was a teenager and the then more-notorious-than-celebrated poet was fifty-four, gray-bearded, and already seriously incapacitated by various ailments. Traubel, like Whitman, had left school at the age of twelve and was in 1888 a clerk in the Farmers' and Mechanics' Bank on Chestnut Street in Philadelphia. As the months of daily visits passed by, he became Whitman's alter ego, factotum, and liaison with the local press and many a visiting stranger, as well as his increasingly overworked amanuensis and, crucially, a manager of the poet's financial and printing affairs.

Traubel's loyalty and the regularity of his visits to the little, ramshackle two-story house were staggering. A passing remark he made toward the end of his four years of service—"Never miss a morning"—was almost true: the days he records not appearing or being out of town are extremely rare. When he did miss a day, it was usually a Sunday. After one Sunday in which he had been absent, Traubel notes that Whitman "greeted me as 'a stranger.'" Once, when he missed two consecutive days, Traubel records that Whitman "called out 'Horace' with great cordiality—took and held my hand—said, 'I had wondered what had become of you: was going to send up to ask tomorrow.' I explained my absence—he assenting, 'I know—it was all right—I am not disposed to question it. But we missed you.'"

Traubel's daily visits were frequently multiple. "Four times there today—8 A.M.—5:30 P.M.—8 P.M. and again on return from Philadelphia at midnight," he records; then, a week later: "The fourth time at W.'s at 12:40." Gradually, however, he concluded there was an ideal time to accost and record: "Eight o'clock is his good hour invariably if there is a good hour in the day. For that reason I have mostly made it the hour for consultation." Rarely did he arrive after 9 P.M. In the event that Walt was not in a consulting mood, Traubel knew well enough to beat a hasty retreat: "I did not prolong my stay," he notes of one April day, "W. not in good talking mood. In such cases I never linger."

The practical responsibilities Traubel began to shoulder grew steadily as Whitman's health continued to deteriorate. Especially onerous was the correspondence he undertook on the poet's behalf. In the days after the first serious health scare of June 1888, Traubel records, "Wrote a dozen replies. Sometime W.'s correspondence gets voluminous and keeps me working steadily until daybreak." In the last months this task made heavy demands: "I suppose 25 or 30 letters in all today." Soon it was encroaching on his break time at work ("Wrote 12 or 20 letters between times at the Bank") and on his home life: "Up home then and the whole evening spent writing letters to W's friends, Europe and home." A couple of weeks later an aghast Traubel remarks, doubtless with a cramped writing hand, "My letter-writing is assuming enormous proportions, but I must stick to it." Sometimes the "news" at Mickle Street would change even before Traubel could get a batch of letters into the mail: "Striking change in W. My many exuberant letters of forenoon already knocked off their feet."

The help of most lasting significance that Traubel offered Whitman, of course, concerned the major publications of these last years: *November Boughs* (1888), the nine hundred–page *Complete Poetry and Prose of Walt Whitman* (1888), and the final, or so-called deathbed, edition of *Leaves of Grass* (1892). The day Whitman formally announced his intention to hand over the *November Boughs* manuscript to a printer, he warned Traubel, "I shall need to enlist you as my co-worker. I am physically helpless. I could not do this work alone: I seem every day to be losing something—some atom of power." This challenge was accepted, spectacularly.

Traubel quickly became the ultimate publishing-world gofer: ferrying proofs, negotiating with and then prodding printers, scouring for the Mammoth Falcon quill pens the poet preferred, dispensing books ordered directly from Mickle Street, and performing all the tasks now associated with publicity agents. Here is Traubel's note for what, one hopes, was an unusually busy day spent on Walt's behalf toward the end of the summer of 1888: "Running about all day for W.—first to Bonsall's house for the Book Maker—then across the river for conferences at different places with Ferguson [electrotyper], McKay [publisher], Magarge & Green (paper merchants), Brown [photo-engraver], Bilstein (plate printers). Struck a paper for seven cents, by which we can save one hundred and forty dollars."

Traubel was not a little jealous about his position of responsibility. When Whitman gave a third party a delivery task, Traubel threw a small fit: "W. had returned yesterday's proofs through Baker today. I kicked. I said I ought to do all those errands myself in order to keep a supervising eye on our affairs. . . . I said to him: 'If I am to work with you it must be on this condition.' He at once came down."

Warm thanks were often expressed for his exertions. When Traubel delivered the first sheets for *November Boughs*, Whitman gleefully contemplated them: "This looks like getting something done: I'll be getting quite proud of myself by and bye—or of you, rather, for you are the one who is oiling the machine and keeping the fires up these days." But no thank-you was more eloquent than the one that came a few days before Christmas in 1888, when Walt presented Horace with an inscribed copy of *November Boughs*. "At home I opened the package: found in it the inscription that follows. It is the first time he has let himself go to me." The inscription read:

> To *Horace Traubel*
> from his friend the author
> Walt Whitman
> & my deepest heartfelt thanks go with it to HT in getting this book
> out—it is *his* book in a sense—for I have been closely imprison'd
> & prostrated all the time (June to December 1888) by sickness &
> disability—& HT has managed it all for me with copy, proofs,
> printing, binding &c. The Volume, & especially *November Boughs* &
> the portraits, could not now be existing formulated as here, except
> thro' his faithful & loving kindness & industry, daily, unintermit-
> ted, unremunerated—
>   WW Dec: 1888—
> Camden New Jersey—

Sometimes gratitude was expressed with more quiet eloquence. In Whitman's last months he observed, "our affairs here belong, after me, to you" and "you are our next necessary self." Just two months before dying, Walt summed up: "I can die easier, seeing these things all in order."

Gradually, it became apparent to Whitman and Traubel that posterity was being served by their collaboration. Horace developed the true archivist's pack-rat instinct—what the poet called "a hungry look"—as he became familiar with the haphazard chaos at Mickle Street.

His fretfulness about the state of the papers in Whitman's second-floor living quarters was frequently met with wry humor by the constitutionally disheveled old party. One day a glimpse was allowed of an envelope with "from Ellen Terry" written on it. Walt, says Horace, regarded him "with a whimsical eye: 'You have a hungry look: I think you want the letter. Well—take it along. You seem to cultivate that hungry look: it is a species of pantalooned coquetry.' I put the letter in my pocket." Over time Traubel's hungry eye began to spot especially tantalizing objects: "I took a look through his old bulgy scrap-book to-night—full—choked—with magazine pages, newspaper extracts, written (the text everywhere scored, marked, commented on) pieces (copied, original)—'the origins, beginnings, if not whole of *Leaves of Grass*—just there,' W. says. A precious volume, which he reads daily, almost."

Whitman's carefree habit of chucking out was slowly tamed, as Traubel explains: "W. sometimes has what he calls 'house-cleaning days.' He puts aside some waste for me on these occasions. I always take along what he gives me. I know what will be its ultimate value as biographical material. He rarely or never takes that into account. For instance today he said [of three rejection letters for poems he had submitted to magazines]: 'I would burn such stuff up—or tear it up—anything to get it out of the road.'" On another day Whitman razzes: "You always come into this room hungry and I always try to feed you, but I don't believe you ever get enough. Did you ever go home satisfied?" He laughs but a moment later grows earnest: "God knows boy you are welcome to the stuff . . . if you think it has any significance—is data for history—take it—preserve it—welcome." Months pass and Whitman was still teasing. Horace tells of Walt saying, "You can throw the stuff away if it's a nuisance" and then laughing: "Knew I wouldn't."

Still, skirmishes over the poet's lackadaisical storage habits occurred now and then: "As I was leaving W. remarked: 'I was destroying some papers today but I saved a few for you.' I kicked at once. 'I knew you would growl—but no matter—you growl but you do not bite. I am, in fact, Horace, saving you all the essential things—the things that make history: what I chuck away or burn up is not worth while keeping either for your purposes or mine.'" Such a remark, of course, makes it necessary to assume that even *With Walt Whitman in Camden* is in some respects (like all of Whitman's own published works) subject to a tendency toward self-concealment. Further, such a remark reminds us that it is now impossible to know the extent to which Traubel, after Whitman's death, *himself* deemed certain personalia not suitable for the eyes of posterity—and so put it in the fire.

Variations on the following vignette doubtless occurred on a regular basis: "Under the stove—an edge suspicioning itself out—was one of the Fredericks (N.Y.) portraits of which—W. seeing it in my hand—he said, 'You had better take it along with you if you want it—you can make your claim to it—if you had not found it, it probably would have been lost anyhow.'" Eventually, Whitman designated "the Horace corner" of his bedroom table as the place for material to be carted off. Horace caused "a lot of merriment" when he began referring to it as "the amen corner."

Not long after, Traubel was able to express satisfaction on the archival front: "No day passes now but W. hands me over some document which he says is for my 'archives.' I said to-night to him: 'You are giving me some great stuff nowadays: I will find real use for it: I'll make a big story out of it some day.' He nodded: 'That's what I want you to do if the world will stand it. In the final sense they are not records of my life—of my personal life—of Walt Whitman—but scripture material applying to a movement in which I am only an episode.'"

More than a year later Whitman found a five hundred–word autobiographical précis among, as the poet put it, "the odds and ends that get nowhere." Traubel includes the valuable document in full and then observes, with obvious pain, that he must be ever vigilant: "He destroys lots of these 'ineffective' pieces—trial songs or trial bits of prose—burns some, tears some up—will reserve sides of some for other articles. Wish I could rescue these—seize, cherish them. When I tell him this he says, 'You may—yes, you may . . . but what good can they do you or anybody? They are but passing showers, shadows.' But did they not go into soil and soul, for creative ends? Which he would grant and so drop. Yet I never knew him to refuse me slips or sheets when I ask."

Over time, the two friends began to acknowledge the obviously biographical import of their interaction. After a few months (the day he signed his first will), Whitman threw out this challenging demand for biographical candor: "Some day you will be writing about me: be sure to write about me honest: whatever you do, do not prettify me: include all the hells and damns." Then, in September of 1888, after handing over his one letter from Oscar Wilde, Whitman impressively and emphatically expressed both his authorization of any future biographical labors and his disinclination to interfere with them: "I am laying aside one thing and another for you from day to day. You will do what you will with them—you will throw them away if that seems best to do—you will use them some way—this way or that (perhaps publish them): I do not wish to tie you up at all—to say what you must or may not do: I prefer to leave you free to dispose of anything I may pass over into your hands as you see fit: put it into the fire, put it anywhere: I feel safe in your hands."

After nearly a year of daily intimacy, Whitman reiterated his awareness of a "poet's life" in progress: "I'm doing all I can from day to day to put you in possession of papers, data, which will fortify you for any biographical undertakings, if any, you may be drawn into concerning me, us, in the future." Another year and a half passes, and Walt acknowledges the unparalleled window into his character that Horace was being afforded: "I see more value in the matter you are piling together in your little article—personal memorabilia, traits of character, incidents, habits—the pulse and throb of the critter himself!" In his transcriptions Traubel undeniably succeeded in conveying the critter's "pulse and throb."

But, it must be asked, did Whitman feel "safe" in Traubel's hands because he trusted him to destroy the kinds of things he had himself destroyed over the years to protect his privacy in very personal, delicate, or potentially embarrassing matters? And did Traubel fulfill that trust by judicious disposal or simply by the decision not to transcribe certain parts of the conversations? A "yes" to both questions is difficult to resist, if only because there is nothing one could legitimately call breathtaking, shocking, or scandalous in all nine volumes of *With Walt Whitman in Camden*. The proprieties are never breached—unless Whitman's calling President Benjamin Harrison a "shit-ass" on one occasion could be thought beyond the pale.

There is one elaborate and fascinating example of an exclusionary principle (be it Whitman's or Traubel's) at work in the transcriptions. Perhaps it can stand for other, more fleeting instances of suppression that we will never know about. This has to do with the Englishman John Addington Symonds and his persistent querying of Whitman, over many years, about whether the forty-five *Calamus* poems, which first appeared in the 1860 *Leaves of Grass*, might express approval of what Symonds called "semi-sexual emotions & actions" between men.

In a letter dated August 3, 1890, Symonds posed to Whitman several boldly phrased questions: "In your conception of Comradeship, do you contemplate the possible intrusion of those semi-sexual emotions & actions which no doubt do occur between men? I do not ask, whether you approve of them, or regard them as a necessary part of the relation? But I should much like to know whether *you are prepared to leave them to the inclinations & the conscience of the individuals concerned?*" Symonds also asserts in this letter his belief that the encouragement of "ardent & *physical* intimacies" in *Calamus* should not be considered "prejudicial to social interests."

Whitman's responding letter is not extant, but a draft of it (endorsed "Aug 19 '90—Sent to Symonds") does exist and was reproduced for the first time in 1969 in *The Collected Writings of Walt Whitman* (1961–84). The letter has become notorious because of the amazing canard Whitman closes with, by way of putting Symonds off his scent: "My life, young manhood, mid-age, times South, &c. have all been jolly, bodily, and probably open to criticism—Tho' always unmarried I have had six children—two are dead—One living southern grandchild, fine boy, who writes to me occasionally. Circumstances connected with their benefit and fortune have separated me from intimate relations." Most who have considered the matter doubt the statement's veracity (the editor of *The Correspondence* volumes in the *Collected Writings* calls it "artfully deceptive").

More to the present point is the nervousness—verging on panic—of Whitman earlier in the letter:

> Ab't the questions on *Calamus* pieces &c. They quite daze me. L of G. is only to be rightly construed by and within its own atmo-sphere and essential character—all of its pages & pieces so coming strictly under *that*—that the calamus part has even allow'd the possibility of such construction as mention'd is terrible—I am fain to hope the pages themselves are not to be even mention'd for such gratuitous and quite at the time entirely undream'd & un-reck'd possibility of morbid inferences—wh' are disavow'd by me & seem damnable.

In a letter of September 5, 1890, Symonds managed to conceal his dis-appointment at such a response; he also forbore to remark that having children proved nothing and that he himself had three daughters. He did, however, show himself unrepentant in his views about sexual be-havior: "It seems to me, I confess, still doubtful whether (human nature being what it is) we can expect wholly to eliminate some sensual alloy from any emotions which are raised to a very high pitch of passionate intensity."

How is this all handled by Whitman . . . and Traubel? In the entry for August 18, much is made of the arrival of a "long letter" from Symonds. Harmless opening news in it is read aloud by Whitman; then he is interrupted for an interview with a census-taker. Afterward Whitman resumes reading. Traubel records: "Suddenly his face paled in the strangest way and he laid the letter down and said, 'I talked with him [the census-taker] too long: it has tired me out.' I stayed till he had recovered himself somewhat—told him he could speak of it again—then left." The next day, when the response quoted earlier was mailed, Symonds and his letter go unmentioned. Though he and his publica-tions regularly arise in the conversations, perfect silence covers this explosive three-letter exchange. Several other Symonds letters are re-produced in full by Traubel, but not these.

Traubel's description of a suddenly ashen-faced Whitman suggests that he may have kept the letter and his response secret even from Horace. But given Horace's free access and eagle eye, it seems very doubtful Whitman could have kept them under wraps. More likely, they were discussed—and the discussion simply kept off the record. Symonds's two letters and the draft have survived (they are in the New

York Public Library's Oscar Lion Collection), and they could only have done so by passing into Traubel's hands. The fact that they do not figure in *With Walt Whitman* must be due to an editorial judgment.

Still, Traubel's overall success with his "accumulations" is undeniable. And it can be chalked up, for one thing, to how well Traubel hewed to the modus operandi he expressed in the introduction to the first volume of *With Walt Whitman in Camden*: "I have only one anxiety. To set down the record. Then to get out of the way myself." But the success of this massive oral history is principally due to Traubel's skill at drawing the famously reticent, sometimes elaborately concealing old poet out into provocative, colorful, revealing conversational forays. Horace observes on one occasion that "W. is wonderfully candid with himself at all times," but the challenge was to get that candor on its feet in conversation. Within days of Traubel's taking up the very visible task of recording the poet's words, Walt praises Horace's skill at wheedling: "I just get going and go and can't even stop myself, especially when you come round, damn you! You have an odd effect on me—you don't ask me questions, you have learned that I hate to be asked questions, yet I seem to be answering questions all the time whenever you happen in."

Horace tells us Walt "laughed at this sally," but a few months later he confided in his notes how well Whitman had put his finger on the techniques used to make him open up: "My method all along has been to not trespass and not ply him too closely with questions necessary or unnecessary. When a lull occurs I sometimes get him going again by making a remark that is not a question." Patience was clearly crucial: "Other times we sit together for long seances of silence, neither saying anything. One evening during which we had not done much more than sit together, he on his chair, I on his bed, he said: 'We have had a beautiful talk—a beautiful talk.'"

With the transcription process comfortably de rigueur after four months, Whitman reiterates his praise, and a kind of affectionate epiphany takes place:

> "Horace, you are the only person in the world whose questions I tolerate: questions are my *bete noir*: even you at times, damn you, try me: but I answer your questions because you seem to me to have a superior right to ask them, if anyone has, which may be doubted. Cross-examinations are not in the terms of our contract but you do certainly sometimes put me through the fire in great shape." He laughed. "Now, Horace, you see how much I love you: you have extorted my last secret. You have made me tell why you are an exceptional person—you have forced from me an avowal of affection." He was quite lively for an instant while making this sally. Then he relapsed—looked miserable, as if to go to pieces. I went to him. "Help me to the bed," he said. This I did. He sank on the pillow. Closed his eyes. I reached down and kissed him. He said "Good night" without opening his eyes. I said "Good night" and

left. As I stood in the doorway an instant he cried: "And you will come tomorrow again? that everlasting, that sweet tomorrow!"

A year more of sweet tomorrows and the stack of transcriptions was assuming ominous, epic proportions.

This was revealed in a droll way when the devoted English Whitmanite J. W. Wallace decided to transcribe some of the poet's table talk in order to "report . . . back to the boys" in Lancashire. He then told Traubel he should do the same: "You, who are with Walt every day, a son—in fact, we might say, an *only* son—ought to take the world into your confidence." Traubel wondered later that day, in his notes, if the secrecy of his project was safe: "Did he suspect I had notes? Had Bucke said anything to him? I think not. Yet I say nothing myself. Displayed all my treasures but these—the greatest treasure of all." When Traubel got back home, he found Wallace there working on his transcriptions. He looked them over and thought them "fine in perception but not quite in touch with W. in the verbal constructive side." He also discovered that his wife had revealed the secret: "I instantly perceived that Anne had left the cat out, so owned up—afterward giving Wallace some specimen pages." Then he adds, deliciously, after revealing his hoard, that "Wallace seemed rather aghast by the extent of my accumulations."

How did Traubel actually operate? In an editorial preface to the fifth volume of *With Walt Whitman in Camden*, his daughter, Gertrude, quotes his wife's summary of his "procedure": "The notes of the visits to Whitman were written on small bits of paper to fit into the pocket of his jacket and were written in what he called 'condensed longhand,' in the dim light of Whitman's room. Within the hour of the words spoken, the material was put into . . . complete form. . . . There was no vacuum of time or emotion, thus preserving the vitality of the original conversations."

To many casual and perhaps cynical observers, the Whitman-Traubel relationship must have seemed a classic example of an idolatrous young acolyte unwilling, as the phrase is, to "get a life" and who chooses instead to devote himself utterly to an august old literary celebrity. This thought may have run through the mind of the poet's Philadelphia publisher, David McKay, when Traubel gave him this letter of introduction from Whitman: "The bearer Horace Traubel is a valued young personal Camden friend of mine—American born, German stock—whom I wish to introduce to you with the best recommendations—He is of liberal tendencies and familiar with printing office matters and the run of books."

But, as the long extract just quoted strongly hints, something more profound and emotionally charged was developing. Love—life-enhancing love rather than mere good-hearted kindness or even great friendship—was clearly in play at Mickle Street. Mundane allusions to the emotional sustenance Traubel's visits afforded occur now and then. For example, Mary Davis, the poet's live-in housekeeper from 1885 until his death, remarks to Horace as he departs, "You seem to have waked Mr. Whitman up. He was dull enough all day." Whitman makes the same point a few days later. When Horace excuses himself, "I've bothered you long enough," Walt forcefully demurs: "You bother me? you couldn't: you never victimize me—you wake me up. I am far more alert this minute, am feeling better, than I have been at any time during the day." Whitman himself muses a few days later, "The instant you came into the room and hung your hat on the bed post I felt better. How do you account for that?"

Though Horace noted once that "W. rarely gives way externally to his extreme emotions," Whitman did prove, in a few unbuttoned moments, far from shy about expressing his strong affection. When a few weeks later Horace asked, "Walt do I come too much?" the poet took his hand and replied, "Does the fresh air come too much? Thank God for the fresh air!" Sometimes this point was made wryly. One day he told Horace that he "naps it" in the evening before his arrival: "I want to be ready for you: you are the oasis in my desert." To which Horace replied, "Do you really feel that way about my coming? I never flattered myself that I am vital to you. I have felt that maybe I was rather the desert in your oasis." Whitman laughed at the notion: "That's witty but there's not a damn bit of truth in it."

Moments of wit and gentle humor are not uncommon in the pages of *With Walt Whitman in Camden*. Once, for instance, Traubel entered the bedroom rather silently, and this exchange followed: "Well—you are my ghostly visitor! If I was in the theatrical business and needed a ghost, I would hire you." "Do I look like one?" "No indeed: it's all in the footstep!" When Whitman complained about a very slow binder ("Oldach is very elephantine"), Horace got a laugh by remarking, "That is just the way he's described you: he said the other day that you were as slow as a Dutch frigate turning a corner." Walt has to agree—"a fellow always gets worst mad seeing his sins in other people"—but ends up asking Horace to tell Oldach that his client should be "humored, like a convict who's to be hung tomorrow." Another day Whitman observes that *Leaves* sells but *Specimen Days* does not and that "to many people *Specimen Days* is the mistake." Horace replies, "To most people, Walt, both books are a mistake, and you yourself are the biggest mistake of all!" Walt laughs, says "I am not prepared to put up an argument against you," and laughs again.

At other times Whitman could strike a more solemn note; here are two examples from the early months of their transcribing routine:

W. was very affectionate in his manner tonight. "Come here, Horace," he said. I went over. He took my hand. "I feel somehow as if you had consecrated yourself to me. That entails something on my part. I feel somehow as if I was consecrated to you. Well— we will work out the rest of my life-job together: it won't be for long: anyway, we'll work it out together, for short or long, eh?"

He took my face between his hands and drew me to him and kissed me. Nothing more was said. I went back to my chair and we sat in silence for some time.

"You are doing much too much for me nowadays. What can I do for you?" "I am not doing anything for you. I am doing everything for myself." W. looked at me fixedly for a moment. Then he reached forward and took my hand. "I see what you mean, Horace. That is the right way to look at it. People used to say to me: Walt, you are doing miracles for those fellows in the hospitals. I wasn't. I was, as you would say, doing miracles for myself: that was all."

Several months later, Whitman phrased his indebtedness more starkly: "I wonder whether you understand at all the functions you have come to fulfill here! that you're the only thing between me and death?—that but for your readiness to abet me I'd be stranded beyond rescue? I want you to understand."

The depth of their emotional and intellectual sympathies, of course, sometimes manifests itself in moments of badinage. When Whitman happens to remark of an acquaintance, "Johnston has some of the failings of the business man," Traubel breaks in, "Yes, and all the virtues of a lover." Traubel then records: "W. shook his finger at me: 'There you are again! Why didn't you let me say that? "Some of the failings of the business man and all the virtues of the lover." Well, that's the truth, even if you do say it.'"

And they were secure enough to sustain arguments large and small. When Whitman gripes about his friend Dr. Richard Maurice Bucke's handwriting ("all up and down angles—sharp, like his voice: I never get used to it"), Horace blithely replies that he has no trouble with it. To which Walt responds, "That's right—contradict me." On another day Horace interrupts Walt in midspout about everything in Homer and Shakespeare speaking "for nature" by asking, "You don't mean to say anyone ever talked like Shakespeare's heroes, do you?" Whereupon Walt "shook his forefinger at me" and said: "You're too damned critical: why don't you keep a few of your scepticisms to yourself?"

When the poet slips into theatrical self-pity, Horace can deftly deflect it with humor: "Some day I'll surprise you and Warrie [the nurse] and Doctor Longaker by puffing out. When you do not suspect it—kick the bucket without warning. I don't think any one of you, or Bucke, realizes what I have come to. It is a far-down peg—far-down." Horace interrupts to ask if he proposes "to slip us before dinner." Whitman "laughed and made merry over 'the bad look that would have.'" When Walt said a few days before his 1890 birthday fete, "This will undoubtedly be my last public appearance," Horace elicited a hearty laugh by remarking, "Like the farewells of actors? You always seem to come around again, whatever your fears."

Considerably more impressive, however, are the occasions when Traubel probed and prodded on more touchy issues. Volume 4 alone contains several superb examples of Horace making Walt squirm. One day the poet remarks that Hamlin Garland strikes him as being "strongly impulsive" and "a little one-idea'd." Horace pounces: "You may think you're not, but you're a little one-idea'd yourself." Walt: "I never heard it put quite in that way: Jesus was one-idea'd, I admit, for instance." Does Walt object to Jesus? "Yes: why not? Emerson had, too: the dear Emerson: he felt that Jesus lacked humor, for one thing: a man who lacks humor is likely to concentrate on one idea." Traubel records, "I parried him again": "Why, that's a familiar charge against you, Walt: didn't even Ruskin say that? and I hear it every now and then from somebody or other." Walt retorts "a little hotly": "Well—you've rather got me: I'm not much good in an argument." Elsewhere, Horace suggests, referring to Whitman's frequent complaints about being ignored in his own land, "Walt, don't you sometimes put that American neglect business a bit too strong?"

Traubel also gives Walt something like hell for thinking kindly of Andrew Carnegie just because the robber baron "showed himself so warm, generous, lavish" to Whitman. At this, the anticapitalist Horace lectures severely: "Walt, that sounds like treason: the knowledge of what he did for you is one thing—the consciousness of what he or his partners did with their workingmen is another thing. I don't think his generosity to you or any individual makes up for his greed towards the people from whom he derives all his money." Walt comes quickly down: "There's your logical faculty buzzing again: you're unbearable when you get going on that tack. . . . Though when you put it that way, Horace, I acknowledge that you shake me a little."

Mention of Whitman's reluctance to agree with Emerson's eloquent embrace of the abolitionist martyr John Brown also gets a rise out of Traubel: "You have a few very weak spots: John Brown is one of them: you never show that you understand Brown." Walt replies, "That's what William [O'Connor] used to say: he would sometimes say to me: 'Walt, you let off the God damnedest drivel on some subjects!' Brown was one of these subjects." Horace, exasperated: "Emerson and you are alike in one remarkable respect: you both resent argument: you simply take your positions and stay there."

Nor were Whitman's opinions safe from the occasional witty charge of hypocrisy. One day he opined, "A boy can do a lot sight worse than have a girl," then added, "he may *not* have a girl—that's a lot sight worse." When Horace retorted, "And that from a bachelor!" Whitman "snapped back half in fun and much in earnest": "Not too much of a bachelor, either, if you knew it all!" Horace notes that "this fling was so dead set with its teeth shut that I thought he might go on some on the subject. But he was silent and I went home."

Only once, however, does Traubel make bold to remark on a consequential flaw in Whitman's character. This occurred when Walt refused to put his name to an autobiographical piece J. M. Stoddart had commissioned for *Lippincott's Magazine* (preferring to let a firmly reluctant Traubel be its author). Stoddart had expressed his awareness that Whitman's will could be changed by the offer of money, and this caused an irked Traubel to write: "I am not sure that his singular weakness for money will persuade him to yield the point he so decidedly negatived with me—to autobiographize for *Lippincott's*. Still, I would not be surprised. He does not need money nearly so much as I do, yet he deludes himself to think he constantly suffers for it. I know of no other radical weakness in his personality, and this is only a very recent development."

Horace's views were also candid when it came to the poems themselves. When Whitman egged him to comment on "My Captain" (a poem Whitman himself several times ridiculed in private), words were not minced: "I think it clumsy: you tried too hard to make it what you shouldn't have tried to make it at all—and what you didn't succeed in making it in the end." Whitman's response was to laugh and say, "You're more than half right." More feisty—and revealing—is Traubel's merciless probing of Whitman's rather tawdry treatment of Ralph Waldo Emerson when the 1855 *Leaves of Grass* appeared (see the Emerson section below).

Walt had his innings, too, though on less momentous subjects. When Horace arrived to see him talking with Mary Davis: "[Walt] greeted me: 'We were just telling each other about you.' I asked, 'Telling *what*?' but he only laughed—in a way to say, 'I guess I won't tell.' " When Horace reminded Walt of his earlier prediction that his young friend would "never know how to write," Walt opined, "You're still a pretty green pippin but you'll ripen."

After nearly a year of his daily appearances, Traubel said flatly to Whitman of all his Boswellian efforts, "That's all there is to my hoarding up these records—as you call it. I don't have any sycophantic regard for you. I don't worship the ground you tread on or kiss the hem of your garment or discover something oracular in everything you say. But I think I know how you are bound to be regarded in the future—not as a man above other men but as one of the spokesmen of a new movement of the spirit." To Traubel's enormous credit, almost every one of the pages of *With Walt Whitman in Camden* bears out this credo of clear-eyed devotion sans sentimental humbug or egregious haloing.

But, to repeat, not sans love of the deepest kind, which is often glimpsed in such fleeting, throwaway observations by Traubel as these:

W. lay on his bed as I left. The tangerines and a book beside him: he played with them. I was happy. He seemed so well.

He was serenely glowing to-night. He stirred me.

Happy this night's 20 minutes with W!

Spent a half hour of significant joy with W. He sat in his room, writing, the crazy quilt tied about his neck.

Seeing me in the hallway—an exclamation—I suppose of joy—"Oh! boy! Oh Horace! Here at last—here again. How good it is to see you again!" and he urged I come right in—holding my hand warmly and firmly.

He slept—we did not disturb him, but I regarded him "long and long."

The depth of this love is powerfully conveyed by Traubel's entries for the days just before and after Whitman's death on March 26, 1892; these are excerpted at length at the end of this volume.

Late in April 1889 Dr. Bucke wrote to Whitman with the suggestion that he move into the Johns Hopkins hospital in Baltimore as a private patient for six months or a year or longer. A few days later Traubel made the following observation, surely a suggestion of the bond of affection that was growing between him and the old poet: "Ever since the note from Bucke proposing the removal, W.'s demeanor towards me has been more tender and marked. This has been decidedly palpable—so much so as to strike me peculiarly." As this hints, Whitman never seriously entertained Bucke's idea. When he finally announced his no to the proposal, he told "with huge enjoyment" the story of a man wandering through a graveyard and coming upon a tombstone that read: "I was well—I wished to be better—I consulted a Doctor—I am here." A few weeks earlier, however, Traubel noted that Whitman had been vocal about the probable real reason for his decision: "He keeps saying all the time: 'It would be difficult for an old fellow like me to conform to rules . . . impossible even.'"

Finally, it must be emphasized that this relationship was not merely platonic—not sexual, of course, but most assuredly physical. An affecting leitmotif of *With Walt Whitman in Camden* is the series of moments when a kiss becomes part of the evening farewell. Whitman, as we have seen, used the word "consecrated" to define the relationship they were forging, and the aptness of that term can be underscored by citing some moments that issued in a kiss. Not surprisingly, these kisses became more frequent and more moving as Whitman approached death.

W. kissed me good night. He said: "We are growing near together. That's all there is in life for people—just to grow near together."

W. said: "Come, kiss me for good night." He was still lying down. I reached over him and we kissed. He took my hand—pressed it fervently. "I am in luck. Are you? I guess God just sent us for each other."

[On the last Christmas Day:] I reached over and kissed him. I could feel his responding lips [wonderfully echoing Whitman's line from

Drum-Taps: "vigil for boy of responding kisses (never again on earth responding)"].

And as I leaned over and kissed him, first on the lips, then on the forehead, he murmured, "Always a blessing, boy. These are long, long days—but they might be longer."

In leaving W. I kissed him. "You are not the least of my comforts, Horace!" he exclaimed. Surprising strong grasp of hand—though hand was cold.

Then, just days before the end: "Every word a struggle. And again I kissed him, and heard him say, 'Bless—bless.' Coughed—choked—breathed heavily. I turned as I reached the door. His eyes opened. He smiled. That smile! And after I had gone I had yet to go back again to see him, to have his smile."

The importance of Traubel's achievement in making possible the nine volumes of conversations is powerfully demonstrated by turning to the somewhat more than a thousand extant letters Whitman wrote during the "Horace years." If this correspondence were our only record of the poet's last years, our sense of his intellectual vitality (what he frequently referred to as his "grip") and still-vigorous powers of articulation would be drastically truncated.

A large majority of these letters are rather short—under two hundred words—and are freighted mostly with repetitive, mundane news about his daily health and routine. And about 75 percent of them are the nearly daily ones he wrote to Dr. Bucke in Canada, to William and Ellen O'Connor in Washington, D.C., (until O'Connor died on May 9, 1889), and to perhaps half a dozen favored others. These usually reported nothing "specially notable" and gave a brief summary of his condition, the day's weather, the whereabouts of his nurse and housekeeper, and perhaps the latest news of his books' progress through the press or of his visitors. A typical example would be this letter of March 21, 1889, to William O'Connor:

> Am feeling pretty well, but it is now the third dark rainy muddy half-raw day—Have just written to Dr B—Hope & pray this will find you better—Have just had a bath & some massage—sitting now in the big chair & wolf skin, sort o' comfortable—Best love to you & N[elly]— W W

Indeed, the correspondence radiates a kind of torpor, as in this paragraph from a letter to Bucke in January 1889:

> 3½ p m—The day moves steadily on—pretty dull and heavy with me here—Mrs. Davis has been in to cheer me up & was very welcome—(she has that definite something *buoyancy of presence*)—Ed is down stairs practicing on his fiddle—For a change I am going to stretch out on the bed, for a little while—I have got so that books

& papers are no recreation to me, almost revolting—no letters today—no visitors . . .

Whitman's letters to Bucke were generally his longest, partly because they faithfully favored the doctor with reports on the diet of his two daily meals, a breakfast and an early supper ("do not eat dinner at all, find it best"): a mutton chop, broth with mutton and rice, Graham bread, and various stewed fruits were among the staples. And on his evacuations, a few variations being "night-rest & bowel action fair to fairish" and "fair bodily secretive & excretive affairs considering."

Horace's assistance, happily, is often acknowledged in these letters, though always matter-of-factly. "Horace is most faithful & invaluable to me, comes every evening, & sees to the printing first rate." "H remains & is perfectly faithful & I depend on him more than words could describe." "Should not get along with it [proofs] or anything without Horace Traubel." But resonant or evocative passages are almost nonexistent in the letters: their editor, Edwin Haviland Miller, sums up, indeed, that Whitman "rarely brought himself to compose" a "personal letter."

And very rare in the letters are the sparks of drollery, earnest debates, and expressions of *saeva indignatio* over some literary or political preposterousness that one finds in almost every one of Traubel's daily entries. When they do surface, they give the usual delight: as when he wrote this note and sent it down to some visitors who were deaf who showed up on his doorstep: "Glad to see you—the doctor prohibits callers nearly altogether—but I suppose because they *talk* too much—wh' I find you do not—but I can only say Hail—& good bye." Or when a reference to a massage from his nurse gives rise to some wit: "Ed gives me a good *currying* every evening—Sleep fairly—Sun bursting forth as I write—the great *burr-r-r* of the Phila. whistles from factories or shores often & plainly here sounding, & I rather like it—(blunt & bass)—some future American Wagner might make something significant of it."

Nor does Walt, in his postmarked writings, concern himself much to convey a sense of the vignettes of his Mickle Street existence that surface regularly in his dialogues with Horace. In one letter to Bucke, though, he does capture nicely the mood at his seventieth birthday celebration in Philadelphia: "The compliments & eulogies were *excessive* & without break—But I fill'd my ice-glass with the good wine, & pick'd out two fragrant roses f'm a big basket near me, & kept cool & jolly & enjoy'd all."

Traubel remarks, amid the conversations, that "W.'s mind never loses its critical force," but that rosy view could not possibly be proved from the correspondence. Here is one of the tiny handful of pungent obiter dicta in all the thousand letters: "I guess [Whitman writes to Bucke] we are now floating on *dead water* in literature, politics, theology, even science—resting on our oars &c. &c.—criticising, resuming—at any rate *chattering* a good deal." A reader of *With Walt Whitman in Camden*, on the other hand, expects such colorful, charming, or trenchant passages with the turn of many a page.

But in one letter to Bucke, dated November 3–4, 1888, there is a most extraordinary passing remark, in parentheses, that surely captures the value of Horace Traubel's tireless transcribing: "Tom Harned & his brother Frank & young Mr. Corning have just call'd & spent a short half hour (I don't know but I find myself *talking more* than I used to—talking perhaps more than ever)." Whitman's most important work in his last years, it could be fairly said, *was* his talk, and we are fortunate that so much of it has been vouchsafed to posterity.

Horace Logo Traubel was born in Camden on December 19, 1858, the fifth of seven children of a Jewish immigrant father from Frankfurt and a Christian mother (neither was practicing). Though an early school-leaver, Horace became an omnivorous reader on his own. Some of his tutelage was at Whitman's side; as Traubel recalled, "My earliest memory of Whitman leads me back to boyhood, when, sitting together on his doorstep, we spent many a late afternoon or evening in review of books we had read." Like Walt, Horace drifted into the publishing trade, becoming a printer's devil and later a compositor, typesetter, and reporter for the *Camden New Republic* and later for the *Camden Evening Visitor*. Subsequently, he was a factory paymaster, then finally landed a clerical position at the Farmers' and Mechanics' Bank, where he worked during his years of closest association with Whitman.

Traubel was, as Walt's letter of introduction to David McKay points out, of liberal political tendencies, which sometimes became too far left and vocal for the poet's comfort. Early in the project, Traubel noted, Whitman jumped on him for his "radical violence" and added, "don't let your dislike for the conventions lead you to do the old things any injustice. . . . Be radical—be radical—be not too damned radical."

Traubel's "liberal tendencies" were impressively demonstrated in the pages of the *Conservator*, a monthly journal of political, social, and cultural commentary that was by no means conservative. He founded it in March 1890 and was its editor for the entire thirty years of its existence. His purpose, he announced in the inaugural issue, was "to welcome all the broader tendencies and ethical growths, in orthodox life as in radical." In addition to essays on such remarkably forward-thinking subjects as divorce, laws criminalizing suicide, vegetarianism, animal rights, the plays of Ibsen, and "sex attraction," passages from the works of such avant-garde cultural and political figures as Wagner, Nietzsche, Shaw, Eugene V. Debs, H. G. Wells, Edward Carpenter, G. K. Chesterton, and Maurice Maeterlinck were featured. Books by such friends of socialism and liberalism as Upton Sinclair, Frank Harris, Frank Norris, Leo Tolstoy, Jack London, and Karl Marx were reviewed in the *Conservator*.

Much verse in the long-lined Whitman style also appeared, large portions of it by the editor himself. His poems carried such titles as "The bread line trails its clouded way into my sunny heart" and "I have taken the bad with the good." Traubel was not shy about running glowing reviews of his own two poetry collections, *Chants Communal* (1910) and

Optimos (1914)—a form of self-puffing that he could say he learned from Walt. But let it also be said that he was not shy about running highly critical reviews as well—for example, H. L. Mencken's devastating roundhouse in the *Smart Set* on *Optimos*. There the famous curmudgeon refers to Traubel's "dishwatery imitations of Walt Whitman," complains, "[a]ll the faults of the master appear in the disciple," and chides his "inability to distinguish between a poem and a stump speech." Likewise, the *Times Review* in New York opined, in a review that Traubel reprints, that his verse is "lacking in nothing but strength and imagination to make it as good as Whitman's own." Mencken and the *Times Review*, most readers now would agree, were not entirely unjust. In the November 1917 *Conservator* appeared an excerpt from a *Philadelphia Press* article on that city's poets. It said of Traubel, critically but also more generously, that he "often is defective artistically, but he is one of the more humanitarian poets America has ever produced. . . . [H]e is an intellectual figure and has fought his way, a typical idealist, a true democrat, editing his *Conservator*."

When the first three volumes of *With Walt Whitman in Camden* appeared, many a rosy encomium was allowed into the *Conservator*. Edmund Clarence Stedman ventured that the project was "the greatest contribution to the record of our grand poet that has or ever can be made." When the second volume appeared, Traubel printed in the April 1908 issue very encouraging words from Walt's old friend Francis Howard Williams that ends, "Whitman is a crescent force in literature and your volumes must help powerfully to bring his fame to fruition." But then Traubel follows this immediately with a reprint of a hatchet job by the *New York Evening Post* that begins, "One volume of Horace Traubel's shirt-sleeve Boswellianism was tolerable, even valuable, a second volume of 563 closely printed pages is too much for patience. What profit there can be in following the record of Whitman's health day by weary day, in reading the diary of his trivial talk night by weary night, we do not see." The *New York Evening Globe* review, also reprinted in the *Conservator*, assesses the volumes more accurately and fairly: "To say that Mr. Traubel's work is comparable with Boswell's in fulness of detail is short of the truth. Boswell's book is a model of literary selection and compression and arrangement compared with these Traubel volumes, which are as big and shaggy and unkempt, and even as untidy, as we have had the picture of Whitman himself in this Mickle street home, knee deep in manuscripts and bills and memoranda and jottings." After the third volume appeared, the *Passaic (N.J.) Daily News* concluded more generously, "It is easy to find fault with it. But fault-finding falls away before the stupendousness of it. When we say that some of the details might have been omitted, that the work might have been made more compact, we have said all there is to be said by way of criticism."

One of the most eloquent reviews of *With Walt Whitman in Camden* at its third-installment stage appeared in the *Yale Review* in January 1915, and Traubel reprinted it in that year's April *Conservator*. It does, how-ever, begin with a complaint that underscores the need for an anthology from all nine volumes such as the present one. Referring to the third vol-ume, the reviewer, John Erskine, says that "unfortunately it continues their [the first two volumes] bad precedent of an inadequate index. To collect so much interesting and miscellaneous information into books of nearly five hundred pages, with indices of nothing but the names of persons mentioned, is to discourage the serious use of this large work." Erskine expresses hope that a general index might eventuate in the full-ness of time, but that did not happen (though it should be said the later indices improved somewhat in quality).

Erskine goes on to express admiration for Traubel's project. "We shall have here—indeed, we have already—through the multiplied illustra-tions of his demeanor the most effective approach to an understanding of Whitman's personality." He later adds, "The length is justified by the great veracity it secures. . . . The best service this more honest, unse-lected record will do for Whitman is to show the kind of mind he had. Where his poems are read there ought to be no question of his intellect, but should there be, this diary will answer for it. The mind here revealed is singularly balanced and judicial, singularly wise in practical affairs, keen in literary opinions and modern in its philosophy." One of Erskine's closing sentences perfectly captures my hopes for *Intimate with Walt*: "It will be a pity if this life of Whitman does not become widely known in America."

Three months later Traubel balanced the score by reprinting the *New York Evening Sun*'s snide swipe: "If somebody will thresh out the wheat a very good loaf of bread may be made out of these gleanings. But Horace won't do that. He loves it all—chaff and straw."

Obviously sharing Whitman's unflappability in the face of harsh criticism, Traubel was also happy to disseminate caustic reviews of the *Conservator* itself. Referring to the "highly emotional journal" and quot-ing some typical Traubel verse, the *New York Evening Sun* harrumphed, "The same familiar stuff has been dribbling forth these twenty years and we have had a surfeit of Mr. Traubel and his countless headshakings."

But Traubel did not shake his head over Mildred Bain's laudatory 1913 biography of himself. His (signed) review ends, "What does matter is that she makes it clear that he has been a helper to those who have struggled against tides. She has done that. That does count. Counts in the man. Counts in the book." Easily one of Traubel's wittiest per-formances in the *Conservator* appeared near the end of its life, when he undertook to "review" the as-yet-unpublished manuscript of David Karsner's biography of him. "I've been allowed to see this bit of gen-uinely good work," Traubel opens, "but is it worth such serious atten-tion?" Aping an old Whitman habit, Traubel speaks wryly of himself in the third person: "I know a lot about Traubel's personal history. When he was a young fellow he was a hot advocate of Whitmanism and went for Walt's enemies baldheaded. Walt himself many times cautioned Traubel to 'hold his horses,' as he used to say. That is, go slow. That is, not claim too much. But Traubel was impetuous in his fiery propaganda." He then goes on to make a modest proposal to the erstwhile author: "If he'll take the manuscript home and substitute some more plausible name for Traubel's throughout I predict he'll find a publisher for it without delay." (The biography did find a publisher, Arens, the next year.)

In the pages of the *Conservator*, Traubel worked strenuously to keep the Whitman flame alight, publishing articles and shorter items on the poet in almost every issue. Many an essay was contributed by such Whitmanites as Bucke, John Burroughs, and William Sloane Kennedy, and among the wide variety of topics addressed were "*Leaves of Grass* and Modern Science," "Walt Whitman's Lack of Humor," "Walt Whitman and Music," "A Peep into Whitman's Manuscripts," "Walt Whitman and Sex," "Whitman and Jesus," "Whitman and Socialism," and "Whitman and Mannahatta." A regular feature for several years was "Recent Study and Criticism of Whitman," and after each year's Whitman birthday celebration on May 31, issues usually carried several Whitman features. The *Conservator*'s last pages always carried advertisements for Whitman volumes.

Books about Whitman were damned or praised in the *Conservator* as need be. Bliss Perry's 1906 biography particularly rankled and suffered several attacks over the years. One reviewer complained of its revised 1908 edition, "Perry's book is vitiated by its malignant falsities and its churlish superciliousness." George Rice Carpenter's *Walt Whitman* fared better, Traubel himself concluding, "Carpenter is mostly on to Walt's curves." On the other hand, the very first concerted attempt to argue the case for Whitman's homosexuality (*Der Yankee Heiland*, by the German Eduard Bertz) is treated witheringly in a June 1907 *Conservator* article on "Whitman and the Germans of Today." "I have no intention of advertising the book," says its author, Amelia von Ende, "by dwelling on its contents."

Poignantly, the *Conservator* survived the Whitman centennial in 1919 by just one month. Traubel's moving and trenchant last editorial on Whitman, from the centennial issue, is excerpted at the end of this volume.

Traubel's antiestablishment views were so outspoken as to cause in 1902 his separation from the bank. Thereafter he was a freelance literary man-of-all-work. He was greatly admired on the political left, most notably and eloquently by the socialist and presidential candidate Debs.

Traubel's association with Whitman lasted nineteen years, beginning in 1873 shortly after the poet, disabled by a paralytic stroke, moved from Washington into the house of his brother George and his wife, Louisa, on Stevens Street in Camden. The Traubel family lived nearby and was acquainted with the Whitmans, so the paths of the two were bound to cross.

Just after Christmas 1888 came some nostalgic reminiscing about their early meetings during what the poet often referred to as the gloomiest period of his life (his beloved mother, Louisa, in her late seventies, had also just died in 1873). "Life was reviving," Whitman says, "I was getting a little like my old self: certainly was spiritually realizing life once more—tasting the cup to the full. Horace, you were a mere boy then. . . . I remember you so well: you were so slim, so upright, so sort of electrically buoyant. You were like medicine to me—better than medicine." Walt also recalls conversations fueled by Horace's rabid reading they enjoyed while lying under trees by the Delaware River: "Oh! you were reading then like a fiend: you were always telling me about your endless books, books: I would have warned you, look out for books! had I not seen that you were going straight not crooked—that you were safe among books."

Horace, for his part, responds by remembering the day three years later when he happened upon Walt just after the poet had attended the burial of his—and his father, Walter's—namesake nephew, Walter Orr Whitman (George's baby son died on July 12, 1876): "Walt, do you remember the day you buried little Walter? How we met—walked a bit: how we had quite a little chat: how you took the car at Fifth Street—at Stevens there: how we met again an hour or so later on the [ferry] boat? I look back and see it all: you said: 'Horace, it does me good—this air does me good: sort of makes me *whole* again after what I have gone through to-day.'" At this Walt was silent. Horace asks if indeed his memory is jogged. "Yes! now I do remember it: not all the details you mention but the circumstances: and I remember what maybe you have forgotten: that on the boat you bought some wild flowers from an old nigger mammy who had been all day trying to sell them in the city and was going home dispirited: you bought her flowers and handed them to me. Do you remember that?" Horace records, "When he spoke of it, yes. W. was palpably moved." Other early memories are more cheery—for instance, of their watching baseball players on the Camden town common: "I can't forget the games we used to go to together: they are precious memories."

The friendship disturbed some busybodies. Traubel sarcastically reminisced in 1908 about Camden's small-mindedness: "People in Camden went to my mother and father to tell them Walt was not quite a safe man for me to go round with. (People of Camden are still of the same eclipse of mind. . . . Walt in the opinion of Camden is still not quite safe for Camden to go round with. But that dont matter to Camden. Camden aint goin to take no moral chances on gambles of that sort.)"

It was only in the late 1880s, however, that the friendship burgeoned well beyond the casual and recreational. Traubel became chief among the circle of Whitman friends and well-wishers: handling financial matters, calling for medical assistance when necessary, hiring and dispatching helpers and nurses, and even (behind the poet's back) supervising some discreet fund-raising. On one occasion he censors a letter he is reading to Walt to avoid revealing this: "I did not read W. the first part of Stedman's letter. He does not know how I am paying for the nurse."

In due course, Traubel became one of Whitman's three literary executors, Thomas Harned and Bucke being the other two. Doubtless his involvement in such publications as the three executors' *In Re Walt Whitman* (1893) and the ten-volume *Complete Writings of Walt Whitman* (1902) was in part responsible for Traubel's fourteen-year delay in commencing the publication of his Mickle Street word-hoard. Traubel was also prominently involved in founding and leading the Walt Whitman Fellowship, serving for two decades as its secretary and treasurer. The Whitman Fellowship held annual conferences on May 31, Whitman's birthday.

By 1890, Traubel was courting Anne Montgomerie, and on November 17 he reported her passing a crucial test with flying colors: "I spoke of reading *Leaves of Grass* last night to Anne Montgomerie; that I hit passages the world outlaws—never winced—nor did she, and W. exclaimed, 'Admirable! Admirable!'" Six months later, on May 28, 1891, Horace and Anne were married in a ceremony that took place in Whitman's bedroom at Mickle Street. How this came to pass is, of course, recorded: "Talked with W. about my marriage tonight. He could not come up to my father's house. Could we all come to him? He seemed greatly pleased, 'Do you wish it? Do you really wish it?' Yes indeed. 'Well then, *come*—yes, come, Horace, boy, all of you. And no formalities? And a minister? Oh! [the Unitarian minister and Whitman partisan John] Clifford—yes, that will do—Clifford will always do—the good Clifford!'" While honeymooning at Niagara Falls, Horace got a letter from Ed's successor as nurse, Warren "Warrie" Fritzinger, who remarked, "How strange it appears not to have you coming in of an eve. Walt said last night that he felt quite lost." A daughter, Gertrude, was born in 1892, and a son named Wallace (after J. W. Wallace) was born the next year but died five years later.

Given the considerable discussion in recent years of the nature of Whitman's sexual identity and its influence on his poetry, there has inevitably been some similar speculation about Traubel. As the examples of Oscar Wilde, John Addington Symonds, André Gide, and many another make clear, marriage and the fathering of children by no means moot the question. Some recent research, indeed, suggests that a shared openness to homosexual affections—what Whitman had long ago identified in his poetry as "adhesiveness"—may have been a significant underlying factor in their remarkable friendship.

Ed Folsom, a leading Whitman scholar and longtime editor of the *Walt Whitman Quarterly Review*, has discovered in correspondence in the Library of Congress that Traubel seems to have had a passionate relationship with a man five years younger than himself. This person, Gustave Percival Wiksell, became a dentist residing in Boston and for many years presided over the Whitman Fellowship there (he also presided over the secular memorial service for Traubel in 1919). In the introduction for the last volume of *With Walt Whitman in Camden*, Folsom describes a "heated correspondence spanning five years (1899–1905)" in which "Traubel and Wiksell poured out their love for each other, often expressing themselves in Whitman's *Calamus* terminology." "Percival, darling, my sweet camerado," wrote Traubel, for example, in a 1902 letter, recalling a recent meeting with Wiksell: "Definitely sweet was one hour & the next while we remained in love's carouse—That day will go with me into all eternities. Send me your words, dear love—your words live. They go into my veins. I do not put you away with a kiss. I hold you close, close, close!"

Wiksell contributed a few items to the *Conservator*. Most redolent and full of irony, perhaps, is the eulogy he offered for Whitman's rebel boyfriend from his Washington days, Peter Doyle, which Traubel reprinted in the September 1907 number. Wiksell's opening describes a true Whitman spirit: "He held no pose. Cared not a hang for anyone's opinion. Lived a free sane life and hated appointments. Spoke only of things in his knowledge. Never faked up any good-sounding phrases."

Sensing, perhaps, the weakness of his heart and the imminence of death in the spring of 1919, Traubel movingly allowed Wiksell the valedictory word on the great influence and love of his life. The last hushed words on the last page of what turned out to be the final *Conservator* are these:

> If all the theologies (guesses about God) were to sink in the quicksands of the word war. If all Greek and Hebrew originals were lost. Out of *Leaves of Grass* would come the flowers of worship satisfying the soul, and forms and ceremonies to meet the use of temples and groves in the religious expression of vital events, as marriage and burial ceremonies. "Whispers of Heavenly Death" hold more comfort for the mourners than any other scripture we have. This explains the mental rest derived from them. We argue no more about God or immortality. Confucius said: "I would that all men might write a book about God. Time so spent would be profitable to the soul." *Leaves of Grass*—biography of a man—is the biography of God.   Percival Wiksell

Joann Krieg—in a fascinating 1996 essay in the *Walt Whitman Quarterly Review* titled "Without Walt Whitman in Camden"—quotes at length from another series of passionate love letters written to Traubel. Also now in the Library of Congress, these date from a few years earlier than the Traubel-Wiksell correspondence and were written by a young American composer and singer, Philip Dalmas. The first extant letter is dated January 1893, and the correspondence begins to wane the next year, when Dalmas spent much time among a circle of homosexual English Whitmanites. One of them, J. W. Wallace, described

Dalmas to Traubel in a letter as "an indescribably lovely and loveable man."

In the spring of 1895 came the sensational and (to homosexuals) intimidating trial and imprisonment of Oscar Wilde. The following November Dalmas wrote Traubel something of a Dear John letter that appears to allude to the event: "in these days of subtle reasoning one's declarations of love can be turned into engines of hate by the loved one's lofty conception of what life is and since the unnatural has gone out of fashion." (Traubel devoted the first *Conservator* to appear after Wilde's May 25 conviction, the June issue, entirely to Whitman. It contains two remarkable defenses of Whitman against the charges of "morbid psychology" then associated with homosexuality: a damning review of Max Nordau's book *Degeneration*, which attacked both Whitman and Wilde, and a long essay by Bucke, "Was Whitman Mad?")

The cooling of the relationship, however, did not mean banishment from the Whitman circle for Dalmas. He remained for several years a member of the Whitman Fellowship. When it convened at the Colonnade Hotel in Philadelphia on May 31, 1900, Dalmas sang four songs he composed to Whitman texts. One of them, "As I Watched the Ploughman Ploughing," was popular enough to be reprised at the fellowship's annual conferences in 1908, 1910, and 1916; it is also included on baritone Thomas Hampson's 1997 compact disc of Whitman songs, *To The Soul* (EMI 55028). Dalmas's songs were published in 1901 in London ("text reprinted courtesy of Horace L. Traubel") and in 1927 in New York (seven other of his Whitman settings remained unpublished).

A remarkable item that appeared in Traubel's *Conservator* perhaps deserves notice in this context. In 1913 Edward Carpenter's pathbreaking study of homosexuality, *The Intermediate Sex: A Study of Some Transitional Types of Men and Women*, was published in New York by Mitchell Kennerley (the previous year the publisher added all Whitman's works to its list). In the February number Traubel included his own review of the book; it is favorable, challenging, and acerbic. "A friend of mine picked Carpenter's book up off my desk. 'He's a brave man to write on that subject.' He's neither a brave man nor cowardly. Just honest. He's not presenting a situation. He's scientific. It is a subject about which most everybody refuses to talk decently." In the course of the review, Traubel notes that "sex is omnipresent and omnipotent. Sex is action. If you lay down and die, then you have ceased to have any relation to sex." He also remarks on how "impossible it is to wholly dissever the masculine from the feminine order" and on how "we are passing on to a new stage" in understanding the subject. Then he asks the rhetorical question, "Dare we say this intervening sex which today is the puzzle of the wise and the horror of the foolish is not performing a vitally inevitable part?" Though he did not dare to say so, it is tempting to think Traubel might have had Whitman in mind when he posed the question. The review ends with a gesture in the spirit of Whitman's wide embrace: "If you shut the door on [Carpenter's book] you don't shut the door on him but on yourself. And it's far worse for you to shut yourself in than to shut him out."

After a long period of heart ailment, Traubel died on September 8, 1919, at the age of sixty-one. Walt's last word was "shift," a request to Warrie for a change of position. Horace's last words—uttered to his wife, a nurse, and a few others—were more antic: "Laugh, for God's sake, laugh." After a nonsectarian funeral service like Whitman's, Traubel was buried in Harleigh Cemetery, not far from the poet's tomb.

I would like to express my gratitude to the heroic editors of *With Walt Whitman in Camden* who came after Horace Traubel and saw this remarkable labor of Whitmaniac love to completion, particularly Jeanne Chapman and Robert MacIsaac, and also to Ed Folsom for his warm embrace of the concept of this edition and valuable suggestions for presenting the text. Dedications are out of bounds for editions of Whitman: not once did he see fit to compose one himself. Being reluctant to spoil my own perfect dedicatory record, however, I would like to offer my editorial efforts on Walt's behalf to Todd Sinclair.

Note on the Text

The selections are presented in five parts. They focus on (I) Whitman personally (his life in Mickle Street, comments on himself and his family, and memories of his early life); (II) Whitman as poet (his views on *Leaves of Grass*, its reception, and the literary and "publisherial" life); (III) Whitman's affectional and social life (his friends, partisans, and idols); (IV) Whitman's wide-ranging, serendipitous views on human nature, culture, and society; and (V) Whitman's health, final months of serious illness, and death.

The sources for all entries—and for all quotations in the introduction, chapter headnotes, and notes to entries—are provided in the Citations. All excerpts are given exactly as they appear in *With Walt Whitman in Camden*, except for a very small number of changes in confusing punctuation or anomalous spelling. All italics are original. All ellipses indicate elision for this edition (Traubel does not employ ellipses). The headings for entries are added editorially, usually employing a phrase from the passage. Where an entry consists entirely of Whitman's words, no quotation marks are used; they are used where an excerpt requires introduction or there is an exchange between Whitman and Traubel.

Part One

Whitman's two-story house on Mickle Street,
Camden, in 1890

The Whitman house, a New Jersey State Historic Site,
after a full restoration completed in 1998.
© *Jeanne Bening, photographer.*

The Mickle Street
Ménage

In March 1884 Whitman moved into and purchased for $1,750 the first and only house of his lifetime. This was the one time he had the funds to swing such an investment, he told Traubel, because "I was making money then— just after the Massachusetts expulsion [of the 1881 Boston Leaves]: the first Philadelphia edition [of 1882] netted me thirteen hundred dollars." The house, which he once referred to as a "little Camden shanty," was a small two-story tenement at 328 Mickle Street in Camden, New Jersey.

Near a noisy ferry and train depot (for service to the Atlantic Coast), the house was looked upon dimly by many of the poet's acquaintances. Elizabeth Keller, who was brought in to nurse Whitman for a little over two months just before he died, registered a comprehensively negative view of the house in her memoir, Walt Whitman in Mickle Street: "It was an unpretentious brown frame structure, sadly out of repair, and decidedly the poorest tenement on the block." Its situation, she adds, "was anything but inviting, and the locality was one that few would choose to live in." She also despised the "uninterrupted racket day and night" of nearby railroad traffic, even the "sharp-toned bell" of a neighborhood church and its "choir of most nerve-unsettling singers." A "disagreeable odor" from a guano factory across the river completed the picture. Inside the house, Keller noted the narrow hallways and staircase and a kitchen "so compactly filled that many people remarked its close resemblance to the cabin of a ship." And she expressed particular scorn for the chaos in Whitman's upstairs front parlor/bedroom, with its "hillock of débris."

The house is now a New Jersey State Historic Site and was recently renovated completely and returned to its state when Whitman lived in it. Mickle Street—except for Whitman's block—has since become Martin Luther King, Jr. Boulevard, and 328 now stands (fittingly, for a poet who made a point of embracing "The crazed, prisoners in jail, the horrible, rank, malignant") opposite a very large penal institution.

Buoyant Dr. Bucke

"His method is peaceful, uncoercive, quiet, though always firm—rather persuasive than anything else. Bucke is without brag or bluster. It is beautiful to watch him at his work—to see how he can handle difficult people with such an easy manner. Bucke is a man who enjoys being busy—likes to do things—is swift of execution—lucid, sure, decisive.

3

Doctors are not in the main comfortable creatures to have around, but Bucke is helpful, confident, optimistic—has a way of buoying you up." Thus Whitman sums up his impressions of Richard Maurice Bucke, one of the most important friends of his last two decades. Though a constant and important presence at Mickle Street, he in fact lived hundreds of miles away in the Canadian province of Ontario. Here, in more formal terms, is how Whitman described him in June 1891 in a letter of introduction to Alfred Lord Tennyson: "let me introduce my good friend & physician Dr Bucke—He is Superintendent (medical and other) of the big Insane Canadian Asylum at London Ontario—he is an Englishman born but raised (as we say it) in America."

Bucke, who visited Camden several times during the *With Walt Whitman* years, alone received an almost daily letter from Whitman in the poet's last years, and his advice on the management of Whitman's health care—and countless literary transactions—was much valued and often even followed. It was his recommendation that led to one of Walt's happiest male nurse experiences. For Bucke's moving farewell to Walt, see the chapter "A Voice from Death."

The friendship began in 1872, and Bucke's tenure as asylum director began in 1876; Whitman made one of his relatively rare long journeys to visit him and his wife there in the summer of 1880. Bucke published his idolizing *Walt Whitman* in 1883 (Whitman actually wrote many of the passages); Walt said of the book in 1889 that it "has my cordial regard" but that "the book is guilty, like the dinner [that honored his seventieth birthday], of being too honeyish." Bucke became one of Whitman's literary executors and in that capacity published two volumes of Whitman letters, *Calamus: A Series of Letters Written during the Years 1868–1880* (1897; these were letters to Peter Doyle) and *The Wound Dresser: A Series of Letters Written from the Hospitals in Washington* (1898).

Spirit of Tidiness: Mary Davis

Mary Davis was Whitman's live-in cook and housekeeper; her instincts for tidiness were regularly frustrated by Whitman's laissez faire attitude toward debris. Cruelly, Davis was chided sometimes by observers for her housekeeping, as Traubel records: "People often criticize Mrs. Davis because of the confusion apparent in the parlor and W.'s bedroom. The fact is W. does not encourage any interference even by her with his papers. She has been cleaning some this week, W. being rather disposed to joke about it. 'I hate to see things after they are "fixed." You get everything out of place and call it order.'" He varied the remark a week or so later, when Davis brought some books up from the parlor: "Now that the room is arranged I suppose I'll never be able to find anything any more."

In Whitman's correspondence from the "Horace years," references to Davis are invariably cordial. In one letter to Bucke, he even ascribes to her "that definite something *buoyancy of presence.*" When she made a rare long trip (two weeks to Kansas City), her presence was missed. In his charming letter to her, Whitman assures her that his substitute cooks are giving him "plenty for my meals & all right." He also includes the droll news that "we've killed one of the roosters (he behaved very badly & put on airs)."

Clearly, Whitman rankled at having to submit to Davis's management: "Mary thinks men ain't much use for taking care of themselves nohow. I am keen about all that myself—jealous of my right to fall down and break my neck if I choose."

Asked about the quality of Davis's cooking, Walt told a visiting Bucke, "Always good—very good." He was reluctant to hurt her feelings, though, and Traubel tells us that, a few days before, Whitman had confided, "Mary's heart is all right—she studies to please me—to feed me right—but she lacks in that finer something or other which the best cooks possess—which is so inestimably precious to a sick man."

Far more treasured were Davis's services as guardian of access to Whitman, especially when someone fell out of favor—as apparently happened to one James Scovel: "Nowadays Mary will not let Jim Scovel come up at all—he is in disfavor! Oh! Mary is invaluable to me in such matters—and Warren [his nurse], too—but Mary, invaluable! The fellows come—they must see Walt Whitman: if only Mr. Whitman would see them for a moment! But no, Mary is inexorable—the Doctor has ordered that nobody see Mr. Whitman: Mr. Whitman is too sick, feeble, to be wearied by visitors, &c.&c. And that is her reception to interlopers."

And Davis had a way with the teakettle: "She hit the medium: tea is only good at one consistency—stronger or weaker than that, either way it is damnable."

But sometimes Davis was too strict, as Traubel notes: "Mrs. Davis yesterday persuaded boys on the street to take their firecrackers around the corner. W. objected: 'Don't send them away, Mary: the boys don't like to be disturbed either. Besides who knows but there may be a sicker man around the corner?'" A few days later, as the Fourth of July loomed, the boys still enjoyed Walt's forebearance: "There's a certain allowance of deviltry in all boys. The boys out in this street probably know there is a sore, nervous old man up in this room, so they fling their malignant rattle-snake poison about with special vehemence. Boys could not get along without that. But let them go on—don't interfere with them. It would worry me more to have that done than to bear the noise." When the Fourth arrived, Traubel reports, "W. stood the noise today heroically."

Rubbed the Wrong Way: W. A. Musgrove

Whitman clearly could not seem to warm to this new nurse at Mickle Street. In July 1888 Horace observed Walt was "Depressed. Change of nurses has something to do with this. Musgrove is a cloudy man. I asked how M. got on. W. evaded the question by some general remark." Later Whitman mentions that he has taken a solitary bath, and Traubel records that Whitman "resents the attentions of Musgrove. . . . Musgrove rubs him the wrong way." But the sign that Musgrove's tenure was not up to cozy camerado standards is the day the rarely formal poet referred to Musgrove as "the gentleman who is here to assist me" (the first allusion to him, Horace notes, in two weeks). After a rousing conversation with Horace, Walt half-jokes, "Mr. Musgrove will step in presently and put me to bed with or without my consent." That Musgrove was strict is also suggested by how Walt laughs when Hamlin Garland overstays the two-minute interview he had been granted: "Mr. Musgrove was on nettles—the man overstayed his leave." On October 26, 1888, a letter from Bucke arrived from Canada; it included this news: "I do not hear good accounts of your present nurse (Musgrove) and I have just written to Horace about a young man whom I can fully recommend who is willing to go from here and take the place. His name is Edward Wilkins." Within a few days, the change is made behind Whitman's back, but Traubel remarks, "W. is eager for the change. Yet he hates to have Musgrove's feelings hurt." When the man's days were clearly numbered, Traubel summed up: "Musgrove is curt, rough, almost surly—creates a bad atmosphere for a sick room. 'He has done his best,' said W., 'but don't quite understand that I'm a peculiar critter mostly determined to have my own way—not to be unnecessarily interfered with even here, even in my incompetencies.'" When Musgrove settled up his pay with Tom Harned (1851–1921), a prosperous lawyer and friend who had charge of many of Whitman's financial affairs, he was "out of humor," which even Walt noticed: "He is put out—indeed I may say, mad." Still, Horace observes, "W. is glad of the change. That is easily seen."

A Touch the Patient Likes: Ed Wilkins

Edward Wilkins arrived at Mickle Street in early November 1888. Bucke clearly knew his man in recommending him. Horace's first reaction: "He was tall, young, ruddy, dynamic. W. regarded him approvingly. Ed had been writing. He stood, his arms folded up, against the foot of the bed. He was in his shirt sleeves. There was half a smile on his face." A few days later Walt remarked, "Ed is very stalwart—handled me well—helped me with the currying." Horace assessed the situation: "He takes to Ed. Calls him 'brawny—a powerful ally.' His first lament over Musgrove was his last." The next day William O'Connor was informed in a letter that Walt was now in the hands of "a clean strong kind hearted young Kanuck man." Walt came to dote on Ed and his ministrations, as these passages show:

I am coming to see that he is just the man I needed: he is my kind: he is young, strong: I felt immediate wholesome invigorating reactions under the spur of his treatment: he gives me a sort of massage. . . .

I don't know what Ed thinks of me: I think he looks upon me favorably: I like him. I wrote Doctor [Bucke] so: he is just what he seems to be—straightforward, not inquisitive, hearty—best of all he is not intrusive: he does not push himself upon me. Does not insist . . .

[Ed undertook the violin while at Mickle Street, Horace reports:] Ed has a violin which he plays round the house. W's favorite piece in Ed's modest repertoire is Rock-a-bye Baby. Ed says quaintly: "I make it long for him—put in the chorus two or three times." [A few days later:] W. told Ed: "Play your violin: play it as much as you choose: I like it: when I am tired I will tell you to stop." Ed at first played in the next room. I advised him to play downstairs. But W. said to me on the side: "I don't altogether like the screeching, but I do altogether like Ed, so I can stand one for the sake of the other."

[Horace to Whitman:] Ed seems to be the right fellow for you here: he suits you to a T. [Whitman's reply:] Yes: he is vital, easy, nonchalant, self-sufficient (in the right sense): he throws out a sort of sane atmosphere: I always find myself at home, at peace, with him.

[Whitman a week later:] Ed is well fit in many ways: he is silent: moves about noiselessly: strong, faithful: has one quality significant above all, essential—the quality of touch: has a touch which the patient likes.

After about a year passed, Wilkins announced his resignation to Horace: "[Ed] told me of his resolve to go back to Canada Oct. 20. Had engaged with a veterinary surgeon to go with him on that date. This rather staggered me, as experience has shown how difficult it is to get a nurse for W. who combines qualities we desire and those which commend him to W." A week later Horace has not had the courage to tell Walt. Two weeks later Horace records, "[Ed] has spoken to W. about it. W. is 'adverse to a change'—greatly likes Ed—but would not advise him to risk his future, if it was risked, as it seemed to be, by staying." When Horace spoke of the virtues of a young black man working for Tom Harned, Whitman said: "Well—I have not the slightest objection in the world to a darky—not the slightest." A possible reason for Ed's defection is perhaps suggested by Horace's remark early in January 1889: "W. is so well now Ed has little or nothing to do. The other day E. complained." Walt, who had doted on Ed, wrote to Bucke, "we are all sorry Ed is going—every thing has been smooth & good . . . no hitch or anything." Amid puzzlement over Ed's returning to a "less than a quarter of a horse town" in Canada and after interviewing several replacement candidates, Warren Fritzinger was engaged on October 21, 1889. Wilkins did indeed become a veterinarian and returned to the United States to practice near Indianapolis, Indiana, for many years.

Noble Drubber: Warrie Fritzinger

Warren Fritzinger was already known at Mickle Street before he was hired for regular service (Mary Davis had cared for Captain Fritzinger, his seafaring father, for nearly ten years). "I like him very much," said Walt in June 1888, "he is such a lusty fellow—has been about the world so much—is a sailor." Walt was also very fond of Warrie's brother, Harry. Just before his marriage Harry visited Mickle Street: "I felt quite solemn about it," Walt wrote in a letter, "(I think more of the boy, & I believe he does of me, than we knew)—He kissed me & hung on to my neck—O if he only gets a good wife & it all turns out lasting and good"; in a letter to Bucke the next day he ends, "One of my two boys 26 yrs old was married last evn'g—he came yesterday to talk ab't it & hung on my neck & kiss'd me twenty times."

Soon Warrie ("my sailor boy") and Walt were on very good terms. After just two days on the job, Walt summarized: "Warrie and I come to understand each other pretty well—*very* well. I like his touch and he is strong, a font of bodily power.... As I was saying, I liked his touch—like to have him around—he has that wonderful indescribable combination—rarely found, precious when found—which, with great manly strength, unites sweet delicacy, soft as a woman's, gentle enough to nurse a child."

Walt particularly relished Warrie's abilities as a masseur: "Warrie rubs me every day—or twice a day—pummels me." "Warrie is a noble drubber [massager] himself: he handles me like a master—and the best thing about him is not his strength but his magnetism: he is electric to the last degree—never man more so. I don't think he can be beat. Ed Wilkins was strong, too—but lacked in many ways Warrie's peculiar gifts." The massages were daily, he tells Bucke, "generally just before going to bed." Walt wrote to Bucke in December 1889, "have had a good currying bout—I sometimes fancy I get the *vitalest* ones I ever had f'm my present nurse—young & strong & magnetic he is." Fritzinger also took lessons from the head masseur of Dr. Mitchell's Orthopedic Hospital to improve his massaging skills.

Young Scamp: Bill Duckett

Traubel records the visit of a lad who had lived at Mickle Street in the mid-1880s: "Bill Duckett came up as I sat there. Had had a sister die. W gave him 10 dollars. 'I am more interested than you know, Bill,' [Walt] said, 'when you get settled in the city, write me how you like it, or come see me.' And after Bill had gone, W. spoke feelingly of the sudden death of the sister and explained the condition of things."

Prior to the *With Walt Whitman* period, Duckett was a helper about the Mickle Street house and occasionally drove Whitman around Camden in a buggy. The baby-faced youngster's stopping by for money bordered on effrontery, for several months earlier Davis had taken him to court for the costs of room and board during the years he actually lived in Whitman's house. In court he said that Walt had "invited" him to live there, and this infuriated the poet: "think of it!—that I invited him here, that he was my guest!—the young scamp that he is! Why, that is downright perjury, outrageous lying." When Horace queried about the invitation, Walt was emphatic: "on the contrary, I resented his presence here from the start." Davis won her case. Whitman must have forgiven Duckett's cheek: $10 was a considerable sum. How was Whitman's kindness repaid? Amusingly: five months later a squib in *Current Literature* reported Duckett saying he had taken notes on Whitman and planned to lecture on him after his death. In October 1889 Walt was at first "amused . . . into great laughter" when news of this appeared in the *Philadelphia Epoch*. Later he fumed, calling the item a "*lie* in big, big type." He also said, with evident satisfaction, "Billy was here to see me the other day, but they [Davis and Warrie] would not let him in."

Pessimist: Nurse Keller

"He was rather disappointed that the nurse was a woman," Traubel reported of Elizabeth Keller. She gave Traubel notes on how the day of December 29, 1891, went; they included this remark of the poet to her: "You will find me very self-willed when you come to know me." On January 8, 1892, Keller told Traubel, correctly as it turned out: "I don't think he will ever get out of that bed."

Horriblest Dog Ever Born

To Horace's consternation, the setter, all too aptly named Watch, never learned to greet the constant visitor silently: "The dog made a terrific howl as I entered—never learns to know me. I said to W jokingly: 'I'll shoot him some night, he don't get over that.' W at once responding: 'And I'll not complain of the deed in the least! He howls a hundred times a day, at all hours. In the night too, generally about one o'clock when the rest of the world wants to keep quiet.'" A week earlier, the dog's noisy greeting to Horace animated Walt: "Well, if there's anyone in the world he ought to know by this time—would know, if he had any sense at all, as he has not—it is you. He is the nastiest, noisiest, silliest, stupidest, horriblest dog that ever was born, a pest, a continual sore in my side! . . . Any useful dog—any manly dog—gets to know his friends, betters—but this dog, never!" Three weeks later, when the dog snarled again: "There are good dogs and bad dogs, like there are good Irishmen and bad. A good Irishman is a tip-top fellow—you want no better: but a bad?—Oh! there's hell to pay!"

Two years later, Watch remained vigilant: "W. had remarked that the dog howled as I came in. 'He never gets to know me,' I explained. 'Nor anybody else,' said W. 'He's dumb as the devil! Don't seem to have any dog intuitions. Why, bawls the life out of us if Warren pulls the bell or opens the door: hasn't yet inner life enough to know Warren. I don't believe he realizes anybody at all but Mary.'" A few days later Horace notes: "The dog had barked when I came in and he had noticed it. 'He is the dumbest dog that ever set foot in America! He never seems to learn to know anything!'"

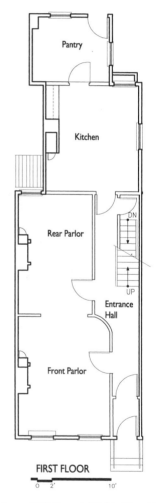

First floor of Whitman's Mickle Street house.
Courtesy Page Ayres Cowley Architects, LLC.

Serendipity:
Visitors and Vignettes

Whitman, at the time of his conversations with Traubel, was a considerable celebrity, though for reasons that ranged from deep "Whitmaniac" devotion to bemused, sometimes sneering curiosity over an incomprehensible, eccentric, and vaguely risqué old versifier. Walt did his best to remain cordial under siege. When the rumor got back to him that a visiting young poet had been unkindly treated, in fact, he got justifiably hot under the collar: "I make every effort to do justice to everyone who comes. If I go downstairs to see them, or see them in the room, I am sure that in 99 cases out of 100 I am kind, courteous. It is true I do not always consent to hear all that people may want to say—I could not: but when they come—young men, girls, whoever, I give the best welcome I can." Among the steady but utterly unpredictable stream of celebrity seekers who showed up at Mickle Street were the famous and notorious as well as the obscure and nameless. Their collisions with a courteous but decidedly cagey old party are often poignant and sometimes hilarious. And even on days when there were no visitors of note, Traubel often recorded fascinating or revealing vignettes.

Suspect Debris

Traubel describes the scene in Whitman's bedroom-cum-study: "There is all sorts of debris scattered about—bits of manuscript, letters, newspapers, books. Near by his elbow towards the window a washbasket with such stuff. . . . He pushed the books here and there several times this evening in his hunt for particular papers." A little self-conscious, Whitman defends his housekeeping: "This is not so much a mess as it looks: you notice that I find most of the things I look for and without much trouble. The disorder is more suspect than real."

Promiscuous Disorder

Months later and untidiness still reigns: "He sat much of the day across the room from the bed working in a mild way. His raw product is about him, on the table, the floor, in boxes and baskets, on chairs, and pretty nearly all things he may need are within reaching distance. At his foot is the pitcher of ordinary (never iced) water, which he takes up from time to time and draws from copiously. Books are piled promiscuously about, his will remains on the box-corner where he placed it when it was drawn up—letters, envelopes, are scattered over the floor—autographed volumes hang on the edges of the table-leaves, chairs, the sofa—everything seeming in disorder."

Motherly Valediction

One day Whitman pulled out a letter and handed it to Traubel, who then "took out the little sheet and read what was on it in trembling letters. I could not say anything. I put it back, holding it irresolutely in my hand: 'Yes: I wished you to take it: it is safer in your hands than in mine.' He was very grave. I still said nothing. 'I was afraid you would ask me something about it,' he said, chokingly. I kissed him good night and left." Traubel then records Louisa Whitman's valedictory words to her son: "farewell my beloved sons farewell i have lived beyond all comfort in this world dont mourn for me my beloved sons and daughters farewell my dear beloved Walter."

Testimonial

Traubel's sharp eye caught and recorded this moment during Whitman's seventieth testimonial dinner at Morgan's Hall in Camden: "How many saw the negro cook there in the hallway rush up to him to embrace and shake hands? He had nursed her husband in the hospital at Washington."

A Quiet Visit

Traubel records: "He had a couple of deaf and dumb visitors today. He was 'considerably interested and amused to have them come. . . . We got along pretty well together—though silently!'"

Room Temperature

On a cold January day in 1891, Traubel arrived and noticed Walt's room "not as cozy as usual" and asked about this, evoking the following exchange: "'I attribute a good deal of my cold, chilliness, discomfort to the variable temperature: now it is hot, now cold—extremely hot, sweaty, roasty—then cold as ice.' I asked him why he did not have Warren attend it more assiduously. The room should have a uniform temperature. 'Warrie does bring the wood in—keeps me in wood.' I expostulated, 'But he ought to keep the fire going too.' W. then, 'Warrie doesn't seem to have a talent for that sort of thing.' It is rare to hear so much of criticism from him. I suggested a thermometer for the room—that Warrie should keep its temperature steady. W. objected, 'But the best thermometer is my feeling.' 'Yes, I know: but Warrie must not have to consult you always.' He laughed slightly, 'You are right—I am convicted.'"

Holey Love

Traubel records: "Some neighbor had sent W. a plate of doughnuts. He put four of them in a paper bag and gave them to me for my mother. 'Tell her they are not doughnuts—tell her they are love.'"

A Square Offer for Kindling

One day Walt handed over the manuscript draft of "Note at Beginning" of the *Complete Poetry and Prose* (1888), saying, "I rescued it from the wood box for you." Horace voices his frustration: "I protested against his profligacy in threatening to throw such treasures away. He was jolly over it. 'Well—there is lots more here prepared to follow it!' I kicked: 'Let's make a swop: I'll furnish paper for the fire if you'll give me the manuscripts!' He cried: 'That's a square offer, sure enough. We'll see, we'll see!'"

An Exceptional Publisher Brings Oscar

The Philadelphia publisher J. M. Stoddart was responsible for the famous meeting of Oscar Wilde and Whitman at Mickle Street on January 18, 1882. Whitman greatly admired Stoddart, who later became the first to publish Wilde's novel *The Picture of Dorian Gray* (in *Lippincott's Magazine* in 1890), and reminisced about him and the meeting thus: "There is no airisfines about him—no *hauteur*. Years back he came over with Oscar Wilde, when Wilde was here in America and the noise over him was at its height. They came in great style—with a flunky and all that. And what struck me then, instantly, in Stoddart, was his eminent tact. He said to me, 'If you are willing—will excuse me—I will go off for an hour or so—come back again—leaving you together,' etc. I told him, 'We would be glad to have you stay—but do not feel to come back in an hour. Don't come for two or three.' And he did not—I think did not come till nightfall. And all I have had to do with him since is equally to his credit."

Walt Whitman Popcorn

On hearing that his portrait had been used on a cigar label, Walt laughed: "Who knows but by and by we'll give a name to some new brand pop-corn or the like? I remember what fun we had a long time ago over the Jenny Lind pop-corn."

Timid as the Rocky Mountains

One day, with Bucke down from Canada to visit, Traubel says a Unitarian minister in Massachusetts has been in touch with him about planning a Whitman evening in his church. Bucke urges the poet to send "a few words for Sunday too," but Whitman declines to do so. "How can we evangelize for you, Walt, if you won't help us?" "I don't want you to evangelize for me, Maurice: neither you nor anyone: I'd rather not have anybody evangelized into a belief in *Leaves of Grass*." Bucke accuses Whitman of being "very literal." "I am only timid, Maurice." "Yes: so you are: about as timid as the Rocky Mountains." Traubel observes: "Walt shrinks from the idea of conversion even to himself: he'd rather have enemies than converts." Bucke calls this nonsense. Whitman: "It does not sound like nonsense to me, Maurice: Horace hits the nail on the head. . . . Oh, Maurice! Maurice! will you never understand *Leaves of Grass!*"

A Preacher amid the Debrisity

Walt reports merrily on a visit by his printer, David McKay, who brought a dismaying guest: "Dave did not come alone. He had his preacher with him—a Presbyterian—up tonight. And do you know, Horace . . . I believe the old man came to me with a set purpose to deliver a speech—to question me about the *Leaves*, about my philosophy, politics. . . . But when he got into the room, the *debrisity* ["what a word!" Traubel inserts] of things—the confusion, the air of 'don't care,' the unusual look and atmosphere—must have struck him, abashed him, staggered him. For he hardly said a word beyond greetings!"

Lost in the Debris: The Great Letter

Probably the most important letter Whitman received in his entire career was the one from Ralph Waldo Emerson congratulating him on his first edition of *Leaves of Grass* in 1855. Whitman made shameless use of the gallant gesture, reprinting it in full, along with a long-winded response, in the second edition of the next year (he even slapped a blurb from it—"I greet you at the beginning of a great career"—on the volume's spine). In January 1891, when Walt allowed as how it might still be floating amid his papers, Horace clearly salivated: "The original is here still. I think I can lay my hands on it. Why, do you want it? You shall have it, without a question from me: if you want it, it is yours." Four days later Horace inquires whether it has been found: "No, but I shall, and it belongs to you: you may have it, now hereafter, instantly it comes to light. I know *about* where it is: today I have been in too bad a way to go searching for it." The next day inquiry is made again: "It will turn up, in some one of my searches, and whatever happens, it is yours, Horace." A week later "W. expressed regret that the Emerson letter had not yet turned up." Ten months later came the denouement, both droll and touching as reported by Horace: "Kicking about the floor—as often—I turned over a couple of yellowed letters fastened by a gum band and, picking them up, found my heart to stand still at the inscription that met my eye! The Emerson 1855 letter at last! And by strangest accident, which no one could have foreseen. Often had he promised me this letter—never knew where it was. 'When it turns up, it shall be yours.' Was always confident he had it, and I doubting. Now to have its thousand eyes look at me from this heap of debris! At the first pause in the talk I extended letter to W. 'I have made a great find, Walt.' 'What's that, Horace?' 'Look!' He took it while I said, 'A letter you have often promised to give to me but which I did not believe you would ever find!' Without for an instant opening it, 'What is that?' 'Emerson's 1855 letter!' Then he took it out of its yellowed Fowler & Wells envelope (it had been sent in their care). 'Sure enough, this is the letter. Did I promise to give it to you?' As if half hoping he had not. 'Yes, often.' 'Well, then I'll keep my promise. But it seems almost too precious to part with.' And with a smile, 'It must not be written of us that we did not keep our promises! However, I will keep it for a day or so—look it over. Do not forget to remind me of it when you come tomorrow!' "

Make Note of the Corn

"I found W. in his room just eating his dinner," Traubel reports. "He sat eating and talking during nearly the whole time of my stay. At one point said: 'I think this is the heartiest meal I have eaten in a fortnight.' Because he was extra well? 'No—not that—but this corn'—munching a little for an instant—'This corn is the cause of it and you can put it down in your notes.' Laughingly: 'I remember when Sidney [Morse, a sculptor] was here—he took lots of notes—always had his pencil ready—and I would say to him—put this down—that down. Now you put down for me—say that Walt Whitman likes nothing on this earth in the way of eating better than good, genuine, sweet corn.' "

Walt (Re)tells a Joke

One day Tom Harned, Walt, and Horace spend nearly half an hour exchanging jokes. Here is one that Walt rehearses some "40 or 50 years" after he first heard it: "A story of some one's falling overboard somewhere and being fished out—handing the Irishman a small coin—a sixpence, shilling, whatnot—the Irishman's scanning it, so [Walt performing a close scrutiny] and the rescued man's question, 'Well—isn't it enough?'—then the [a]cute reply—a blast in itself—'Ach, Soor—I was thinking as how I might have been overpaid!' "

Police Mitts Arrive

Traubel records Whitman "amusedly" asking him: "You have not seen my new mittens, have you? There—see these! Ain't they fine! What struck me most was their seamlessness—their one-piecedness." Whitman then spoke of his "growing sensitiveness" to the cold and of Davis getting them for him because "they were recommended to her there in the city as policeman's mitts. So, you see the new category I am included in!"

Spring Chicks Exercise Their Right

One Sunday Davis brings in two tiny chicks, and Walt is tickled: "Oh! What mites! And black ones, too! O you dearies! Are you glad you have come? . . . I have nothing here for you, darlings—nothing at all—nothing but *Leaves of* Grass—and *Leaves of Grass*. When you come to want them at all you will want the genuine, which, unfortunately, we have not about us here. How serene! . . . just as if they had a right to be here!—which is the most beautiful feature about it all."

Taking the Edge off Marriage

Traubel breaks the news that his sister, Agnes, will be married five weeks hence, and Whitman, we are told, "took this very seriously—exclaimed, 'Dreadful! Dreadful!' and murmured again, 'All the young fellows are to get married.' I put in, 'She is going to marry a Whitmanite, at any rate.' He laughed, 'Well, that takes the edge off it, to be sure!'"

A Tipple with the Cork In?

Traubel records this exchange on a Sunday outing to the Harned household: "My sister Agnes remarked: 'The drives are certainly doing you good—you show it.' He assented: 'They do indeed, yes they do. I have been out each day now for three or four days. . . .' He turned to Tom: 'I say Tom what's the matter with that tipple? Did you put in the cork again? What's the good of a tipple with the cork in?' Then after his glass was filled. 'Well, I forgive you. I forgive everybody: I am in a good mood for gentle things: the beautiful day, my hearty reception here, all of you about me: there's no room left for malice.'"

Violets and Verse

On an April day in 1889: "Mrs. Davis came in with violets in a tumbler—beautiful fresh stems: she had them from the backyard; handed them to Walt with a few words from the Lincoln poem—and took from the table the old bunch. W. protested as to the last: 'You are going to take them, Mary? But don't throw them away—they are too good still'; and put the others to his face an instant, inhaling their fragrance, ere placing before him on the table. Mrs. Davis departed—he looked long and pleasedly at the pure new stalks."

Voting on a Title

During another Sunday visit to the Harneds, Whitman very unusually put an artistic question on the table: "I want to take a vote on an alternative of titles for the poem section of *November Boughs*. Should it be 'Sands at Seventy' or 'Sands on the Shores at Seventy'? . . . I am at a loss about it." Everyone present—Horace; Rev. Clifford; Tom Harned; his wife (and Horace's sister), Augusta; and Anne Montgomerie (Horace's future wife)—voted for the shorter title, and Walt said, "So I see—I am agreed too." Tom Harned quizzed Whitman about this surprising event, "I thought you always did things in your own way without advice?" "So I do. Did I take any advice? It happened that you all agreed with me on that title. Suppose you hadn't? What would have happened? Tom, what would have happened?" Harned laughed heartily and said, "I suppose you would have cast your one vote against all our votes and declared your motion carried!"

Name-dropping

Whitman did not shy from salting his table talk with the names of celebrities he had met. On at least one occasion Traubel was able to top him. Whitman recalled about General Grant, "I have seen him, talked with him, a number of times: Grant's great feature was his entire reserve—his reserve behind reserve: his horse sense, I may say: he never set himself apart in an atmosphere of greatness: he always remained the same plain man—the unwavering democrat." Horace then recounted *his* meeting with Grant, on a Camden ferry boat as Grant was returning to Washington. He "asked me for the time. He set his watch by mine. Later I found my watch wrong. I said to W.: 'I felt as if I had set the United States of America wrong.' He laughed: 'That's a good boy story. I can appreciate your remorse!'"

Horace's Thirtieth

The day after Horace turned thirty this exchange was recorded: "W. was inquisitive—congratulatory—saying of my health so far (I have never been in a doctor's hands): 'Certainly that is the whole story: it seems to me that tells all: the thirtieth year! and health, vim, hope! What is there more than that?' He humorously questioned me. Had I no rules of life—no dietary doctrine? No. 'Good! good!' 'Except,' as I put it, 'no tobacco, no whiskey.' 'Ah! that is wise—a wise precaution: should say, persevere on that point—everything is to be gained by it, nothing lost!'"

An Ocular Debate

Traubel observes: "W. is always saying to me—'I am nearly blind.' He does have trouble with his eyes. But he sees things, too. Tonight he said: 'One of the worst signs is my eyes—they seem to be going back on me entirely—I can't see an elephant with 'em.' Right afterwards while I was looking at a photograph . . . W. remarked: 'And do you notice [John Addington] Symonds himself is down there by the shed, large as life?' I did notice Symonds. But he wasn't large as life. He was so small it would take divination or a magnifier to see him. I said so to W. and added, rallying him: 'And you are the man who says he is blind!' To which W. testily replied: 'Who should so well know he is blind as the man who can't see!' I laughed and was about to ask him another question but he would not let me. 'Take your questions to court—don't bother me with them: you ought to be a detective or a lawyer!'"

Siren from Ulyssean Seas

The entry for an August Saturday in 1890 ends on this evocative note: "There's a whistling buoy at Kaighn's Point which is often heard over this entire neighborhood. It sent forth its cry today—W. listening intently—then smiling, 'It has a sound as if from Ulyssean seas.'"

Walt in Eruption

One day Traubel happened in to find a livid Whitman shaking a letter furiously and muttering, "Goddamn your soul to hell! Damn you! Damn you!" Catching sight of his visitor, the poet launched a series of apoplectic rhetorical questions at him: "Have you ever had one near you who was a persecution, a perpetual filch, a damned lazy scoundrel—full of pretense, hypocrisy, lies, sneakiness? A hog, a poison, a snake, a dog, a beast? A person who defies honor? . . . A man who trades on your anxieties, preys on your good nature, whose presence is a loitering, whose whole life is hollow to all high and excellent purpose? . . . [A] man, arch in hypocrisy, double-dealing, a scaramouche of the worst sort, *nowise* related to me, who is a constant spear in my side . . . a man who almost shames me and my gospel of the divinity of evil." Who could evoke this highly uncharacteristic vitriol? Charles Heyde, the husband of his sister Hannah (they lived in Vermont). The feckless and cadging Heyde, Traubel notes, "is a perpetual worry and pain to W."

An Understated Visitor

One day a young man visited and talked so quietly that Whitman, whose ears had long since begun to fail him, could not hear his questions. The next day he observed, "What a quiet young man that was you brought yesterday!" Traubel reports that the friend said afterwards, "Curiously, W never answered one of my questions." Traubel then adds in his notes, "I am often asked when I take strangers there [to Mickle Street], why it is I cast my voice to such a [loud] pitch."

A Quaker Gift

I had a visitor—a Quaker lady—to-day. . . . She was here but shortly—explained that she had been out a while since, called on a friend: while waiting in the parlor had hit upon *November Boughs* on the table there: she had read it. . . . The old lady—she must be quite old—is poor, not famous: not intellectual, not even literary: but with a face remarkably gentle, sweet: and she 'thee'd' and 'thou'd' me—tickled me much: I own up to it. . . . When she came to go she took my hand, put into it a little folded piece of paper—so—and said "Don't open it till I'm gone—this is not for thee alone but for me": passed out. When I looked, lo! she had left me a two dollar and a half gold piece. The whole manner of it was characteristic: much the way of the Friends. It is a singular feature in men, that to simply confess a love is not enough: there must be some concrete manifestation of it.

A Namesake Visits

A son was born to Warrie Fritzinger's brother on Christmas Day 1891. He was named Walt Whitman Fritzinger, and the poet left $200 to be invested for the boy. On January 4, 1892, the boy was presented to Walt and laid upon his breast. Whitman's instincts for a photo opportunity never left him: "We ought to have our pictures taken."

Prying Baby—Cumbersome Critter

Traubel records this visit, with Whitman wheeled in his chair by Ed Wilkins, for Sunday dinner at the Harneds: "He got up the front steps with considerable difficulty, saying: 'I am considerable more cumbersome than I thought I was. . . . I am not for getting prizes for agility—foot-races—any longer!' He . . . rejoiced exceedingly in having the baby on his lap. As the boy played with his beard, he said: 'Never mind—he is only trying to discover what kind of a critter I am—let him pull whatever he chooses. . . . The dear babies! It is the Whitman trait to love women, babies, and cattle: that is a demonstrated feature.'"

A Dusty Tramp

A tramp—"a curious character—an itinerant poet"—appeared at Mickle Street and read some of his verse. "Lord pass him, what stuff!" was the response. But Whitman reflected to Traubel afterward : "When I said goodbye to the tramp I was envious: I could not see what right he had to his monopoly of the fresh air. He said he was bound for some place in Maryland. I shall dream of Maryland tonight—dream of farm fences, barns, singing birds, sounds, all sorts, over the hills." The next day: "I am still jealous of that tramp: I suppose he's bummin' along somewhere on the road eatin' apples and feelin' drowsy and doin' as he pleases." But the next day Whitman assured Traubel, "I no longer envy the tramp. . . . I thought he had taken everything he had brought away with him again: but I was mistaken. He shook some of his dust off on me: that dust has taken effect."

A Load of Prohibition

Tom [Harned] was here tonight with a couple of gentlemen—one of them is to lecture on prohibition down here at the church—and it was no small addition to the tedium to have him here, lightening himself of his load of doctrine.

Postal Efficiency

One day a letter arrived from abroad. It was simply addressed "Walt Whitman, America," and the poet was pleased that it got to him "sharply."

Walt Gets Hell, Calmly

A woman broke in on me years ago, one day, when I was alone: I was downstairs, at the window, where I used to sit so much. She came in innocently enough, talked awhile innocently enough, then suddenly broke loose on *Children of Adam*—on me—giving us hell from A to Z: I was surprised, almost scared. . . . She accused me of a deliberate desire to ruin boys, girls, people, by my flagrant philosophy—went on in that strain. . . . I never said a word. . . . My silence seemed to astonish her. "Haven't you a single thing to say in your own defense?" she finally asked me. I said: "Madam, I need no defense: I only need to be understood." That mystified her. She said: "No one would suppose, Walt Whitman, from looking at you that you are the sort of a man your books show you to be." She didn't intend that for a compliment but I enjoyed it as such. Finding she could make no impression, that I was not inclined to debate with her, she withdrew. I said quietly: 'Come again.' . . . So you see things do happen, some things, now and then, even here, in this Quaker household.

A Young Emissary from Harvard

One afternoon a young Harvard student appeared. He lingered for only fifteen minutes, but Whitman had to work rather hard to keep the conversational ball rolling, asking "some questions he cared nothing about" and admitting to "the most curious lack of curiosity about Harvard" and to always getting "Harvard and Yale mixed in my mind." As Whitman graciously autographed two copies of *Leaves of Grass* the boy had brought (and searched for a loose title-page photograph, which he also signed), the visitor remarked that "there are many of the fellows up there who have the same feelings about you I do. They would like to see you: I am lucky." Whitman replied, "Give my regards to them all: I know what it is for one man to meet another—what personal contact means: the magnetism of being present with your man. In the absence of that, in the presence of an impossibility, give them my love." After the visitor left, Traubel records, "W. was as usual serene. The stranger young, with the New England accent. Slender, agile—complexion sallow. When he was gone W. said: "I rather like him—don't you? a modest, engaging fellow."

No Pun Intended

One day Walt handed over to Horace a Civil War souvenir, a safe-conduct pass from 1862, saying as he did so, "it won't pass for money." Horace laughed and expressed his surprise at the apparent play on words, but Walt insisted, "Did you ever know me to pun? It's not in my line at all. I am guilty of most [of] the real bad sins but that bad sin I never acquired."

Small Request

Traubel records: "W. received what he calls 'one of my funny notes' a while ago. A young man in Richmond, 'a Southern boy'—writes a novel—say publishers refuse it because it shocks etc. Asks W. to read it—it is only 109 pp. Legal cap! Of course W. never answered."

A Note from Ellen Terry

Bram Stoker had arranged for Whitman to send an autographed copy of *Leaves* to the actress Ellen Terry, and she wrote him back, "Since I am not personally known to you I conclude Mr. Stoker 'asked' for me—it was good of him—I know he loves you very much."

In Longhand, out of Mischief

In December 1890 Walt received a letter from New York composed on a "type-writer" and was curious: "I wonder how they go? But of course I am too old—too old! Besides—I really have not much writing to do—and what I do tends to keep me out of mischief."

A Beautiful Boy

"There was some kind of labor agitator here today—a socialist, or something like that," Whitman told Traubel one day. "Young, a rather beautiful boy—full of enthusiasms: the finest type of man in earnest about himself and about life. I was sorry to see him come: I am somehow afraid of agitators, though I believe in agitation: but I was more sorry to see him go than come. Some people are so much sunlight to the square inch. I am still bathing in the cheer he radiated. O he was a beautiful, beautiful boy! . . . Oh he was a beautiful boy—a wonderful daybeam: I shall probably never see his face again—yet he left something here with me that I can never quite lose."

The Harned Baby

At a Sunday dinner with the Harneds, Whitman "was immensely taken" with the baby: "Generally, in the first year or two—the babies fear me: but they get bravely over that." When the baby smiled at him: "How instinctive they are! How they divine us—expose us! And yet I think even more so later on, after the first year or so is over." When it was excused for being noisy: "Oh! let it go on! A baby is not a baby who is denied that privilege!"

Whitman said one day of his regular Sunday visits to the Harneds (with Harned present): "they spoil me: it has come to be with me an essential point: I get expecting it. I am greedy—never satisfied: their house is an oasis in my domestic desert." Harned urges him not to "put it on too thick," and Walt replies: "Don't get conceited, Tom: that's not meant for you—that's meant for Mrs. and the children and the cook!"

Montaigne Varied

Traubel recalled how Michel de Montaigne, being amused by his cat, paused to wonder if he amused the cat. Whitman responded: "I remember that a long time ago, down at Timber Creek—I would go along the stream, looking, singing, reciting, reading, ruminating—and one fellow there—a splendid sapling—I would take in my hands—pull

back—so-so: let it fly, as it did with a will, into position again—its up-
rightness. One day I stopped in the exercise, the thought striking me:
this is great amusement to me: I wonder if not as great to the sapling? It
was a fruitful pause: I never forgot it: nor *answered* it. I suppose this is a
new strophe—Montaigne in other dress."

Scarey Question

Traubel ends his entry for June 1, 1891, with this parenthetical:
"(Nearly a fire in W.'s room the other night. He slid his chair about—it
ignited a match—which in turn fired papers. I discovered and stamped
it out. W. seemed to see nothing of it. If I had not been there, what might
not have happened?)"

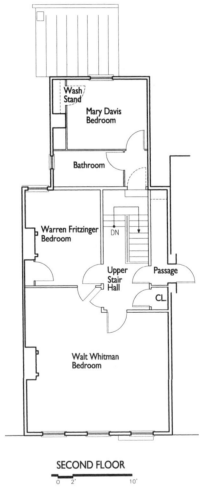

SECOND FLOOR

0 2'   10'

Second floor of Whitman's Mickle Street house.
Courtesy Page Ayres Cowley Architects, LLC.

Walt on Walt

Whitman never seriously considered the notion of writing a full-dress auto-biography, not least because his poems are relentlessly autobiographical (perhaps also because he was able to insinuate more than his two cents worth, anonymously, in the one biography published on him during his lifetime). The episodic compilation of 1882, Specimen Days, appears to have satisfied Whitman's self-singing urge in prose. Fortunately, Traubel was able to evoke countless self-descriptive exchanges during his talks with Whitman; many of these passing remarks, even some that at first seem quite mundane, are quite revealing of the author of Leaves of Grass.

His Almost Essential Name

I used to be Walter—started that way: then I became Walt. My father was Walter. He had a right to Walter. I had to be distinguished from him so I was made Walt. My friends kicked: Walter looked and sounded better: and so forth, and so forth. But Walt stuck.

Some of my friends still hold on to the belated "Walter": some do even worse—say "Mr." Whitman. Could anything be more out of place than "Mr." Whitman?

[At a Sunday dinner at Tom Harned's, one of his host's children asked how he came by "Walt":] It was to distinguish me from my father originally and then the name held. "Walt"—it is a good name, to me! But Mr. Whitman does not surprise or startle me: I take quite naturally to that, too—though my friends young and old—the real intimates—those, as I say, of the inner circle—all call me Walt—and there is no better way!

The "Walt" has come to seem almost essential.

In spite of it [Oliver Wendell Holmes's dislike of the four-letter word], "Walt" grows: I am "Old Man," "Kris Krinkle," now even "Walt" to the boys in the street. I think of one boy in particular—he always calls me "Walt"—"How are you, Walt?"—always with feeling and respect, I am not deceived—and he is a handsome boy—one of the handsomest I ever did see!

I like best my name in full—Walt Whitman—not Whitman alone nor Walt alone!

Halcyon Days

Traubel's reply to Whitman's query about his own health evoked a definition of the prime of life that was, autobiographically, very accurate: "Your invariable answer is 'well,' always 'well.' Are you always so well? It is so great—so superb—to be always well. However, these are your years to expect it—from eighteen to forty-five [1837 to 1864 for Whitman]—halcyon days, sure enough—and if there's anything in a man, physically or mentally, it's sure to come out, to give an account of itself, along through that stretch of life."

A Superb Start

In fibre, muscle, organically: in build, arm, leg, chest, belly—I started superbly—no one more so—more gifted, blessed.

Quaker Affinity . . .

Whitman spoke of his "conviction that a thing is because it is, being what it is because it must be just that—as a tree is a tree, a river a river, the sky the sky. A curious affinity exists right there between me and the Quakers, who always say, this is so or so because of some inner justifying fact—because it could not be otherwise. I remember a beautiful old Quakeress saying to me once: 'Walt—I feel thee is right—I could not tell why but I feel thee is right!'—and that seemed to me to be more significant than much that passes for reason in the world."

. . . but Not Completely

The Quakers are very clannish, though I am not that way myself. I am like the cabbage in the fable which forgot it was a cabbage: a very varied experience has washed me clean of that fault.

Unhurried

"Hurry" was never another name for Walt Whitman.

I seem to be remarkably constituted in one way—for being slow to affect things or be affected. I would never take a disease in a hurry—never make a convert in a hurry.

I'm no hurrier: I couldn't hurry if the house was on fire. . . . William [O'Connor] said to me more than once: "Walt, you're as fast as frozen molasses!"

New Light on Mickle Street—and on Walt

Traubel records: "At the near corner from W.'s house (4th St) they are planting an electric light pole. Said W. amusedly: 'Little shall I care for it—I always did shrink both from getting into a great light and from being a great light.' 'Yet,' I put in, 'did not some anyhow contend you were a light?' To which—'Yes: the sort of light that says, Beware!'"

Rooted in Socrates . . .

I can see why [the Unitarian minister John] Clifford said the other day that I made him think of Socrates. I never was nervous or quick. On the other hand I had, I may say, an unusual capacity for standing still, rooted on a spot, at a rest, for a long spell, to ruminate—hours in and out sometimes.

. . . and Rabelais?

Some people think I am someway, in some part, Rabelaisian. I do not know where it comes in—just what induces the belief. But after all, I know little of Rabelais—have looked at him, picked him up, but have never given him any close attention. William O'Connor's explanation of Rabelais was that he became disgusted with the cant of intellect, scholarship, in his time, and went off to his characteristic work as a protest. But people do not agree: I remember another claim pressed upon me for Rabelais . . . that his motive was spiritual; not of revolt alone, though that also, but affirmation. I don't know where I stand—I suppose I don't take sides.

Undemonstrative

I am not a demonstrable being, even to my intimate friends. . . . It is not a part of me: demonstration.

Uncorrespondent

I am not much of a correspondent—never was—always wrote when I had something definite to say but never for the sake of writing—never for the sake of keeping up what is called a correspondence.

I never was a fulsome correspondent myself—wrote no superfluous letters: wrote very deliberately: often made a draft of my notes. I rarely do that now—very few people do it. . . . I have given you drafts of several of my old letters: you have seen how extra-cautious I was: that was long ago. It involved a lot of useless work—made a man a slave: a long letter was half a day's job: God! I used to sweat over it even in cold weather.

Bad Temper, Perfect Control

There's one thing about me, however, which I don't think my best friends know—not you, not Bucke: inherently I have a bad temper—I have always known it—but I am just as sure that I have nearly perfect control of it—that it never runs away with me—that I am its master, not it mine. My dear mother knew it well—warned me of it, counseled me. And it was not without effect.

Intellectual Hospitality

If there's anything I pride myself on, it's my toleration, hospitality. Bob [Ingersoll] puts it well, "intellectual hospitality." I take in all the fellows—omit no one—as I take in all religions—seeing that they are all necessary to the scheme—all "divine facts" . . . not to be sneezed away. That is perhaps the only difference there is between Bob and me. I am quite as radical as he is, quite as set against the conventional, quite as determined to oppose the horrible phantasmagoria of creeds, religions (so-called)—yet have no quarrel with them—rake them too hard—from always having in mind their necessity.

An Evolutionist Party

My leanings are all towards the radicals: but I am not in any proper sense of the word a *révolutionnaire*: I am an evolutionist—not in the first place a *révolutionnaire*. I was early in life very bigoted in my anti-slavery, anti-capital-punishment and so on, so on, but I have always had a latent toleration for the people who choose the reactionary course.

Freakish Character

I interest the newspaper men as one of the strange fellows—they look for freakish characters—it is among these I come. . . . There was Emerson—they never could hold him: no province, no clique, no church: and there was Lincoln, who did his duty, went his way, untrammeled: but there are few others. I slipped out, avoided the beaten paths, tried a way of my own—that was my experiment. Has it failed or succeeded?

Oceanic Critter

I am not surprised to have friends in Australia—I am a sort of Pacific, Oceanic, Californian critter, anyway.

Clothes Make the Individual

Whitman told Traubel it was "damnable" to be "tailorized" or "hatted" after a "mode." A few days later, a hatter came to Mickle Street, and Whitman reported comically: "It was a young man who came. He spoke like one in authority. I liked him: he was direct, emotional, frank, seemed to understand me—best of all seemed inclined to follow the instructions I gave him—which is surprising in a hat or tailor man anytime. . . . I made the order very plain—wrote it out for him—pinned it to the old hat, which he took away with him—and warned him: 'Now look you out: if it's not just as I ordered it, I'll let it remain on your hands.'"

No Flag-waver: Sartorial

"This stars and stripes business is new and false. I never heard the story before, but ["with a merry laugh," Traubel notes] I have heard as bad and worse." Such was Whitman's response to this report in the

Advertiser of January 10, 1892: "He was almost the first to make the now fashionable fad of the flannel shirt in Summer his all the year round convenience and comfort, and the broad collar was turned over a silk American flag. His ordinary wear was a neat suit of working-man's clothes. . . ." Still, there can be no doubting that Whitman's outlay for clothing was extremely modest by any standards; in October 1890, in a letter to both Bucke and Traubel, he says Warrie Fritzinger has gone to Philadelphia "to take my aged white hat (25 y'rs old & more) to be done over, if possible."

Humorist

The idea that anybody imagines I can't appreciate a joke or even make jokes seems preposterous. Do you find me as infernally impossible as that, Horace? [William Cullen] Bryant said to me in one of our chats: "The most humorous men I have met have been the lightest laughers." You can't always tell by a man's guffaws whether he is a real humorist or not.

A short time later Whitman asserted, "I pride myself on being a real humorist underneath everything else." But word was about that Whitman lacked a sense of humor, and Traubel later probed again: "I told him of people who had asked me if W. ever laughed himself—could appreciate a joke. Had they heard his laugh at this they would have been convinced. 'That is very funny. My intimate friends would have their best fun with a man who brought them such a doubt!'"

Egotist

Traubel reminds Whitman of Bucke's long-standing suggestion that the poet keep autobiographical notes and adds that the idea seemed "farcical," given that "all *Leaves of Grass* and the prose was autobiographical if anything." Whitman agreed and "merrily" elaborated: "That after all is said by the others, I will pursue my *own* way; that the worm, the tortoise, the snake, the whatever, will leave its trail wherever it goes. The show of autobiography everywhere in my work. I read 'Old Poets' last night again . . . and I can see now why it should be an offense to some people. It's *egotism*—egotism: that is the trouble. It is somewhat scrappy, very gossipy and terribly egotistical—and that is its trouble with some. But it is my vein, and I must flow in it."

Note: "Old Poets" is a short overview essay of Whitman's that first appeared in the *North American* in 1890, later as part of *Good-Bye my Fancy* in the 1892 *Leaves*.

No Bower and Scraper

I have always been taken for a great quarreler—almost a brawler—rather than a bower and scraper: I was never accused before of being willing to train in with other people. My dear mother used to say to me:

"Walt—does thee not sometimes—just sometimes, Walt—look for differences where there are none?" Dear mother!

Specimen Days: *Confessional*

The best biographical material of all—if you wished it for your article—is in *Specimen Days*: there is no mistake about that—no "interpretation": what is there is confession.

Note: *Specimen Days*, a collection of short prose memoranda (a "way-ward book" Whitman called it), was published as part of the 1882 edition of *Leaves*; it includes a brief autobiography, some war memoirs, and a potpourri of nature pieces, travel recollections, and thumbnail essays. Whitman's remark to Traubel is one of many indications that they assumed something biographical would issue from their relationship.

Catechizers and Interrogators

I am always uneasy about the inquirers when they come buzzing about: they get on my skin and irritate me!

He [William Ingram] is a questioner—a fierce interrogator: I am disturbed by his boisterous questions: rattled by them, as the boys say: I am not fond of being catechized—indeed, rather run from it: I am not fond of questions—any questions, in short, that require answers.

For thirty years my enemies and friends have been asking me questions about the *Leaves*: I'm tired of not answering questions.

Traubel observes: "W. is a slow answerer but he always answers to the point. That is, if he wants to answer at all. Sometimes he don't. Then he will say he don't want to in so many words or will tell you what a long tail that cat has and so get off your chase."

God Almighty how I hate to be catechized!

Traubel reiterates, "He hates to have anyone fire a fast question at him." One day Traubel told Whitman what the Unitarian minister John Clifford said when he heard that John Addington Symonds had written a letter inquiring about poems the poet had banished from later editions of *Leaves*: "It is good he is 3,000 miles off: it saves him the disappointment of putting his questions to Walt and having them avoided." Whitman's response: "So Clifford has heard I dislike to be asked questions" "Not *heard* of," Horace replied, "but has observed it himself." In a letter to William Sloane Kennedy, Whitman alluded to the steady stream of "talkers bores questioners (hateful)" at his door.

They ["questioners"] are my abomination: I'd as lief be buffeted so and so and so—right in the mouth—as be constantly submitted to catechism. It is always: what do you think of [presidential candidate James] Blaine? or, what do you think about religion? or, what are your opinions about politics? or, do you believe in immortality? and so on, with a list that sets me sick.

His Master's Voice

I was a great spouter in my early days—even later on—had my favorite pieces. . . . Yes, "A Voice Out of the Sea," my own piece was one—one of many. I always enjoyed saying it—saying it to the winds, the waters, the noisy streets—on stage-coaches. And one has love for the sound of his own voice—somehow it's always magnetic.

Note: He got the title of the favorite poem wrong: it was "A Word Out of the Sea" (becoming in 1871 "Out of the Cradle Endlessly Rocking").

His Memory

It plays some tricks—but then it always did: it is not a marvellous, only a decently good, memory.

Not Inertial

On the occasion of the poet's seventieth birthday banquet, his long-time partisan John Burroughs sent a festive letter. Its text was to be included in the pamphlet marking the occasion, *Camden's Compliment to Walt Whitman*. In the letter Burroughs asserts about the American character, "We lack mass, inertia, and therefore, power," and then suggests Whitman possesses these qualities. Not catching the physics of the point (which pleased Traubel), Whitman rankled at "inertia," clearly because it subverted a central element of the persona he had projected for decades: "I am inclined to question that use of the word—and yet, provided a result is had, provided we can clearly take hold of a writer's intention, I rarely quarrel with peculiar manipulation of the language. I have always associated inertia with what is dull, sluggish, I may say dead. . . . It is a word that has been used to express lack of verve—a lack of fire: it does not fully or even friendlily recommend itself to me."

Language Skills

I never knew any other language but English. I never liked text books— could never study a foreign language. Did I say I never knew any language but the English? My enemies would even dispute my knowledge of the English.

Anarchist Tramp: His Politics (and Horace's)

It seems as though all the square round fellows were getting to be Socialists: sometimes, I think, I feel almost sure, Socialism is the next thing coming: I shrink from it in some ways: yet it looks like our only hope. I'm a sort of an anarchist tramp, too: and you? well, you are a lot like me (or am I like you?): but things drive us on—the God-damned robbers, fools, stupids, who ride their gay horses over the bodies of the crowd. . . . Horace, you'll be in the thick of the fight after I'm gone: my days are few: but you have years ahead—years of vicissitude—of active agitation: you are one of the rebels: you will have to take your part in the fight. God bless you whatever you do. I know that what you do for yourself, for others, in those days you'll also do for me. God bless you!

Warm Abolitionist

The abolitionists at that time [prior to the Civil War] were split up: some of them endorsed Lincoln, others accused him of temporizing, and called for a more radical policy—wished the engine driven at full spped, no matter what was on the road. I myself, coming in contact as I did with everybody, was right in the midst of a little group of inveterate abolitionists, never endorsing them or accepting their methods—though always an antislavery man—but there with them, rubbing up against them—hot abolitionists, which I never was myself.

Aquatic Loafer

I always hugely enjoyed swimming. My forte was—if I can say it that way—in floating. I possessed almost unlimited capacity for floating on my back—for however long: could almost take a nap meanwhile. . . . I was a first-rate aquatic loafer.

Candor

"Some day you will be writing about me: be sure to write about me honest: whatever you do, do not prettify me: include all the hells and damns." Whitman said this on the day he signed his will.

A Pair of Nobodies (W. W. and E. D.)

I do not seem to belong to great show events—I am more like nobody than like somebody, as some funny man says—I was more used to being kicked out than asked in: I always went to the big pow-wows with the crowd, to look on, not with the nabobs, to perform.

Note: The first stanza of the famous Emily Dickinson poem is: "I'm Nobody! Who are you? / Are you—Nobody—Too? / Then there's a pair of us? / Don't tell! they'd advertise—you know!"

Omnivorous

I used to thrust papers, things, into my pockets: always had a lot of reading matter about my person somewhere: on ferries, cars, anywhere, I would read, read, read: it's a good habit to get into: have you every noticed how most people absolutely waste most all of their spare time?

Procrastinator

I am more famous for procrastination than for anything else: you write to him—tell him that Walt Whitman will be along by and bye—is rather lame in the legs and in several other things: is harder to move round than a sick elephant.

One day Whitman spoke regretfully of a long-mulled study of the Quaker preacher Elias Hicks he had long venerated: "My infernal laziness, neglect, inanition, for thirty years or fifty or more has put this off and off till now it is no longer possible. My fatal procrastination has tripped me up at last."

Unexplosive Northerner

When Walt gave Horace an inscribed copy of *November Boughs*, still warm from the press, he excused his inscription for being "not very strong, very emphatic." Horace quotes Emerson to excuse him: "The superlative is the fat of expression." The poet warms to the idea and elaborates: "That's the Emerson I knew: sinew without fat: if anything (though I guess not) too much sinew: reserved, reticent, always sweet, almost a disciple of silence. You know me and know I never quite go off about things—am not explosive, extravagant. Gesticulation, physical emphasis, facial grimacing, more prevalently distinguishes southern peoples than peoples north."

Cautious Stayer

I am what the boys call a stayer—I am very cautious: my caution has kept me out of many scrapes: has saved me from this death scrape [the minor strokes of spring 1888]. Thirty years ago or more a circle of *cèlébres* in phrenology gave my head a public dissection in a hall—for one point marked my caution very high.

Under Control

"You always seem so equable. Don't you ever get mad?" Traubel asked. "This warmed him up." Whitman responded: "Mad? I boil: burn up: but often I keep my mouth shut: I am a slow mover: I don't hurry even in my tantrums: my passions are all ready for action but—well, there are many 'buts.'"

Between the Lines

"Oh! I use ruled paper, but I don't write on the lines!" This was a tendency Whitman shared with Oscar Wilde, whose "huge and sprawling" hand at Oxford "took no notice of lines" in examination books.

Slow Fruit Is Best

One day Whitman received a remarkably poised tributary letter from an eighteen-year-old. Walt's response clearly had an autobiographical resonance, given his late arrival at a chosen profession: "That sounds very ripe for a boy of eighteen, ripe enough already to shed fruit. It is singular how soon some natures come to a head and how long it takes others to ripen, though I believe, as a rule, the slow fruit is the best." Some months later he paraphrased this view: "it's mainly the slow maturers who mature to stay—mature to grow."

Snubber

I had a way in the old times—as I have not now—of saying something very snubbing to a fellow I thought impudent.

No More Theater

I am no longer a theatre-goer—perhaps I have lost the theatrical perspective—I have not seen plays for a long time.

Open Air, Water

I am an open air man: winged. I am also an open water man: aquatic. I want to get out, fly, swim—I am eager for feet again! But my feet are eternally gone.

Walt on the Whitman Family

Whitman spoke rarely about his father, Walter (1789–1855), but often, and in the most effusively venerating terms, about his mother, Louisa Van Velsor Whitman (1795–1873). He rarely alluded to his many siblings in his published works, one exception being his brief memoir, in Specimen Days, *of a trip with his brother Jeff to New Orleans in 1848. On several affecting occasions, however, Traubel was able to get the poet going on the subject of his family, and the impression left is of Whitman being very loving but also very sensitive to their lack of comprehension of his art . . . and of his personality. Whitman's family consisted of his mother, father, and siblings Jesse (1818–70), Mary Elizabeth (1821–99), Hannah (1823–1908), Andrew Jackson (1827–63), George Washington (1829–1901), Thomas Jefferson (1833–90), and Edward (1835–92).*

Family and "Family"

A man's family is the people who love him—the people who comprehend him. You know how for the most part I have always been isolated from my people—in certain senses have been a stranger in their midst: just as we know Tolstoy has been. Who of my family has gone along with me? Who? Do you know? Not one of them. They are beautiful, fine: they don't need to be apologized for: but they have not known me: they have always missed my intentions. Take my darling dear mother: my dear, dear mother: she and I—oh! we have been great chums: always next to each other: always: yet my dear mother never took that part of me in: she had great faith in me—felt sure I would accomplish wonderful things: but *Leaves of Grass?* Who could ever consider *Leaves of Grass* a wonderful thing: who? She would shake her head. God bless her! She never did. She thought I was a wonderful thing, but the *Leaves?* oh my, hardly the *Leaves!* But she would put her hand in mine—press my hand—look at me: all as if to say it was all right though in some ways beyond her power to explain. I was saying our family is where we are loved—understood: by all the real tests the O'Connor family was my family: you, Rossetti, anyone near to me, is my family. I have been giving you the letters—the avowal letters, we have called them: they are my family—the avowers: blood tells sometimes against a man as well as for a man: they say that blood is thicker than water: but what does blood mean in a case like this?

Defeated by Leaves

"No one of my people—the people near to me—ever had any time for LG—thought it more than an ordinary piece of work, if that." Even his mother, Traubel asked: "No—I think not—even her: there is, as I say, no one in my immediate family who follows me out on that line. My dear mother had every general faith in me; that is where she stopped. She stood before LG mystified, defeated." And his brother George, Traubel asked. Whitman smiled, "You know that George believes in pipes, not poems."

A Curio of Sorts

Traubel and Whitman speak one day about the poet's father, Walter: "I asked: 'And at what time was it your father died?' '1855.' 'Just your entrance year?' 'Yes.' 'Then he did not live to see any of your great work?' 'No—and I don't suppose it would have made much difference if he had.' 'But,' I pursued, 'have none of your folks grown into an understanding of it?' 'I hardly think so—surely not: they sort of accept me—do it as a matter of course—but with a feeling as though not knowing why or what I am: a feeling, a wish, that I might be more respectable. . . . Even today they look on me, I am sure, as untamed, stubborn, too much bent on my own ways—a curio of sorts.' 'Then there's not one in the bunch who can be regarded as being in touch with what you have written?' 'Not one of them, from my dear mother down—not one of them: on the contrary, they are dead set against my book and what it stands for.' "

Ignorant

One day Traubel came across an early photograph of Whitman and asked after its date: "Do you think your family would know about it?" Whitman: "My family know nothing at all: not one of them." Later, Traubel summed up about Whitman's family, "You will drag them all to immortality"; this "made him laugh though he said nothing in direct reply to it."

Parents

My father was not, properly speaking, a Quaker: he was a friend, I might almost say a follower, of [the Quaker orator and reformer] Elias Hicks: my mother came partly of Quaker stock: all her leanings were that way—her sympathies: her fundamental emotional tendencies.

Rheumatic Sister Mary

She married a mechanic named Van Nostrand—I do not hear from her often: she is old, sickly—younger than me, but now frail. In the beginning she was vigorous enough, as we all were—but rheumatism has sapped her. And do you know, Horace, I often sit here and wonder why I am exempt from rheumatism—for both our parents had it, and the children more or less—but except for the slightest incidental hints of it, I do not know what it is.

Note: Mary Whitman married in 1840 and moved to Greenport, Long Island, where Whitman frequently visited. She is almost never mentioned in conversation.

Accidental and Actual Brother Jeff

Jefferson Whitman, an engineer who specialized in water projects and lived in St. Louis, paid a short visit to Camden in February 1889, and Walt reports: "His visit was quite a short one: he came in the forenoon: then I thought he would come back again before going off but he did not: he goes straight West again." Traubel remarks, knowing he was Walt's favorite sibling, "You must have been overjoyed to see him." We are told Walt responds quietly: "I don't say overjoyed: but Jeff and I are actual as well as accidental brothers."

Traubel tells of seeing Jeff's obituary, then going to Mickle Street: "Was aware of the death of Jeff. 'I had a telegram here,' he said, and relapsed into a great quiet—not for five full minutes disturbed. Then he spoke of the beauty of the day: 'How good it must be to be free to live out of door.'" Whitman reported Jeff's death thus in a letter to Bucke: "Gloomy & depressed enough these two or three days—My brother Jeff died Tuesday last at St Louis—typhoid pneumonia—was in his 58th year—was very much with me in his childhood & as big boy greatly attached to each other till he got married—(I was in 16th year when he was born)." Jeff named a daughter Manahatta, doubtless to please Walt.

Dear brother Jeff was a mild enough man—careful, never over-stepping the caution of speech. . . . [Radical] but radical after a quiet, not aggressive fashion. Not that he would hide his thought, hypocritize, no, that would have been impossible. But you will notice with the best engineers, scientists, that whatever their un-orthodoxy, they make no parade of it—are quiet, not assertive—though very firm. Of course in men of their kind—the whole class—there is no lingering with the old ideas. They quickly discover their falsity—dismiss them. . . . Dear Jeff! He loved a long walk—always enjoyed an hour's stroll: was self-contained, quiet, radical, without display in any way.

Distant Brother George

George and I—well, we were never quite so near: not that I have anything against George or that he has anything against me: no: but we were never cheek by jowl, as Jeff was with me, I with Jeff, always. Being a blood brother to a man don't make him a real brother in the final sense of that term.

George once said to me: "Walt, hasn't the world made it plain to you that it'd rather not have your book? Why, then, don't you call the game off?" I couldn't give George any reason why which he would have understood. Then I remembered that he was my mother's son, my brother—not my counsellor. I said nothing: George was disappointed: he said: "You are stubburner, Walt, than a load of bricks."

George was a waterpipe inspector, first in Brooklyn, then in Camden. In 1884 he and his wife moved to a farm about twelve miles outside of Camden. Though in relatively close proximity, the brothers had absolutely nothing in common. Not a single lively word from or about George is contained in all of *With Walt Whitman*. This Traubel entry is typical: "George Whitman in to-day. Saw Walt for a minute. Never stays long. Makes brief inquiries. In nearly every day." One day George's wife, Louisa ("a comforting woman"), visited, Traubel afterward remarking, "You get more out of her than out of George." Walt agreed emphatically: "I get nothing out of George or absolutely nothing: I get much out of her."

George could never overlook the *Children of Adam* poems: he has of course never understood them—I doubt if he ever really read them, though he says he did: he thinks them of 'the whore-house order,' as he has said to me: what mystifies him is the fact that I wrote the poems: he finds it impossible to realize them as mine: he don't believe evil of me—yet the poems seem to him to be evil poems: it's quite a puzzle which he has told me more than once he absolutely gives up.

I think George has always had more or less suspicion of my sanity. I think George would have been pleased, better pleased, if I had written in rhyme. He said this to me in a burst of confidence: "Damn it, Walt, I think you have talent enough to write right: what are you up to, anyhow?" Then he waited as if I had something to say—as if I was bound to give away my secret! I made no reply . . . finally he broke in again: "I say, Walt—have you nothing to say?" I nodded: "Nothing, George: I just did what I did because I did it: that's the whole secret." . . . He only said: "You're as stubborn as hell, Walt." So we abandoned the subject.

Helpless Brother Eddy

One day Traubel suggests that Whitman preserve the manuscript of *November Boughs*—and Walt acquiesces. A discussion follows of the value of taking such care, which leads to discussing Eddy, his brother with mental and physical disabilities. Walt promised his mother he would look after Eddy, who lived with her until her death in 1873: "The first manuscript copy of *Leaves*—1855—the first edition—is gone—irretrievably lost—went to the ragman: the copy for the Osgood edition [of 1881–82] I think is still somewhere. But I make nothing of that—of the money value of the manuscripts—attach no importance to curios. The collectors are inflamed with the curio desire but to me the appetite is unwholesome—at least never excited even my momentary interest. And yet, for Eddy's sake it might be wise for me to husband such stuff—though I don't know: even that seems to me rather wide of the mark. I have for years done so many things with reference to Eddy—have stinted, spared, saved, put by, cherished, watched—so that I might not slip cable some day with him unprovided for. Eddy is helpless . . . was a poor, stunted boy almost from the first. He had the convulsions—it was all up with him—the infernal, damnable fits that left him not half himself from that time on forever."

A few days later, Eddy happens to stay overnight at Mickle Street as he is being transferred from Moorestown to Blackwood, New Jersey. Horace records: "The meeting between the brothers mostly and impressively silent—Eddy mentally inarticulate, W. sadly ruminative. They talked in monosyllables. I noticed that while Walt will kiss Jeff he merely takes Eddy's hand and holds it and says nothing. . . . As the evening wore on W. grew more and more uncommunicative as towards Eddy. Finally he said to Mrs. Davis: 'I think you had better go now,' and to Eddy: 'Good-bye, boy—I will send for you soon again: you shall come whenever you choose: good-bye! good-bye!' W. saying of it to me: 'Eddy appeals to my heart, to my two arms: I seem to want to reach out and help him.'"

The cost of Eddy's care at Blackwood, paid for by Walt, was $45.50 a quarter. In a letter to Susan Stafford, the mother of his friend Harry Stafford, he says Eddy "is well, & seems to be off & satisfied." The only extant letter from Walt to Eddy, dated November 28, 1890, begins: "It is pretty sad days just now for me here—our dear brother Jeff died last Tuesday at St Louis, Missouri, of typhoid pneumonia. . . . I often think of you & hope you have comfortable times—I have heard you have a good kind attendant who has been there some time in the asylum. . . ."

Mysterious Brother Jesse

Whitman's silence about his year-older sibling, Jesse, clearly puzzled Traubel. This was notably shown the day Whitman gave him a short letter, calling it a "family memorandum" and saying nothing else. It was written by an assistant physician at the Kings County Lunatic Asylum in Flatbush, Long Island, and was dated March 22, 1870. It read, in full: "Your brother Jesse Whitman died very suddenly yesterday from the rupture of an aneurism. As it is uncertain whether this reaches you or not we shall bury the body tomorrow." Traubel read it and records: "He said nothing. Looked rather serious about it. 'Do I understand that I am to take this?' 'Yes—take it—put it away where it will be preserved.' I left shortly after."

Pregnant Quaker Force

Too much is often said—perhaps even by me—about my Quaker lineage. There was some of it there, but back, altogether among the women, with my own dear mother and grandmother and her mother again. It is lucky for me if I take after the women in my ancestry, as I hope I do: they were so superior, so truly the more pregnant forces in our family history.

Family Politics: Deep-dyed Heretics

All Republicans, Jeff, George: all of us: we were originally Democrats but when the time came we went over with a vengeance: it was no role, no play for us: we were at once what the church would call—what orthodox Democrats would call—deep-dyed heretics.

So Much for the Family Diamonds

Would you say that George was capable of giving you any ripe views on *Leaves of Grass*? I would say, God bless George my brother: but as to George my interpreter, I would ask God to do something else with him. When I think of what my own folks by blood didn't do for me and what you fellows not of the blood royal have done for me, I don't make much of the family diamonds or the inherited crown. Now you must not set this down for a growl: it's not that: I never feel unhappy over what is unavoidable: I have no more right to expect things of my family than my family has to expect things of me: we are simply what we are: we do not always run together like two rivers: we are not alike: that's the part and whole of it.

The Horace Family

I say again, Horace, *you* are my family: if love and being in *rapport* together makes two men of one family, then you are my family and I am yours.

Walt on Images of Himself

Probably no American writer—certainly none in the nineteenth century—
courted the image-makers of the day more than Whitman. He gave a remarkable number of painters and photographers access to his visage. One
day he gave a rough estimate of the number of photographs: "I suppose I
have had at least a hundred and fifty taken . . . perhaps a good many more."
The number may have been so large because the poet was typically disappointed with the results and hoped for better. The visit of one portraitist,
John White Alexander, led to a characteristic outburst: "I give the painters
all the rope they want: I humor them every way I know. Alexander came,
saw—but did he conquer? I hardly think so. He was here several times,
struggled with me—but since he left Camden I have heard neither of him
nor of his picture." (Whitman then compared Alexander to the one living
painter he cottoned to: "I thought Alexander would do better, considering
his reputation. Tom Eakins could give Alexander a lot of extra room and yet
beat him at the game. Eakins is not a painter, he is a force. Alexander is a
painter." Later Whitman said of Alexander's portraits, witheringly, "I hear
they are bad, bad—good for art, but bad for truth—good, but no portraits."

The Gamut

No man has been photographed more than I have or photographed
worse: I've run the whole gamut of photographic fol-de-rol.

They have photographed me all ages, sizes, shapes: they have used me
for a show-horse again and again and again.

I suppose I have had at least a hundred and fifty [photographs] taken—
quite that many—perhaps a good many more. They would make a big
gallery of themselves.

I have been photographed, photographed, photographed, until the
cameras themselves are tired of me.

Elusive

I am persuaded that my painter has not yet arrived. I know I have been
very successfully taken—taken in all sorts of habits and hours—but
somehow there is an elusive quality which so far no one has caught.

Risky Business

Nothing can be predicted of a photo—it hits if it hits, not otherwise. It seems true of all photos, that you can't start out to produce any certain effect: you must submit to circumstances.

Trouble for the Camera

There are difficulties, too—my red, florid, blooded complexion—my gray dull eyes—don't consort well together: they require different trimmings: it is very hard to adjust the camera to both. . . . Startle, strikingness, brilliancy are not factors in my appearance—not a touch of them. As for me I think the greatest aid is in my *insouciance*—my utter indifference: my going as if it meant nothing unusual.

Solicitous Sitter

I am always subjected to the painters: they come here and paint, paint, paint, everlastingly paint. I give them all the aid and comfort I can—I put myself out to make it possible for them to have their fling: hoping all the time that now the right man has come, now the thing will be done completely once and for all, and hereafter I can hood my face.

Giant Lover

Whitman hands Traubel a photograph of him by the eminent New York celebrity photographer Napoleon Sarony and asks, it would appear rhetorically: "How does that strike you? Take it along. It is one of the strongest of my good-humored pictures. Some of my pictures are strong but too severe—don't you think so? This is strong enough to be right and gentle enough to be right, too: I like to be both: I wouldn't like people to say 'he is a giant' and then forget I know how to love. It would be no consolation to me to be a giant with the love left out."

No Guts

Whitman's comment on a painting of him by Anne Gilchrist's son Herbert: "his picture is very benevolent, to be sure: but the Walt Whitman of that picture lacks guts."

Too Much Rabelais: The Eakins Portrait

Eakins' picture grows on you. It is not all seen at once—it only dawns on you gradually. It was not at first a pleasant version to me, but the more I get to realize it the profounder seems its insight. I do not say it is the best portrait yet—I say it is among the best: I can safely say that. I know you boys object to its fleshiness; something is to be said on that score; if it is weak anywhere perhaps it is weak there—too much Rabelais instead of just enough.

Of all portraits of me made by artists I like Eakins' best: it is not perfect but it comes nearest being me. I find I often like the photographs better than the oils—they are perhaps mechanical, but they are honest. The artists add and deduct: the artists fool with nature—reform it, revise it, to make it fit their preconceived notion of what it should be. We need a Millet in portraiture—a man who sees the flesh but does not make a man all flesh—all of him body. Eakins almost achieves this balance—almost—not quite: Eakins errs just a little, just a little—a little—in the direction of flesh.

But over time Whitman warmed to the Eakins; here he compares it favorably to the bust of him done by the sculptor Sidney Morse: "Eakins! How nobly he conforms to the Carlylean standards!—the standards which declare: you will come to this first in doubt, chagrin, perhaps: but here is an art that is nature—that will grow, grow, grow upon you: develop as you develop—is finally all opened to you as a flower! Who can look at Eakins at the start and be satisfied?—but looking longer, revelation comes—little by little discovery, discovery. Oh! there is no doubt Eakins is our man!"

Note: Apropos a discussion of photo-engraving Eakins's portrait, Traubel remarks that "W.'s friends in the main resent E.'s picture. But he is obdurate." Whitman stands up for it: "For my part I consider that a masterpiece of work: strong, rugged, even daring."

Particularly Idiotic

When Whitman hands him an old Matthew Brady photograph, circa 1862, Traubel remarks on its "rather ascetic look." Whitman responds, "So it has—a sort of Moses-in-the-burning-bush look. Somebody used to say I sometimes wore the face of a man who was sorry for the world. Is this a sorry face? I am not sorry—I am glad—for the world: glad the world is as it is—glad the world is what it is to be. This picture was much better when it was taken—it has faded out: I always rather favored it. William O'Connor always said that whenever I had a particularly idiotic picture taken I went into raptures over it. There may be good reasons for that: how often I have been told I was a particularly idiotic person!"

Don't-Care-a-Damnativeness

Looking over an early picture of himself, Whitman said, "what hits me so strong about it: its calm don't-care-a-damnativeness—its go-to-hell-and-find-outativeness: it has that air strong, yet it is not impertinent: defiant: yet it is genial." Walt admired this trait in others, notably Emerson (he "begets a healthy don't-care-a-damn-ness") and Anne Gilchrist ("gifted in a rare degree with a necessary "don't-care-a-damn-ativeness").

Love-seat Photo with a Rebel Friend

One day Traubel comes across "a picture from the box by the fire: a Washington picture: W. and Peter Doyle photoed together: a rather remarkable composition: Doyle with a sickly smile on his face: W. lovingly serene: the two looking at each other rather stagily, almost sheepishly. W. had written on this picture, at the top: 'Washington D.C. 1865— Walt Whitman & his rebel soldier friend Pete Doyle.'" Traubel records what ensued: "W. laughed heartily the instant I put my hands on it (I had seen it often before)—Harned mimicked Doyle, W. retorting: 'Never mind, the expression on my face atones for all that is lacking in his. What do I look like there? Is it seriosity?' Harned suggested, 'Fondness, and Doyle should be a girl'—but W. shook his head, laughing again: 'No—don't be too hard on it: that is my rebel friend, you know' &c. Then again: 'Tom, you would like Pete—love him: and you, too, Horace: you especially, Horace—you and Pete would get to be great chums.'" It is likely that the photograph was actually taken in 1869.

Photographer's Art

The art is growing with strides and leaps: God knows what it will come to: some of the smart wide-awake fellows even back in that Lincoln time had a knack of catching life on the run, in a flash, as it shifted, moved, evolved.

The human expression is so fleeting—so quick—coming and going—all aids are welcome.

Portrait or Photograph?

The photograph has this advantage: it lets nature have its way: the botheration with the painters is that they don't want to let nature have its way: they want to make nature let them have their way.

Portrait or Bust?

Whitman pondered, as usual, very carefully about the image of himself that would go into *November Boughs*: "I have wavered between Eakins [the portrait] and Morse [the bust]: Morse's, on the whole, seems to me best: is better for this purpose—as a distinct portrait. I think we should have the proper photos taken experimentally at once from the bust. . . . I am a little doubtful about getting the view I desire: I want your man to try and try and try again until the right one is secured. It is like ordering a suit of clothes: I can give the tailor a hint of what I want, but he must lumber out his stock—wait for me to recognize the right piece. I don't believe in the 'great' photographers—the swells with reputations—I think the other fellow is just as apt to hit it."

Whitman may have liked the bust created by Sidney Morse, but he certainly thought the sculptor's life pathetic: "So much of Sidney is abortive—he don't get anywhere: he is a child of *ennui*. . . . Sidney lacks altogether the world faculty—the power to turn the world to his uses . . . it is half tragic—the life he leads: the starts made—the ends that never come."

Please, *Not Glum*

Whitman hands over to Traubel a photograph of himself that he clearly feared would leave the wrong impression: "Does it look glum—sickish—painful? Has it that in it? They say so. I hate to think of myself as pensive, despondent, melancholy. . . . No man has any excuse for looking morose or cruel: he should do better. . . . That is so important to me: to not look downcast—cloud up things. . . . Be sure to say Walt Whitman was not a glum man despite his photographers."

Memories of Long Island, Brooklyn, and Manhattan

If there is one surprise amid the pages of With Walt Whitman in Camden, *it is that interesting and substantial reminiscing about the past does not occur more often. When Whitman does float back to what he called his "halcyon days," the re-reading of an old letter or the contents of one he has just received is usually the evoking factor.*

Long Island Home

Whitman urged an English friend planning a trip to Long Island to visit his birthplace near Huntington: "The best way to jaunt is in a carriage. A day ought to be devoted to West Hills. One of the things to remember is that our old house is on a flat—that the Hills proper are a little distance off—where my father and his and his and his were born and lived. . . . The old house is kept by a family named Jarvis—and very nice folks they are too. . . . I was there several years ago—they were very kind to me—I was in a carriage—went with Dr. Bucke—did not alight, but their invitation was very cordial."

Founding the Long Islander

It must have been about '39 or '40—long before *Leaves of Grass*—before it was thought of, even. I was a mere boy, then—it was in fact my boyish exuberance put into concrete manifestation. It was non-partisan, no party affiliation, independent—not neutral—travelling its own road. And successful, in a way, I suppose, from the very first—a good property now without a doubt.

Big Rivers

My own favorite loafing places have always been the rivers, the wharves, the boats—I like sailors, stevedores. I have never lived away from a big river.

Cities of Romance

Camden was originally an accident—but I shall never be sorry I was left over in Camden! It has brought me blessed returns. But Washington, New Orleans, Brooklyn—they are my cities of romance. They are the cities of things begun—this is the city of things finished.

Center of Gravity

New York's the place! If you wish the profound, generous, encompassing things, New York is your natural center of gravity.

The Big Affairs on Broadway

Horace speaks of the crowd of "drunken gentlemen and respectable roughs" he has seen celebrating Harrison's victorious election in 1888 in Philadelphia, and this takes Walt back: "Many, many a time have I enjoyed such crowds—experienced the thrill of the crowd: for what, from what, who can tell? I am at home in such places: I respond sensitively to the life of the street—its almost fierce contagion: it seizes you in spite of yourself, even against your sympathies, your dreams: I remember the big affairs on Broadway, many of them memorable, all of them historic: I never missed one of them. What you tell me goes to confirm my old faith in the masses. The good nature, the nonchalance, of the people— what may not come of that? I hope for all things from the crowd—the crowd needs no savior: the crowd will be its own savior."

A Looker-on at Pfaff's

Pfaff's, a below-street level tavern on Broadway near Bleecker Street, was a frequent haunt of Whitman and his circle circa 1859–62: "My own greatest pleasure at Pfaff's was to look on—to see, talk little, absorb. I never was a great discusser, anyway—never. I was much better satisfied to listen to a fight than take part in it." Some months later a Boston friend conveys in a letter this kind offer from one of Whitman's old Pfaff's colleagues: "Would you not like in the house a nice fireplace where you could sit and toast your toes . . . ? If the idea pleases you, my friend, Jack Law, the Chelsea tile-maker, would like to send you a handsome set of tiles for it. Law knew you in the old Pfaff days, when he was a landscape painter, but says you probably would not recognize him by name. Very likely you might remember his vigorous expletives and great enthusiasm!" Of Pfaff's Whitman later reminisced, "We talked [there], discussed: all sorts of questions were up. It was a place, say, like this room, with an area extending under the pavement: considered famous in its time: all now obliterated."

Wonderfully Open City

I found New York wonderfully open to every influence—opportunity— marvellously so, in its complex make-up.

Absorbing Theatres

I spent much of my time in the theatres then—much of it—going everywhere, seeing everything, high, low, middling—absorbing theatres at every pore. That was a long, long time ago—seems back somewhere in another world. In my boyhood—say from nineteen on to twenty-six or seven—New York was in its prime for theatricals—still possessed the fine old extra-efficient stock companies. In these days the stage is made up of giants and nobodies: back in that other time nobody was a nobody—there were reasons for the existence of everybody concerned in the production of a play. I gradually found myself alienated from the stage: there was the best justification for my withdrawal, too. The reality that was has ceased to be. The true old comedies and tragedies have given way to lightness, frivolity, spectacle, dazzle: the expression of power—of mind, of body—of stately manners, of noble bearing—is no longer required, called for or approved if they appear.

Coney Island, Broadway Reader

It [reading aloud] arouses people—arouses the reader. . . . I know I did my best reading when I was alone that way—off in the woods or on the shore. Long ago, when I was a young man, Coney Island was a favorite spot. At that time Coney Island had not the reputation it has now—it was then a desert island—nobody went there. Oh yes! when I read, it was in solitude, never in frequented places—except perhaps, Broadway, on the stage-coaches, where a little more noise more or less made no difference.

Walt's Bookself

I first discovered my bookself in the second-hand book stores of Brooklyn and New York: I was familiar with them all—searched them through and through. One day or other I found an Epictetus—I know it was at that period: found an Epictetus. It was like being born again.

New York Literary Life

New York is a dampener to everything like enthusiasm. It tones everybody down, insists that art is cold, is judicial to the point of extinction. The demand is for smart men—for good writers. There seem to be periods in the world harmonies when our native forces are cropped very close—where convention curbs all down—and this is one of them.

"It is life to the letter but death to the spirit. It is a good market for the harvest but a bad place for farming." Whitman was here referring to "the New York crowd of scrawlers."

New York is ahead in engravings, in printing, in certain of the fine arts—in enterprise, business—in venture, hazarding for trifles: but in all big things, in the heroics, it is left without a sign. I can see no future for literature in New York. All seems so hedged in—closed, closed.

I have just been reading [a] piece . . . in *Lippincott's*: it is full of the snarl and bite of dogs—full. Unworthy, cowardly, I was going to say. The whole atmosphere—literary atmosphere—there in New York is charged with it.

The main matter—defect—with the New York fellows is . . . that they lack guts: they are afraid of great voices, ideas, men.

. . . this whole crowd, of which [Edmund] Stedman is the pick and treasure, is bitter—bitter with New Yorkism: not one of them seems spared, not one.

New York Lifestyle

Let a man go to New York with whatever, soon he is a changed being. Everybody going to New York, getting into the swim of its affairs, is born again, remade—seems given a new lease, but not a better. And its secret—what is its secret? To me a horrible show, strain—disgusting, ruinous, promising nothing. The very bottom principle corruption itself. Think of it—the games they play—the travesty! To them life is but a game—a play, a frolic, devil-take-the-hindmost business. . . . To a New Yorker life is not lived a success if it be not planted in a background of money, goods: curtains, hangings, tapestries, carpets, elegant china. . . . And yet it is not New York in any special, or exclusively special, sense. I might say, it is *America*—the land, time—speculative, prone to display, to count success in dollars . . . a money civilization can never last. We must find surer foundations. Not to disdain goods, yet not to be ruled by them—not to dawdle forever in parlors, with luxury, show.

One reason Walt idolized Robert Ingersoll was that New York living could not taint him: "He is one of the men New York cannot touch—he is not spoiled—all these years, and yet he is safe—he is *unspoilable.*"

High up in New York Theatres

I always went in my early days to the 25-cent place in the theatre, and it was my breath of life, what I got there, however cheaply secured. What opportunities were tallied! What gates opened! . . . I, too, used to meet and make new friends in the galleries. Often we would go in parties. We heard the best plays, operas, in that way. My early life especially was full of it. I suppose the average man doesn't object to high prices because he only wants to go to the theatre about twice a year. I suppose that satisfies him, but for the wanderers, for the Bohemians we are—many, many times are not too many. The time came when I was on the papers, when I had a pass, by which means I fell literally from my high estate—from gallery to parquet, and it *was* a fall—I felt it to be such. It was comfortable to have the seat reserved, I admit *that*, but something was lost—the greatest something. Besides, it was at the top I heard best—got the greatest distance, effect—*ensemble* most impressive.

Fatal Velocity of City Life

One day the subject of the sudden death of Secretary of Treasury William Windom in New York, just after delivering a dinner speech, arises, and Whitman indulges in some urban sociology: "It was the reaction—the sudden fall of pulse. And I do not wonder—not at all. All that sort of life is *double*-life: they live it hard and fast: all that is called the high life of cities. It is two or three days crammed into one, years into a year—pressed close and more; and men go under it. I often think of myself compensated for simplicity, obscurity: I get peace, satisfaction— deepest joy."

Note: Windom's collapse, after an elegant and lavish dinner at Delmonico's restaurant, was extensively reported in the *New York Times* of January 30, 1891.

Part Two

Frontispiece engraving of Whitman in
Leaves of Grass, 1855, left,
and the spine of the second edition, 1856.

Credos

Whitman left behind plenty of "official" announcements of the artistic commandments by which he lived—in his many prose prefaces and introductions, in the poems themselves, even in a few unsigned rave reviews of his early editions of Leaves of Grass. *But in Traubel's pages are a number of off-the-cuff observations and throwaway lines that, as he would say, "cut to the marrow" and illuminate the seminal influences and the central principles of Whitman's oeuvre.*

Scorners

Why shouldn't we just let go—let life do its damnedest: take every obstacle out of the way and let go? Why should being thought foolish or unreasonable or coarse hold us back? We can go nowhere worth while if we submit to the scorners.

Come-outers

All my sympathies are with the radicals, the come-outers.

Minority Voice

One day Bucke asserted, "Walt, you seem determined to be in the minority." Walt's response: "Yes, I do: that's the only safe place for me."

Song of the "High-falutin"

Whitman's first great French devotee, Gabriel Sarrazin (1853–1935), sent a short celebratory essay on him as his contribution to the seventieth birthday festivity in 1889. Traubel and Whitman gave the essay to one of the circle, Harrison Morris, to translate, and Morris made the mistake of remarking that Sarrazin's take on the poet was "extravagant" and "high-falutin." At this Whitman, who much admired Sarrazin, laughed and launched into the following aria: "Yes—I suppose he is high-falutin!—and so is God Almighty! God Almighty is very high-falutin! All his ways, globes, habits—high-falutin! I suppose in all our millions of population—our 80 millions—teeming, spreading—there are not a dozen men—not a dozen, even—who realize—really realize—realize in the sense of absolutely picturing, nearing, participating in it—vibrating, pulsing—that this earth we inhabit is whirling about in space at the rate of thousands of miles a minute—going on in a hell of a way: that this earth is but one of a cluster of earths—these clusters of clusters of clusters again—and all again, again, again, circulating, whirling about a central system, fact, principle—movement everywhere incessant immense, overwhelming. Now—I doubt if there are a dozen men who really sketch that to themselves—perceive, embrace, what it means—comprehend in the midst of what a high-falutin extravagant creation we live, exist. And yet things go on and on—keeping up their high-falutin course! . . . [T]he literary fellows like Morris, [Joseph] Gilder, all look too much at conventional things—at the usual order: they lack and do not understand in others, vigor—vigor. Yet there is a brave penetration about Sarrazin which beats anything heretofore . . . the largest, most liberal investigation so far, particularly in what he says evil—of evil, not for itself but as an essential of the orbic system—the cosmos. There has been no such word spoken elsewhere."

Dirty People

[Matthew] Arnold always gives you the notion that he hates to touch the dirt—the dirt is so dirty! But everything comes out of the dirt— everything: everything comes out of the people, the everyday people, the people as you find them and leave them: not university people, not F.F.V. [First Family of Virginia] people: people, people, just people!

Unrespectable

Respectability has no use for me: I suppose the distaste is mutual.

Road to Truth

[A] Canadian preacher . . . was bound to make me define my attitude towards [Robert] Ingersoll—to condemn him, show our disagreements— which I would not do. The fellow finally made me mad. I said to him substantially: "I think it a great thing to have a man who will tell the truth, irrespective of where it leads him—of what it leads him to deny or affirm: to me [that is] the recompense of everything or anything that had to be lost in the process."

Quaker Spirit

I am a great believer in every fellow's setting-to and doing what he feels he ought to do—following out the Quaker spirit; so if you must, you must!

The Right Books

In May 1889 Whitman launched into what Traubel called a "considerable quiet statement of his conception of the function of books in our civilization." It began: "What we want above all—what we finally must and will insist upon—in future—actual men and women—living, breathing, hoping, aspiring books—books that so grow out of personality, magnificence of undivided endowment, as themselves to become such persons, stand justly in their names."

Whitman eloquently offered an almost identical credo, specifically identifying *Leaves* with it, in a letter to Bucke on May 27, 1891: "the preparatory all-enclosing continual theory of L of G is *myself, opening myself* first to the countless techniques, traditions, samples, items, knowledges, &c. &c. &c. as a fund and interior battery, magazine & identity : sphere, nothing too small to be despised, all welcom'd, to be digested & formulated by *my own living personal emotionality,* wh' shapes & stamps the L[eaves] birth marks f'm *Personality* down below every thing else."

Idiosyncrasy

You mustn't think I object to odd views when they come natural to a man—are a part of a man. I only object to them when they are put on for effect.

Oh! I hope that is the keystone of the arch of my teachings—allowing a place for every man's personality, idiosyncrasy.

Just after war's end, in a letter to a "loving soldier-boy," Whitman wrote of the throngs at the Attorney General's Office, where he worked, reiterating his taste for the idiosyncratic: "There is a perfect stream of Rebels coming in here all the time to get pardoned. . . . Many old men come in here, and middle-aged and young ones too. I often talk with them. There are some real *characters* among them—(and you know I have a fancy for any thing a little out of the usual style)."

When someone had the nerve to call his beloved Dr. Bucke "that Canadian crank," Whitman was, as Traubel says, prompt in his resentment: "Bucke is no crank at all—he is simply individualistic. If to be individualistic is to be a crank, then he is one—not otherwise."

Sweet Deference to the Minority

I think the world has never paid enough deference to that principle of Quakers, which, in their meetings, prevents a mere majority from deciding policies, actions. One vote or several not being sufficient to make a rule operative. Always suggesting to me a silent sweet deference to minorities, to the spirit: not doing all out of awe of numbers. I am sure it is a rebuking contrast to all that is accepted in the methods of legislation. Let us keep it in mind.

Morals and Moralists

It's a profound problem: teaching morals: they should be taught—yet also not taught: sometimes I say one shouldn't teach morals to anybody: when I see the harm that morals do I almost hate seeing people good.

I more and more make morality so-called take a back seat—relegate it—subordinate it.

I always mistrust a deacon—a typical deacon—a church functionary. . . . I thoroughly disapprove of—hate—yes, even fear, institutional, official, teleological, goodness. I would any time rather trust myself in the hands of an avowed secular merchant. He is less likely to do you up.

Alimentary

Life is like the stomach—it needs for things now and then not with reference to digestion—stimulation—but for the purpose only to flush, to cleanse. Doctors tell me that and it works its own confirmation.

His Own Valuations

I always designate my price when I submit a piece: it is far the simplest way: I make my own valuations. There was the "Twilight" poem, printed in *The Century* (a good many of my pieces are like it—only a few lines—a touch)—that was a mere thumb-nail, a hint—yet I named my sum and got it.

How to Pronounce "Pumpkin"

Why everybody here says "punkin"—even some who think themselves great "punkins" too! I know it is not right, but sometimes a fellow is glad not to be right: he gets into the way of the locality, the people, allows their habits, phrases—and better to do so, too! I have no doubt I often offend—often horror-strike people—in parlors—in all ways.

In Nature's Arms

The great thing for one to do when he is used up, is to go out to nature—throw yourself in her arms—submit to her destinies. Many years ago I passed some time down on Timber Creek . . . down here a little ways—a matter of 8 or 10 miles or so. . . . My friends the Staffords lived away from the town—had a farm. They were quite a family—farm folks—father, mother, children, boys and girls. It was six months or so after I came to these parts [from Washington]—I was in a poor way—a sad plight—had been doctoring a good deal. Now I ceased all that—simply gave myself over to nature. Have you ever thought how much is in the negative quality of nature—the negative—the simply loafing, doing nothing, worrying about nothing, living out of doors and getting fresh air, plenty of sleep—letting everything else take care of itself?

Earth Hunger

One day Whitman received a letter from his English follower William Rossetti describing his nature walks; after asking Traubel to read it aloud, Whitman enthused: "Oh! that's so fine—so fine, fine: he brings back my own walks to me: the walks alone: the walks with Pete [Doyle]: the blessed past undying days: they make me hungry, tied up as I am now and for good in a room: hungry: hungry. Horace, do you sometimes feel the earth hunger? the desire for the dirt? to get outdoors, into the woods, on the roads? to roll in the grass: to cry out: to play tom fool with yourself in the free fields?"

Indifference

I must see to it, rather, that I am suited than that the public is suited. I don't know if a fellow ought to say it, but if it might be allowed I would say: so I please myself I don't care a damn what the public thinks of me.

No Confinement: Hugo versus Hawthorne

Hawthorne's method would never be satisfactory [to "take Lincoln's measure"], though to the literary craft—to the men who look upon literature as a thing in itself, clear-cut writing, phrasing, mastery of expression an end—Hawthorne would have to be an eminent figure—among the best, consummate. But these are to some of us things of the past. We have had men in our century who have taken the wind out of all theories of literature that confine it, restrict it, belittle it: for literature in its deepest sense defies measurement, rules, standards. Victor Hugo was one of these men—daring with the daring. Oh! who could say, doing how much good!

Brotherhood

During a political discussion at the Harneds one Sunday, Whitman spoke heatedly in favor of free trade and was then asked, "But isn't it our first duty to take care of ourselves—our America?" Whitman's reply: "Take care of your family, your state, your nation—that's right from a certain standpoint: some people seem ordained to care for one man, for a dozen men, for a single nation: and some other people—of whom I hope I am one—to care for them all. All sounds so damned much better than one—don't you think? The whole business done at once instead of a little patch of it here and there! I don't want the brotherhood of the world to be so long a-coming. I can wait till it comes—it is sure to come—but if I can hurry it by a day or so I am going to do so.

Pruded Away

One day Whitman extolled the "spontaneity" of his fiery defender Robert Ingersoll: "It is rare in any age—I think particularly rare in ours. And in such a time, when everything is toned down, veneered, hidden, lied about, *pruded away*, it is well to have the giants make free with life."

Stepping across the Line, Tipsily

After a well-lubricated Sunday meal at chez Harned, Whitman allowed as how he might have drunk too much, then said on second thought: "but then a fellow must once and a while be allowed to step across the line." When it was suggested that his hosts led him away, he (half) jested: "nobody ever led Walt Whitman away but Walt Whitman himself. That is the whole story, if story there be."

No Artifcial Agencies

I have always been best pleased with what seems most to disregard literariness: the artistic, the formal, the traditional aesthetic, the savor of mere words, jingles, sound—I have always eschewed: language itself *as* language I have discounted—would have rejected it altogether but that it serves the purpose of *vehicle*, is a necessity—our mode of communication. But my aim has been to so subordinate that no one could know it existed—as in fine plate glass one sees the objects beyond and does not realize the glass between. My determination being to make the story of man, his physiological, emotional, spiritual self, tell its own story unhindered by artificial agencies.

Dangerous Books

A newspaper review that calls a book "dangerous" is mentioned, and Whitman responds: "If that is so then I must read the book: it must be one of our books. . . . Yes, it certainly must be one of our books if the preachers are against it."

Overmastering Verve

One day the question arose of whether the name "Walt Whitman" was too big on the title page of the "complete" edition. Whitman allowed the size to stand, making this utterly characteristic analysis: "Walt Whitman is so positive a force in the book that this arrangement of the title seems well in accord with his general methods and principles. I am accused of egotism—of preaching egotism. Call it that if you choose—if that pleases you: I call it personal force: it is personal force that I respect—that I look for. It may be conceit, vanity, egotism—but it is also personal force: you can't get me to quarrel over the name. It is of the first necessity in my life that this personal prowess should be brought prominently forward—should be thrown unreservedly into our work. . . . I am one with [William Sloane] Kennedy's opinion, that a writer, to reflect life, nature—be true to himself, to his art (if we may say that)—must throw identity, overmastering identity, personality, verve, into his pages. . . . To throw a live man into a book: you, your friend, me, anybody else: that is the background, the heart-pulse of *Leaves of Grass.*

True Spirituality

Horace calls attention one day to a short article by John White Chadwick on the spirituality of Tom Paine and Robert Ingersoll, evoking this pronouncement from Walt: "Well, that depends on what a man means by spirituality. What Chadwick means by spirituality is his spirituality. But what a little part of the world he is! Here is a world of individuals, each with some fresh, peculiar demonstration of it. Whose is to count—or *all*? . . . I throw myself back on Elias Hicks in *all* matters of this kind. Elias would say we are *all* spiritual, by the very necessities of our natures, every man in his measure: we can no more escape it than the hearts that beat in our bosoms. I haven't the least doubt that here he touched bottom. Think of Bob [Ingersoll]: the grand glorious justification of Bob is that from head to foot he is *flushed with the square*—every line of him—of his books—bathed in justice, love of right, human generosity, to a degree I fail to find in any other."

Note: Hicks was one of Whitman's early heroes; a biographical work on him by Whitman was a much talked of project during the Traubel years but never commenced.

Saying the Big Things

Time was when I had to say big things about myself in order to be honest with the world—in order to keep in a good frame of mind until the world caught up. A man has sometimes to whistle very loud to keep a stiff upper lip.

American Oratory

It has always been one of my chosen delights, from earliest boyhood up, to follow the flights particularly of American oratory. I went into the courts—when there was a good preacher about, went to church—heard all the best specimens of Southern speaking—the big lawyers, Senators—Congressmen—but none of them brought such conviction to me as [Robert] Ingersoll . . . such suavity, ease, suppleness, capacity—such power to say, yet not to appear to know all the gravity and wonder of his power. It was a revelation—brought me conviction of many stray thoughts, observations—was in itself confirmation of my philosophy, if I may be said at all to have a philosophy—of the doctrine to keep close to nature. . . . Great speaking, what we call great speaking, is plenty—we know it in many peculiarities—the Websterian grandeur—all that; but speech like Ingersoll's—this gravity, linked with such joy—holding the words at tongue's end—is a divine gift, a divine fire.

Spontaneous . . .

To be spontaneous—that is the greatest art—art of arts—the only art that excites respect.

. . . but with Care

One day talk turned to "the question of spontaneity of public speaking," and Whitman recalled his talks about this with the spectacularly eloquent reforming preacher Henry Ward Beecher (1813–87). He is here, unwittingly, describing the essence of his own poetic style: "Beecher said his main point after all was *contact*, touch with his audience—even to depend upon that—to trust to the communications of the moment—to feel the throb—joy, sadness, expectancy—of the people gathered together. But, along with this, preparation of the subtlest sort—of course to get soaked with the subject—to know the main lines of attack—to even go into partnership with every incident—turn incident to profit—not to be nonplussed—to keep absolute open door for occasion. There was—never is—the spontaneity people imagine in a speech, even the best. It must have something back of it—something—and care—oh! such care! . . . Men like the signs of spontaneous utterance—they like to be approached direct. I remember vividly the long talk with Ward Beecher about this. I haven't the least doubt but he himself was full of re-source—reserve—and our friend the Colonel [Ingersoll]—who knows but he, too, is full of art that is not art."

Asinine

My old daddy used to say it's some comfort to a man if he must be an ass anyhow to be his own kind of an ass!

Living a Life

After Horace reads aloud an 1882 letter from an English disciple, the literary critic Edward Dowden, he guesses that one sentence in it hit Whitman hard: "You annex your friends so closely that your health and strength becomes part of theirs." He is right: "You fire right home—that's the thing. Isn't that better than writing books?" But Horace asks, "don't it come to you because you have written a book?" Whitman mulls this, then replies: "It might be put that way but I prefer to say, *because I have lived a life*. Don't you think *living a life* the most important thing of all?" Horace adds, "I accepted his amendment."

Brotherhood

Literature is big only one way—when used as an aid in the growth of the humanities—a furthering of the cause of the masses—a means whereby men may be revealed to each other as brothers.

Affluence versus Real Work

This whole crowd, of which [Edmund] Stedman is the pick and treasure, is bitter—bitter with New Yorkism: not one of them seems spared, not one. All the tendency seems to be to a surrender . . . [to] the sense of the presence of materials, riches, ten thousand [dollars] a year—all that; the feeling as though this was the necessary accompaniment of art, lit-erature. Oh! it is there—there—in the politics, art, society, religion—all are dominated by it. Yes, I would be even more extreme—say that it even touched Emerson at points—that Emerson*ism* inevitably leads [to] it. Yet I regard it hopefully, too, look upon it as a step in the process. The American literary fellow—the American himself—is too smart, [a]cute, sensible, to be totally entrapped. Someday he will shake the whole burden off. But as things are now, none of them possess or even respect the simple, elemental, first-hand, Homeric qualities which lie se-cure at the base of all real work—of all genuine expression. Of course I do not undervalue the canny qualities, either: the disposition to keep some background in goods, money; it has its place—but no first place—no superior place.

Egotism

A certain amount of egotism is necessary—but for having it, we never could have endured the strain—passed unharmed through the fire—especially in the years when *Leaves of Grass* stood alone, unfriended but by me.

Agitation

I am in favor of agitation—agitation—agitation and agitation: without the questioner, the agitator, the disturber, to hit away at our complacency, we'd get into a pretty pass indeed.

Manhood = Authorship

Beware of the literary cliques—keep well in the general crowd: beware of book sympathies, caste sympathies. Some one said here the other day—who was it?—"Mr. Whitman you seem to have sympathy for manhood but not for authorship?" It seems to me that all real authorship is manhood—that my sympathy for manhood includes authorship even if it don't make authorship a preferred object of worship. What is authorship in itself if you cart it away from the main stream of life? It is starved, starved: it is a dead limb off the tree—it is the unquickened seed in the ground.

Montaignesque = Whitmanesque

One day Traubel quoted to Whitman this sentence from a review of a volume of Montaigne's essays: "'Myself am the groundworke of my booke': such were the Whitmanesque words with which old Montaigne concluded the preface to his immortal essays just 309 years ago, and such the reason for their perennial freshness and charm." Traubel then records, "W. said at first: 'I do not recognize the relevancy of the *Whitmanesque*,' but when I repeated the sentence, he said: 'Oh! now I begin to see there is reason for it.'"

Battling the Granitic Stupidities

It is best for any man to be tried by fire, to draw all the shot of the reactionaries, the wise conservatives and the fool conservatives, the asses in authority, the granitic stupidities of the average world. . . . I want the full fire of the enemy. If the work we try to do cannot stand up against the total opposition we may be sure we have gone off on a false scent.

Status Quo—Plus Agitation

I think things are as good as they can be—all right as they are . . . *including the agitation, including the agitation!* especially the agitation! Indeed, I might think agitation the most important factor of all—the most deeply important: to stir, to question, to suspect, to examine, to denounce!

Perfect Health

"Perfect health is simply the right relation of man himself, & all his body, by which I mean all that he is, & all its laws & the play of them, to Nature & its laws & the play of them. When really achieved (possessed) it dominates all that wealth, schooling, art, successful love, or ambition, or any other of life's coveted prizes, can possibly confer, & is in itself the sovereign & whole & sufficient good, & the inlet & outlet of every good. In perfect health . . . sometimes I think it is the law flower and fruitage of civilization & art, & of the best education." This statement was written in Whitman's hand on a "dirty slip of paper" that he handed to Traubel, asking him to read it aloud because it was pertinent to their conversation that day (January 20, 1889); for more of that conversation, see the "*Leaves* and Letters to the Boys" entry under "About *Leaves of Grass*," p. 72.

Wrong Is No Hurt

I do not lack in egotism, as you know—the sort of egotism that is willing to know it self as honestly as it is willing to know third or fourth parties. Why shouldn't a man be allowed to weigh himself? He can't do worse than go wrong: going wrong is no hurt.

Dudes, Dandies, Dawdlers

It is well to allow a liberal margin to the dudes, dandies, dawdlers: I know the probabilities are against you: the average is likely, almost certain, to disappoint you: yet your man may be there.

Joyful Conclusions

Whether it is constitutional or what not with me, I stand for the sunny point of view—stand for the joyful conclusions. This is not because I merely guess: it's because my faith seems to belong to the nature of things—is imposed, cannot be escaped: can better account for life and what goes with life than the opposite theory.

Mundane Heroism

The common heroisms of life are anyhow the real heroisms, the impressive heroisms: not the military kind, not the political kind: just the ordinary world kind, the bits of brave conduct happening about us: things that don't get into the papers—things that the preachers don't thank God for in their pulpits—the real things, nevertheless—the only things that eventuate in a good harvest.

Light-hearted

I don't want to figure anywhere as misanthropic, sour, doubtful: as a discourager—as a putter-out of lights.

A Solid Free-trader

Traubel remarks on how often Whitman blows steam on the subject of free trade: "Protection rubs his fur the wrong way. It's like a perpetual sore with him." On this day the subject evokes this remark on a life's preoccupation: "Why am I a free-trader? a free-trader in the large sense? It is for solidarity: free-trade makes for solidarity: the familiar, full, significant word: and I hope, oh I hope, there has been no failure to manifest the fact in my books. I know in my own heart that every line I ever wrote—every line—not an exception—was animated by that feeling."

Life's Work

Whitman recounts the story of an old woman: "she insisted, every woman born, man born, had his or her mate, somewhere—if they could but find out where! I suppose that should be the whole matter of life—the whole story: to find the mate, the environment—what to be— then, adjustment!"

Necessary Ill

I am a great contender for the world as it is—the ill along with the good. Indeed, I am more and more persuaded that the ill, too, has its part to subserve—its important role—that if ill did not exist, it would be a hopeless world and we would all go to the bad.

Walt on the Literary Life

There are numerous passing remarks in the conversations not specifically concerning the poems in Leaves of Grass *but rather descriptive of Whitman's habits and experiences as a writer, as well as his generally jaundiced views on the American literary scene. His reactions to the critics of his writing are also lavishly expressed, but these trenchancies are presented separately in a subsequent chapter.*

Ambitions—Fulfilled?

Horace remarks that Walt does not "seem to be disturbed by literary ambitions," and Walt clarifies the point: "I have had ambitions: no one is without ambition: nothing can be done without it: but I had no notion of simply shining—of doing something brilliant, showy, to catch the popular imagination: I can say I never was bitten by that poisonous bug: but I had ambition: there were some things I wanted to do—some things I wanted to say: I was very eager to get my life according to a certain plan—to get my book written so, according to a certain plan: I was very resolute about that: that was my ambition: to get certain things said and done." Walt adds, "Have I done it? Have I fulfilled my ambition? God knows. Here I am about stepping out with the case still undecided." Horace queries about the answer he expected, and the reply is: "On the whole, yes: sometimes no: but on the whole, yes."

Genius

All genius defies the rules—makes its own passage—is its own precedent.

Howl

Now and then a man steps out from that crowd—says: "I will be myself"—does, because he is, something immense. The howl that goes up is tremendous.

Autobiography

Bucke urges me to autobiographize myself! Well—well!

A Poet's Secret...

If a fellow is to write poetry the secret is—get in touch with humanity—know what the people are thinking about: retire to the very deepest sources of life—back, back, till there is no farther point to retire to.

...and Another

And the secret of it all is to write in the gush, the throb, the flood, of the moment—to put things down without deliberation—without worrying about their style—without waiting for a fit time or place. I always worked that way. I took the first scrap of paper, the first doorstep, the first desk, and wrote—wrote, wrote. No prepared picture, no elaborated poem, no after-narrative, could be what the thing itself is. You want to catch its first spirit—to tally its birth. By writing at the instant the very heart-beat of life is caught.

Circumspection

Who more, who ever so much as Emerson, demanded, was entitled to a reserve? *Every* man needs it. I have found even in myself the call for care, circumspection. I cannot go to Philadelphia—or could not when I got about—without guarding myself against questions, comers, strangers, reporters, writers, intrusions varied in kind.

Retrospect

One's life is not always the thing it is supposed to be—has its periods and periods—dark, light, dark again—spots, errors, damned foolishnesses. Looking back over my own time—looking into the period starting with '61—'62—I have nothing to regret, nothing to wish reversed.

Catawauling the Words

One day Whitman gives Traubel a manuscript draft of a poem evoked by President James Garfield's assassination in 1881, "The Sobbing of the Bells" (it was written on the back of a letter the poet had received from John Boyle O'Reilly, the celebrated Irish journalist and poet then living in Boston). It clearly showed chaotic revising, and Walt preened: "Some of my enemies who think I write in the dark without premeditation ought to see that sheet of paper: there ain't a word there that seems to have had an easy time of it—that wasn't subject to catawauling. I tell you, Horace, it's no fun for words when they get in my hands, though the howlers may not know it."

Tinkering

Whitman remarks that he added a paragraph at the opening of *Democratic Vistas* when it was republished, but then he mulls whether the change was wise: "I have never been able to settle it with myself whether that change was an improvement or not: often the first instinct is the best instinct." Then he recalled how Bucke and O'Connor detested changes in the *Leaves of Grass* text: "Both object but O'Connor is worse than Bucke: O'Connor gets mad, mad!"

Speaking of a charcoal portrait Traubel's father had made of him, Whitman said: "I hope he has not touched it since I saw him—it seemed to me on the whole there was nothing more to be done. The devil in artists is to keep pegging away at a thing after it really is all done—pegging away at it *done*, till it is *undone*."

Self-promotion

In early January 1889 Traubel managed to get a rise with this remark: "Walt, some people think you blew your own horn a lot—wrote puffs on yourself—sort of attitudinized and called attention to yourself quite a bit." (Horace notes that Walt was "quizzy over this.") The response: "Do they? Who are some people? What are puffs? I have often talked of myself: I talked of myself as I would of you: blamed and praised just the same: looked at myself just as if I was somebody else: I am not ashamed of it: I have never praised myself where I would not if I had been somebody else: I have merely looked myself over and repeated candidly what I saw—the mean things and the good things: I did so in the *Leaves*, I have done so in other places: reckoned up my own account, so to speak. I know this is unusual: but is it wrong? Why should not everybody do it? You, anybody?"

Note: Whitman wrote at least two unsigned reviews of his first edition of *Leaves*; as it happens, they are exceedingly, not to say boisterously, favorable.

Self-questioning

Traubel asked if the poet ever had moods in which he doubted himself, and Whitman replied: "Yes—sometimes: at least moods in which I put myself through a series of the severest questions. It does a man good to turn himself inside out once in a while: to sort of turn the tables on himself: to look at himself through other eyes—especially skeptical eyes, if he can. It takes a good deal of resolution to do it: yet it should be done—no one is safe until he can give himself such a drubbing: until he can shock himself out of his complacency. Think how we go on believing in ourselves—which in the main is all right (what could we ever do if we didn't believe in ourselves?): but if we don't look out we develop a bumptious bigotry—a colossal self-satisfaction, which is worse for a man than being a damned scoundrel."

Scribble, Scribble

In most of us I think writing gets to be a disease. We scribble, scribble, scribble—eternally scribble: God looks on—it turns his stomach: and while we scribble we neglect life.

Biographers, et al.

What lying things, travesties, most all so-called histories, biographies, autobiographies are! They make you sick—give you the bellyache! I suppose it can be said the world still waits for its honest historian, biographer, autobiographer. Will he ever come?

News of publication of a life of Jesus causes Whitman to reiterate his low opinion of the genre: "Poor Jesus!—to have come down these eighteen hundred years, to be biographized by us moderns! He hardly deserved it!"

Chary Punctuation

While reading proofs of William Sloane Kennedy's essay "The Quaker Traits of Walt Whitman," Walt noticed "attar" spelled with one "t": "I hesitated for a minute, was going to say, perhaps better out. But I suppose in that case it ought to be inserted. I am in favor of short spelling whenever that will do. I like the modern tendency that way, and in punctuation, too. I have followed it right along, myself—often to the horror of my friends."

In his later *Leaves* editions, Whitman indulged in a thorough and systematic lightening of his punctuation (deleting many an em dash, semicolon, and ellipses and relying mainly upon the comma). One month after the preceding excerpt, he was delighted to find himself in the company of the author of his beloved novel *Consuelo*. Traubel records: "He asked me, 'You like the *chary* punctuation of *Leaves of Grass?*' I mentioned a letter in which George Sand had taken much such ground as his and he seemed pleased, saying, 'That is new to me, but *good.*'"

No Memorizer

I don't know my poems that way: any one of you fellows probably could repeat more lines from the *Leaves* than I could. I never commit poems to memory—they would be in my way.

Overdoing the Cake

I avoid at all times the temptation to patch up and refine, preferring to let each version or whatever go out substantially as it was first suggested. This does not mean that I am not careful: it only means that I try not to overdo my cake.

No Acrobatics

"I am not a reciter. Every now and then some woman or man comes in here and chats a while with me—doing most of the chatting themselves, most of them—and then go off and picture me as standing out in the middle of the room and spouting my own poetry. I am not a poetic acrobat—not in the least. When the visitors come—you see lots of 'em yourself—I sit very still and try to be good—don't I?" Many months later Whitman offered a succinct reason why he did not recite his poems: "I don't recite because I don't know them." Traubel also noted, "W. rarely reads his poems to anybody. To-night read 'An Evening Lull' to me. His voice was strong and sweet. He never recites a poem (his own). I never had him do it for me. Occasionally he will cite a line or two."

The Right Ugly Word

I like any word which sharply defines its object: I prefer the ugly to the beautiful words if the ugly word says more: ugly words you'll often find drive more immediately to their purpose.

Style

When you talk to me of "style" it is as though you had brought me artificial flowers. Awhile ago, when I could get out more, I used to stop at Eighth Street there, near market, and look at the artificial flowers made with what marvellous skill. But then I would say: What's the use of the wax flowers when you can go out for yourself and pick real flowers? That's what I think when people talk to me of "style," "style," as if style alone and of itself was anything. . . . style is to have no style.

Respectability

A sculptor named John Boyle was involved in the planning of Whitman's burial house at Harleigh Cemetery. These comments on him brought the poet back to his own career: "I should think the danger of his work—as of the work of all sculptors (and others, too, for the matter of that) is in the temptation to make their work genteel—to bow before the gentility of the world—and you know there's no one in the world more despises all that. I am a confirmed enemy to gentility, respectability. . . . How much the artists, writers, surrender to gentility! It is astonishing—the extent of the sacrifice. I am so opposed to respectability, they think I'm not respectable!"

Plan to Have No Plan

My friends could never understand me, that I would start out so evidently without design for nowhere and stay long and long.

That has mainly been my method: I have caught much on the fly: things as they come and go—on the spur of the moment. I have never forced my mind: never driven it to work: when it tired, when writing became a task, then I stopped: that was always the case—always my habit.

Beware the Literary Conscience

There are consciences and consciences—a moral conscience, an aesthetic conscience—all that—but these are quite different from that conscience of which Elias Hicks so often spoke—the conscience of consciences, that conscience which ordered the largest measure of fact—

that penetrating, fibrous, spinal quality which over-arches all. The literary conscience is a leaning, a surrender—sacrifices itself to other consciences, and here it is John [Burroughs] has been touched. It is the spirit of Emersonianism, which is the spirit of culture, of knowledge, of elegance. Not that Emerson had it in the least, but that Emersonianism leads straight to it, and it is dangerous, Horace—dangerous from the start—it is playing with fire.

Whitman bemoaned the waning powers of John Burroughs as a thinker and writer and spoke thus by way of explaining the decline. Whitman elsewhere expresses several times his fear that Burroughs fell under the taint of the New York literary crowd. Shortly after making the preceding remark, Whitman said more bluntly, "the John Burroughs who wrote the early books [including *Notes on Walt Whitman, as Poet and Person* in 1867]—who was convinced, who commanded—is not the John Burroughs we know now. The old John Burroughs is much thawed out—much melted."

Poetical Debate
It is the very worst sort of logic to try a poem by rules of logic—to try to confirm a round world by square tests—to sit down and argue a poem out, out, out, to an end—yes, to death.

The Author Class
I in the main like traders, workers, anyone, better than authors. The author class is a priest class with esoteric doctrines: I do not easily mix with it—I refuse to condone it.

Self-pity Punctured by a Sassy Boss
Whitman predicts that he will not live long enough to learn that his life's work is a "failure," and Horace calls him on it: " 'O pshaw!' I exclaimed: 'You don't think you've been a failure: what's the use of putting on airs? Why don't you get humble and reconcile yourself to your success?' He exploded over this. 'You're damned sassy, boss: yes you are: but I'll obey: I'll be humble: forgive me.' "

Inscriber with Scruples
Asked to inscribe John Burroughs's 1867 book on him, Whitman declined: "I always object to putting my name in a book about myself. I know it may be thought a mere prejudice—a kink—but somehow it hangs on to me—I do not violate it."

Fame—Up in Smoke
When Horace brought in the logo for a line of cigars named after him, Whitman "laughed much over it" and said, "That is fame!"

After the Bucket Is Kicked

Whitman responds to Traubel about a bibliographical project on Whitman contemplated by William Sloane Kennedy: "I can see no . . . unmitigated necessity. After I have kicked the bucket there may be more decisive reason for the thing, but while I am about and kicking myself [he "laughed heartily" at the play on words] I can see no call. I see more value in the matter you are piling together in your little article [a probable reference to "Walt Whitman at Date"]—personal memorabilia, traits of character, incidents, habits—the pulse and throb of the critter himself. Oh! how I have looked for just that matter in connection with great men, some of whom I have met, some not, yet it is the thing we get least of—is really a desideratum." Here Traubel asserted, "The real life of a man can often be written of the scraps the formal biographer refuses." Whitman agreed: "That is striking—it is what I am trying to say."

Posterity

I know how, after a man disappears, the mists begin to gather, then fallacy of one degree or another, then utter myth, irresistibly mystifying everything. It is a lamentable twist in history.

Walt Whitman Societies

The German-Japanese Whitmanite Sadakichi Hartmann was in 1887 busy in the Northeast trying to establish a Walt Whitman Society, but the honoree threw a wet blanket over the idea. "What do they want of a Walt Whitman Society, anyway? Are they to dig a hole for me and close me in?" Horace (who was to become a pillar of the Walt Whitman Fellowship in later years) told him they were "bound to come," at which the poet cried, "Then God help me—I am lost!" No, he will be *found*, says Horace. Walt is still nervous: "Do you justify a *Leaves of Grass* creed?—boards of explicators?—this line means this, and that line means that, and God damn you for a fool if you don't say so too?" Only when Horace assures him that these societies will "go in for fraternity without a creed—love without a creed" does the poet relax: "I stand for that if I stand for anything—fraternity, comradeship: and I suppose that if you can make societies that stand for the same thing (if you can, do you hear? if, if) then I am bound to wish them luck."

The Rest Is . . .

I get humors—they come over me—when I resent being discussed at all, whether for good or bad—almost resent the good more than the bad: such emotional revolts: against you all, against myself: against words—God damn them, words: even the words I myself utter: wondering if anything was ever done worth while except in the final silences.

Before Leaves of Grass

Considerable—one might almost say complete—mystery surrounds Whitman's precise activities in the several years prior to 1855, during which the gestation of the spectacularly inimitable first Leaves of Grass *occurred. To judge from the very few (and usually grudging or dismissive) reminiscences about his pre-1855 activities as a writer of various kinds of grist for the newspaper mill, Whitman did not care to have much known about them. With Traubel, he largely succeeded in keeping his old poems, short fiction, editorials, and feature articles in a skeleton's closet. Perusal of the scholarly editions of* The Early Poems and the Prose Fiction *and* The Journalism *will perhaps explain his bashfulness about what he thought of as his juvenilia.*

Wrestling among the Masses

In these older years of my life, I see how lucky I was that I was myself thrown out early upon the average earth—to wrestle for myself—among the masses of people—never living in coteries: that I have always lived cheek by jowl with the common people.

Short Story Writer

Horace passes on a query about certain stories in the files of the *Democratic Review* from circa 1842 signed "Walter Whitman." Were these his? "Yes—I guess there's no doubt of that—they're mine, if I want to claim them—as I do not! I don't think much of 'em—they're better forgotten—lain dusty in the old files."

Whitman speaks some time later of "days when I was writing stories to fill in corners, gaps, in the magazines—stories of no importance to anybody but me, and of no importance to me, but for the fact that they supplied me with necessaries—grub, a living."

On His Temperance Novel Franklin Evans

"Dr. Bucke is wild for a copy. . . . It's not worth getting. I'm glad he hasn't been able to get a copy. Yet it's probably in existence, procurable in some New York second-hand store." Would it not appear, Traubel asks, some day as his? "It's not impossible, but it's a bad fate to look forward to!" Traubel then tells of someone possessing a volume of

Whitman's old short stories and being ready to publish them: "Probably waiting for me to peg out. I should almost be tempted to shoot him if I had an opportunity."

Youthful Designs

I was at that period full of designs that were never executed: lectures, songs, poems, aphorisms, plays—why, even stories: I was going to write stories, too, God help me! It took me some time to get down, or up, to my proper measure—to take my own measure—that is, a long time to really get started—though I think that after I had made up my mind and got going I kept up a pretty steady pace in that one direction.

About Leaves of Grass

The most important reason to read the conversations of Mickle Street, obviously, is for the poet's unguarded observations on Leaves of Grass— *observations his benign, avuncular, "good gray" image of the late 1880s prevented him from making in public. Thanks to Traubel, we are permitted to overhear Whitman's candid, provocative comments, complete with some "hells and damns," on the gestation of* Leaves of Grass; *the purposes it had (and did not have) and retrospects on specific poems, poem sequences, and editions; the physical design of these editions; the readers he hoped for and those he thumbed his nose at; and the American literary scene it never entirely ceased to discombobulate.*

The Title

I am well satisfied with my success with titles—with *Leaves of Grass*, for instance, though some of my friends themselves rather kicked against it at the start as a species of folly. "Leaves of Grass," they said: "there are no *leaves* of grass; there are *spears* of grass: that's your word, Walt Whitman: spears, spears." But *Spears of Grass* would not have been the same to me. Etymologically *leaves* is correct—scientific men use it so. I stuck to leaves, leaves, leaves, until it was able to take care of itself. Now it has got well started on its voyage—it will never be displaced.

Whitman's sensitivity as to "leaves" and "spears" of grass was shown when a German translation of *Leaves of Grass* appeared under the title *Grashalme*. Traubel records that, "as so often before," Whitman asked him, "and *Grashalme* means Leaves or Spears of Grass?"

A year and a half later Whitman recalled another instance of the debate over "leaves": "What a fight I had for that name . . . for 15 or 20 years, everybody objected to it—even my friends. . . . I remember one ardent friend I had—Theodore something or other—a poet, a man of parts. He asked, 'Who ever knew of a *Leaf* of Grass? There were *spears* of grass— but leaves?—Oh! no!' There was one night the question came up; a very erudite—a scientific man—a botanist, in fact—having stood it as long as he could—spoke out—set me quite up—said that, whatever the case in literature, in science *leaves* of grass there were and doubtless would be." Whitman continued, "My critic gave all the intellectual reasons in the calendar, but the emotional, the sympathetic, he could say nothing—nothing!" Whitman's final point, though, was that of the practiced editor he had been: "A headline should be large—capacious—expansive—should cover its subject, explicitly—then something more."

Autobiographical

I should say that anyone, to get hold of me—the bottom of the big book—all I have written—would see that all my work is autobiographical—yes, and that this autobiography finds its center and explication in the poems—in *Leaves of Grass*.

One day Traubel reminded Whitman of Bucke's "old suggestion that he should write autobiographical notes etc. I thought it would be almost farcical to write any autobiography deliberately, when all *Leaves of Grass* and the prose was autobiography if anything. W laughed and said, 'You are right about it—right.' "

Breakneck Speed

I was once driven down a steep hill by a friend of mine: he hurried the horses along at a breakneck pace, I protesting. "Ain't you afraid to go so fast?" I asked. "No—not a bit of it" he answered: "I'm afraid to go slow. That's the only way I can overcome the difficulties of the road." So it is with the *Leaves*—it must drive on, drive on, without protest, without explanations, without hesitations, on and on—no apologies, no dickers, no compromises—just drive on and on, no matter how rough, how dangerous the road may be.

Leaves *and Letters to the Boys*

I have found you another letter to Hugo [Fritsch]: a draft: one of the first drafts: I always kept the original. I would like you to read it to me before you finally take it along: to-morrow if you choose: now if you have time. We were just talking of personal things—of the *Leaves*—the complete book: we insist upon the personal: well, you have it in these letters too: they, too, demonstrate me—my theory, philosophy, what I am after: they too. If you want to know what I mean watch what I do.
Note: The long letter, written from Washington and dated October 8, 1863, was to Hugo Fritsch, one of Whitman's New York chums.

Emerson: Early Friend with a Blind Spot

Whitman received a very cordial letter from Ralph Waldo Emerson on his first edition of *Leaves* and famously made bold to print it and extract a blurb from it for his second edition. Glowing though all of Whitman's subsequent public comments on Emerson were, in private he never ceased to rankle at Emerson's attempt, during a walk on Boston Common, to urge a taming of his more daring poems. Almost three decades later, Whitman summed up: "He did not see the significance of the sex element as I put it into the book and resolutely there stuck to it—he did not see that if I had cut sex out I might just as well have cut everything out—the full scheme would no longer exist—it would have been violated in its most sensitive spot."

Persona Non Grata

Over the years Whitman made many comments about the "enemies" of *Leaves of Grass*. Reminiscing at the age of sixty-nine, he summed up: "For a long time all I got out of my work was the work itself and a few amens like that [in a letter Traubel had just read aloud]: I was not only not popular (and am not popular yet—never will be) but I was *non grata*—I was not welcome in the world."

Happy Ending

How might Whitman have reacted to acceptance of *Leaves of Grass* at long last? In the summer of 1888 the thought evoked a little hilarity: "I wouldn't know what to do, how to comport myself, if I lived long enough to become accepted, to get in demand, to ride on the crest of the wave. I would have to go scratching, questioning, hitching about, to see if this was the real critter, the old Walt Whitman—to see if Walt Whitman had not suffered a destructive transformation—become apostate, formal, reconciled to the conventions, subdued from the old independence."

For the Underdog

If I have any doubts at all about *Leaves of Grass* it is in the matter of the expression of my sympathy for the underdog—the vicious, the criminal, the malignant (if there are any malignant): whether I have made my affirmative feeling about them emphatic enough. You see, Horace, I agree with you new fellows who do not believe that the criminal classes so known are the cause of themselves: I see other causes for them: causes as to which they are no more guilty than we are.

Dedicated to Criminals

"It is a book for the criminal classes. . . . The other people do not need a poet." "Are you in the criminal class yourself?" Tom Harned then inquired. "Yes, certainly. Why not?"

Symphonic

Leaves of Grass is not intellectual alone (I do not despise the intellectual—far from it: it is not to be despised—has its uses) nor sympathetic alone (though sympathetic enough, too) nor yet vaguely emotional—least of all this. I have always stood in *Leaves of Grass* for something higher than qualities, particulars. It is atmosphere, unity: it is never to be set down in traits but as a symphony: is no more to be stated by superficial criticism than life itself is to be so stated: is not to be caught by a smart definition or all given up to any one extreme statement.

Average

If *Leaves of Grass* is not for the average man it is for nobody: not the average bad man or average good man: no: the average bad good man: if I have failed to make that clear then I've missed my mission for certain.

Crude Offender

Leaves of Grass may be only an indication—a forerunner—a crude offender against the usual canons—a barbaric road-breaker—but it still has a place, a season, I am convinced.

Polish Routed and Damned

Oh! I expect the day to come . . . when all these things will be scattered to the winds—literariness, polish, grammaticalism, all that—routed and damned, by some daring spirit, some bold, bold personality, full of defiance, straight in communication with the elemental forces. [Here Traubel interrupts to ask if perchance *Leaves of Grass* has "done much such work."] I don't know: it is not for me to say. The new man will have a flavor all his own, like a new climate, a fresh breath of northern air.

Revisions

How William [O'Connor] would storm and cry out if I made a change in *Leaves of Grass*—a comma, even. He was worst of all. And Bucke next, easily next—though not quite as bad. And even Mrs. Gilchrist, who, if she ever showed passion at all, came nearest it in the matter of revisions. . . . Bucke probably does not know that long long ago, before the *Leaves* had ever been to the printer, I had them in half a dozen forms—larger, smaller, recast, outcast, taken apart, put together—viewing them from every point I knew—even at the last not putting them together and out with any idea that they must eternally remain unchanged. Bucke mistakes the danger: there was no danger. I have always been disposed to hear the worst that could be said against the poems—even the most rasping things—everything, in fact which would serve to give me an honest new point of observation. That was a necessary part of my career.

Spinal Purpose

One day Whitman insisted on holding Traubel's very cold hand when he arrived: "It *is* cold, therefore I keep it. It is a reminiscence of the open air, the sky, the sea, and no one knows how precious these are—have been—to me. And indeed, it is to surcharge *Leaves of Grass* with them that was my presiding spinal purpose from the start." Later Traubel remarked that *Leaves* was "important in the things it leads out to, not in any outright gift." To which Whitman responded, "Yes, perhaps. And that is in fact the true spinal thing in all books." The point was reiterated a few days later: "LG is less accomplishment than preparation."

Improvisatory

Whitman informs Traubel that *Harper's Bazaar* had rejected a poem, later published as "A Christmas Greeting": "Did I tell you I got my piece back from *Harper's*? Well—I did! They write that it is too much of an improvisation! As if all *Leaves of Grass* was not improvisation!"

Escaping the Taint

I suppose every man has his purposes. I had mine—to have no purpose—to state, to capture, the drift of a life—to let things flow in, one after another, take their places, their own way. My worst struggle was not with ideas, anything of that sort, but against the literariness of the age—for I, too, like all others, was born in the vesture of this false notion of literature, and no one so born can entirely—I say entirely—escape the taint. Though, as for me, looking back on the battleground, I pride myself I have escaped the pollution as much as any.

Mother Dearest

In August 1888 Whitman spoke of the influence of his mother, Louisa: "The reality, the simplicity, the transparency of my dear, dear mother's life was responsible for the main things in the letters [Whitman wrote to her] as in *Leaves of Grass* itself. How much I owe to her! . . . *Leaves of Grass* is the flower of her temperament active in me. My mother was illiterate in the formal sense but strangely knowing: she excelled in narrative—had great mimetic power: she could tell stories, impersonate: she was very eloquent in the utterance of noble moral axioms—was very original in her manner, her style. It was through my mother that I learned of Hicks: when she found I liked to hear about him she seemed to like to speak. I wonder what *Leaves of Grass* would have been if I had been born of some other mother and had never met William O'Connor?"

At the Opera

Whitman several times invoked opera as an important influence on the early editions of *Leaves of Grass*. On August 21, 1888, he reminisced: "My younger life was so saturated with the emotions, raptures, up-lifts, of such musical experiences [as hearing the tenor Cesare Badiali] that it would be surprising indeed if all my future work had not been colored by them. A real musician running through *Leaves of Grass*—a philosopher musician—could put his finger on this and that anywhere in the text no doubt indicating the activity of the influences I have spoken of." In his 1882 memoir, *Specimen Days*, Whitman wrote that "certain actors and singers" had "a good deal to do with the business" of gestating *Leaves of Grass*: "I heard, these years, well render'd, all the Italian and other operas in vogue."

Fiery Speculation

Traubel put this question, "Suppose the whole damned thing [*Leaves of Grass*] went up in smoke, Walt: would you consider your life a failure?" and Walt cried out "with intense feeling": "Not a bit of it: why my life? why any life? No life is a failure. I have done the work: I have thrown my life into the work: in those early years: teaching, loafing, working on the newspapers: traveling: then in Washington—clerking, nursing the soldiers: putting my life into the scale—my single simple life: putting it up for what it was worth: into the book—pouring it into the book: honestly, without stint, giving the book all, all, all: why should I call it a failure? why? why? I don't think a man can be so easily wrecked as that."

Funny Book

Talk on January 30, 1889, turned to the notion, then abroad among the public, that Whitman had no funny bone. The poet begged to differ: "I pride myself on being a real humorist underneath everything else. There are some people who look upon *Leaves of Grass* as a funny book: my brother George has often asked me with a wink in his eye: 'I say, Walt, what's the game you're up to, anyway?' So I may go down into history, if I go at all, as a merrymaker wearing the cap and bells rather than a prophet or what the Germans call a philosoph." This view may help to explain why, the previous year, Whitman was willing to admit that *Leaves* left some room for satirical wits to play: "I am aware that *Leaves of Grass* lends itself readily to parody—invites parody—given the right man to do it."

Civil War Boys

Whitman told Traubel that going off to the Civil War was "the very centre, circumference, umbilicus of my whole career." One day a few months later, when he was seventy, Whitman came across the draft of a letter written to one of his Manhattan friends from Washington over a quarter century earlier. In it he described his hospital work and reminisced about his profit from these harrowing ministrations: "What did I get? Well—I got the boys . . . then I got *Leaves of Grass*: but for this I would never have had *Leaves of Grass*—the consummated book (the last confirming word)."

Anti-moralist, but Indefinite

Though Whitman in fact had toned down some of the potent sexuality of the early editions of *Leaves*, he spoke very differently in March 1889: "had I *Leaves of Grass* to write over again, knowing what I know now, I do not think I should in any way touch or abate the sexual portions, as you call them: but in the other matter, in the 'good' and 'evil' business, I should be more definite, more emphatic than ever. All moralism, metaphysicalism, theologicality—pulpits, teachers, all of them—seem to go down on that snag. . . . Yet I do not know: perhaps it is good I am *not* to write the book again: no doubt all is best just as it is: *Leaves of Grass*, anyhow, does not teach anything absolutely: teaches more by edging up, hinting, coming near, than by any definite statement."

The "Idiocrity" of Leaves

When an "error" in *Leaves* was drawn to his attention one day, Whitman responded: "I see—I see: it must be wrong—but that is one of my idiocrities—to put it there and let it be, wrong or right. Maybe what is wrong for him is right for me: such things, too, do happen."

Unhallowed Ground

Leaves of Grass takes the ground from under the churches as churches.

Room for All

The open-armed essence of *Leaves of Grass* was insisted upon by Whitman many times. On May 26, 1889: "In my philosophy—in the bottommeanings of *Leaves of Grass*—there is plenty of room for all." In August 1890: "*Leaves of Grass* . . . is based on no less than the world, man in *ensemble*—not his parts, not special races, religions." And the next fall he remarked similarly: "*Leaves of Grass* has its own eligibilities—has no narrow tendencies—at least, I hope it has not" and "Catholicity—receptiveness—welcome: that is *Leaves of Grass*."

The Patriotism of Leaves

Leaves of Grass has its patriotism too, but patriotism of the common kind is a narrow principle at the best—a sort of *boost me and I'll boost you; take care of me, I'll take care of you; our interests, our purses, to hell with the rest of the world! Leaves of Grass* has nothing to give to that principle—nothing. I think . . . our patriotism has never been better defined than by Paine—he hit it off in several places. For instance, where he says *the world is my country, to do good is my religion.* That is the whole gospel of politics, life.

Damn Art and Let Fly!

In May 1891 Traubel tells Whitman of a debate on the future of American literature during which one suggestion is for building on "some great English model." Whitman erupts: "Damn the Professor! Damn the model! Build on hell! No, no, no—that is not what we are here for—that is not the future—that's not *Leaves of Grass*—opposite to all that. . . . Here, Horace—here in *Leaves of Grass*—are 400, 430 pages of *let-fly*. No art, no schemes, no fanciful, delicate, elegant constructiveness—but *let-fly*. A young man appears in the Western world—the new world—is born in the free air, near the sea—lives an early life in the early life of a big city—absorbs its meanings, the past, history, masses of men, whores, saints, sailors, laborers, carpenters, pilots—goes liberal-footed everywhere—has no erudition—reads books, reads men—

prepares himself a great ground—travels—takes everywhere—every sign a sign to him, every treasure his treasure—nothing denied—lives the life of a war—unmistakably the greatest war of history—passes through camps, enters the hospitals—using gifts of penetration (Horace, they told me my penetration would damn me!)—accumulates, accumulates—then lets fly—lets fly—no art—no, *damn* art!" Immediately after this ebullition, Whitman tied his performance in *Leaves* to several kinds of overmastering vocal performance in the following excerpt. Whitman uttered a variation on his "damn art" theme in an "Autobiographic Note" included in *Camden's Compliment to Walt Whitman* (1889). In this he says that in 1855 he "Commenced putting *Leaves of Glass* to press, for good—after many MS. doings and undoings—(I had great trouble in leaving out the stock 'poetical' touches—but succeeded at last.)"

Let-fly Voices

Here is the kernel—this is the seat of the explanation: the tremendousest let-fly in this, our history here, perhaps in all literature. Understand me, I mean that men shall proceed in all they do out of a knowledge of life—as great actors act, orators speak, singers sing—as in [Italian contralto Marietta] Alboni's voice, perhaps the greatest singer ever breathed—as in [Junius Brutus] Booth—the old Booth—I don't know but the grandest actor the world has seen or will see—as in Ingersoll—voice, vitality, and so on—full—overflowing—with accumulation of fact, feeling, actual palpitating experience—crowded into them, as crowded into me, by resistless forces of a proud pure ancestry—intricately woven from hardy, to hard, purposes—splendid effects.

The Painter for Walt

Whitman saw the rural landscapes of Jean-François Millet (1814–75) in person for the first time on a trip to Boston; he was deeply moved, especially by *The Sower*. Later he told Traubel, "The *Leaves* are really only Millet in another form." Three weeks later he elaborated, "Millet is my painter: he belongs to me: I have written Walt Whitman all over him." Three months later: "Millet excites all the religion in me—excites me to a greater self-respect. I could not stand before a Millet picture with my hat on." Again, several months later he praised Millet in words that he might have liked to hear applied to *Leaves of Grass*: "Millet's color sense was opulent, thorough, uncompromising, yet not gaudy—never gilt and glitter: emphatic only as nature is emphatic. I felt the masterfulness of 'The Sowers' [*sic*]: its dark grays: not overwrought anywhere: true always to its own truth—borrowing nothing." Traubel includes a long list of nearly a dozen remarkable parallels between the lives of Millet and Whitman that Bucke had drawn up. Most notable was Millet's painting his signature work, *The Sower*, at the age of thirty-six, which was Whitman's age when the first *Leaves* edition appeared in 1855. Whitman found the list "Not convincing . . . only interesting." Millet was known for his portraits of peasant life, his most famous pictures being *The Sower* (1850), *Gleaners* (1857), and *Angelus* (1859). Traubel drew Whitman's attention to the following sentence in an article, "Recollections of Jean-François Millet," in the May 1889 isue of *Century* magazine: "Two Americans have reminded me of Millet—George Fuller [the noted painter, 1822–84] in the general appearance of his figure, and Walt Whitman in his large and easy manner."

There is one of Millet's pictures—not so well known—I have seen it—which seems to me the gem of his creations—at least, of such as I have known. The plot of it was simply this—a girl going home with the cows of an evening—a small stream running lazily along—the cattle tempted forward to the water, mildly drinking. I can conceive of nothing more directly encountered in nature than this piece—its simplicity, its grand treatment, the atmosphere, the time of day: not a break in the power of its statement. I looked at it long and long—was fascinated—fastened to it—could hardly leave it at all. This picture more than any other to my judgment confirmed Millet—justified his position, heroism—assured his future.

No Cut and Dried Philosophy

In June 1889 Whitman strongly asserted the lack of an "agenda" in *Leaves of Grass*: "I do not teach a definite philosophy—I have no cocked and primed system. . . . He who goes to my book expecting a cocked and primed philosophy will depart utterly disappointed—and deserve to! . . . The last thing the world needs is a cut and dried philosophy, and the last man to announce a cut and dried philosophy would be Walt Whitman."

Nearly a year later Whitman reiterated this conviction: "I have no axe to grind—no philosophy to offer—no theory to expound in *Leaves of Grass*: all I have written there is written with reference to America—to the larger America—to an America so inclusive, so sufficient, no phase of life, no nationality can escape it.

Heaven and Hell

While discussing "theological matters," Whitman asserts, "The idea of ministers seems to be that without the theory of heaven and hell—particularly of hell—society would not be safe—things would not go on—we would collapse!" This reminds Traubel of Whitman's earlier remark that, as he aged, morality has "more and more relegated itself"—and that Goethe had made a similar confession. Whitman's response: "Yes, and not only Goethe but all the fellows that amount to anything. . . . That is the creed of *Leaves of Grass*, the in-working, through-working principle."

Fair Warning

Whitman, on October 1, 1889, warned of the challenge presented by his lifework: "I almost pity the young man (or woman) who grapples with *Leaves of Grass*. It is so hard a tussle."

Turning Quaker

One day Whitman recalled a time early in life when he considered becoming a Quaker. In the end, he said, "I put it aside as impossible: I was never made to live inside a fence." Traubel then asked whether Whitman thought *Leaves* could have been written if he had "turned Quaker," and he replied, "It is more than likely not—quite probably not—almost certainly not."

No China Spared

Whitman had good reason to boast on March 28, 1890, that "*Leaves of Grass* is an iconoclasm, it starts out to shatter the idols of porcelain worshiped by the average poets of our age."

Song of the Real Me

In June 1890 Whitman asserted one of the most obvious characteristics of *Leaves*, namely its richly autobiographical impetus: "I should say that anyone, to get hold of me—all I have written—would see that all my work is autobiographical—yes, and that this autobiography finds its center and explication in the poems—in *Leaves of Grass*."

Deep Exposé

At his seventy-first birthday party on May 31, 1890, held at Reisser's restaurant in Philadelphia, Whitman delicately suggested that he had carefully veiled some of the autobiography in *Leaves*: "Often it is by the things unsaid, rather than the things said, that give importance to speech, to life. I have kept the roots well underground. *Leaves of Grass*, be they what they may, are only in part the fact—for beneath, around, are contributing forces, which do not come out in the superficial *exposé*."

Unpleasant Facts

[Henry Ward] Beecher declared once—in a company—I was one of them—that he did not know one drunk from another—boasted of it. I think—thought at the time—that the fling was at me. But though it excited an inward retort, I said nothing—held my peace. But what I thought was this: that it was very much as if a doctor would boast "I know nothing of your guts, blood, excrement, urine, wounds, sores—it is all unelegant, forbidding, nauseous to me: I am the doctor of your proprieties" . . . all this leads to what I was going to say . . . [Edmund] Stedman should know me, know *Leaves of Grass*, well enough to see that we look to reflect, to stand for, *fact*. Not *pleasant* fact only, but fact: and fact means all tempests, horrors, hoggishnesses—everything—whatever! I am *always* curious in just such points—complexion, the color of a man's hair, eyes, voice, legs, arms, trunk, port—all that goes to make him himself.

Phenomenal

On September 28, 1890, at supper with a piece of chicken suspended on his fork, Whitman paused to speak further of the implicit meanings of *Leaves of Grass*: "It can never be understood but by an indirection. . . . It stands first of all for that something back of phenomena, in phenomena, which gives it all its significance, yet cannot be described—which eludes definition, yet is the most real thing of all."

Healthy Appetite

On October 9, 1890, he said his main purpose was "to leave men healthy, to fill them with a new atmosphere." A week later, on October 20, he asserted that "there is no delicatesse, no aestheticism, about the *Leaves*."

Plus Ça Change

On January 27 of his last year Whitman offered this response to news that *Leaves of Grass* was still banned from the library of Harvard College: "I am not astonished—the action would probably be duplicated in many quarters." Early in his conversations with Traubel, Whitman summed up his fate on campus: "College men as a rule would rather get along without me . . . they go so far, the best of them—then stop: some of them don't go at all." He also fared poorly in one of America's major emporiums, John Wanamaker's in Philadelphia, which had long been notoriously shy about *Leaves of Grass*. Just weeks before his death, when Whitman heard that Wanamaker's would take orders for *Leaves of Grass* but not keep it in stock, he laughed and said, "It is an old story—a pull on the old string."

Humble Request

If these fellows would only read *Leaves of Grass*—read it through with their eyes rather than through their prejudices: but when they condemn it without reading it—that's what nettles me.

Bob the Embodiment

It should not be surprising that I am drawn to Ingersoll, for he is LG. He lives, embodies, the individuality I preach. LG utters individuality, the most extreme, uncompromising. I see in Bob [Ingersoll] the noblest specimen—American-flavored—pure out of the soil, spreading, giving, demanding light.

Individual Power

My *Leaves* mean, that in the end reason, the individual, should have control—hold the reins—not necessarily to use them—but to possess the power: reason, the individual—through these solidarity (the whole race, all times, all lands)—this is the main purport, the spinal creative fact, by which we stand or fall.

Solidarity

Late in 1890 Horace recorded Whitman's speaking of "'the idea of human solidarity'—which was essential *Leaves of Grass*, and to leave which out would destroy these poems. Spoke earnestly of this, in tone eloquent and strong." Later Whitman reiterated, "Solidarity—human solidarity—is not that *Leaves of Grass?*"

Animality

. . . the heroic animality of the *Leaves* . . . How these damned saints affect a carriage of anti-animality! Well, our *Leaves* stand against all that: we are solidly for healthy appetite!

Autobiographicality

A letter from Bucke expressed a view about *Leaves* that Whitman eagerly embraced: "Doctor seems impressed with the autobiographicality of the book—that from the beginning to end it is autobiographical: not in the usual sense—but in a sense that makes it strikingly mine." On the same day, December 20, 1888, Whitman wrote to Bucke: "yes it is mainly all *autobiographic* environ'd with my time & deeply incarnated & tinged with it, & the moral begetting of it (I hope)."

Ultimate Mystery

"*Leaves of Grass* is a mystery to me—I do not pretend myself to have solved it—not at all. Doctor [Bucke, in his book on Whitman] starts off with great vehemence to assert—*Leaves of Grass* means this and this and this and this and this—oh! stamps it down with the hammer of Thor! But even he, much as he really *does* know about it, has never caught this—that *Leaves of Grass* never started out to do anything—has no purpose—has no definite beginning, middle, end. It is reflection, it is statement, it is to see and tell, it is to keep clear of judgments, lessons, school-ways—to be a world, with all the mystery of that, all its movement, all its life. From this standpoint I, myself, often stand in astonishment before the book—am defeated by it—lost in its curious revolutions, its whimsies, its overpowering momentum—lost as if a stranger, even as I am a stranger on this earth—driving about with it, knowing nothing of why or result. . . . This way, you see, I am a spectator, too." Ingersoll, in a lecture on Whitman, offered one plausible reason for this "mystery" of *Leaves*: "One of the valuable features to me is its *indirection*—how much ground it covers that is not set in the *letter* of it—is not suspected by casual, careless readers." Ingersoll was surely unaware that among Whitman's notes to himself was "This indirect mode of attack is better than all direct modes of attack."

Individual Poems and Sequences

Once a poem was finished, it pretty much went out of Whitman's head (except, that is, when a new edition of Leaves *was being prepared; then he was not above going back to make revisions). He was, to judge from the conversations, not a constant or doting revisitor of his works, and this may partly explain why individual poems were not often discussed at Mickle Street. When they do surface in the dialogue, the tone is more usually one of wittiness than of emotion recollected in tranquillity.*

"Crossing Brooklyn Bridge"

Traubel, having just read the poem, queries about the "objections often urged that W. was too indirect, too suggestive, presumed too much in powers behind" the verse. Whitman's answer: "I suppose no one but a habitue could grasp fully—even measurably—the pictorial significance of the piece: no one who has not been there as I have been, a frequenter of ferry ways, boats, wharves, men, bustling commerces. I have been there in the presence of all its thousand and one changes of color: mine was no casual contact, but the contact of years, love, association—of childhood, boyhood, manhood, maturity—the sailing on the waters, the going out with the pilots in their pilot boats, the tripping it to the sea and back again—Sandy Hook, down to Navesink. Only by such gathered lights and shades can anyone really know, appreciate, enter into, the fine tones of meaning: that is, by actually living, breathing, bathing, in the life of it!"

Children of Adam

In the first few days of their project, Whitman showed Traubel a friendly letter from Robert Buchanan in England dated January 8, 1877. In it, Buchanan drew the line at the *Children of Adam* poems: "I shall ever regret the insertion of certain passages in your books (*Children of Adam* etc). . . . I think your reputation is growing here, and I am sure it deserves to grow. But your fatal obstacle to general influence is the obnoxious passages." Hearing this read aloud, Whitman responded: "*Children of Adam* stumps the worst and the best: I have even tried hard to see if it might not as I grow older or experience new moods stump me: I have almost deliberately tried to retreat. But it would not do. When I tried to take those pieces out of the scheme the whole scheme came down about my ears."

She [Anne Gilchrist], too, like [William] Sloane Kennedy . . . shied at the *Children of Adam* poems at the start. Sex is a red rag to most people. It takes some time to get accustomed to me, but if the folks will only persevere they will finally feel right comfortable in my presence. *Children of Adam*—the poems—are very innocent: they will not shake down a house.

It has always been a puzzle to me why people think that because I wrote *Children of Adam*, *Leaves of Grass*, I must perforce be interested in all the literature of rape, all the pornograph of vile minds. I have not only been made a target by those who despised me but a victim of violent interpretation by those who condoned me.

Calamus: Timber of the Leaves Ship

"Calamus" is a Latin word—much used in Old English writing, however. I like it much—it is to me, for my intentions, indispensable—the sun revolves about it, it is a timber of the ship—not there alone in that one series of poems, but in all, belonging to all. It is one of the United States—it is the quality which makes the states whole—it is the thin thread—but, oh! the significant thread!—by which the nation is held together, a chain of comrades; it could no more be dispensed with than the ship entire. I know no country anyhow in which comradeship is so far developed as here—here, among the mechanic classes.

Calamus: Upright, Emotional

Traubel recalled, during an excursion to Pea Shore, a shallow bay of the Delaware River, Walt pointing to the stands of deep water-grass running all through the flats and exulting: "Leaves of Grass! The largest leaves of grass known! Calamus! Yes, that is calamus! Profuse, rich, noble—upright, emotional!"

Note: Whitman named the most potently autobiographical sequence of poems he ever wrote after the *calamus aromaticus* plant (its small effloresence is shaped like an erect phallus). The sequence appeared first in the 1860 *Leaves* edition.

Calamus *and Curious Mr.* Symonds

On April 27, 1888, Traubel records an unusually long talk ("an hour or more") about John Addington Symonds's persistent questions, in letters over many years from England, about the *Calamus* poems. Though calling Symonds "a royal good fellow," Whitman says he has not enjoyed this third degree: "What does *Calamus* mean? What do the poems come to in the round-up? That is worrying him a good deal—their involvement, as he suspects, is the passional relations of men with men—the thing he reads so much of in the literature of southern Europe and sees something of in his own experience. He is always driving at me about that: is that what *Calamus* means?—because of me or in spite of me, is that what it means? I have said no, but no does not satisfy him. But read this letter [dated February 7, 1872]—read the whole of it: it is very shrewd, very [a]cute, in deadliest earnest: it drives me hard—almost compels me—it is urgent, persistent: he sort of stands in the road and says: 'I won't move till you answer my question.'" Traubel reads the long letter, which does focus on Whitman's same-sex "adhesiveness" and "comrade-ship." The discussion that follows is remarkable. Traubel allows that he sees no "driving you hard" in the letter, that Symonds "asks the questions mildly enough." Whitman: "I suppose you are right—'drive' is not exactly the word: yet you know how I hate to be catechized. Symonds is right, no doubt, to ask the questions: I am just as much right if I do not answer them. I often say to myself about *Calamus*—perhaps it means more or less than what I thought myself— means different: perhaps I don't know what it all means—perhaps never did know. My first instinct about all that Symonds writes is violently reactionary—is strong and brutal for no, no, no. Then the thought intervenes that I maybe do not know all my own meanings."

Note: Symonds's memoirs, published nearly a century after his 1893 death, reveal the cause of his persistence: he was convinced *Leaves of Grass*, and the *Calamus* poems in particular, played a crucial role in coming to terms with his homosexuality. Symonds tells of beginning in the late 1860s to write for his own eyes—as a "kind of mental masturbation"—a cycle of poems "illustrating the love of man for man in all periods of civilization." Then he explains, "very early after the commencement of this cycle, I came across W. Whitman's *Leaves of Grass*. I was sitting with F. M. Myers in his rooms at Trinity, Cambridge, when he stood up, seized a book and shouted out in his nasal intonation with those brazen lungs of his, 'Long I thought that knowledge alone would content me' [*Calamus* #8, 1860 ed.]. This fine poem, omitted from later editions of *Leaves of Grass*, formed part of *Calamus*. The book became for me a sort of Bible. In- spired by *Calamus*, I adopted another method of palliative treatment, and tried to in- vigorate the emotion I could not shake off by absorbing Whitman's conception of com- radeship. The process was not without its bracing benefit. My desires grew manlier, more defined, more direct, more daring by contact with *Calamus*. . . . I can now declare with sincerity that my abnormal inclinations, modified by Whitman's idealism and penetrated with his democratic enthusiasm, have brought me into close and profitable sympathy with human beings even while I sinned against law and conventional morality."

Later, a thirteen-year-old letter from Symonds is mentioned: "He harps on the *Calamus* poems again—always harping on 'my daughter.' I don't see why it should but his recurrence to that subject irritates me a little."

On February 21, 1891, Symonds wrote to Traubel: "I exchanged some words by letter with Walt lately about his *Calamus*. I do not think he quite understood what I was driving at. Yet that does not signify. I wish you would tell me what you & your friends feel to be the central point of this most vital doctrine of comradeship. Out here in Europe I see signs of an awakening of enthusiastic relations between men, which tend to assume a passionate character. I am not alarmed by this, but I think it ought to be studied." Symonds's letter became a matter for secrecy, as Horace recorded: "[Harrison] Morris had asked me to see Symonds' letter, to quote from it for Literary World. Showed him the letter but advised that he not quote—it would seem out of confidence, etc. W said, 'You were quite right—I am sure we should guard well these inner utterances—often they are only and simply for us.'"

Calamus: *Botanical*

The visiting Englishman J. W. Wallace expressed the desire to take some calamus back as a souvenir, and Whitman advises: "Well, that is easily done—there is plenty of it here. But you must be careful how you look it up. There's counterfeit calamus, which is only a rush—has no root. But calamus itself, the real thing, has a thick bulby root—stretches out—this way—like the fingers spread. And it is a medicinal root—is often brought in town by the niggers—some boiling it even, some chewing it. It always grows in damp places, along runs of water—lowlands. You can easily get it—it pulls up. Oh! yes! You will know it by the root, which is really the *only* way to know it."

Calamus: *Manly Affections*

Whitman hands over to Traubel the draft of one of his chatty letters written from Washington to Hugo Fritsch, one of his New York circle, with these emotional words: "I want you some day to write, to talk, about me: to tell what I mean by *Calamus*: to make no fuss but to speak out of your own knowledge: these letters will help you: they will clear up some things that have been misunderstood: you know what: I don't need to say. The world is so topsy turvy, so afraid to love, so afraid to demonstrate, so good, so respectable, so aloof, that it sees two people or more people who really, greatly, wholly care for each other and say so. . . ."

Note: For the full, vigorous condemnation of what would now be termed homophobia, see the entry "Demonstrative Men," p. 171.

"O Captain! My Captain!"

Traubel brings Whitman a newspaper squib that suggests "the world would be better off today" if the poet had written a volume of "My Captains" instead of filling "a scrap-basket with waste and calling it a book." Whitman lets fly: "I'm honest when I say, damn 'My Captain' and all the 'My Captains' in my book! This is not the first time I have been irritated into saying I'm almost sorry I ever wrote the poem. . . . *I* say that if I'd written a whole volume of 'My Captains' I'd deserve to be spanked and sent to bed with the world's compliments." A few days later Horace is handed the very manuscript of "My Captain" with these words: "I ought to have destroyed it, but your face always hovers around to rebuke me when I think of destruction so I laid it aside for you . . . if you promise not to bring the manuscript back I will promise to let you take it away." Walt keeps it a few more days, then relinquishes it with further deprecation: "The thing that tantalizes me most is not its rhythmic imperfection or its imperfection as a ballad or rhymed poem (it is damned bad in all that, I do believe) but the fact that my enemies and some of my friends who half doubt me, look upon it as a concession made to the philistines—that makes me mad." A typical philistine of the day was Thomas Wentworth Higginson (Emily Dickinson's dismal confidant), whom Whitman despised ("poor water enough"). In an article titled "Literary High-Water Marks" that came to Walt's attention in November 1890, Higginson utters the sort of comment on "Captain" that turned the poet against it: "In some cases, as in Whitman's 'O Captain, My Captain,' the high-water mark may have been attained precisely at the moment when the poet departed from his theory and confined himself most nearly to the laws he was wont to spurn."

"So Long!"

Traubel asks about the origin of the poem's title phrase; Whitman replies: "It was very prevalent when I was a boy among the lower orders, so-called, in New York—the laborers on the wharves, stevedores, boatmen, the street boys, particularly the sailors: So long! So long! So long! It was prevalent, too,—and this would rather detract from it for some— among the prostitutes, the loose women, of the town."

"Passage to India"

There's more of me, the essential ultimate me, in that than in any of the poems. There is no philosophy, consistent or inconsistent, in that poem . . . but the burden of it is evolution—the one thing escaping the other—the unfolding of cosmic purposes.

"As a Strong Bird on Pinions Free"

I made that singular excursion to Dartmouth—delivered the little poem you see here. I wonder how it happened that I was chosen for the poem there? It was never quite clear to me. But I went—was royally received. When I returned to New York I produced this little volume [the 1872 collection with the title taken from this poem]. Nobody wanted it—nobody cared for it—even my friends mostly left it unread—and so five hundred copies or so fell into my hands—five hundred, which I have given away right and left.

Tell her [Mrs. Joseph Fels] for me that that is a hard nut to crack—the hardest nut of all. . . . "As a Strong Bird"—that is a great task for any one to assume to understand. The poem is a puzzle.

"A Riddle Song"

A running joke of the conversations is Bucke's "long puzzlings" over the riddle in this poem. Walt confides to Horace, "About *that* you must remember the secret in 'Diplomacy'—that there *is* no secret. It is important to remember—even necessary." Three months later, the same subject evoked an important statement of the mode of indirection in Whitman's verse. Walt, Horace reports, "roared when I told him B[ucke] thought I should watch for some hint of a solution [to "A Riddle Song"] before W. slipped away from us." Whitman responded, "Doctor would find after all, that it is the old story, 'diplomacy,' again—the secret: that there is no secret. Some of my simplest pieces have created the most noise. I have been told that 'A Child Went Forth' was a favorite with Longfellow, but to me there is very little in that poem. That is one of my penalties—to have the real vital utterances, if there are any in me, go undetected."

"The Dismantled Ship"

Whitman tells Traubel the following about "The Dismantled Ship," a five-line poem about a hulk that lies "rusting, mouldering" on "some unused lagoon," which would appear in *November Boughs*: "Yes, it was suggested by the picture in Harned's parlor: that's me—that's my old hulk—laid up at last: no good any more—no good—a fellow might get melancholy seeing himself in such a mirror—but I guess we can see through as well as in the mirrors when the test comes."

"To the Sun-set Breeze"

It is part of our history to say that this poem was refused by *Harper's* as an "improvisation," refused by the *Nineteenth Century* for general reasons, accepted and paid for by Stoddart, of *Lippincott's. Improvisation!* I wonder if they ever heard of the other things I have written? I should not know what else to do but "improvise"!

Note: Whitman's inner circle particularly rejoiced in this rather rare late poem of high quality, which appeared in *Lippincott's* in December 1890. Bucke wrote to Traubel, "It is a wonderful poem, one of the greatest of these later poems of W.'s."

Printing Leaves of Grass

If there is one regular topic of conversation in Traubel's pages that sometimes does more than threaten to become tedious, it is the interminable debate and dealings with all the "publisherial" artisans and contractors responsible for producing November Boughs *(1888), the nine hundred–page* Complete Poetry and Prose *(1888), and the "deathbed"* Leaves *(1892). Then there were the numerous "poemets," little squibs, and articles placed by Whitman in newspapers, as well as special items like the elaborate pamphlet* Camden's Compliment to Walt Whitman, *which appeared in the fall of 1889 and recorded the festivities on the poet's seventieth birthday. Much time is devoted to the finer points of printing simply because Whitman was so scrupulous about the physical presentation of his work. As Traubel sums up, "He is stubborn about having his punctuation, abbreviations and general arrangement strictly followed." Still, there are some memorable ebullitions and execrations in* With Walt Whitman *that suggest the publishing world did not change all that much in the following century.*

The Orphan of 1855

It is tragic—the fate of those books. None of them were sold—practically none—perhaps one or two, perhaps not even that many. We had only one object—to get rid of the books—to get them out someway even if they had to be given away. You have asked me questions about the manuscript of the first edition. It was burned. [Andrew] Rome kept it several years, but one day, by accident, it got away from us entirely—was used to kindle the fire or to feed the rag man.

Note: The first edition of *Leaves of Grass* came from a press situated at Cranberry and Fulton Streets in Brooklyn. In an 1885 letter Whitman responded to a query about this edition by stating, "The first *Leaves of Grass* was printed in 1855 in Brooklyn New York—Small quarto 9 by 12 inches, 95 pages—in the type called 'English'—was not stereo-typed—800 copies were struck off on a hand press by Andrew Rome, in whose office the work was all done—the author himself setting some of the type." An invoice survives from the binder, Charles Jenkins, and it confirms there were 795 copies in various bindings.

I don't think one copy was sold—not one copy. It was printed in Brooklyn—I had some friends in the printing business there—the Romes—three or four young fellows, brothers. They had consented to produce the book. I set up some of it myself: some call it my hand-work: it was not strictly that—there were about one hundred pages: out of them I set up ten or so—that was all. The books were put into the stores. But nobody bought them. They had to be given away. But the ones we sent them to—a good many of them—sent them back—did not want them even on such terms. . . . [Horace asks what became of the first edition.] It is a mystery: the books scattered, somehow, somewhere, God knows, to the four corners of the earth: I only know that they never have been in my possession.

I had a funny experience with a publisher in my early days—with the first edition. A fellow there was willing to print it but for a couple of lines which he construed into a disrespectful reference to God Almighty. It has always seemed to me *very* funny because I have never heard a word of complaint against them: nobody has picked them out, though they have picked out nearly everything else.

When Traubel told Whitman that a book sale catalog listed an 1855 edition for $15, the poet poked at the fire and laughed: "They say—some of them—that the first edition sold—sold through the good Emerson's letter—but that's not true: nobody would have them, for gift or price: nobody: some even returned their copies: editors—others."

One day Whitman drew Traubel's attention to an English book sale catalog that included rare and autographed Whitman volumes for prices up to £12: "I wish I had a few hundred of the books myself now—they would set me up! When I *did* have them, no price was low enough to persuade the world that they were to be desired!"

Making a Book

I do not think even intelligent people know how much goes to the making of a book: worry, fret, anxiety—downright hard work—poverty—finally, nothingness! It is a story yet to be told.

Superviser

I like to supervise the production of my own books: I have suffered a good deal from publishers, printers—especially the printers, damn 'em, God bless 'em! The printer has his rod, which has often fallen on me good and powerful.

No Slouches

"I am sensitive to technical slips, errors—am as ready as anyone to have everything shipshape. . . . I abhor slouchy workmen—always admonish them in offices doing my work: don't put on a slouchy printer." Whereupon Traubel adds: "W. is always saying to me such things as these: 'Look out that the binders don't get slouchy,' 'avoid the slouchy mechanic, whatever you do.' "

Foresight

Having been a printer myself, I have what may be called an anticipatory eye—know pretty well as I write how a thing will turn up in type—appear—take form.

Book Making

I sometimes find myself more interested in book making than in book writing: the way books are made—that always excites my curiosity: the way books are written—that only attracts me once in a great while.

Pica and the Best Stock

I often think that pica is, after all, my type: it is so ample, so satisfies the eye; and then I am inclined for quite narrow margins, plenty of ink, good genuine paper—the best stock. This goes a great ways in all particulars.

Design: Open Space Preferred

On noticing that his autobiographical prose preface in *November Boughs* ended at the foot of a page, Whitman repined, "If I had been a little more vigilant I should have cut out five or six lines. I like chapters in books to end short of a page—it pleases my eye better so."

Whitman asked Traubel about a page of poems in *November Boughs*: "Does it seem crowded? Yes? Well, we can throw a line away." Traubel asks, "Don't you love your lines too much for that?" "No—not enough to let them spoil the page."

Compacter

It is wonderful how much of one's manuscript a few compact pages of type will chaw up—consume—do away with: sometimes it is a terrible astonishment and ordeal for a poor writer to go through.

Proofreaders

What a tribe the tribe of proofreaders is! I think some men, some writers, owe a great part of their reputations to the excellence of their proofreaders—to their vigilance, their counsel. Who can do justice to the [a]cute, keen intellects of men of this stamp—their considerate patience, far-seeingness?

Very few people know—very few readers of books—literary people—what we owe to proof-readers—the indefatigable proof-reader. I knew one, Henry Clark, a man not of extraordinary appearance—plain—but a man who seemed the deeper, more expansive, the more a fellow looked. He was a Boston man—the reader of the final proofs of the Boston edition [1860] of *Leaves of Grass*.

He is an important critter—the most important, I often think, in the making of a book. It is easy enough to have good material—a plenty of everything—but to put all in its rightful place and order!—oh! that is another thing!

"I have great respect for the decided opinions of good printers, proofreaders—am disposed, every time, to yield to them. Long experience has taught me their wonderful [a]cuteness. Accent and all that is always a foggy latitude to me. I never feel certain of myself in it." Whitman was referring to a query about accenting the final letter in "finale." Traubel reported of a proofreader at *Lippincott's*: "This man in a great rage about W's inconsistent punctuations, and spellings and abbreviations." On another occasion, Whitman autographed a title page and told Traubel to give it to the proofreader at Bilstein's, his publisher: "I have great emotional respect for the background people—for the folks who are not generally included—for the absentees, the forgotten: the shy nobodies who in the end are best of all."

No Perfect Book

It is a saying among the proofreaders that there never has been a book without a mistake—never—never—from the earliest records of printing: never a book absolutely correct—technically, mechanically.

Publishers

Authors always growl about publishers, probably with a good deal of reason, too.

I am familiar with the small economies, meannesses, of publishers.

What a[n] [a]cute—devilishly [a]cute—lot the publishing wolves are.

Editors

There is no appeal from the editor: he is a necessary autocrat.

This time it was an editor fool not a preacher fool, Horace, though, as you know, as we know, both sorts of fools are plentiful.

Note: Whitman is sniping here at a newspaper editor who published a "nasty snarling thing" about his beloved Robert Ingersoll.

Apostrophes

In his later editions, Whitman systematically changed his suffix "-ed" to "-'d" in his past-tense verbs. Compositors questioned this when *November Boughs* was being set, and the poet explained: "So they wonder about my use of the apostrophe, do they? I use it . . . because it seems like reason to do so. The practice comes to me legitimately from the old dramatists—yes, and there is a reason nearer home. I have so accustomed myself to it in my verse that I extend it to my prose for uniformity's sake. Besides, the closening of words—'wisht' for 'wished' and such like—is not alone an old literary form but a wise one—in line today with current phonetic tendencies. . . . I believe in getting rid of all superfluities—penetrating to the root sense of the matter."

Printers

Why in the world do the printers—like the tailors—always pursue their own way, regardless of what others want or of what is best?

It seems to be taken as one of the inalienable prerogatives of some of the best mechanics to get drunk: you know how true this is of the printers: often of the very best of them: then there are the hatters: they too I am told are tremendously addicted to the cup: there must be something in these confining occupations which induces thirst.

Lots of Ink

Leaves of Grass looks better, reads better, *is* better when black-inked—when the ink has not been spared.

A Slow Binder

"That book has been there about a month: it should be done: what must we do to get it? Go there: don't hurt him: ram a needle in his ass—not too far: not far enough to hurt him—only far enough to wake him up." Traubel adds that Whitman "was so funny about this I burst into a furious laugh. This broke him loose, too, and he haha'd till the tears flowed down his cheeks like rain."

All the Interferers

Everybody interferes, advises, threatens: printers, binders, worst of all publishers. If a fellow could safely get through all that, many a battle would be saved: trouble: quarrel: loss.

All the Editions

"What a sweat I used to be in all the time over getting my damned books published! When I look back at it I wonder I didn't somewhere or other on the road chuck the whole business into oblivion. Editions! Editions! Editions! like the last extra of a newspaper: an extra after an extra: one issue after another: fifty-five, fifty-six, sixty-one, sixty-seven—oh! edition after edition. Yes, I wonder I never did anything violent with the book, it has so victimized me!" Horace records, "I broke into a broad 'Ha! ha!,'" and Whitman responded: "What the hell! What are you breaking loose about now?" "Oh! I was only thinking how the poor victim is still making edition after edition: now, even, in eighty-eight—thirty-three years after fifty-five." Horace records that Whitman chuckled at this: "It does seem rather laughable, don't it? But the fact is, the bug bites: we can't help ourselves: we are in a web—we are moths in flames: all of us." The bug bit Traubel, too, as Whitman then unwittingly predicts about

With Walt Whitman in Camden: "You, too, damn you! you'll have your bug some day: then maybe you'll have some sympathy for me!" Was there a favorite edition? "They all count—I like all—I don't know that I like one better than any other."

Chronological Debate

Traubel records: "Drifted into a long discussion anent my statement that Bucke was in favor of a chronological arrangement of *Leaves of Grass*. W. spoke freely, 'What was the ground you took?' [Traubel responded:] 'That the spiritual—the present—was better than any chronological arrangement—that you wished the book to remain in the form you have put it yourself.' He then: 'That was right—I do wish it as kept—it is my final request. All my close friends have taken a lick at this chronological business—Mrs. Gilchrist for one, now Bucke. But I charge that matters be left where they are. . . . The unitary principle is there—was there from the start—the scheme—the rest followed. I take it—want it that the latest poem embraces the first, as the first the last.' "

A *Folio* Leaves

Some of the fellows have been at me to produce a folio of the *Leaves* as they are today. It is a favorite notion of Talcott Williams: to have a big broad page to save me as much as possible from breaking my long lines. But it is only a pleasant dream—it is impossible: at present I must meet the case as I find it. The real case amounts to this: that it's all I can do to get the book out in any form.

Note: A folio—the most famous example being the 1623 Shakespeare folio—is a book with large pages, the paper sheet being folded once to make two leaves. The largest *Leaves* edition was the 1855, a quarto (the sheet making four leaves); the smallest, the 1856 (a sextodecimo, or sixteen leaves to a sheet).

A *"Junior"* Leaves

The concept of a "selected" *Leaves* edition was floated several times. Whitman was averse: "any volume of extracts must misrepresent the *Leaves*. . . . The whole theory of the book is against gems, abstracts, extracts: the book needs each of its parts to keep its perfect unity."

Arthur Stedman, a minor literary figure not greatly liked by Whitman, later undertook to produce a volume of poems selected from *Leaves of Grass*. Just weeks before he died, Whitman told Traubel he wanted to convey to Stedman "a suggestion if it's not too late." What might this be? "That he call it *Leaves of Grass, Jr.*" Traubel deflected the apparently serious notion by asking if Whitman had heard of the Walt Whitman Jr. who was writing for the English labor newspapers: "Yes, and I am told he is a bright fellow." When Bucke got wind of the idea, he wrote to Traubel: "*L. of G. Junior* that would damn the book before it was born—

and W. would just as soon do that very thing." Stedman's volume appeared in 1892, after Whitman's death.

Dedicatees Not Needed

Whitman not once affixed a dedication to a publication of his. Pressed about this by Traubel, he responded: "I do not know why—probably there was no why. Dedications have gone out of vogue—are no longer regarded as necessary."

Of Proper Margins and Stubbornness

This exchange occurred when Traubel arrived to find Whitman had pasted up a sample of the margins he wanted for *November Boughs*: "That may give them an idea—but I mainly leave it to them." Horace breaks in: "What nonsense, Walt: you mainly leave it to nobody: you want it your way and you'll have it that way though the heavens fall." Walt smiles and replies, "How did you find that out? you're damned [a]cute—too damned [a]cute to live!" Whitman finally says of the margins: "We want the margin the narrowest that comports with decency . . . not as broad as he chooses but as close as he chooses: like the hair on the head of a prize fighter: close enough to get rid of superfluities but not close enough to expose the scalp." Earlier, this little debate transpired when Traubel asked Whitman why he "resented margins in books." "Do I?" he responded, and asked Horace's opinion, which was: "I like open-spaced leaded liberal margined books. . . . For the same reason maybe that I like lots of windows in a house: they let the air in and the light." Whitman: "It's a picturesque argument even if it fails to convince me." Horace: "I didn't present it as an argument but as an impression. I couldn't prove it. I could only feel it." Whitman, relenting a little: "I admit that 'feeling' goes way beyond 'proving' most of the time."

Pocket Books

All my own tastes are towards books you can easily handle—put into your pocket.

I have long teased my brain with visions of a handsome little book at last . . . a dear, strong, aromatic volume, like the *Encheiridion* [of Epictetus], as it is called, for the pocket. That would tend to induce people to take me along with them and read me in the open air: I am nearly always successful with the reader in the open air.

Note: The only *Leaves* edition that fit this bill, however, was the small 1856 sextodecimo edition.

Flaws

Books are like men—the best of them have flaws. Thank God for the flaws!

Banned in Boston versus "Keep off the Grass"

They were trying times—the '82 times: back there: the Yankee went back on us: we had to come to slow Philadelphia for an asylum: and after all the slow things are often or mostly the surest.

In 1882 Whitman told, in a letter to a Philadelphia supporter, about one who stood up for him when Boston enforced an antismut law on the 1881 *Leaves*: "George Chainey, the free lecturer and preacher of Roxbury, Mass. lately preached in Boston a Sunday discourse, calling it 'Keep off the Grass,' in explanation & defence of Walt Whitman, especially of the meaning of his poem 'to a Common Prostitute,' which was quoted in full. When Mr. Chainey had the lecture printed, the printer refused to print the poem."

Taboo

When Traubel happens to remark in November 1890 that he saw no copies of *Leaves* on the counters of Lippincott's or Porter and Coates's bookstores, the poet says, "Walt Whitman is undoubtedly taboo in the bookstores as in other places."

Catalogue of Impecuniosities

Traubel records: "Laughingly [Whitman] told me [David] McKay had been over a few days ago—'paid me royalties between 50 and 60 dollars: think of it!—for *Leaves of Grass* and *Specimen Days* both! It is a long story of woe—a catalogue of impecuniosities—this record of my printed labor!' But there were other ways in which he was 'compensated'—'in best friends: friends, few, but the *better* of which the world never saw.'"

The 1892 Edition

This, of course, is the edition I swear by . . . the only authentic and perfect.

This is now my own personal, authenticated volume. . . . It is my ultimate, my final word and touch, to go forth now, for good or bad, into the world of the future.

The point is, to substitute *this* for all other editions—to make of it my final, conclusive utterance and message—a declaration of my realized intentions.

Leaves of Grass *and the Critics*

Whitman was subject to more abuse and contumely from the literary estab-
lishment than any author in the history of American letters. As he said on
countless occasions and in many charming ways, he got used to it—thrived
on it. "He is very cordial towards the enemy," Traubel was bound to note.
Praise was far from unknown to Whitman, but on one summer evening with
Horace, Walt got quite jocular about how he would react to open-armed
acceptance: "I would have to go scratching, questioning, hitching about, to
see if this was the real critter, the old Walt Whitman." Then he comments
poignantly and eloquently: "I have adjusted myself to the negative condi-
tion—have adjusted myself for opposition." The heat surrounding Leaves
of Grass *was considerable, as Whitman granted when he said of reviewers,*
"I seem to make them mad—rile them." Traubel varied the point neatly,
when he observed, "A man can't be an upholder of W.W. and be altogether a
man of peace." Following are a number of amusing and incisive variations
on this insouciant attitude toward his literary adversaries.

Dizzying

It's astonishing how many different sorts of reasons have been given by
some people for liking and by many more people for not liking *Leaves of*
Grass: then you'll find one person liking in it what another person dislikes in it: it makes me dizzy trying to straighten out these extraordinary
contradictions.

Great Expectations

I expected hell: I got it: nothing that has occurred to me was a surprise:
there probably is still more to come.

The Gamut

I get many curious things: some adulation—a little (a little's enough):
some cussing: now and then somebody goes for me—gives me hell. If I
had made a collection of such documents I'd have had some queer stuff
for you to preserve.

Whipper-snappers

Every whipper-snapper of a reviewer, instead of trying to get at the motive of a book or an incident, sets out sharply to abuse a fellow because he don't accomplish what he never aimed for and sometimes would not have if he could.

Friends and Enemies—Perfect Balance

Horace, there are some things in the world too big for it: they seem to crowd it out at the sides—to demand more room. I have had to spend a good deal of time for thirty years thinking of my enemies: they have made me think of them: even when I have tried to forget I had any enemies, have been compelled to reckon with them. But when I turn about and look at my friends—the friends I have had: how sacred, stern, noble they have been: the few of them: when I have thought of them I have realized the intrinsic immensity of the human spirit and felt as if I lived environed by gods. I do not mean to be extravagant—to say too much—Horace: you know how much I hate gush, effusion, flattery: but I can't help acknowledging that while I have had the worst enemies that ever were I have also had the best friends that ever were: perhaps the one comes to offset the other—the passionate love to offset the venomous hate . . . how I have been bedeviled! how I have been blessed!

Early Foes (Bless 'Em)

Leaves of Grass has had this advantage: it has had a stormy early life. Nothing could make up for the loss of this—it was a priceless privilege. Ease, comfort, acceptation would have ruined us. Even now the storm is not all down—perhaps better *not* down. However, we will not let the new kindness spoil us: there's yet to see!

Despised and . . .

I think everything that could happen to a rejected author has happened one time or another to me.

Two Kinds

Some of my opponents are fairly on the other side—belong there, are honest, I respect them; others are malignants—are of the snake order.

An Exception to the Hooters

Henry Clapp was always loyal—always very close to me—in that particular period— there in New York. . . . Clapp stepped out from the crowd of hooters—was my friend: a much needed ally at that time (having a paper [the *Saturday Press*] of his own) when almost the whole press of America, when it mentioned me at all, treated me with derision or worse.

Note: Traubel includes a warm Clapp letter to Whitman, dated March 27, 1860; its postscript: "I need not say, we are all anxious to see you back at Pfaff's, and are eagerly looking for your proposed letter to the crowd."

Exegesis

If there are 301 different ways of interpreting a passage—300 right, 1 wrong—the great mass will hit upon that wrong interpretation, insist upon it, dogmatize.

A Venemous Pursuer

Sour, dissatisfied disgruntled: it has been so with him—that has been his humor—for many years. . . . I am sure when I kick the bucket he will be ready with some columns of obituaries just as vinegary, fault-finding, mean. . . . That type of man is particularly devilish to me: is not big, ample, inclusive: rather drives away than invites. . . . [Richard Henry] Stoddard has pursued me with a sort of venom always. . . . On one occasion especially, on Broadway . . . [he said] "if it was not for the sympathy he, Walt Whitman, gets from a few of you men who really stand for something, he would have no currency whatever—would disappear": said that to the gentle [editor Richard Watson] Gilder, who, though always my friend—God bless 'im!—was never rabidly bitten by Whitman.

Silent Treatment

It seems to be a principle with some of the fan-dams of literature to treat me right (as they think) by not treating me at all. They look on me as a passing phase—that soon Walt Whitman will be done, his work done: that silence is therefore wisely imposed.

Barbarous, Bastard . . . Whatever

Whitman's response to a passage on Whitman in an essay by the English critic Edmund Gosse: "I liked one of his phrases. He speaks of *Leaves of Grass* as 'barbarous jargon.' That was quite good. . . . No, that's not just the phrase: 'bastard jargon'—that's it; and very good . . . almost gave sign that he had been reading *Leaves of Grass*. . . ."

Note: Traubel a few days later made a point of visiting his usual newsstand and recording the admired sentence, which contained both words: "And although assuredly the bastard jargon of Walt Whitman, and kindred returns to sheer barbarism, will not be accepted." Gosse (1849–1928), the English man of letters, greatly admired Whitman early in life but, with increasing respectability (he became librarian of the House of Lords), later fell away.

Thanks, I Needed That

Whitman hands over a hostile clipping from the *Chicago Herald* with these equable words: "That is a slap in the face that does a fellow more good than a kiss. They sail into me in great style—but that is the great test: if I cannot stand their attack I might as well go out of the *Leaves* business."

Opponents with Reasons—and Not

We have enemies and enemies. I find there are opponents of *Leaves of Grass* with reasons and without reasons: some without reasons who have not a leg to stand upon, men who, like a row of defective houses, no one of which could stand alone—any wind, any unusual disturbance would ruin them—but which, braced by each other, very well hold their heads up. ·

A Verbose Windbag

I got a letter from a doctor up in New England—a small town—he was an alienist or something: he assured me that there was a screw loose in me somewhere: he said I was a subject for a pathologist—that he had gone into *Leaves of Grass* definitively: that nothing else could explain its jumble of sense and nonsense, of the sublime and the ignoble: that I assuredly had a squirt or two of talent but that on the whole I was simply a verbose windbag. I was amused over his letter.

The Natively Antipathetic

You know, Horace, there are some who in the natural order couldn't accept Walt Whitman—couldn't appreciate the inmost purpose of his art: it is the absence of affinities. [James Russell] Lowell, with his almost steel-like beauty, and [Thomas Wentworth] Higginson, with his strict, straight notions of literary propriety—I could call them enemies, creatures natively antipathetic.

Later Whitman thus swatted Higginson: "Oh! I take no note of Higginson—he amounts to nothing, anyhow—is a lady's man—there an end!" Higginson was the editorial ogre who sat so dismissively and unpresciently upon the poems that Emily Dickinson sent him. There are, of course, no Whitman references to Dickinson in the conversations: she had died in 1886 with fewer than a dozen of her nearly 1,800 poems published—and those anonymously. Dickinson, however, refers to Whitman in a letter to Higginson dated April 25, 1862: "You speak of Mr Whitman—I never read his Book—but was told he was disgraceful." Higginson doubtless encouraged this view. When Whitman heard that Higginson might attend the 1890 Lincoln lecture, he said, "Oh! damn Higginson!" When he was told Higginson was staying with Agnes Repplier, an author Whitman despised, he elaborated: "and damn Miss Repplier—damn 'em both: that's my compliment to *them*!" Later: "Higginson has always been mere sugar and water. He lacks all else."

Sticking to Business

No matter what the fellers said, didn't say—no matter for the curses, the blessings—no matter for anything, I had to stick to my business. If I had stopped to dispute with my enemies, even to dally or luxuriate with my friends, the book would have gone begging. The book—the book: that was always the thing.

Gnats, Mosquitoes

There are a thousand and one gnats, mosquitoes, camp-followers, hanging about the literary army, and each one of 'em thinks he must have a fling at Walt Whitman. They know nothing about him—maylike never read or even looked at his book—but that's no matter: that, in fact, seems to be taken as a special qualification for their carpings and crowings. Walt Whitman is a rowdy, rough—likes common people: is apt to write about indecent, indelicate things—is odd, dresses informally: they all tell you that, get hold of that—then are done for.

Just Deserts for a Rumpus

The fact is I have been about as well received as I expected to be, considering the proposition I set forth in the *Leaves*, considering the rumpus I made, considering my refusal to play in with the literary gang.

Best of Enemies

It is a good and safe rule always to take care to be introduced to the fellow you don't expect, or don't want to meet. These do us the most good. It is not a man's friends from whom he gets the most benefit . . . but often the man who despises you, won't have you on any terms, is most rich in benefits.

Views from Abroad

We are always curious to know what is being said of us—particularly by the man who views us from the outside. Even if we realize that he don't grasp us, we see an importance in his statement.

Note: Whitman is speaking of a five-page notice on him by one Rudolf Schmidt, an admirer in Copenhagen. Unfortunately it was in Dutch: "We must certainly get some translation of this."

Obscene

The world now can have no idea of the bitterness of the feeling against me in those early days. I was a tough—obscene: indeed, it was my obscenity, libidinousness, all that, upon which they made up their charges.

Three Bespattered Editions

Leaves of Grass is made up of six or seven stages of [my] life, three of which—the first three—have had that inestimable benefit which comes of being fought against, bespattered, denounced.

Note: Whitman refers here to the three first editions of *Leaves* (1855, 1856, and 1860), which were written during his "halcyon days" as a Manhattanite and Brooklynite.

Rhinoceros Hide

I have the hide of the rhinoceros, morally, and in other ways—can stand almost anything.

Expert Opinion: Insane

In July 1889 a short article, "Insanity Experts: Some Amusing Opinions in a Will Case," appeared in the *Philadelphia Public Ledger* reporting on a New York City case that required expert testimony on insanity. This caused some hilarity at Mickle Street, Whitman saying of the squib, "isn't that a curio? I think it has been a long time since I heard anything so funny as that!" It ran, in part:

> Dr. William R. Birdsall, a visiting physician at Bellevue Hospital, expressed the opinion that certain letters in evidence betrayed the writer's insanity, giving as one reason for his opinion certain poetical tendencies which the letters displayed, and he was then asked if he considered all poets insane.
>
> "Well, not exactly," he replied, "but I do decidedly when I find that this poetry is not logical. I think Walt Whitman insane."
>
> "How about Milton?"
>
> "Well, I think Milton was insane."
>
> "And Shakespeare?"
>
> "Well," answered the witness deliberately, "from what I have heard I should consider Shakespeare as having rather a superior mind."

The Worst

Traubel tells of someone, upon hearing Traubel knew the poet, asking if this was the Whitman who wrote "dirty books." Whitman's response: "The world at large might suppose I am sensitive. . . . But there are three or four of my very most intimate friends—those nearest, best understanding me—who thoroughly realize that my disposition is to hear all—the worst word that is said—the ignorantest—whatever."

"I am sure this will amuse you," Whitman tells Traubel of a letter from Canada, "here is a woman who is afraid I am to be damned—bless her! There's nothing in the letter: it's of the same parcel with others I get from day to day."

I don't mind the fellows who say without a tremor: "Here, damn you, Walt Whitman, what do you mean by all this nonsense. To hell with you, Walt Whitman: to hell with you! to hell with you!" That don't sound bad—on the contrary it sounds very good—it is tonic. But when a fellow comes along, convinced and not convinced, hungry for your society and afraid of your society, blowing hot and cold, with praise on his lips that had better be blame, you are at your wit's end to know how to meet him.

Short Shrift

Whitman's response to Robert Louis Stevenson's critical essay on him was compact: "It amounts to nothing."

Still on Trial

This little burst of rancor was evoked by the re-reading of a rejection letter from *Harpers' Magazine* from twelve years before: "I suppose I'm thin-skinned too, sometimes: I never get it quite clear in my old head that I am not popular and if [newspaper and magazine] editors have any use for me at all it can only be among the minor figures of interest. I do not rank high in market valuations—at the best I am only received on sufferance: I have not yet really got beyond the trial stage."

Hasty Obit

An obituary for Whitman, prepared ahead of time, came to the attention of Mickle Street, its purport being that the poet was "a rowdy Emerson."

Formal-cut Men

I do not value literature as a profession. I feel about literature what Grant did about war. He hated war. I hate literature. I am not a literary West Pointer.

Of "literary men" Whitman summarized: "They are mainly a sad crowd: take the whole raft of them."

Literary men learn so little from life—borrow so much from the borrowers.

Arthur Stedman [was moved] to print me in his biographical index as "Walt" and the "er" in parentheses. It is parlor logic, yet characteristic of the literary man of our time. Oh! you can have no idea of the intensity of this feeling unless you come into direct contact, conflict with it! It is the spirit which wants marble busts on ebony niches in corners—fine porcelains—the assumed necessities of luxuries, enervations—elegance.

When asked how "formal-cut men in literature" could comprehend *Leaves*, Whitman replied: "They do not—they could not: They like portions, beauties, what they would call 'gems'—do not see more. But it took more than *that* to compass *Leaves of Grass*. The thread connecting all was never penetrated by such men."

He [one Nathan Dole] is a good refined fellow, but phantasmal—an Edmund Gosse-ish sort of critter . . . wall-flowers, I call them!

Grove of Academe

College men as a rule would rather get along without me: they go so far, the best of them—then stop: some of them don't go at all.

Harvard never wanted me. . . . I am not quite the sort: I need toning down or up or something to get me in presentable form for the ceremonials of seats of learning. You must understand that I never blame anybody or any organization or any university for discovering my cloven hoof. I am like the diplomatists who are *non grata*. I can't be tolerated by the kings, lords, lackeys, of culture: in the verbal courts of the mighty. I am mostly outlawed—and no wonder.

The Eastern Literary Establishment

. . . that dreadful press and pull of New York professional literary life . . .

These New England men—supercilious, overbearing—sensitive about their own rights—not so sensitive about another's. . . .

He [O'Connor] was first of all *literatus*—yet a literatus of the highest type—not the New York ilk.

The real New Englander *façades* all that—oh!—two, three, four bricks thick . . . [Whitman then goes on to speak of a good friend, George H. Baker, who had no such New Englander's façade. He was] not four bricks façaded . . . his heart so took you up, beat close to you. He had such an air of genuine love.

Silent Treatment

I have asked myself in the face of criticism of my own work: "Should I reply—should I expose, denounce, explain?" But my final conviction has always been that there is no better reply than silence. Besides, I am conscious that I have peculiarly laid myself open to ridicule—to the shafts of critics, readers, glittering paragraphers: yet I am profoundly sure of one thing: that never, never, has even calumny deflected me from the course I had determined to pursue.

Down . . . but Not Out

It has been a rallying cry with a little group of men in the country: down with Walt Whitman—down him in any way, by any method, with any weapon you can—but down him—drive him into obscurity, hurry him into oblivion! But suppose Walt Whitman stays, stays, is stubborn, says again, says again, will not be downed?

The West

Hamlin Garland wrote to Whitman on November 24, 1886, when he was twenty-six, describing himself as "a young man of very ordinary attainments. . . . I am a border-man . . . a child of the western prairies. . . ." This evoked one of Walt's many expressions of affinity for the western reaches of the United States. Speaking of Garland's letter, he enthused, "Did you notice, too, that he speaks of himself as a borderman?—a child of the western prairies? That appeals to me—hits me hardest where I enjoy being hit. That country out there is my own country though I have mainly had to view it from afar. I always seem to expect the men and women of the West to take me in—what shall I say—oh! take me in one gulp! Where the East might gag over me the West should swallow me with a free throat."

I answered an autograph letter the other day—an unprecedented act: it was from the far west: from one of the territories, I think: there was something in it which moved me.

Editors

They do the best they can. Besides, I am an incongruity to most of them—I make the sort of noise they don't like—I upset some things they do like: why should I expect to be received? . . . I used to worry over it, just a little—resent it, too, just a little: I am past that now.

Kicks and Pats

We are not always patted on the back—sometimes we are kicked on the behind: and who knows but the kicks do as much good as the pats?

Whitman Man under Conditions

Thayer is a very likable young man—has been here. He is in one sense a Whitman man: that is to say, a Whitman man under conditions. He won't accept the critter just as he stands—yet has a kindly disposition our way.

Note: William W. Thayer and Charles W. Eldridge were the two young Boston publishers (still in their twenties) who made bold to publish the third edition of *Leaves of Grass* in 1860. In the June 1914 *Conservator* Traubel published, posthumously, Thayer's brief memoir of the venture.

No "Club" Author

When told that a Whitman Club in Boston had "petered out," Walt responded, "I never wish to be studied that way. I seem to need to be studied by each man for himself, not by a club."

Leaves *at Wanamaker's*

The store [Wanamaker's] is full of goody-goody girls and men—full of them: people who have been foully taught about sex, about motherhood, about the body. It is easy to see what *Leaves of Grass* must look like to such people with such eyes. The *Leaves* do not need any excuse; they do need to be understood. If I did not understand them I would dislike them myself, God knows! But all this fear of indecency, all this noise about purity and sex and the social order and the Comstockism particular and general is nasty—too nasty to make any compromise with. I never come up against it but I think of what Heine said to a woman who had expressed to him some suspicion about the body. "Madame," said Heine, "are we not all naked under our clothes?"

No Popular Sinner

Whitman, Traubel records, "had a good deal of fun" over a sentence in a letter from a Boston Whitmanite that ran, "One man said you had early had your head turned by excessive adulation": "I've been accused of many sins, been accounted for in many ways, but that, as pure novelty, goes ahead of all the rest of the interpretations!" Bucke, who was present, then added, "The time will come soon, Walt, when there will be no enemy," and Whitman replied, "God help us when that happens, Maurice!"

Suspectors

Traubel remarks, "You seem to think you have enemies at Concord," to which Whitman responds, "Enemies? I may not call them that: maybe not that: but suspectors, certainly."

Open Arms

After decades of critical opprobrium, Whitman paused to imagine how he would respond to thoroughly favorable reception: "I wouldn't know what to do, how to comport myself, if I lived long enough to become accepted, to get in demand, to ride on the crest of the wave. I would have to go scratching, questioning, hitching about, to see if this was the real critter, the old Walt Whitman—to see if Walt Whitman had not suffered a destructive transformation—become apostate, formal, reconciled to the conventional, subdued from the old independence. I have adjusted myself to the negative condition—have adjusted myself for opposition, denunciation, suspicion: the revolution, therefore, would have to be very violent, indeed, to whip me around to the other situation." He laughs: "But I guess there is no immediate danger: I am not very near such a crisis." To be sure, Whitman was not above a little preening over favorable reception late in life. To Bucke he wrote on October 16, 1889: "The main wonder-fact of all is that L of G seems quite decidedly to have, or begin to have, a real and 'respectable' and outspeaking clientelage."

No Elemental Flame

Whitman on the study of him by his acquaintance Edmund Stedman: "Stedman is [a]cute but hardly more than [a]cute—not a first hander—a fine scholar, with great charms of style, fond of congregating historic names, processional, highly organized, but not in the windup proving that he is aware of what all his erudition, even all his good will (he has plenty of that, God bless him!), leads up to. I should not say such things, should I? I am a hell of a critic." A few days later Whitman added to his assessment: "With all its scholarliness, its kindliness, its receptivity, its genuine and here and there its striking talent. It still lacks root—still misses a saving earthiness: what shall I call it?—a sort of brutal dash of elemental flame, which burns."

A Dozen of Me

"I meet new Walt Whitmans every day. There are a dozen of me afloat." This comment on the public's tendency to multiply—and falsify—perceptions of celebrities caused Whitman immediately to think of Lincoln: "Now, there's Abraham Lincoln: people get to know his traits, his habits of life, some of his characteristics set off in the most positive relief: soon all sorts of stories are fathered on him—some of them true, some of them apocryphal—volumes of stories (stories decent and indecent) fathered on him: legitimate stories, illegitimate: and so Lincoln comes to us more or less falsified."

A Wonder

"It is a new wonder to me, day by day, how much is put into *Leaves of Grass* that I never intended to be there. I am discovered in all sorts of impossible guises. We must submit, there is no defense against that!" Small wonder, then, that Whitman would in the fall of 1891 express whimsical fear of what future critics might do to him: "It is one of my dreads, that there may come a time, and people, to *exposit, explicate, Leaves of Grass.*"

Damned Definiteness

Walt expresses his dismay over critics being so certain in their explications, even critics who were dear friends like Bucke: "What I quarrel with is the Doctor's damned definiteness—and it is *very* damned! I often pull him up short when he is here. He is explicating this, that, the other, as if there was no doubt in the world about it. . . . Doctor, I may say to you, yes, this meant a certain something yesterday, it means a certain something today. I am most troubled by it of all—yet sure, too, that it has entrance *some* where. The *Leaves* often defy me to turn them."

The Admirable Ones

I admire a good many of my enemies more than I admire some of my friends.

"Queer" Readers

Whitman professed to be amused at "the respectable army of *Leaves of Grass*-ers" and "not surprised" to learn that a reader of *Leaves* should be thought "queer" by his friends.

The Catalogues

I am not in the least disturbed by that [criticism of "cataloguing"]. Do you know, of all the charges that have been laid at my door, this has affected me least—has not affected me at all, in fact. I have gone right on—my bent has remained my bent, everything remained as it would have remained otherwise. In Doctor Bucke all this—this peculiarity of mine—falls like seed on good ground—he has caught the significance of it. Bucke is a Doctor himself, a scientist, free, exuberant—and he has happily comprehended (and this is essential, the crowning requisite) the *physiological Leaves of Grass*—the *Leaves of Grass* nursed in these native occurrences, facts—the occupations, habits, habitats of men.

Advice from Emerson

"You have a great pack howling at your heels always, Mr. Whitman: I hope you show them all a proper contempt: they deserve no more than your heels."

Critical Weakness

Every time I criticize a man or a book I feel as if I had done something wrong. The criticism may be justified in letter and spirit—yet I feel guilty—feel like a man who ought to go to jail. I guess I am weak just there—the love in me breaks loose and floods me. I hate to think any man may not write the best books—any man. When I find any man don't I am disappointed and say things. How lucky is the man who don't say things!

Fired

My dismissal from employment in 1865, by the Secretary of the Interior, Mr. [James] Harlan, affords too true a specimen of the high conventional feeling about it still. The journals are many of them inveterately spiteful.

Burst-forther

Toward career's end, Whitman did have to field favorable effusions, but it was often done with humor, as here in this remark to Traubel: "I had a paper here—a San Francisco paper—California—in which they said that Wagner, [the great Italian actor Tomasso] Salvini, Walt Whitman were the burst-forthers of our time. Did not use that word—burst-forther—but words to that effect."

Ah, but Self-criticism!

It does a man good to turn himself inside out once in a while: to sort of turn the tables on himself: to look at himself through other eyes. . . . It takes a good deal of resolution to do it: yet it should be done—no one is safe until he can give himself such a drubbing: until he can shock himself out of his complacency. . . . If we don't look out we develop a bumptious bigotry—a colossal self-satisfaction, which is worse for a man than being a damned scoundrel.

Satisfactory Conclusions

I have suffered all my life from the misjudgments of people who looked with suspicion upon all I do. I am not concerned to please them, but I am anxious to come to conclusions satisfactory to my own soul.

Advice

Oscar Wilde enjoyed his cozy visit with Whitman at Mickle Street on January 18, 1882, more than a dozen years before the premiere of his play An Ideal Husband. *One flippant line in that play, however, perfectly captures Whitman's habitual attitude toward advice, whether from enemies or friends: "I always pass on good advice. It is the only thing to do with it. It is never any use to oneself."*

Good Advice

"Take my word for it—don't take advice!" Four days later: "'And you, Horace: listen to this: Take one more piece of advice and then stop.' What piece? 'Never take advice!' W. laughed heartily."

Preacher's Advice

To vary the monotony of my life I received a long letter of advice yesterday from a preacher up in Maine who said if I wrote more like other people and less like myself other people would like me better. I have no doubt they would. But where would Walt Whitman come in on that deal?

Doctors' Advice

It is one of the admonitions of my Doctor not to see people—not to talk: but I am a disobedient subject: I only regard professional advice so far—not farther: I decide limits for myself after all.

Mushrooms' Advice

I have another letter from an adviser today. It's queer how the advisers spring up everywhere like mushrooms. I used to think God was everywhere. I was wrong: the adviser is everywhere!

Moderate Advice

Be cocky, you young quarrelers—be cocky, be cocky, don't be too damned cocky!

Be individualistic, be individualistic, be not too damned individualistic.

Be bold, be bold, be not too damned bold!

The conventionals, on their side, are generally too timid; we, the radicals of us, on our side, are often too cocky.

Ministerial Advice

On May Day 1888 Traubel records that Whitman "laughed a bit and broke into a little recitative" about a visitor he had had that day: "A minister was in here today—he came to give me advice—he said he had come from St. Louis, or Denver perhaps (I forget which), to give me his opinion of *Leaves of Grass*. I told him that was hardly worth while—that I had plenty of opinions of *Leaves of Grass* nearer home—all sorts of pros and cons: damns and hallelujahs. But he didn't laugh or seem deterred—he went right on with his message. I must have done something to make him think I was inattentive—I didn't do it purposely—for he suddenly stopped: 'I don't believe you're hearing a word I say, Mr. Whitman,' he said. It was a good guess. I didn't mind his knowing it—so I said: 'I shouldn't wonder—I shouldn't wonder.' That seemed to open his eyes a little. He went very soon after that, saying to me: 'I was told you wouldn't take any advice—even good advice.' I said again: 'I shouldn't wonder—I shouldn't wonder,' and while he was trying to intimate his disgust I added, 'You know I get so much good advice, and so much bad advice, so much nearer home.' The thing seems incredible: I don't believe anybody but a minister of the gospel would do such a thing—would have been guilty of so egregious and impertinence. When he was all gone I had a long laugh all to myself. . . . The ministry is spoiled with arrogance: it takes all sorts of vagaries, impudences, invasions, for granted: it even seizes the key to the bedroom and the closet."

Imperative Advice

I do not object to advice but to having it made imperative. I claim the final privilege—claim the right to pass upon the advice that is passed up to me. I can honestly say that I like to hear all that is to be said in criticism of my work, my life: but you know well enough that it is impossible for a man to get down on his hands and knees before the advisers.

Threatening Advice

One day Whitman receives a letter from "a Western professor" with some "sound advice" on the prosody of *Leaves*, and Traubel jokes, "What a shame you did not call a council of the school-masters before you wrote your book" and asks about all the letters of advice the poet gets. Whitman lets fly: "Lots of 'em! and not all of 'em mere letters of advice. Some of 'em are even threatening. You take this advice, Walt Whitman, or, God damn you, we'll know the reason why!" Still in the whimsical vein, Traubel asks why he doesn't just do what they demand: "I would—I would—but they can never agree together as to what they want. Some don't like my long lines, some do: some don't like my commas, some do: some cuss my long catalogues, some think them holy: some call *Children of Adam* decent, some call *Children of Adam* obscene: and so on, and so on, and so on. Nothing I have done but a lot of somebodies have objected—nothing I have done but a lot of nobodies have praised. What's the use? What's the use?"

The Advantage of Ignoring It . . .

Take the last edition of *Leaves of Grass* [in 1881–82]: some of the fellows think my changes have not improved the book: yet it is my final judgment that the book is just right as it is now—that it should be permitted to stand. One advantage a thing has if a man disregards the advice of his friends—it is all his own—an expression purely of his own personality: free of blemishes nothing could be, but freedom from alien influences: ah! that is necessary.

. . . even Advice from Emerson

Traubel asked, "Don't you think that maybe Emerson was as glad in the end as you were that you refused to expurgate your book?" Whitman's response: "Horace, there—that's it: you've hit the nail on the head: I think he was—yes, just as glad: he liked me better for not accepting his advice. He must have known as well as I knew that it would have been decenter to throw the book away than to mutilate it."

Ultimate Advice

When you write do you take anybody's advice about writing? Don't do it: nothing will so mix you up as advice. If a fellow wants to keep clear about himself he must first of all swear a big oath that he'll never take any advice.

Expurgation

A perusal of the reviews of the early Leaves *editions shows what tremendous pressure Whitman was under to retreat from his avant-garde ramparts. The* Boston Christian Examiner *said his work "teems with abominations."* Frank Leslie's Illustrated Paper *(New York) fumed: "The only review we shall attempt of it will be to thus publicly call the attention of the grand jury to a matter that needs presentment by them, and to mildly suggest the author should be sent to a lunatic asylum and the mercenary publishers to the penitentiary for pandering to the prurient tastes of morbid sensualists." And the* London Literary Gazette *review opened, "Had it been called 'Stenches from the Sewer,' 'Garbage from the Gutter,' or 'Squeals from the Sty,' we could have discerned the application." On all sides, Whitman was urged to tame himself. Comparison of successive versions of many poems shows that, in fact, he did perform a retreat. But when the subject of expurgation or self-censorship came up, his views were largely unminced and eloquent—though he continued to perform expurgatory revisions of* Leaves of Grass.

Dirty Book

Damn the expurgated books! I say damn 'em! The dirtiest book in all the world is the expurgated book.

No Apology

I have heard nothing but expurgate, expurgate, expurgate from the day I started. Everybody wants to expurgate something—this, that, the other thing. If I accepted all the suggestions there wouldn't be one leaf of the *Leaves* left—and if I accept one why shouldn't I accept all? Expurgate, expurgate, expurgate! I've heard that till I'm deaf with it. . . . Expurgation is apology—yes, surrender—yes, an admission that something or other was wrong. Emerson said expurgate—I said no, no. I have lived to regret my Rossetti "yes"—I have not lived to regret my Emerson "no." Expurgate, expurgate—apologize, apologize: get down on your knees. . . . Expurgation and justice do not seem to go together.

Censorship

I want the utmost freedom—even the utmost license—rather than any censorship: censorship is always ignorant, always bad: whether the censor is a man of virtue or a hypocrite seems to make no difference: the evil is always evil. Under any responsible social order decency will always take care of itself. I've suffered enough myself from the censors to know the facts at first hand.

I hate all censorships, big and little: I'd rather have everything rotten than everything hypocritical or puritanical, if that was the alternative, as it is not. I'd dismiss all monitors, guardians, without any ceremony whatsoever.

When the Philadelphia postmaster (the very John Wanamaker) threatened to suppress Leo Tolstoy's *Kreutzer Sonata*, it seemed like déjà vu to Whitman, whose 1881 *Leaves* had fared thus in Boston. Horace records a predictable reaction: "W. asked me 'And what has [Wanamaker] been saying of Tolstoy?' And when I answered, 'That the book is not a fit one for boys and girls to read,' he retorted— 'And now they ought to read it!'" Thus primed, Whitman was bound exult in the novel—and he did: "it's a masterpiece—as great a masterpiece as *Othello*—by as great a master. I don't know but greater than *Othello*—certainly more fitted to the intricacies of modern life." Shortly after: "It is a mighty book, a vast book: it has property from the highest sources. . . . It's throbbing, vital with fidelity." And then: "It is like a magnificent nigger—superb, powerful, true to the first shred of nature—not to be admired because of his beauty, but because of his truth."

Note: Whitman's casual use of the offensive term was not unusual in the nineteenth century.

On the 1868 English Leaves

With the poet's encouragement, William Michael Rossetti prepared a selection of *Leaves* poems for publication in England. When Whitman began to recognize the mode of selection amounted in some respects to expurgation, he tried to insist on a "complete" edition, but printing was too far advanced to allow this. After Horace reads the draft of an 1867 letter to Rossetti, he asks Walt if he felt at the time the Rossetti selection was "in effect an expurgated edition": "Yes I did: I never gave my assent to any abbreviated editions which I didn't live to regret. After all, the Rossetti book was a piecemeal affair—an apology: it said to the British public: here you are good respectable readers, here is this American Walt Whitman pruned so as to make a decent member of your household: your sons and daughters are safe with this book: we have shaved off the mane of the lion, we have drawn his claws and teeth: now, behold, you have one of yourselves, whom you may welcome with an unfearing heart."

I now feel somehow as if none of the changes should have been made: that I should have said, take me as I am or not at all: I should have assumed that position: that's the only final, logical position: take me as I am: my bad and good, my everything—just as I am: to hell with all the cuts, all excisions, all moralistic abridgements. . . . Rossetti himself used his margin with great tact, consideration, delicacy: was miraculously circumspect. But an expurgation means a lot more always than it looks as if it is meant—has far-reaching consequences: like one move on the chessboard that moves so much else with it—imposes other moves: so we must look out—must not compromise unless it's a life and death issue.

Final Word

More than a month later, an old letter to Rossetti about the English edition, dated December 3, 1867, surfaced and was read aloud. It contains this stern warning: "I cannot and will not consent of my own volition to countenance an expurgated edition of my pieces. I have steadily refused to do so here in my own country, even under seductive offers; and must not do so in another country." Traubel then asked Whitman if the letter contained "the last thing you feel like saying on the subject of expurgation." The poet let fly: "It's a nasty word: I do not like it: I don't think I ever thought expurgation in my life: Rossetti wished to cut out or change a few words: only a few words: I said yes, do it: that was long ago: if the question came up today I would say, no, do not do it: I think as time has passed I have got an increased horror of expurgation. . . . Censorship: I don't like it: even the censorship of a man who is his own victim: it's all bad, all wrong, all corrupt: it reduces a fellow to a cipher: seems just like an apology, a confession: it's a sort of suicide."

Waning Powers

Whitman did not enjoy Shelley's or Pushkin's luxury of dying tragically young—say, for example, of some terrible infection contracted in the military hospitals in Washington in the early 1860s. Instead, he died at the reasonably ripe age, for the time, of seventy-two, and like many another great writer he survived long after he had reached the height of his artistic powers. Countless newspaper reviews and magazine articles told him this, as did some of his closest and dearest friends. Whitman told himself—and Horace—the same thing on several occasions. The subject of Whitman's waning powers naturally arose now and then (especially when one of his late "poemets" was submitted to a newspaper or magazine and rejected, as several times happened). Many of the poems Whitman wrote during the With Walt Whitman *years appeared eventually in* Good-Bye my Fancy, *a sixty-six-page pamphlet that was published in the spring of 1891. In a May 1891 letter to Bucke, Whitman responded to William Sloane Kennedy's view that it had none of the "sign-marks of early L of G": "f'm my own point of view I accept without demur its spurty (old Lear's irascibility)—its off-handedness, even evidence of decrepitude & old fisherman's seine character as part of* the artism *(f'm my point of view) & as adherence to the determin'd cartoon of Personality that dominate or rather stands behind all of L of G. like the unseen master & director of the show."*

Losing Grip?

While mulling whether to carry his *Sands at Seventy* poems annexed in *November Boughs* over into *Leaves of Grass* proper, Whitman reflected aloud on how his later poems related to his early career: "I often ask myself, is this expression of the life of an old man consonant with the fresher, earlier, delvings, faiths, hopes, stated in the original *Leaves*? I have my doubts—minor doubts—but somehow I decide the case finally on my own side. It belongs to the scheme of the book. As long as I live the *Leaves* must go on. Am I, as some think, losing grip?—taking in my horns? No—no—no: I am sure that could not be. I still wish to be, am, the radical of my stronger days—to be the same uncompromising oracle of democracy—to maintain undimmed the light of my deepest faith. I am sure I have not gone back on that—sure, sure. The 'Sands' have to be taken as the utterances of an old man—a very old man. I desire that they may be interpreted as confirmations, not denials, of the work that has preceded."

Ecstatic Beginnings

A letter is found among the Mickle Street clutter written by a Boston friend and writer, John Townsend Trowbridge, eleven years earlier; in it, he writes, "I am astonished that these latter-day critics should have so little to say of the first *Leaves of Grass* [editions], or venture to speak of them only apologetically." Whitman responds: "Do you know, I think almost all of the fellows who came first like the first edition above all others. Yet the last edition is as necessary to my scheme as the first edition: no one could be superior to another because all are of equal importance in the fulfillment of the design. Yet I think I know what T means, too: I do not consider his position unreasonable: there was an immediateness in the 1855 edition, an incisive directness, that was perhaps not repeated in any section of poems afterwards added to the book: a hot, unqualifying temper, an insulting arrogance (to use a few strong words) that would not have been as natural to the periods that followed. We miss that ecstasy of statement in some of the after-work—miss that and get something different, something in some ways undoubtedly better. But what's the use of arguing the unarguable question?"

Bucke expressed a view similar to Trowbridge's in his first known letter to Whitman, dated December 2, 1877: "Lately I have got a copy of the 1867 edition of LG, and I have compared the 'Walt Whitman' ["Song of Myself"] in that with the same poem in the 1855 edition, and I must say that I like the earlier edition best." When the subject of Whitman's artistic decline arose, Traubel's inclination was toward loyalty: "Did not agree with [Walt's first biographer] John Burroughs that W's late work lacked in the poetic." Traubel went even further a few weeks earlier: "I thought W had written no nonsense pages. Every minor writer has plenty of them."

Tremendous Drop

One day Whitman, without comment, gave Traubel a letter from Bucke, dated March 24, 1891. It contained this candid assertion: "Of course you do not write now as you did in the 'Song of Myself' days—in power there has been since then a tremendous drop—but that drop occurred in the early '60s."

Lacking in Poetic

Traubel "laughingly" tells Whitman of speaking with the poet's biographer of yore, John Burroughs, and of Burroughs's opinion that "W.'s later poems lacked the poetic." "W. throws in quickly with a laugh, 'And the earlier, too! Ask anybody!'" The next day, when Traubel revived the lacking "in the poetic," Whitman rejoined, "So does it all, that was one of the hardest jobs in my early life—to get the *poetry* out: but I did it." Note: Two months earlier Traubel and John Burroughs "Discussed somewhat W.'s strength—whether *Leaves of Grass* had in that respect declined. B. thought . . . especially the later poems of marked lesser calibre. 'I do not mean, however, to say they are weak; he could not be weak; but they lack in poetic possession.' "

Composure

I was a great deal more vehement years ago than I am now—Oh! I know I was! In my old days I take on the usual privilege of years—to go slow, to be less vehement, to trust more to quiet, to composure.

Ironic

Now that I can no longer write I have a certain vogue.

Rejection

Whitman sent "Passage to India" to the editor of the *Overland Monthly* in San Francisco, Bret Harte. In a letter dated April 13, 1870, Harte communicated a blunt rejection: "I fear 'Passage to India' is a poem too long and too abstract for the hasty and the material minded readers of O.M."

O'Connor Kicks

Whitman's great admirer William O'Connor did not care for the new poems that appeared in *Sands at Seventy*, and the poet faced up to the criticism stoically: "O'Connor kicks against them—is unfavorable—seems to regard the new poems as in some sense a contradiction of the old—alien to the earlier poems—as if I had gone back on myself in my old age. I do not feel that way about them." Editors were increasingly of O'Connor's mind. In June 1890 a smarting Whitman wrote to William Sloane Kennedy, "Did I tell you my last piece (poem) was rejected by the *Century* (R W Gilder)—I have now been shut off by *all* the magazines here & the *Nineteenth Century* in England—& feel like closing house as a poem writer—(you know a fellow doesn't make brooms or shoes if nobody will have 'em)."

Even the Dotard Essential

I don't say a man's old age is as important as his youth or less important than his youth. . . . I only say that in the larger view, in the scheme originally laid down for the *Leaves*, the last old age, even if an old age of the dotard, is essential (if I live to old age) as the record of my first youth.

More of That?

A week after Whitman's very wistful eleven-line poem about a leftover funeral wreath appeared in a New York periodical in January 1891, this exchange took place: "We spoke of 'The Pallid Wreath' in *Critic* of 10th. W. said, 'I am just sending it to Doctor [Bucke] in the letter there on the bed.' Then shaking his head, 'He will not like it. He will say, write us no more like *that*.' I interjected, 'No, no, no: he won't think it morbid.' This word seemed to catch W. He asked eagerly, 'And *you* do not?' I laughed at his eagerness: 'No, not a bit—and further it is another poem precisely in the vein which fits your age and condition, and that is what *Leaves of Grass* ought to do.' W. thereupon, 'You are right: that is a profound thought—and belongs with us—is part of us.' "

Part Three

Whitman with Peter Doyle, 1865.
Courtesy Bayley Whitman Collection,
Ohio Wesleyan University.

Avowal Letters

The daily arrival of mail was perhaps second in importance only to the arrival of Horace himself at Mickle Street. "W. loves to receive letters," Traubel records, "any letters, provided they are in the true sense human documents. He is always disappointed if the postman passes without stopping." Upset of the mail's movement was one of the few events that could anger Whitman, as Traubel notes one day: "Mrs. Davis tells me of a minute's passion in W. yesterday because a letter he had thought mailed had been neglected; unusual."

Discussion of the mail takes up a substantial part of Traubel's transcriptions. Naturally, Walt and Horace began, over time, to divide the mail into categories. A regular aggravation were the requests from "autographites" for the poet's signature. One day Ed Wilkins bet that a suspect letter was one such. "This it proves to be," Horace reports, "W. retaining the stamp and destroying the rest at once." Whitman summarized to Traubel, "I suppose one-sixth of the letters I receive are of the worrisome kind—letters for autographs, letters begging for money (they have heard I am a kindly old man!)—letters for literary advice." Nasty anonymous letters also sometimes arrived; one day there were two and Horace asked what happened to them. Whitman smiled and pointed to the stove: "Gone up in smoke."

The most eagerly perused letters were doubtless what came to be called "avowal" letters—missives variously expressing kindred-spiritedness, affection, or admiration for the poet and Leaves of Grass. On one occasion Whitman referred to these as "love letters": "I receive many queer letters— a couple of weeks ago there was one from an Englishman . . . it was very gushing, very. Yes, I have received love letters—many of them—especially years ago—plenty—even now, having one occasionally." Traubel told Walt, "O'Connor thinks you should collect all your comrade letters in a book: he says they exemplify your revolutionary sympathies." The idea was declined: "Ah! that is his idea? they seem so personal: it might be done but not by me: I would not be the best one for such a delicate task."

Sometimes there came avowals within avowals. One Hiram Ramsdell, for example, included a third party's expression of delight, and Walt wrote back to Ramsdell, reaching out in pure Leaves style for emotional contact with the reader-stranger: "I value George Alfred Townsend's appreciation of L. of G. It was magnificent. Where is Townsend now? I hope it may happen one

*day that I may have him near at hand, that we get to be friends—such is
in my mind."*

*And sometimes the avowal letters went overboard. Whitman received
such a letter from a consul in Colombia: "one of the enthusiastic sloppy
letters I sometimes get." (Walt carefully removed its stamps for stamp-
collecting Ed Wilkins and a local boy.)*

From a Beautiful Unknown

It's a letter from one of the beautiful unknowns—the beautiful unknowns: they get nearer to me, I get nearer to them, than any others:
they have no axes to grind, no wires to pull, no games to play: there's no
nigger in their woodpile: they're just Amos and Miranda: Amos who,
Miranda who, does not seem to matter.

Note: Whitman was referring to one of the many letters he received from out of the
blue, this one from a Louisa Snowdon of Hampstead, England.

Love Never Wrong

Horace refers to a packet of avowal letters that Walt had given him as "a
mine of great treasure,"and the poet tries to capture their spirit: "Do you
think so? Well—so do I. Love is always a great treasure—always: these
fellows may be wrong in what they say of my book but they are not
wrong in their love: love is never wrong."

Confessions of Love

Whitman shows Traubel a letter from a Helen Williams in Chicago
dated May 21, 1882, in which she says, "No man ever lived whom I have
so desired to take by the hand as you. I read *Leaves of Grass*, and got new
conceptions of the dignity and beauty of my own body and of the bodies
of other people; and life became more valuable in consequence." After
Traubel read the letter over, Whitman said: "I like these letters from
people I don't know, from people who don't know me, these confessions
of love, these little 'how do you do's' that appear every now and then out
of mysterious obscure places. I know some people will damn me and
some will save me—the big guns who noise about the world: I don't
know as it affects me either way. But such a letter as this has a verity, a
sureness, a solid reason for itself, which gives it special value. I confess it
pushed clean into my vitals."

Beautiful Thing

W. gave me another one of the "avowals." He said: "It is a beautiful
thing. . . ." I had to read the letter to him of course.

Apiary Invitation

"Now, Mr. Whitman, I am not wealthy, but will be proud to have you
come here and live with us . . . I have a copy of your LG. You have always been my favorite poet, and I think it a shame that you should be
left in need."

Note: Harry L. Dwight, a "Manufacturer and Jobber of Bee-Keepers' Supplies" from Friendship, New York, wrote thus in a letter to Whitman on hearing of his straitened finances.

A "Nob" in Algiers

Whitman remarked to Traubel on certain "odd letters" he would get from "strangers who invoke or extend confidences." He then described an example posted from Algiers by someone "who wants to acknowledge an indebtedness: it is warm, almost fervid. . . . A young fellow, an Englishman—it would seem a 'nob' . . . he has lost his girl: grieves, is restless: turns away from home—travels—gets to Algiers. Whether he took it with him, or found it there, or some one directs him to it—somehow he falls upon a copy of LG: reads it—says he is helped by it: that it braces him up to bear his sorrow: is enthusiastic—feels he must write— must have me know!"

Affinite Soul: Susan Garnet Smith

One of the earliest and most extraordinary avowal letters Whitman kept about him came from Susan Garnet Smith, a resident of Hartford, Connecticut; it is dated July 11, 1860. Smith, who says she is thirty-two and "not beautiful," tells of a friend "carelessly" lending her *Leaves of Grass* and of her reading it on an hour's walk. She describes a rapturous epiphany: "I feel a strange new sympathy! a mysterious delicious thrill! what means it? It is the loving contact of an affinite soul blending harmoniously with mine." Written in a somewhat unhinged, surreal— dare one say Dickinsonian—style, Smith invites Whitman to give her a child: "The world demands it! It is not for you and me, *is our child*, but for the world. My womb is clean and pure. It is ready for thy child my love." After Traubel reads it aloud, he probes with some daring, asking first why Whitman wrote "? insane asylum" on the nearly thirty-year-old letter. "Isn't it crazy?" "No: it's *Leaves of Grass*." "What do you mean?" "Why, it sounds like somebody who's taking you at your word." Whitman: "I've had more than one notion of the letter: I suppose the fact that certain things are unexpected, unusual, makes it hard to get them in their proper perspective: the process of adjustment is a severe one." At which Horace, in a burst of feistiness, remarks: "You should have been the last man in the world to write 'insane' on that envelope—but the question mark saves you. . . . You might as well write 'insane' across *Children of Adam* and the 'Song of Myself.'" "Many people do." Horace, triumphantly getting the last word: "Yes, they do—but you don't."

Shaking off the Shackles: Bram Stoker

Two extraordinary letters written to Whitman from Dublin by Bram Stoker, the author of *Dracula* (1897), are included in full by Traubel. The first one, dated February 14, 1876, when Stoker was twenty-eight, is read aloud, and the poet remarks that one sentence in it "hit me hard." Horace says he can guess which one, namely, "I write this openly because I feel that with you one must be open." Whitman responds, "That's it: that's me, as I hope I am: it's *Leaves of Grass* if *Leaves of Grass* is anything." With this letter Stoker included the draft of another he had written four years earlier but never had the nerve to send. It is more powerfully confessional and effusive: "You have shaken off the shackles and your wings are free. I have the shackles on my shoulders—but I have no wings." Stoker also speaks of being "naturally secretive to the world" and of reading *Leaves* "with my door locked late at night." It ends, "I thank you for all the love and sympathy you have given me in common with my kind." After hearing the draft read aloud, Whitman said, "Horace, I call that an extraordinary occurrence: that he should have let himself go in that style. . . . It all sounds easy and informal to me—not verbally stiff in the joints anywhere." To the "dear young man" Whitman responded with a letter dated March 6, 1876: "You did so well to write me so unconventionally, so fresh, so manly, and so affectionately, too."

Note: In 1878 Stoker married Florence Balcombe, to whom Oscar Wilde first proposed before marrying Constance Lloyd.

Tender and Noble Love of Man: Bayard Taylor

Poet, journalist, and author Bayard Taylor wrote to Whitman on December 2, 1866, when he was forty-one, expressing admiration for *Leaves*: "I have had the first edition of your *Leaves of Grass* among my books, since its first appearance, and have read it many times. I may say, frankly, that there are two things in it which I find nowhere else in literature, though I find them in my own nature. I mean the awe and wonder and reverence and beauty of Life, as expressed in the human body, with the physical attraction and delight of mere contact which it inspires, and that tender and noble love of man which once certainly existed, but now almost seems to have gone out of the experience of the race. . . . There is not one word of your large and beautiful sympathy for men, which I cannot take into my own heart, nor one of those subtle and wonderful physical affinities you describe which I cannot comprehend." Later, it appears, Taylor renounced this enthusiasm, which concerned Whitman: "Taylor has been of recent years quoted against me—especially against the sex poems. Now, it is precisely on that point that the declarations of his letter are the most unqualified and decisive. What are we to believe?"

Drawn toward You: Edmund Gosse

Traubel includes a letter from twenty-four-year-old Edmund Gosse from London dated December 12, 1873. It includes this passage: "The *Leaves of Grass* have become part of my every-day thought and experience. I have considered myself as 'the new person drawn toward' you." After reading Gosse's letter aloud, Traubel asks Whitman if Gosse's enthusiasm lasted: "Who knows? I think he does—but I would not be surprised if he does not: I am used to defections—especially of the young enthusiasts that grow old—yes, old and cold." Gosse did indeed grow colder toward Whitman as he aged, writing a decidedly dubious essay on the poet the year after his death. In it Gosse asserted that "discomfort and perplexity" await anyone entering the "little room called 'Walt Whitman'" in the castle of literature. Whitman took his revenge for Gosse's lapse in admiration. When Gosse, thoroughly aristocratic, wrote on "Democracy in Literature," Walt said Gosse was "no more able to grasp [that] than a neat cockroach w'd one of Kepler's principal laws." Walt later said snippily, "It is dangerous for a man like Gosse, having so little butter, to attempt to spread it over so much bread—it comes up very thin."

With Sugar in It: John Swinton

"This letter is almost like a love letter—it has sugar in it," Whitman said as he handed Traubel a letter from John Swinton dated January 23, 1884 and written from East 38th Street in Manhattan. "John, you know, is stormy, tempestuous," he adds; "raises a hell of a row over things— yet underneath all is nothing that is not noble, sweet, sane." The letter, included in full, contains this passage: "My beloved Walt. You know how I have worshipped you, without change or cessation, for twenty years. While my soul exists, that worship must be ever new. It was perhaps the very day of the publication of the first edition of the *Leaves of Grass* that I saw a copy of it at a newspaper stand in Fulton street, Brooklyn. I got it, looked into it with wonder, and felt that here was something that touched the depths of my humanity. Since then you have grown before me, grown around me, and grown into me."

One of the Just-comers: Lionel Johnson

An Englishman schoolboy, Lionel Johnson, wrote to Whitman in 1885: "I have lived as yet but eighteen years; yet in all the constant thoughts and acts of my last few years, your words have been my guides and true oracles . . . the help and exaltation I have won from [*Leaves of Grass*] have been won by many another boy and young man." The poet's response to hearing the letter read: "It's not the least flattering feature of my experience that I have been most successful with young people, the just-comers, and least successful with the full done and over done literary masters of ceremony."

Note: Johnson later became a friend of Oscar Wilde; he wrote of his first meeting with his fellow Oxford undergraduate: "He discoursed, with infinite flippancy, of everyone: lauded the *Dial*: laughed at Pater: and consumed all my cigarettes. I am in love with him."

A New World in the Old: W. C. Angus

In October 1888 W. C. Angus wrote from Glasgow: "When a young man I read your *Leaves of Grass* 1855 edition. It revealed a new world to me—

the world within myself. Your *Specimen Days* I regard as the most humane book of the present century. . . . I regard your *Leaves of Grass* as being the most original of American books." He concludes with the request: "If you would write your name upon my 1855 edition, which I intend to present to a public library, I should send it to you. . . ."

A Leaf from the Inmost Bosom: Allen Upward

One of the lengthiest and most over-the-top avowal letters arrived in March 1884 from Allen Upward, an English resident of Dublin. It begins: "O Walt! Take this Calamus leaf at the hands of him thou hast sought for. Lo! I am he. What shall I say, or how shall I utter, the radiant feelings that gush from my heart at the magical words thou hast sung to the unknown?" He later prefaces some autobiographical pages: "Let me unroll the extensive panorama of my own personality." Upward says he has been a freethinker, Buddhist, and Darwinian, as well as a liberal, radical, socialist, and anarchist. Now he is a Whitmanite of startling passion, as the letter's closing paragraph suggests: "This is the Calamus leaf which the Englishman Allen Upward (Upward, ought I not to be proud of the name?) plucked from the soil of his inmost bosom to send to Walt Whitman, the American, poet, writer and lover." Horace remarks that this is "the biggest job you've ever given me in the reading line" and asks Walt what he makes of the letter. Whitman mulls a while, then: "Nothing: taking it as a whole, nothing definite: I have feelings about it but no conclusions: it's so youthful, so green, so little, so big, so spontaneous, so stagy, so bulging with vanity, so crowded with affection." The letter, he adds, reminds him of Stoker's performance: "The same impertinence, and pertinence, too? the same crude boy confidence, the same mix-up of instincts, magnetisms, revolts? In both cases there's the curious, beautiful self-deception of youth . . . they were really writing more definitely to themselves."

A Gaze: William Hawley

In August 1869 William Hawley wrote to Whitman from Syracuse, New York: "I would I could grasp your hand, look in your eyes and have you look in mine. Then you would see how much you have done for me. Yours with a brother's love."

A $1,000 Bill: Nellie Eyster

Nellie Eyster wrote a letter from Washington, D.C., dated June 14, 1870, to say, "I closed your book revelation a wiser and more thoughtful woman than when from idle curiosity I first opened it. . . . I thank you Sir, with all my heart, and pray for you the abiding Presence and hourly comfort of the divine *Pure in Heart* whom you worship." Whitman's reaction on hearing it read aloud in April 1888: "Would a thousand dollar bill do you as much good as that? I think I never got a letter that went straighter to what it was aimed for: it's better than getting medals from a king or pensions from Congress."

Bernard O'Dowd

One day Whitman gives Traubel what the latter calls "a curious letter" dated March 12, 1890; it began: "Dear Walt, my beloved master, my friend, my bard, my prophet and apostle." "Enthusiasm abounding," Traubel observes. Whitman then said: "Take it with you, read it: then let us send it to Dr. Bucke." One wonders why, unusually, Traubel does not include the text of the "curious" avowal letter. This is one of the hints one ekes from *With Walt Whitman* that perhaps Traubel indulged in some censorship in producing his transcriptions. Bernard O'Dowd (1866–1953), though Irish, wrote from Melbourne, Australia, where he became a noted poet-democrat and perhaps Whitman's most active disciple there.

Interrogating Enthusiast: Edward Carpenter

Edward Carpenter, the eminent English social reformer, author, and apologist for homosexuality, wrote Whitman several times. Handing a very long one to Traubel, dated January 3, 1876, to read aloud, Whitman called it "one of Carpenter's early fine letters. He was never nobler than then, in that period of interrogating enthusiasm." It included these passages: "Dear friend, you have so infused yourself that it is daily more and more possible for men to walk hand in hand over the whole earth. . . . What have we dreamed? a union which even now binds us closer than all thought high up above all individual gain or loss—an individual self which stands out free and distinct, most solid of all facts, commensurate with all existence—love disclosing each ever more and more. See, you have made the earth sacred for me. Meanwhile, they say that your writings are 'immoral.' . . . Need I say that I do not agree with them in the least. I believe on the contrary that you have been the first to enunciate the law of purity and health which sooner or later must assert itself. After ages perhaps man will return *consciously* to the innocent joyous delight in his own natural powers and instincts which characterized the earlier civilizations."

Earlier Traubel had received a Carpenter letter dated December 19, 1877 (Whitman had written "Splendid letter" on it). One reason for this assessment was doubtless Carpenter's singling out for praise the poems that had caused such a rumpus among American prudes: "I want to say how splendid I think your *Children of Adam*. I was reading those pieces again the other day, and of course they came back upon me, as your things always do, with new meaning. The freedom, the large spaces you make around one, fill me with continual delight."

Arc of Comradery: Charles Warren Stoddard

An old letter, dated March 2, 1869, written by Charles Warren Stoddard from Honolulu, is found among Whitman's papers and is re-read and discussed. *Leaves*, Stoddard says, has had a liberating effect upon him:

"for the first time I act as my nature prompts me. It would not answer in America, as a general principle, not even in California, where men are tolerably bold." He also tells of his experiences sleeping on mats at night with a Hawaiian "lad of eighteen or twenty years" with "his arm over my breast and around me." Whitman's reply says he was deeply touched to learn about "those tender and primitive personal relations away off there in the Pacific islands." Whitman sums up about such letters: "true it is that a man can't go anywhere without taking himself along and without finding love meeting him more than half way. It gives you a new intimation of the providences to become the subject of such an ingratiating hospitality: it makes the big world littler—it knits all the fragments together: it makes the little world bigger—it expands the arc of comradery."

In a later letter to Whitman dated April 2, 1870, and included by Traubel, Stoddard wrote from San Francisco of another trip he planned, this one to Tahiti; his allusion seems to be to that location's indifference to forbidden sexual behavior: "I must get in amongst people who are not afraid of instincts and who scorn hypocrisy. I am numbed with the frigid manners of the Christians; barbarism has given me the fullest joy of my life and I long to return to it and be satisfied." This leads Whitman to make a poignant and revealing comparison of Stoddard and Traubel (certainly glancing at Whitman's own self-image, perhaps glancing, implicitly, at the subject of sexuality identity): "I have had other letters from him: when they turn up you shall have them: he is your kind of a man some ways. . . . [H]e is of a simple direct naive nature—never seemed to fit in very well with things here: many of the finest spirits don't—seem to be born for another planet—seem to have got here by mistake: they are not too bad—no: they are too good: they take their stand on a plane higher than the average practice. You would think they would be respected for that, but they are not: they are almost universally agreed to be fools—they are derided rather than reverenced: why, Horace, you are a good sight such a sort of a fool yourself." Thinking this might hurt, Whitman laid his hand on Traubel's and added, "You know what I refer to in you? I mean your other worldliness, as they call it: you have that in you: the disposition to sacrifice yourself to others—ideas, ideals—all that: it means hell for you maybe here and there but heaven too for sure. Stoddard was, is, that sort of a man, they tell me: I have felt it in his letters."

Penetrating the Remotest Parts: Standish O'Grady

Traubel is handed a letter to Whitman from "a young man of great spirit." It is from Standish O'Grady in Dublin and is dated October 5, 1881. It includes this passage: "I find as I change I cannot so change as that I do not meet in you the expression of every changing ideal penetrating even the remotest parts of my nature with a profound sympathy as of his who knew what was in man."

Beautiful Brotherliness: Hamlin Garland

Garland's first letter to Whitman came in 1886, when the budding American author was twenty-six. The first Garland letter Traubel reproduces—about Garland's class "of forty ladies" in Waltham, Massachusetts, and how he urges them to "come at you through *Specimen Days*"—is dated November 9, 1888. Whitman, though dubious about being approached through his prose ("it's best to let the people take the plunge at once"), grants, "I respond heartily to Garland's beautiful brotherliness: that takes right hold of me."

Some Shucks: Louis Sullivan

A February 3, 1887, letter from the great architect, Louis Sullivan, then in his early thirties, arrived from Chicago. Its opening paragraph read: "It is less than a year ago that I made your acquaintance so to speak, quite by accident, searching among the shelves of a book store. I was attracted by the curious title: *Leaves of Grass*, opened the book at random and my eyes met the lines of 'Elemental Drifts.' You then and there entered my soul, have not departed, and never will depart." Walt's remarks on hearing the letter again: "Ain't that catchin'? It sounds like something good that comes along on the wind for them as know enough to suck in. I'd say that feller's some shucks himself. . . . He's an architect or something: and he's a man for sure."

Three of You, Walt: Logan Pearsall Smith

Whitman was close to the local family of Robert Pearsall Smith for several years but later (after the family moved to England) experienced an estrangement that troubled him. Only the son, Logan (1865–1946), who was gay and who became a prolific author and critic, remained "quite warm for Walt," as Bucke observed. Traubel reproduces a letter dated August 8, 1891, that Logan wrote from Haslemere, "We have just had a visit from Dr. Bucke, and we were so glad to hear from him all about you. In furnishing our house here we have got three of those New York photographs of you framed together, hanging in our dining room, and it almost feels as if you were with us sometimes." Much later, in 1938, Smith published a memoir, *Unforgotten Years*, in which he alluded rather candidly to the liberating impact *Leaves of Grass* had for young homosexuals in the late nineteenth century: "Much that was suppressed in the young people of my generation found a frank avowal in *Leaves of Grass*; feelings and affections for each other, which we had been ashamed of, thoughts which we had hidden as unutterable, we found printed in its pages, discovering that they were not, as we had believed, the thoughts and feelings of young, guilty, half-crazy goblins, but portions of the Kingdom of Truth and the sane experience of mankind."

Walt and His Inner Circle

The principal members of Whitman's inner circle are a regular presence in With Walt Whitman in Camden, *whether in person or, notably with Dr. Bucke in Canada, through frequent correspondence. Though Whitman gratefully and cheerfully received visits from women—usually relations of his men friends—this circle was thoroughly masculine. Throughout his adult life, it is clear, the jovial, sociable poet's circles of male friends in and around New York, Washington, or Camden sustained him emotionally and creatively. Indeed, this tendency toward friendly camaraderie clearly formed a surrogate for the wife and children he never had.*

Walt Whitman Sociable

When planning was begun, several months ahead of time, for a birthday party on May 31, 1890, Whitman put in his two cents: "Do what you think best. No doubt in some way—if it is quiet, unpretentious—I will connive at it in some way. I accept the spirit in which such things come; could not, consistently myself, disregard them. But as I have said, simplicity, simplicity—informality—no brass bands! [I am] thoroughly sensitive, responsive to the enjoyabilities of such a compliment. You know, I love the good things—am awake to personality, contact, sympathy, emotionality at all times, anywhere." As the day drew nearer, Whitman expressed concern about an avalanche of gush: "My fear is of a deluge of soft soap—that I may go down in the flood. . . . Above all we must avoid flattery—the tendency in anyone to pile it on and on till a fellow no longer shows his honest *self* at all!"

The Entourage

Traubel records: "'Do you know, Horace,' he said as I got up and was about to leave, holding my hand in his own, 'the public has no notion of me as a spiritualistic being. Apart from a few—a very few—of you fellows—my *entourage*, household—you, Doctor [Bucke], perhaps several others—no one understands that I have my connections—that they are deep-rooted—that they penetrate shows, phenomena.'"

The Boys

I often recall the old times in New York, or on Broadway, or at Pfaff's—
and the faces and voices of *the boys*.

Visitors and Us

"Tell Anne Montgomerie that if she don't come to see me soon I shall
think she has gone back on me. I know I have said I wouldn't see visitors:
she is not a visitor—she is one of us." Whitman was by this time already
making sly remarks about his suspicion that Anne and Horace were an
item. Their marriage did not take place until nearly three years later, in
May 1891.

Our Crowd

Symonds has got into your crowd in spite of his culture: I tell you we
don't give away places in our crowd easy—a man has to sweat to get in.

Our Circus

"He is loyal beyond loyalty. . . . I have always felt that Johnston belonged to our circus." Whitman said this of a New York friend, John H.
Johnston.

No "Master"

Any "gush," either in letters or in person, made Whitman fidgety. One
day a letter from Symonds was read aloud; it concluded, "Believe me,
dear master, to be, though a silent and uncommunicative friend, your
true respectful and loving disciple." The following exchange took place.
Traubel: "There's 'master' again, Walt." Whitman: "It does not sound
good to me anywhere: I appreciate the reasons why but I can't condone
them. I have the idea that if we sat here together and they called me
'master' I'd feel like a fool." Traubel: "Suppose I called you master, or
Bucke came and did it, or Tom [Harned], or O'Connor, how would you
take it?" Whitman: "I'd send you home till you learned better manners:
maybe I'd give you hell right then and there!"

Whitmaniac

"Dick was a Walt Whitmaniac in the common ways of life . . . hospitable
to all sorts of men, all forms of thought, all contrasts of life." This was
spoken of Dick Spofford, who had recently died. Later Whitman said
of Spofford, "Poor Dick! Good Dick! Dick was one of the dead earnest
men—Italian in that—risking all for a conviction."

Walt among the Nice Jewish Boys

When Traubel said he had an order from Morris and Jacob Lychenheim
for two copies of the *Complete Poems and Prose*, Whitman responded:
"Hebrews? If I keep on in this way I shall by and by have a Hebrew

clientage—and I do not see why I should not—I see every reason why I should: for am I not a Biblical fellow myself—born and bred in Hebrewism—the old forerunners, teachers, prophets?" A few days later he referred again to "my Jew constituency": "It does me proud to think they listen and share me! Who knows but after all the youth are my natural friends?" When Jacob Lychenheim later was anxious to get and pay for a picture of Whitman to hang on his wall, Whitman insisted, "No—I should prefer to give him a little token. . . . And he shall have it tomorrow, if you wish. I'll make it up for you [autograph it]. The boys must be humored—Oh! we all love the boys!"

A Friend "In at the Birth"

[James] Redpath was one of the men in at the birth: just see when that was—1860: I had few friends back there: I was practically alone. What Redpath was then he was always: he stayed so: he helped me in many ways: he was not only loyal—he was militantly so: he was a perpetual challenge: he would say: if you don't like this Walt Whitman I'd like to know the reason why: yes, why? why? and he would hold people up—make them stand and deliver. I was never of that sort myself—always felt rather like slinking away.

Drop-outs

The young fellows seem rather bowled over by me: they get respectable or something and I will no longer do. . . . I suppose I don't wear well—that's what's the matter: I fool 'em for a time, when they're in their teens, but when they grow up they can no longer be deceived—they take my true measure.

[Edward] Dowden has lasted, still formally adheres to his original view. I have seen many defections—have had quite an experience of that sort: young fellows who take to me strong, then, as they get older, recede, sometimes come to entirely disavow me. Dowden is still haunting the corridors.

The young fellows come—the old men go—often, often: they serve an apprenticeship with me, in their youth, when they are getting their roots well in the soil—then they die, maybe become professional, adopt institutions, find that Walt Whitman will no longer do.

Two Unshakable Lovers

My relations with Nelly and William [O'Connor] were quite exceptional: extended to both phases— the personal, the general: they were my unvarying partisans, my unshakable lovers—my espousers: William, Nelly: William so like a great doing out of the eternal—a withering blast to my enemies, a cooling zephyr to my friends.

Whitmanic Forever?

One day Whitman speaks of Hamlin Garland's strong "Whitmanic endorsement and adhesion," but he then mulls whether the young partisan can stay the course and withstand the cultural pressures for apostasy: "Garland looks like a man who is bound to last—to go on from very good to very much better: but you never can tell: there are so many dangers—so many ways for the innocent to be betrayed: in the clutter, clatter, crack of metropolitan ambitions, jealousies, bribes, so many ways for a man, unless he is a giant, unless he is possessed of brutal strength and independent—so many ways for him to go to the devil. I look for Garland to save himself from this fate."

Transportation Men

"It seems to me that of all modern men the transportation men most nearly parallel the ancients in ease, poise, simplicity, average nature, robust instinct, firsthandedness: are next the very a b c of real life. . . . I am *au fait* always with wharfmen, deckhands, train workers." Whitman's sharp eye for handsome working men remained peeled on Mickle Street. In a letter to Bucke (July 18, 1890), he wrote: "As I glance out in the street I see the great young-mid-aged ice man going ab't his work *bare headed* under the sun, up & down, spry & stout & contented."

Thespian

These actor people always make themselves at home with me and always make me easily at home with them. I feel rather close to them— very close—almost like one of their kind. . . . The actors have always been more friendly to me than almost any other professional class.

"I have a weakness for actors—they seem to have a weakness for me: that makes our meetings rather like family affairs." Whitman made this remark when he was visited by a young actor from New York, Nestor Lennon, who came with a proposal to raise money on the poet's behalf: "I know a hundred actors in places about and in New York who would like to get together and give you a benefit." "W was visibly touched," Traubel noted, but he declined the offer, saying, "Tell all the boys what I have said to you about that—give them my love." He then recalled some of the actors he knew, and Lennon responded, "Yes, I know, Mr. Whitman: they *like* you, no doubt, but we—we *love* you."

I have always had a good deal to do with actors: met many, high and low: they are gassy: you'll have to be aware of that, to take account of all that.

New York to Washington

When I went to New York [during the Civil War] I would write the hospitals: when I was in the hospitals I would write to New York: I could not forget the boys—they were too precious.

Calamus *Correspondence*

Whitman's Washington–New York connections are strikingly shown in a preliminary draft of a letter he had written circa 1863 from Washington to Hugo Fritsch from his New York circle. He gave it to Traubel to read aloud, along with these marching orders: "I want you someday to write, to talk, about me: to tell what I mean by *Calamus*: to make no fuss but to speak out of your own knowledge: these letters will help you: they will clear up some things which have been misunderstood: you know what: I don't need to say." Traubel had trouble reading the long draft—it was so criss-crossed and interlined—but did so; its contents are powerful. They include reminiscing of a lately deceased friend named Charles Chauncy ("his handsome face, his hilarious fresh ways, his sunny smile, his voice, his blonde hair, his talk, his caprices"), of "the delight of my dear boys' company and their gayety and electricity," of fancying himself laughing and drinking with them, "tumbled upon by you all, with all sorts of kindness, smothered with you all in your hasty thoughtless magnificent way. . . . Ah if one could float off to New York this afternoon." When Traubel looked up from reading the letter, he observed that "Walt's eyes were full of tears. He wiped the tears away with the sleeve of his coat. Put on a make-believe chuckle."

Three weeks later Whitman turned over another big early draft of a letter to Fritsch (dated October 8, 1863), saying "We were just talking of personal things—of the *Leaves*—the complete book: we insist upon the personal: well, you have it in these letters too: they, too, demonstrate me—my theory, philosophy, what I am after." The strain of the letter is again strikingly effusive, Whitman saying, "Dear comrade, you must be assured my heart is much with you," promising a "tremendous letter to . . . my own comrade Fred" while fancying having "a good heart's time with him & a mild orgie" and wheedling for gossip: "tell me mainly about all my dear friends, & every little personal item, & what you all do, & say &c." Hearing the letter leaves Whitman silent, but then: "The letters, the letters, sent to the boys, to others, in the days of the War, stir up memories that are both painful and joyous. That was the sort of work I always did with the most relish: I think there is nothing beyond the comrade—the man, the woman: nothing beyond: even our lovers must be comrades: even our wives, husbands: even our fathers, mothers: we can't stay together, feel satisfied, grow bigger, on any other basis."

Note: Traubel chose to end volume 3 of *With Walt Whitman in Camden*, the last volume he supervised, with the reading of this letter and the "fired up" and "almost defiant" discourse on his life's work that it evoked afterward.

Two Whitmaniacs Compared

John [Burroughs] is not so outright, so unreserved, so irrevocable, so without exceptions, as William [O'Connor]: he is more submissive to the exactions of the traditional world.

Greek Fraternity

Walt on the essence of ancient Greek culture: "The key to the Greek character is this—freedom, expression, candor, passion, weeping, laughing—yet all these reined in, reason prevailing over all, reason, understanding, the last, the preserving, the balancing, the governing, quality."

Rev. J. Leonard Corning, one of Whitman's circle, said to Whitman: "The Greeks still make excellent wines." To which the poet replied, alluding to their notorious sexual proclivities: "Then you see they are not altogether degenerate!"

Whitman, speaking of John Clifford, a liberal Unitarian preacher in Philadelphia given to quoting *Leaves* from his pulpit: "Clifford is quite Greek, isn't he? Even decidedly, markedly Greek?—what I call gay-hearted, buoyant—especially gay-hearted. I am fond of calling *Leaves of Grass* gay-hearted—I wonder if it is?"

Greek culture also came up, unsurprisingly, apropos the *Calamus* poems. Traubel reports of a discussion at a Whitman meeting: "There was the subject of *Calamus*, which had been much discussed—Sulzberger questioning the comradeship there announced as verging upon the licentiousness of the Greek. W. took it seriously, saying thereto: 'He meant the handsome Greek youth—the one for the other?—Yes I see! and indeed I can see how it might be opened to such an interpretation. But I can say further, that in the ten thousand who for many years now have stood ready to make any possible charge against me—to seize any pretext or suspicion—none have raised this objection. . . . "Calamus" is a Latin word. . . . I like it much—it is to me, for my intentions, indispensable—the sun revolves about it, it is a timber of the ship.' "

On January 26, 1892, the Englishman T. W. Rolleston wrote a letter from Wimbledon that included discussion of Greek culture. After Traubel read it, Whitman responded, "On *Greek* culture? Read that again—read it slow. . . . Horace, that is one of the best of our recent letters. It goes near bottom." Obviously, the poet found appealing this passage, in which Rolleston complains that there is not "enough genuine culture" in America: "I mean the culture gained from absorbing the spirit of the great Greek poets & thinkers—the men who faced the problems of the world & its phenomena in the freest and sincerest spirit ever known."

Those Lancashire Chaps

They are a group of good fellows—those Lancashire men: they put sweet hooks in on me.

In the 1880s Whitman developed extraordinarily close and affectionate ties with a group of *Leaves of Grass*–lovers living in and around Bolton, a town near Manchester in England. Notable among these were

Dr. John Johnston and J. W. Wallace, who were both among the very few persons with whom Whitman regularly and often corresponded. In a letter to Bucke on June 25, 1891, Whitman summed up his feelings about what he sometimes jokingly called "the Bolton College" (and about the kind of response to *Leaves* he most delighted in): "what staunch tender fellows those Englishmen are!—when they take a turn—I doubt if ever a fellow had such a splendid emotional send-back response as I have had f'm those Lancashire chaps under the head of Dr. J. and J W W—it cheers and nourished my very heart." The journeys of Johnston and Wallace to Camden are memorialized in their book, *Visits to Walt Whitman in 1890–1891* (1917).

English Rescuers

I meant to make plain there [in a manuscript later published as "Some Personal and Old-age Jottings Memoranda"], as never before the sense of the debt I feel for my English rescuers in the dark years of my Camden sojourn. . . . No one can know as I know the depth of the need, the nobility of the response. It was veritably a plucking from the fire, as I describe it. No one, not my best friends—know what it means to me. It was life or ruin—to this side continuance, to that wreck—and these men saved me—and with true sacrificing zeal, espousal. I know that London is full of cads, flunkeys, fools, evil-doers—all that—but here, too, were several hundred as generous, devoted souls as men could know.

Two Great Friends Compared, Contrasted

O'Connor is distinguished first of all by an abysmic flavor—an Irish bardic ardor centered in him out of six generations of patriotism, national aspirations. It made a vast heart. But William had no such *intellectual* powers as we see in Bob [Ingersoll]—though he was not a fool, either: had it in all necessary measure when the time came. In Bob it is the fruit of his long law experienced, based, at last, savingly, in an almost unparalleled spontaneity—a calmness, too—and certainty, suavity. . . . The quality which to us is their greatness: to others is a rock of offense. But that undying childhood in both—that is *illimitably* important.

A Leaves of Grasser, *Tainted by New York*

Burroughs is still what he was in the early days—true to *Leaves of Grass* and his original instincts. Of late years something has been added to him—sophistication, I may call it. He has mixed too much with the New York literary crowd. . . . Still, John is too deeply rooted—the soil in him is too firm not to resist the pressure of that gang: he is too natural, too truly endowed. John's style has grown somewhat more refined— perhaps a little more literary, bookish—with time, but is still essentially rooted in the woods, the chipmunks, the trapperies—the first-hand causes and effects. John was with the original *Leaves of Grassers*—in the first rank (the body guard)—has never wavered that I know of.

Note: John Burroughs (1837–1921), who became a prolific author and one of America's leading late-nineteenth and early-twentieth-century nature writers, became Whitman's first biographer with the publication of *Notes on Walt Whitman as Poet and Person* in 1867 (many passages therein actually composed by Whitman). They first met in Washington, D.C., in 1864.

John [Burroughs] was never satisfied to remain out of doors—to view field-life—report it. He always had a hankering after problems, explanations, metaphysicalisms—to me an obvious weakening. . . . The attempt to unite the life out in nature—the life of the woods, of the fields, of the rivers—with what is called the intellectual life—often with the metaphysical tinge—is always bad—always.

Attracting Men

When J. W. Wallace visited Philadelphia and Camden in the fall of 1891, he and Traubel spoke at length about Whitman's appeal. Traubel rehearsed the gist of a conversation had while on a Delaware ferry: "His [Wallace's] whole reverence was rather sympathetic than intellectual. W. had revolutionized his being. Life was quite another thing with this new factor—this new man. Carlyle and Emerson had been and were much to him—but W. overarched all—took immediately and positively the dominant place. We compared notes as to W.'s power to move, to attract men. Rather companionship than reverence, I argued. W. had helped me to freedom. I seemed proved in W. He seemed to seal my identity. All great teachers given this power."

After Wallace visited Whitman, the poet exuded: "Wallace was here—spent well on to an hour with me. Good fellow! What a tenacious rascal he is, too! You would not think it, to look at the little fellow. Yet he takes hold, sticks, sticks, sticks like the devil—yes, sticks like a true Briton!"

Loving, but Inquisitive Symonds

John Addington Symonds wrote numerous letters to Whitman, which Whitman summed up as "warm (not too warm), a bit inquisitive, ingratiating." The first one, dated October 7, 1871, carries this introduction—"I am an Englishman, married, with three children, and am aged thirty"—and includes a poem, Symonds says, "in which you may perchance detect some echo, faint and feeble, of your *Calamus*." He also asserts that "since the time when I first took up *Leaves of Grass* in a friend's room at Trinity College Cambridge six years ago till now, your poems have been my constant companions."

Whitman greatly admired Symonds. He said to Horace that Symonds "is the quintessence of culture: he is the culture of culture of culture—the essence of an essence." This was in spite of Symonds being decidedly of the literary aristocracy: "Symonds, of the literati a distinguished member—among the most distinguished . . . a man of books about whom it cannot be said, 'he don't know what he's talking about.'" The admiration was mutual. In Symonds's memoirs, finally published ninety years after his death in 1893, he wrote that Whitman's "concrete passionate faith in the world, combined with the man's multiform experience, his human sympathy, his thrill of love and comradeship, sent a current of vitalizing magnetism through my speculations." Symonds makes clear that, in spite of the poet's reticence, reading *Leaves of Grass* significantly helped him find "contentment in love—not the human kindly friendly *love* which I had given liberally to my beloved wife and children, my father and my sister and my companions, but in the passionate *sexual love* of comrades."

Later, as Whitman remarked, Symonds's letters became "more intimate, more personal, more throbbing." The last Symonds letter was written from Davos, Switzerland, "in the deep night" and is dated February 27/28, 1892, just one month before Whitman died. In this letter (written to Traubel), certainly one of the most moving of all the avowals, Symonds asserts that "I might have been a mere English gentleman, had I not read *Leaves of Grass* in time." Alluding to his own homosexual activities, the married father of three children also lauds Whitman for making him "love my brethren, & seek them out with more perhaps of passion than he would himself approve." Whitman reacted emotionally to the reading of this letter, as Traubel records: "Several times he cried out, 'Loving Symonds! Dear Symonds!' and several times he had me reread passages. [Horace asks,] 'Do you hear it all?' 'Every word, every word—I am attentive to every word,' which was very evident—the tears gushing out of his eyes, and his whole body and brain evidently stirred by the words of the letters."

Though Walt had deep affection for Symonds the man, he could still be harsh on Symonds the critic. Of an essay, "Democratic Art, with special reference to Walt Whitman," the poet snidely commented, "I doubt whether he has gripp'd 'democratic art' by the nuts, or L of G. either." He also spoke of the "ponderosity" of Symonds's books and of their being "deep, heavy, bookish, [they] infer not things or thoughts at first hand but at third or fourth hand, & after the college point of view—the essays are valuable, but appear to me to be elderly chestnuts mainly."

A Flaminger Soul:
William Douglas O'Connor

*Whitman loved and enthused rapturously over no personal friend more than
he did William Douglas O'Connor (1832–1889). They were both authors
published by the Boston firm of Thayer and Eldridge (Whitman his third
Leaves edition, O'Connor his one novel), and they met there in 1860. But
their period of closest acquaintance was 1862–72, when both were in
Washington, D.C. O'Connor was then a clerk in the Treasury Department.
They lived near each other, and Whitman socialized regularly with him and
his wife, Ellen, throughout the decade: "How much I owe them!—not alone
for scriptural hospitality—for Oriental [luxurious] food and raiment—
but for that other force, accretion, gift, effulgence—soul-force, let us call it,
for want of a better word: the making of my poetic self, such as it is!" Later
O'Connor edited the* Philadelphia Saturday Evening Post, *subsequently
returning to Washington as an official in the Life Saving Service. His forty-
six-page pamphlet,* The Good Gray Poet *(1866), was the first clarion defense of the poet; it was occasioned by Whitman's being dismissed from his
clerical position by the secretary of the interior for having authored the
shocking* Leaves of Grass. *Whitman's gratitude for O'Connor's relentless
and eloquent knight-errantry never waned, even during the decade of 1872–
82, when political differences led to a chill in the friendship. A rapproche-
ment fully restored their warm relations, and Whitman wrote O'Connor
almost daily in his later years, until O'Connor died on May 9, 1889.*

Twenty Thousand Niagaras

There is hilarity one day when a visiting Englishman remarked that,
having seen Walt Whitman and Niagara Falls, "I can fairly say I have
been to America to some purpose." But when Walt learns that the Englishman had been to Washington and had not met O'Connor, he exclaimed: "I was amazed when he told me—it seemed such a woeful
omission: twenty thousand Niagaras would not make up to me for one
O'Connor."

Open Air

William will die with a hurrah on his lips. . . . William always has the effect of the open air upon me. Next to getting out of my room here is to

stay in my room and get a letter from William. I don't know which contains the most open air—William or out-doors.

Human Avalanche

William says . . . "It will go hard if I cannot make such a cloud belch thunder." He made it belch many thunders: William had unlimited capacity for raising hell: I don't mean he was a gratuitous fighter: far from it: I mean that when aroused, when there was occasion for it, he could do the job—he was a human avalanche: nothing could defy him.

Piercer to the Vitals

William is in the best sense an orator—is eminently passionate, pictorial, electric. I'd rather hear O'Connor argue for what I consider wrong than hear most other people argue for what I think right: he has charm, color, vigor: he possesses himself of the field: he pierces you to the vitals and you thank him for doing it. I think he learned all that in the antislavery school—whether for good or bad I do not know—learned it all there, in the clash of classes—won his spurs in the struggles of the abolition period.

Intensely Afire

I wonder if there ever lived a flaminger soul than our William—a man who was for all in all more intensely afire for justice: a man who was more willing to sacrifice his own peace, his own profit, for an idea, for some cause, for some person, he loved?

One of the Fascinators

William is one of the fascinators: you can't escape him: he fixes his eye on you like the Ancient mariner: then you are his subject—you do his will.

All to the Fore

William would talk alive with a dagger in his heart: it's impossible to minimize him: he's always all of him to the fore: I can't conceive of anything that would dethrone his buoyant cheer.

Cat in a Strange Garret

He had an ideal so high—a human, literary, social, moral, religious aspiration so pure—a passion for right, justice, the race, so intense—a disdain for mere literary craft and skill so overwhelming—he seemed out of place in the modern world, its so-often mean ambitions. A cat in a strange garret indeed. The grand O'Connor! Who can take his place today? Who can take his place for me?

Note: Whitman uttered this the day after O'Connor's death.

Catholic Mind

His was the most catholic mind I knew—a mind catholic in the large generic sense of that word—a democrat of democrats—above all, a lover of freedom—freedom of mind— especially of literary freedom: oh! how all-inclusive was his judgment of writers—poets, all!

Boundless Catholicism

I need not tell *you* how . . . his hospitality was boundless—how *catholic* he was, beyond all else, persons else. . . . But then O'Connor had discrimination, too: it will not do to think him a mere panegyrist; he was more—higher—broader. To make a bull, he had the most wonderful natural artificiality which ever possessed a man in literature. Yes, I think I make no exceptions whatever. He had the greatest receptivity, freedom.

Full of Bestnesses

He undoubtedly was the born orator—born to be a *great* orator. He was full of a subject, once it had thoroughly nipped him. And then such fire, enthusiasm—what blows! Certainly he was greater than any of the men who were famous in older times—our old times. . . . He was orator in the best antique sense—*any* sense, in fact—all times, lands. Was gifted to speak, exult, appeal, full of bestnesses—potent for victories, glowing successes.

Magnificent Potencies: Robert Green Ingersoll

Easily the most stentorian and vigorous of Whitman's partisans late in life, Robert Green Ingersoll (1833–99) was a Radical Republican and a lawyer with offices on Wall Street in New York City (Traubel includes an amusing and affecting description of his visit with Ingersoll there in December 1890). Whitman's first contact with him was when he and Bucke attended Ingersoll's lecture in Camden on May 25, 1880, and spoke with him afterward. Ingersoll was attorney general of Illinois from 1867 to 1869, a colonel in the Civil War, and a noted public speaker who commanded enormous fees. Notorious for his views on religion, Ingersoll was known as "the Great Agnostic"—hence the handwringing that occurred when his being the principal speaker at Whitman's funeral was planned. With the exception of Abraham Lincoln and William O'Connor, no man of Whitman's day received more exuberant and elaborate praise from the poet.

Lethargically Forceful

Damn if I don't think the Colonel is always magnificent. . . . He is the same man to-day [as in 1882, when the Boston *Leaves* was expelled], only a little more so if anything: inevitably, tremendously, yet almost lethargically forceful, like a law of nature.

Every Sentence a Dagger

Ingersoll is the man of men—in America, our days, reaching highest, surmounting all the difficulties of speech—the most marked man, yet made so by means of a most astonishing simplicity. He is never passionate in the outward sense, yet every sentence is a thrust in itself— a dagger—a gleam—a fire—a torch, vital and vitalizing—full of pulse, power, magnificent potencies.

Tremendous Singer

"He has a tremendous way of saying tremendous things—*singing* them: is full of light. I don't know but his highest quality is *receptiveness*, sweetness, sympathy: he receives everyone, everything: is gentle, sweet, caressing, mellifluous, at all times. I often think these things are his forte— his power, his master-genius." Just before this, Whitman referred to Ingersoll in a letter as "one of *the very few first class individual American typical men* of the present time, wholly worthy of the land and day."

Rich in Indirection

On October 21, 1890, Ingersoll was the featured speaker at a benefit for Whitman in Philadelphia that netted $869.45. Whitman, who had appeared on the stage and spoke very briefly at the end, was bowled over. Later he commented on the printed version of the speech, which was widely circulated: "Bob is very [a]cute. The best part of the address is that you like it better the second reading than the first, and better the tenth reading than the second. Your liking ascends: it is so rich in indirection, no penetrating eye can fail to catch a part of the treasure." Whitman thus assessed the event's media impact in a letter to Bucke: "the Ing[ersoll] affair seems to be largely newspaperially comment on pro & con, & reported everywhere—shoals of vermin enemies of W W are roused too with their strange shocking slanders ('at wh' innocence itself is confounded' as O'C[onnor] used to say)." Of Ingersoll's performance before the audience of about 1,800, Traubel recorded, "I have known him to speak with more dash—never with more absolute force and eloquence. . . . The peroration was a masterpiece of language, feeling, sense and utterance." The full text is appended to volume 7 of *With Walt Whitman*. Two years before, when Whitman nearly died, Traubel notes, he and Bucke were worried about just two questions: where would Whitman be buried and could the famous atheist be "decently" invited to speak at the funeral? Harleigh Cemetery solved the first problem, and the great success of the October 21 speech solved the other. "We felt the relief of this," Traubel writes—and Ingersoll did in the end provide the climactic funeral oration.

Virile and Sublimed

When Traubel told Whitman that someone has said "Walt Whitman and Ingersoll have nothing whatever in common," the poet begged to differ: "Oh! that is a great mistake, a *great* mistake—we have about *every*thing in common. If Ingersoll comes [to lecture at a Whitman benefit], it will make the fur fly. Not that I hanker to see fur fly, but that I face the truth. Such a man, a man so strong, so virile, so himself, so poised, sublimed in his own individuality—of necessity is an agitation: to many a dread, fear, horror." In the event, fear and horror led the Philadelphia Academy of Music and the Union League to deny the anticlerical Ingersoll a platform in their halls; finally, Horticultural Hall agreed to host the event. In reporting the denials, the *Philadelphia Press* referred to Ingersoll as "the famous atheist."

Tongue of Fire

Ingersoll is a free man, free to his individuality, as all first-class men have been from the start. Fearless, frank, eloquent, with tongue of fire. These are things which stir him to genius. In all essential ways, Ingersoll's work and mine converge: I think even my intimate friends are disposed not to see this.

Magnetic Voice

He has that undefinable thing called magnetism to such an extent, I question if I ever saw its like in a man before. And his voice? I think for music, for change, freedom, ease, it is the best organ ever known—so flexible, so surpassing in its range, and flowing in, over, through you, without stop, without leave or hindrance.

Point of Difference

Horace, I consider the friendship of men like Symonds and Ingersoll a great plume in our cap—great. . . . Bob—I might say he represents the doctrine—if I may speak of it that way—of "one world at a time." Men and women, sense, love—all in a majestic high sense, too. If I had any difference with him at all, it would be at this point: *Leaves of Grass* would say the stamp has been put on these things for something deeper yet— for something yet to come. If there is any lesson nestling down, down— it is that.

Lubricant Humor

Bob has humor—that last quality—not fun, not jollity, which too much narrows its meaning—but humor, in the sense of lubrication— has it richly, superbly. I think reformers often miss it altogether, but he has it to the last degree!

Complicated with Leaves

If ever we had any, Ingersoll is our man. . . . [Such men] are always complicated with the purpose of *Leaves of Grass*.

Walt and His Boys

*Whitman was an ardent and apparently quite skilled schmoozer, as one
of his shortest but most characteristic poems, "To You" (1860), perfectly
captures: "Stranger! if you, passing, meet me, and desire to speak to me,
why should you not speak to me? / And why should I not speak to you?"
His notebooks record countless brief acquaintances made—largely with
blue-collar types and virtually never with women—while traveling on
East River ferries, Broadway stages, Washington horsecars, and Delaware
River ferries. Many chance meetings blossomed into jolly friendships and a
few into deep relationships (notably the ones with Peter Doyle and Harry
Stafford). Often, Whitman's manuscripts leave behind only a first name and,
perhaps, a few notable features ("bad teeth good eyes" or "thin face superb
sonorous voice" or "broad-shouldered, six-footer, with a hare-lip"). However, some of Walt's reminiscences, even if only fleeting, give us a full name
and insight into the poet's character and tastes.*

Ned Wilkins

One day Whitman reminisced at length about Ned Wilkins, one of his
most vigorous defenders from his Pfaff's café and Broadway heyday.
Walt's recollection reveals a queasiness at any ambiguity of gender
roles: Wilkins was "noble, slim, sickish, dressy, Frenchy—consumptive
in look, in gait: weak-voiced: oh! I think the weakest voice I ever knew
in a man. But Ned was courageous: in an out and out way very friendly
to *Leaves of Grass*: free spoken—always willing to let it be known what
he thought: in fact, was what we nowadays call a dude: kid-gloved,
scrupulous—oh! squeamish!—about his linen, about his tie—all
that." Traubel says, "But evidently not intrinsically a dude." At which
Whitman continued, "Oh! no—no—not intrinsically. It illustrates
what I said to you the other night—that we should not take too much
for granted—not too hastily discard a man on appearances. . . . Ned's
dressiness was immense—almost painful: his perfume, washedness,
strangely excessive: yet in spite of all that he was a man one would call
notable: and Ned was always plucky. He was always plucky. . . . He had
a most sickish voice, as I have said: a habit of waiting till a room was all
silence, quiet, then interjecting some remark in weak, frail, drawling,
Dundrearish tones. . . . But let me say this: I never heard Ned say a fool-

ish thing." How, Traubel asks, to explain his liking for *Leaves*: "Ned himself was naturally weak, loose-jointed, thin in the girth: illish: he realized it himself—felt the need of something strong, virile, life-giving." Whitman then added this sad coda on Ned: "You know, he died within a couple of years. . . . Such a defender at that time was appreciated. I don't know if you have ever realized it—ever realized what it means to be a horror in the sight of the people about you: but there was a time when I felt it to the full—when the enemy . . . wanted for nothing better or more than simply, without remorse, to crush me, to brush me, without compunction or mercy, out of sight, out of hearing: to do anything, everything, to rid themselves of me." That the butch/femme dichotomy presented some dilemmas for Whitman is also suggested in his remark that "William [O'Connor] gets on Watson's nerves—William is so virile, Watson so feminine (I don't mean disrespect by that word—I don't mean what people mean when they say 'sissy')."

Elijah Douglass Fox

In September 1888 Whitman gave Traubel the draft copy of a letter he had written to Elijah Douglass Fox, a young soldier he had met on a Ward G of one of the Washington hospitals. It is written from Brooklyn, where he was visiting his mother, on November 21, 1863. Its salutation: "*Dear son and comrade.*" In this long and emotional letter Whitman confesses, "I have had enough of going around New York—enough of amusements, suppers, drinking, and what is called *pleasure.*—Dearest son: it would be more pleasure if we could be together just in quiet, in some plain way of living, with some good employment and reasonable income, where I could have you often with me, than all the dissipations and amusements of this great city." Later he writes, "Douglass I will tell you the truth. You are so much closer to me than any of them ["my dear friends and acquaintances here"] that there is no comparison—there has never passed so much between them and me as we have—besides there is something that takes down all artificial accomplishments, and that is a manly and loving soul." At the end, not sure of Douglass's whereabouts but suspecting Michigan, Whitman adds, "I hope you are quite well and with your dear wife, for I know you have long wished to be with her. . . . the blessing of God on you by night and day my darling boy." Traubel and Whitman discuss this letter, Traubel saying that the "letter to Elijah Fox you gave me the other day is better than the gospel according to John for love." Whitman comments on his letter in a "very fervent" manner: "The letter does not seem like words—it seems like life: it is the collateral for *Calamus*—the thing that made *Calamus* possible or went to verify it." Later Traubel got another long hospital letter, this one dated November 8, 1863, and written from Brooklyn to a Lewis K. Brown. In it he writes, "Lew I wish you would go in ward G and find a very dear friend of mine in bed 11, Elijah D. Fox if he is still there. Tell him I sent him my best love and that I made reckoning of meeting him again, and that he must not forget me, though that I know he never will. . . . Lewy I wish you would go to him first and let him have this letter to read if he is there."

Benton Wilson

One day Traubel asks Whitman, "What comes before comradeship?" "Nothing." And after comradeship? "Nothing again." This exchange, we are told, is "apropos a letter he gave me. It was one of the rough drafts a few of which he seems to have kept." The text is given in full; it is to Benton Wilson and is dated April 15, 1870, when the poet was still in Washington, and responds to a Wilson letter of the previous December 19. It begins "*Dear loving comrade*" and includes this remarkable passage: "I have been and am now, thinking so of you, dear young man, and of your love, or more rightly speaking our love for each other—so curious, so sweet, I say so *religious*—We met there in the Hospital—how little we have been together—seems to me we ought to be some together every day of our lives—I don't care about talking, or amusement—but just to be together, and work together, or go off in the open air together." In closing, he asks "how is the little boy—I send my love to him and to your wife and parents." Traubel then records what happened when he looked up from silently reading the draft: "There were tears in my eyes. I said: 'You did not ask me to read that aloud and I'm glad you didn't.' 'You mean you couldn't have read it?' 'Yes—and that you couldn't have heard it read.' His face was very grave. 'Horace—it is true—it is true: I can't live some of my old letters over again.' I said: 'These letters of yours to the soldiers are the best gospel of comradeship in the language—better than the *Leaves* itself.' 'Comradeship—yes, that's the thing: getting one and one together to make two—getting the twos together everywhere to make all: that's the only bond we should accept and that's the only freedom we should desire: comradeship, comradeship.'"

Peter Doyle
NO WRITER

In October 1891 Whitman was surprised to learn that Peter Doyle was then based in Baltimore: "Well, it was entirely new to me. I did not know of the change! The noble Pete! I hear but little from him. Yet that is not wonderful, either—I never did hear much." Traubel asks if Doyle's letters were frequent. "Oh no! Never! He is a mechanic—an instance out of the many mechanics I have known who don't write, won't write—are apt to get mad as the devil if you ask them to write. But of course I always humored Pete in that. It was enough for me to *know* him (I suppose, too, for him to know *me*). And I did most of the writing."

Note: The correspondence between Whitman and Doyle (published in 1897 by Bucke as *Calamus: A Series of Letters Written between 1868–1880*) and various other statements by Whitman make it clear that the relationship with Doyle was one of the most important affectional events of his life. Doyle (1843–1907), an Irish immigrant, fought for the South and was captured and interned in Washington. After the war, in 1865 or 1866, Whitman met him one night when he was a brakeman on a streetcar route that ran from Georgetown to the Navy Yard. Doyle later worked in various railroad positions between New York and Washington, living in Philadelphia and Baltimore. See the editor's *Walt Whitman: A Gay Life*, pp. 206–14.

NOT AT ALL PERT.

One day in late spring of 1888, apparently after several small strokes, Whitman was found by Traubel in a delirium: "Then he went astray again talking weird things about his friends, seeming to get them all jumbled together. Once he mentioned Peter Doyle. 'Where are you Pete? Oh! I'm feeling rather kinky—not at all pert, Pete—not at all.'" Interestingly, a few days later Doyle appeared (summoned by Traubel?). A sense of a cooled relationship between the two is suggested in Whitman's remark, in a letter to Bucke dated June 15, 1888: "Pete Doyle was over this evening—I was real glad to see him—he only staid two minutes."

A ROUNDED MAN

I have been reading over an old letter from Pete Doyle: so simple, true, sufficient: without even the knowledge of professional things—yet a rounded man. The real Irish character.

PETE'S CANE

A week later: "Peter Doyle was in yesterday and brought some flowers. 'It was Pete who gave me the cane,' explained W, 'the cane with a crook in it. I always use Pete's cane: I like to think of it as having come from Pete—as being so useful to me in my lame aftermath.'" A few weeks afterward: "This cane was given to me by Pete Doyle," Whitman reminded Traubel, "Pete was always a good stay and support."

WALKS WITH PETE

It was at that time, in Washington, that I got to know Peter Doyle—a Rebel, a car-driver, a soldier. . . . Ah yes! we would walk together for miles and miles, never sated. Often we would go on for some time without a word, then talk. . . . Washington was then the grandest of all the cities for such strolls. . . . Oh! the long, long walks, way into the nights!— in the after hours—sometimes lasting till two or three in the morning! The air, the stars, the moon, the water—what a fulness of inspiration they imparted!—what exhilaration! . . . I remember one place in Maryland in particular to which we would go. How splendid, above all, was the moon—the full moon, the half moon: and then the wonder, the delight, of the silences. . . . It was a great, a precious, a memorable, experience. To get the ensemble of *Leaves of Grass* you have got to include such things as these—the walks, Pete's friendship: yes, such things: they are absolutely necessary to the completion of the story.

Some months later Traubel read over a letter from England in which William Rossetti described his nature walks. Whitman reminisced: "Oh! that's so fine—so fine, fine, fine: he brings back my own walks to me: the walks alone: the walks with Pete: the blessed past undying days.

A MASTER CHARACTER

I found everybody in Washington who knew Pete loving him: so that fond expression [in the famous photograph of Doyle with Whitman in a love seat], as you call it, Tom [Harned], has very good cause for being: Pete is a master character . . . a rare man: knowing nothing of books, knowing everything of life: a great big hearty full-blooded everyday divinely generous working man: a hail fellow well met—a little too fond maybe of his beer, now and then, and of the women: maybe, maybe: but for the most part the salt of the earth. Most literary men, as you know, are the kind of men a hearty man would not go far to see: but Pete fascinates you by the very earthiness of his nobility.

NOT DEAD

"I was quite staggered here," Whitman said to Traubel as he arrived one day, "it knocked the breath out of me—to read a headline—'The Death of Peter Doyle'—here in the paper: but it was not *our* Peter Doyle: it was some old man, somewhere, given the same name. Oh! our good Pete— a rebel—not old—big—sturdy—a man, every inch of him! such a fellow—and such health! . . . it was a shock!"

DEAR PETE!

When the famous picture of Doyle and Whitman facing each other in a love seat is found on the bedroom floor, Traubel notes that William O'Connor called it "silly—idiotic." Whitman asks Traubel, "What do you think of it: is it a likeness?" Traubel responds affirmatively, and the poet adds, "I know it is good of Pete—it is first-rate: the best I have. . . . Dear Pete! Many's the good day (night) we have known together."

BIRD OF PASSAGE

"He has not been here for some years," Whitman says in 1891. "He is a bird of passage—always on the wing. He has not been to see me as often as I like. I would not know how to reach him now."

Harry Stafford

In the mid-1870s Whitman had an intense emotional relationship with the teenager Harry Stafford (born in 1858, the same year as Traubel), whose family lived in a rural area southwest of Camden. Through Harry he became very close to the entire family, especially the mother, Susan. When news of the father George's serious illness reached Walt, he remarked to Traubel: "Poor old fellow! But they say he is better. I have known them all so well, especially Harry. I take a great interest in them still. I was most intimate with Harry, but I love all—all."

Traubel reports: "Harry Stafford in to see W. the other day and rather puzzled and offended because W. seemed 'changed'—that is, reticent." Stafford's puzzlement is understandable, for some of Whitman's fondest memories were of idyllic rustic interludes spent with Harry in and around the Stafford family home near Timber Creek (see *Walt Whitman: A Gay Life*, pp. 214–19). Several remarkable letters between the two can be found in the *Correspondence*. The reason for Walt's aloofness may be suggested by what he wrote in a letter to his former nurse Ed Wilkins in Canada (March 20, 1890): "Do you remember Harry Stafford—He is quite sick—has fits of being out of his mind." A few days later he writes to Bucke of Harry, "he is poorly—the *mind-clouding* was temporary—(the worst of course is the eligibility of returning & worse)."

Traubel records: "After Stafford had been here the other day W. said to Mrs. Davis, 'Mary, why do you let everybody come upstairs? I don't know but I'll have to close all my friends out.'"

"Harry Stafford's wife and the little children. You have not seen the children? We love them—we do: Oh yes! tenderly!" Harry, apparently still miffed, was notably not along for this visit. There was clearly some unspoken, unresolved tension between Harry and Walt, for two weeks later Whitman expressed the desire to strike out of his will the clause giving Harry his gold watch. When he was told this would require a new will, he said, "Never mind, let it go"; but on January 1, 1891, a new will *was* drawn up in which the watch was bequeathed to Traubel.

William Swinton

"He was one of my earliest friends—a *true* one, too—a sweet attractive fellow—gemmie—I always loved him. What! The new friends drive out the old? Not unless the old drive themselves out. Yes, I knew him before any of the others—O'Connor, Burroughs—and ours was a real intimacy, too. How is he, Horace? Is he still large, handsome, fascinating? Oh! In the old times he was all that and more—and *au fait* with all the best things, too." Traubel recorded after this remark, "Swinton in Philadelphia—being treated for insomnia —looked to me shattered—yet with flesh, too, and a strong hand."

Ed Lindell, Ferryman

Give my love to the boys: tell Lindell, at the ferry, that I often think of him, as I lie here—of his damned old fiddle—I wish I could hear him again.

"W. knows I am on friendly terms with the men at the ferry and on the boats," Traubel notes. "Made explicit inquiries to-night of many of them by name, of some of them descriptively: knows many of them by name however. 'Pilot' this and 'engineer' that and 'deck-hand' the other: and then he said: 'Tell me about Ed Lindell.' " Traubel says of Lindell, "a gate-keeper on this side—a great friend: the only man there who reads W.—used to talk to him daily."

Traubel records Whitman speaking "hopelessly of the thought of getting out. 'But give my love to all the ferry boys—to Ed Lindell, to Tommy—Tommy Logan—to Foxy, to Eugene Crosby.' "

In May 1891 Whitman commiserated with Lindell, who was absent from the ferry because of "lassitude and bad stomachic conditions." In September Walt inquires about Lindell and is told Ed will not visit for fear of disturbing "the old man." When Walt says, "Tell him it'll do for an excuse," Horace insists Lindell was serious: "Tell him it'll do for an excuse. Ed will appreciate the humor of it."

Note: Lindell's last appearance is redolent: Traubel and the visiting Englishman J. W. Wallace found him "chewing on a bit of calamus root. He had bought it of some negroes crossing the ferry."

Joe Adams, Streetcar Starter

Perhaps Joe Adams can stand for all the other transport men of Whitman's more-than-passing acquaintance. In May 1889 Whitman realizes Adams has dropped out of touch and sends Horace out in search of him: "There was a fellow over there on the Market Street lines: I knew him well—loved him—and he me, too, I am sure: Joe Adams was his name. He was a starter there. Occupied quite a humble, working, laboring man's position there—what they call a starter. We used to be on good terms together. He was an asthmatic fellow—had a wife and family: it struck me—is Joe still alive? You can ask—make inquiries in my name." After a few days' fruitless search, Whitman reminisced further: "We struck up quite a friendship. Joe is not a young man anymore— is of middling size, has a sandy, red beard, is rather pale. He has a family— I think a daughter of 22 or more—and there is a son, too—a son named for me—Walt Whitman Adams. . . . Joe is a genuine fellow of the soil— has about him the flavor of woods, grass, fences, roads. It is uplifting to get near him." With this, Adams vanishes from the conversations.

Walt's "Big Secret"

A tantalizing—and occasionally hilarious—running theme of the conversations concerned a mysterious, presumably scandalous "secret" from his past life that Walt regularly threatened to divulge to Horace. Did it turn into a wild goose chase? The following passages are arranged in chronological order.

A Hint Dropped?

Traubel records that one day Mrs. Davis remarked upon the "charming, winning face" of a woman in a portrait over the mantlepiece in Whitman's room. Pleased, Whitman says, "Some day when I feel more like it than I do now I will tell you about her. She was an old sweetheart of mine—a sweetheart, many, many years ago." The question whether she was still alive "seemed to stir W. profoundly. He closed his eyes, shook his head: 'I'd rather not say anything more about that just now.'"

Still in Suspense

Horace to Walt: "I came today prepared for my surprise—but you have not yet surprised me. Am I still to be kept in suspense?" Walt laughs quietly: "I am afraid so—it looks that way."

Waiting for the Surprise

"Said again to W: 'I am still waiting for that surprise.' 'Why, so you are—I had almost forgotten. A day or two more and you may come to your own.'" Four days later: "I reminded W that I was losing sleep and meals in my anxiety over the 'surprise' that he still held back. 'Still harping on my daughter?' he exclaimed and said no more." Three days later Walt says, "And by the way, our 'surprise' that we have talked so much about has threatened to be a boomerang." Traubel records: "I pricked up my ears. Was the revelation about to come? He saw my interested face. 'Are you ready for it?' I laughingly replied: 'I'm leanin' up against myself strong!'" But on this occasion the "surprise" is only a few old letters from Bayard Taylor expressing his affinity for *Leaves of Grass*.

The Whole Story

Traubel records: "W. said to me mysteriously tonight: 'Some day when you are ready and I am ready I will tell you about one period of my life of which my friends know nothing: not now—not tomorrow—but some day before long. I want to tell you the whole story with figures and all the data so that you may make no mistake about it.' I have no idea what he refers to. He saw my blank face. 'Of course you do not understand an allusion so vague—but you ought to know: I have made up my mind to confide in you to the fullest extent.' I looked for more but he added nothing."

Unraveling the Cat's Tail

Horace raises the subject of "the big story" again: "You'll hear that in due time—not to-night. That cat has too long a tail to start to unravel at the end of an evening: we'll need a whole night for it."

Big Story

Horace reminds Walt of "that big story you were going to tell me: that's not coming very fast." Walt becomes "grave at once. Took my hand in his looked me straight in the eye: 'That couldn't come fast, Horace—that's too serious, yes—sacred: that must come in its own way, in its own time: but it will come.' W's 'good night' more than usually tender. He kissed me. Said again: 'That must come in its own way, in its own time.'"

The Long Cat's Tail Again

Three weeks later, Traubel asks: "Walt, are you in earnest in saying you have a big story to tell me some day?" Growing at once "very grave," Whitman says: "Yes, Horace—dead in earnest: you have no idea, no suspicion, of it, but you ought to know it all. I find it hard to steady my nerves for it—it means so much to me, will mean so much to you, means so much to others. The cat has a long tail—a very, very long tail. . . . We won't go on with it to-night: it involves so much—feeling, reminiscence, almost tragedy: it's a long, long story: and I don't want you to know only a part of it—I want you to know it all: when I start I want to finish: so we must let it go over to some day, some night, when I am just in the exact mood to speak and you are just in the exact mood to listen."

Entanglement

Traubel notes: "W. referred to his 'big secret' this evening again: 'I am daily more anxious to have you know the story—all of it: it belongs to you by right of our sacred association—and when the proper moment comes you shall be made acquainted with all its facts. There are best reasons why I have not heretofore told you—there are also best reasons why I should tell you now. It's not so much that I desire to confide a secret to you as that I wish you on general principles to be made familiar with the one big factor, entanglement (I may almost say tragedy) of my life about which I have not so far talked freely with you.' I waited for more but that was all he said—except that, seeing inquiry on my face, he concluded: 'Not to-night, Horace, dear boy—not to-night.'"

Big Pow-wow

Traubel continues his pursuit: "Just before I left I said to W. (it came into my head without warning): 'You haven't yet told me your great secret or even alluded to it lately.' He at once grew serious. Looked at me gravely. 'No, I haven't, but I will: you must know it: some day the right day will come—then we'll have a big pow-wow about it.' As I left he took hold of my hand extra hard. 'Good night!' he said: 'Some day—the right day.'"

A week later Traubel mulls over this portentous reticence: "W. still refusing to tell me his 'secret,' as he called it. I don't know what to make of it. I wonder what it is? Sometimes I think it is just his playfulness. Then again I get the feeling that he really has something serious to say to me. But I can't push him." Two days later: "I mentioned the 'great secret' this evening again. He grew grave at once. 'Yes, it belongs to you: you are entitled to know it: some day: some day soon.' I laughing replied: 'Maybe it's like the Diplomatic Secret: the secret being that there is no secret.' He shook his head, but was very quiet a bit. 'There is a secret: you will sometime see that there is a secret.' That was all." Three weeks later and still nothing: "I nudged him a bit about the 'secret,' 'You haven't said anything about it, Walt.' He was serious at once: 'But I have not forgotten: I want you to know it—know all about it: you.' I can't make it out. He has something on his mind."

Not To-night

Walt and Horace tease each other: "He said to-night playfully: 'You must always answer my questions even though I don't always answer yours.' I said: 'You don't answer my questions—that's true. That question about the great secret—you've never answered that.' He asked: 'You haven't forgotten that yet?' 'Do you want me to?' 'No.' There was a pause. Then he said again: 'No: I want you to keep on asking till I answer: only not to-night—not to-night.'"

Wrong Mood

Traubel again offers a willing ear: "As I was about leaving, while he held my hand, I said: 'That secret that you were to divulge: you haven't told it to me: is it still too soon?' He became serious. 'No—it's never too soon: but I'm still not in the mood to talk.'"

Denouement . . . or Not?

Traubel, in November 1891, reports that Whitman is "very specific with Tom [Harned] about his affairs" and then reveals the poet's information to Harned: "told him mainly what he told me, with additions to this effect (what he had written Bucke vaguely in letter I have seen): that he had two dead children whom he wished to put into the tomb [at Harleigh Cemetery]; further, that he had had five children, presumably from the one woman, of which woman, and these affairs generally, he wished to make some statement to Tom (Harned thinks deliberately for signature) to be held as history, authentic, and for emergencies. Says he has grandchildren, one of whom, a young man, wishes to come here. (Evidently the young man of whom he told me several years ago.) And this the 'long story' which he then said he wished to tell me but to which he never had recurred."

Nasty Story

Much later Walt began to allude to the possibility that the secret involved the fathering of children in shocking circumstances (this being similar to the almost certain lie he told Symonds about fathering six children in order to distance himself from the same-sex implications of the *Calamus* poems). Four months before Whitman's death Traubel records, "Harned has not yet got from W. the statement regarding his children. When I broached it the other day, W. returned, 'I am not in good condition today. Let it go for another time. It is a nasty story anyway.'" More than a week later: "He [says he] has grandchildren, and they seem to want to come and take care of him. He hears regularly from one young man." Traubel adds, accurately, "Suppose W. would die before it was divulged."

Telling All

Traubel records that Bucke put the subject to rest on a pessimistic note: "I brought up that matter of the children. . . . But he seemed to question whether they would ever assert themselves. He said to me what he said to you, that the women were high-born—proud. And he said further that he did not think there was the least probability that they would ever come forward—ever make any claims—that on the contrary their inclination was to keep quiet, to stay away. Walt don't seem at all averse to telling it, but I don't think he wants to tell part—he feels that a *part* would put him in a wrong light. . . ." Traubel then asks Bucke if he thinks Whitman would ever tell all: "No, I don't think he will. I don't believe he will ever be *able* to tell it."

Part Four

Whitman with Warren Fritzinger, 1890. *Courtesy Library of Congress.*

Views of America

By the time of his death, Whitman had succeeded remarkably in transforming himself from the very bad boy of poetry of the 1850s and 1860s—who left reviewers bandying such epithets as filthy, vulgar, beastly, rank, loathsome, blasphemous, and disgusting—into the benevolent, grandfatherly Poet of America. This he did largely by moving away from his pungent, daring preoccupations with passion and sexuality of the 1855, 1856, and 1860 editions of Leaves of Grass toward more abstract paeans of a political and social nature. The bad boy become "good"—very good. His dear fiery soul mate, William O'Connor, in fact, ushered him into this new persona with his brilliant example of literary spin control, The Good Gray Poet of 1866 (it was inspired by Whitman's dismissal by Secretary of Interior James Harlan). This later Whitman style is too often marked by cheery-cheeked boosterism, rhetorical inflation, and a higher level of abstraction. This is the Whitman of "With All Thy Gifts" (1873)—

> With all thy gifts America,
> Standing secure, rapidly tending, overlooking the world,
> Power, wealth, extent, vouchsafed to thee . . .

—or "Thou Mother with Thy Equal Brood" (1872)—

> Sail, sail thy best, ship of Democracy,
> Of value is thy freight, 'tis not the Present only,
> The Past is also stored in thee . . .

Whitman's comments on the American way of life in the privacy of Mickle Street, however, present a bracingly different picture. While he is still capable, on occasion, of the superbly affirmative little dithyramb on this or that, there are countless coruscating explosions of uncharacteristic fury in With Walt Whitman in Camden. Some have the flavor of his rather Juvenalian or Swiftian social diatribe, Democratic Vistas, of 1882. Whitman, in fact, said one day to Traubel, "To know me to the full, they must not know only the poems, but the story there in prose, too—Democratic Vistas, certainly, if none other." Following are many superb fulminations in the style of that devastating anatomy of America's dark side.

161

America's Meaning

America means above all toleration, catholicity, welcome, freedom.

The point with us in this country is the removal of impedimenta, the throwing off of restrictions: what we most need, must always have, is a clear road to freedom.

America's Intestinal Glory

When Traubel suggested that Emerson, Lincoln, and Whitman ("a trinity of giants") most captured America's achievement in literature and art, Whitman replied: "I should make a better reply: I should say the glory of America is in its possession of 40 million high average persons, the brightest, [a]cutest, healthiest, most moral hitherto. . . . America is not so great in what she has done as in what she is doing, as great, as I am fond of saying, because of her intestinal ebullitions—her cleansingness, so to speak.

American Society

Certainly, in our social life all is villainy and dollars and cents—it is rotten to the core—men grasping, grasping, toiling, fighting, full of venom and bitterness. . . . The state of society—of our society—at this stage—is deplorable—deplorable beyond words.

American Gentility

I may concede that something is to be said for broadcloth, finger bowls, service—even Presbyterianism: I hate them like the devil myself, but they are genteel (the dude-life, collar, tie, make-up)—and one half—oh! three quarters—of the sociology of America consists in keeping genteel. The crowd sleeps—yet it will wake up.

American Politics

The best politics that could happen for our republic would be the abolition of politics.

I do not seem inspired by anything that's happening in politics nowadays. In fact, nothing *real* is happening.

It's coming about that we need a new politics—something of the human to supplant the political order: and it will come, too—maybe not soon, maybe not for some time: but it will come—it must come: without it our democracy will go to the devil—nothing can save it.

The Two Parties

No man can look into what we call party politics without seeing what a mockery it all is—how little either Democrats or Republicans know about essential truths.

Politicians

The whole gang is getting beyond me: I find it harder and harder every year to reconcile myself to the exhibit they make: they narrow, narrow, narrow every year: after awhile I'll be altogether without a political home unless I build one for myself.

The American Plutocracy

I see the real work of democracy is done underneath its politics: this is especially so now, when the conventional parties have both thrown their heritage away, starting from nothing good and going to nothing good: the Republican party positively, the Democratic party negatively, the apologists for plutocracy. You think I am sore on the plutocracy? Not at all: I am out to fight but not to insult it: the plutocracy has as much reason for being as poverty—and perhaps when we get rid of the one we will get rid of the other.

Suspicion

In April 1891 Whitman was visited by an English con man who was masquerading as the brother of the novelist Walter Besant. He came away from a Mickle Street visit emptyhanded: "I did not bite. I suppose I might have been more suspicious but for me dislike for one of our liveliest American qualities—suspicion: to suspect this, that, the other, everything—and this leads me to, in the main, take men for what they seem till other things occur."

America's Full Belly

Restrict nothing—keep everything open: to Italy, to China, to anybody. I love America, I believe in America, because her belly can hold and digest all—anarchist, socialist, peacemakers, fighters, disturbers or degenerates of whatever sort—hold and digest all.

America is for one thing only—and if not for that for what? America must welcome all—Chinese, Irish, German, pauper or not, criminal or not—all, all, without exceptions: become an asylum for all who choose to come. We may have drifted away from this principle temporarily but time will bring us back.... America is not for special types, for the castes, but for the great mass of people—the vast, surging, hopeful army of workers. Dare we deny them a home—close the doors in their face—take possession of all and fence it in and then sit down satisfied with our system—convinced we have solved our problem? I for my part refuse to connect America with such a failure—such a tragedy, for tragedy it would be.

American City Names

One day Walt fulminated about the habit of giving cities Old World names, speaking of "the drunken pedagogue who gave names to the

New York towns" like Ithaca, Troy, and Utica. "The South beats us all hollow—look at Memphis—a fearful name—with no smack of the soil whatever—yet hundreds, thousands, like it! . . . The great Indian names lost, like so many opportunities!"

Execrable names of towns . . . Glendale, Rosemont, Rosedale and the like—thousands of them—glens this and that—of the least consequential order . . . [we] secured no benefit by a desertion of Indian names.

America's Prairies

The prairies typify America—our land—these States—democracy—freedom, expanse, vista, magnificence, sweep, hospitality.

Salvation from the Civilizees

Since the war I have sat down contentedly, convinced that we were to be righted at last. Oh! there is no doubt of it! And not the most to this end is to come of the civilizee himself—the man of cities, knowing as he is, and prosperous—for civilization, cities are also a great curse. I know in the armies the clearest-brained, cleanest-blooded of all the soldiers were the farmer-boys. In them was the future—democracy—America.

Grabbings and Poverty

The great country, the greatest country, the richest country, is not that which has the most capitalists, monopolists, immense grabbings, vast fortunes, with its sad, sad foil of extreme, degrading, damning poverty, but the land in which there are the most homesteads, freeholds—where wealth does not show such contrasts high and low, where all men have enough—a modest living—and no man is made possessor beyond the sane and beautiful necessities.

Nation of Lunatics

One day Traubel picks up "a stained piece of paper" underfoot and shows it to Whitman. He looks it over and says, "That's old and kind o' violent—don't you think—for me?" Possibly, Traubel might have said (but didn't); it read: "Go on, my dear Americans, whip your horses to the utmost—Excitement; money! politics!—open up all your valves and let her go. . . . Only make provision betimes, old States and new States, for several thousand insane asylums. You are in a fair way to create a nation of lunatics."

American Place Names

The names of two railroad stations outside of Philadelphia—Wingohocking and Tulpehocken—come up in conversation, and Whitman discourses: "They are beautiful names; they should be kept: they still have some reason for being. Why should we give up the native for borrowed names? Down in the country—right here, near us—there was a place called Longacoming: the name was fine, fine—the mere sound of it: yet they got it into their fat heads that the name was not satisfactory: they met, put the old name aside for a new name: changed Longacoming to Berlin: oh God!"

The Real Americans

In Canada I was always astonished to hear people speak of us as Americans—as if they were not as really American as we were. Of course there is no difference at all—we all acknowledge it—and yet we go on calling ourselves exclusively American at somebody else's expense. Why not all Americans—Canadian, Mexican, the Panamanian, the Nicaraguan—what-not! It affords an astonishing instance of how corruptions get legitimized—gain currency—become orthodox and are defended.

American Humor

Speaking about American humor, Whitman excoriated "that damnable idea of humor which thinks that to misspell or be idiotic or vulgar is to be funny."

American Cleanliness

The American people wash too much. . . . They like nice white hands, men and women. They are too much disturbed by dirt. They need the open air, coarse work—physical tasks: something to do away from the washstand and the bathtub. God knows, I'm not opposed to clean hands. But clean hands, too, may be a disgrace. It was the disgraceful clean hands I had in mind.

The American Idea of a Good Time

Warrie Fritzinger's report of a visit to the bustling seaside resort Atlantic City set off this debate in Whitman's mind, which he related to Traubel: "Perhaps I took it all too seriously. The new thought—the *fear*, I was going to say—has vexed, followed me since. The rush, din, delirium, passion of life there—the visitors—all of them with lots of money— the whole bent of things towards fun—simply fun—the American idea of having a good time. Warrie described the shore, bathers, not hundreds of them, but thousands—perhaps ten thousand—and the costly liquors drank, clothes worn, food eaten—the whole thing impressing me as pandemonium—a horrible medley—with conceptions of life rather vulgar than true or profound. But there was more than cloud, too—light, as well as shadow: for instance, the freedom—there seemed no drunkenness. And there was a prevalence—a general prevalence— of suavity, good humor—everybody prepared to think, say, do the best-natured thing. I confess when he told me this many of my first impressions were sent flying or at least thrown into doubt. Perhaps here was a new solvent—the very good-nature itself the major stroke for freedom, progress. . . ." Still, rueful about "the frivolity—the shallow impress put upon character, personality," Whitman concludes that "the American ideal of pleasure, joy, seems set so low." The next day Traubel notes Whitman's recent particular vitality: "Have this week had the best talks in months."

Low Comedy versus Leaves

One day an actor named Francis Wilson paid a visit, and Traubel noticed that Whitman showed no "enthusiasm or warmth," as he usually did with actors. Traubel identifies him as a "low comedian," and this sets Whitman off: "But that is the stuff the world now seems to want—the absinth, burning, burning—strong liquors. A plain cup of water is an insult—bread and butter, anything less than the toppiest flavors— artificiality." Traubel suggests it is "a passing phase." Whitman: "I don't know—but I have no doubt it is one reason for the enmity which *Leaves of Grass* excites—a strong, potent reason."

America's Gift to Music

Our best work so far seems to be in the direction of nigger songs, some of these are superb—"Old Folks at Home"—"Old Black Joe" and such. Exquisite specimens, some of them, out of the heart of nature—hitting off nigger life South there with wonderful expression.

American Presidents

I never knew a president to totally fail. ["Even Johnson?" Traubel asks.] Even Andy Johnson. In all the line of Presidents I do not think we have had one absolute failure—I think every President so far has made more or less honest use of the office.

If they had all of them except Lincoln been inadequate, impossible, he would have redeemed, justified, the tribe. But there have been other forcible goodsized men: there was Jackson: he was a great character: true gold: not a line false or for effect—unmined, ungorged, unanything, in fact—anything wholly done, completed—just the genuine ore in the rough. Jackson had something of [Thomas] Carlyle in him: a touch of irascibility: quarrelsome, testy, threatening humors: still was always finally honest, like Carlyle: Jackson was virile and instant. Look at some of the other Presidents: take Andy Johnson and Frank Pierce, who were the worst of the lot: they tried every way they knew how to steady up—to redeem themselves from their weaknesses. Take Buchanan: he was perhaps the weakest of the President tribe—the very unablest: he was a gentleman—meant to do well—was almost basely inert in the one crisis of his career.

The Presidency

We are too apt to pause with particulars: the Presidency has a significance, a meaning, broader, higher, than could be imparted to it by any individual however spacious, satisfying. There is no great importance attaching to Presidents regarding them simply as individuals put into the chair after a partisan fight: the Presidency stands for a profounder fact: consider that: detached from that it is an incumbrance indeed, not a lift, to the spirit. We need to enclose the principle of the Presidency in this conception: here is the summing up, the essence, the eventuation, of the will of sixty millions of people of all races, colors, origins, inextricably intermixed: for true or false the sovereign statement of the popular hope.

Presidential Tuft

A little, snarling, pecking administration, with a big tuft of pretended dignity. . . .

Note: Whitman's description of the Benjamin Harrison administration could be applied to several others.

The Nation's Capital

Washington is corrupt—has its own peculiar mixture of evil with its own peculiar mixture of good—but the evil is mostly with the upper crust—the people who have reputations—who are better than other people.

The copy of an 1868 letter written from Washington was discovered among Whitman's papers and included by Traubel; in it he wrote, "this is a stupid place compared to New York."

Though agreeing with Traubel that the cost of living in Washington was high, Whitman said, "Yet no city I would better like for living than Washington—it is so open—so little crowded—so unrestricted. Yet Washington is no longer the place for the Capital: fifty years from now the Capital will be elsewhere—off towards the great West—to the Mississippi or beyond. There'll be a devil of a row, but it'll be done.

Impeachment

There was a group of us—O'Connor was one, I was another—who felt, insisted upon it, from the first, that the impeachment of [Andrew] Johnson was a mistake . . . the Republicans were hot for impeachment then.

American Oratory

It has always been one of my chosen delights, from earliest boyhood up, to follow the flights particularly of American oratory. I went into the courts—when there was a good preacher about, went to church—heard all the best specimens of Southern speaking—the big lawyers, Senators—Congressmen—but none of them brought such conviction as [Robert] Ingersoll. . . .

American Masters

The ornamental classes make a lot of noise but they create nothing: you may crack a whip over men and you may be useless nevertheless: lots in business that passes for ability is only brutality: don't forget that—you masters: you are not so damned clever as you think: you're only coarse, cruel, wanton: that's all.

American Sculpture

I have seen most of the statutes in Central Park and off through the city there, and must say of them, as I would of those in our Fairmont Park [in Philadelphia], that they are nearly all pretty bad. I don't think the American genius has so far run into effective sculptural work.

Gap Between Rich and Poor

Traubel tells of a visiting Japanese friend saying that his "first strong impression received in America is of the fearful gap between its rich and poor." Whitman's response: "I am convinced that he put his finger on the sore spot at once. I always come back to the same idea myself: there is the itch—the trouble . . . the fact of the matter is the situation is growing worse and worse. . . . It is seen at its damnedest in the big cities—New York, Philadelphia, Chicago: but it is bad no matter where. America has got to clean house some day!"

Foreign Arbitraments

I am even opposed to Congress petitioning the Czar to investigate Siberia—even that is out of our province. We can never be in a position to arbitrate—enforce our arbitrament—in European contests.

American Press

According to the papers I am crazy, dead, paralyzed, scrofulous, gone to pot in piece and whole: I am a wreck from stem to stern—I am sour, sweet—dirty, clean—taken care of, neglected: God knows what I am, what I am not. The American newspaper beats the whole world telling the truth, the whole truth and nothing but the truth!

It seems to be a penalty a man has to pay, even for very little notoriety—the privilege of being lied about. Yet I rest the case finally on the good sense of my friends—their knowledge that, of printed matter anyhow, fully half—three-quarters perhaps—even a greater proportion, is lie—is admitted to be such.

American Publishers

I wonder that America . . . does not raise a race of publishers the finest, the broadest, the world has so far seen—publishers typical of our life here. Instead of having done this so far—instead of having raised one such man—we have had to get along with the most miserable, mean, tricky, circumscribed, hedged-in specimens the world has known.

The Stupid Public

The people are lethargic—let things go—suffer themselves to be milked and thrown away by a class of political scoundrels—they are so patient, often so stupid—blind to their own divine descent—but finally they revolt—are up in arms—raise hell. Then look out! But they are so slow—so slow! This year or some year the people will do some new things for America—hardly this year—the soil is not yet sufficiently prepared—but some year. I wish the people believed in themselves as much as I believe in them!

Money's Clutch

God help our liberties when money has finally got our institutions in its clutch.

Note: Whitman was speaking here of newspapers falling into the hands of millionaires.

American Avarice

The trouble here with us is our devil of a craze for money—money in everything for every occasion—by hook or by crook, money: and, on top of that, show, show: crowning all that, brilliancy, smartness unsurpassed, repartee, social wishwash, very misleading, very superficial: the whole situation one to discourage the more efficient factors of character.

We are growing: this present mad rush for money—every man robbing from every man—cannot last. Our American people after all have enough sense to revise themselves when there is need for it. [Traubel remarks, "You are quite a revolutionist."] If that is revolution I am a revolutionist! But the word hardly applies. I don't expect an upset—I expect a growth: evolution.

Scotch, Teutonic Influences

Traubel raises the question of "German contributions to our nationality," and Walt says, "I like the Scotch: it always draws me—even its clannishness has an element of love, home, moral fibre—but the German? Ah! Yes! I can see in it all the wider, widest spiritualist tendencies of time—of civilization—a depthless moral background, vast capacity for seeing, generous inclusiveness, acceptivity. Of course I speak of that whole branch of Teutonism, which is a big, fine, true stock, past measurement."

American Prosperity: A Warning

The Greeks—nearly all of them: the writers, the race traditions—are full of this idea: the idea that the gods hate prosperity—this sort of prosperity: the idea that when men sit heaped all round with possessions, loot, then the end is near—then look out!

Whitman wrote to Robert Pearsall Smith (June 12, 1890) in a similar vein: "What I am afraid mostly ab't America is that we are too prosperous & and too infernally *smart.*"

Wealthiest Country on the Globe

Traubel reports in late 1891 that Whitman "suddenly roused himself to fire pitch because of assertions now in papers that the United States was 'the wealthiest country on the globe'": "Everything looks damned fair till a few figures are exhibited—then the pretty theory vanishes. I don't know what the unspeakable rush for money means—will lead to—on this continent. Unmentionable degradation—rottenness—the foulest, perhaps, taking it politically, ever known, ever written of in history. Wealth unbounded, greed as unbounded, one man feasting on the ruins of another! Look at politics—stinking, dripping, with the last filth, experiences. Often and often I used to look at Brooklyn, New York City—see all that transpired there—a perfect carnival of fraud—and now Camden. . . . Bribery everywhere—show, show of virtue—all as hollow as a shell."

American Lawyers

It comes of the damned pettifogging lawyers. . . . Our lawyers . . . do not seek the manifest integrity of a case, but the trifling lapses—the weak points—the little indefinitenesses here and there that are bound to occur, whatever the caution: for no more is a law perfect than lawyers. . . . The great lawyer is the sun—shining to illuminate, not to distract. I sometimes think that this is the dark and damned spot of our national character: pettiness, prettiness, quibbling, finery. We have everything—we are big, heroic, grand, smart—oh! as for smartness, *damned* smart! too damned smart: but after our heroism, *this.*

Note: This fulmination was evoked when Whitman learned that Samuel Tilden's will, which bequeathed his fortune to establish a great public library in New York, was successfully contested by his relatives (one heir relinquished her share, and this became the nucleus of the New York Public Library's Tilden Foundation).

Affection, Love, and Sex

As suggested in the introduction, the nine volumes of transcriptions are very well behaved: plenty of plain, sharp-edged talk but no slander, libel, or veerings into lubricity. Still, there are several passages, sampled below, that touch on the sexes, sexuality, and amative emotions in ways that elaborate on and illuminate his more candid and courageous poems, especially those that appeared in the first three editions of Leaves of Grass.

Extremely Unselective

Someone was here the other day and complained that the Doctor [Bucke] was extreme. I suppose he is extreme—the sun's extreme, too: and as for me, ain't I extreme? Ask my enemies if I ain't extreme. It seems to be the notion of some people that I should "select" my friends—accept and reject and so forth. Love, affection, never selects—just loves, is just affectionate.

Demonstrative Men

"The world is so topsy turvy, so afraid to love, so afraid to demonstrate, so good, so respectable, so aloof, that when it sees two people or more people who really, greatly, wholly care for each other and say so—when they see such people they wonder and are incredulous or suspicious or defamatory, just as if they had somehow been the victims of an outrage. For instance, any demonstration between men—any: it is always misjudged: people come to conclusions about it: they know nothing, there is nothing to be known; nothing except what might just as well be known: yet they shake their wise heads—they meet, gossip, generate slander: they know what is not to be known—they see what is not to be seen: so they confide in each other, tell the awful truth: the old women men, the old men women, the guessers, the false-witnesses—the whole caboodle of liars and fools." Whitman uttered this fiery allusion to what is now termed homophobia on Christmas Day 1888. Horace's response was to say, "That's eloquent enough for Congress and true enough for the Bible!" Walt, shaking a fist at him, replied, "What do you know about either, anyhow?"

The Root of Leaves . . . and the Uproar

We have got so in our civilization (which is no civilization at all) that we are afraid to face the body and its issues—when we shrink from the realities of our bodily life: when we refer the functions of the man and the woman, their sex, their passion, their normal necessary desires, to something which is to be kept in the dark and lied about instead of being avowed and gloried in. . . . Sex: sex: sex: whether you sing or make a machine, or go to the North Pole, or love your mother, or build a house, or black shoes, or anything—anything at all—it's sex, sex, sex: sex is the root of it all: sex—the coming together of men and women: sex, sex. . . . always immanent: here with us discredited—not suffered: rejected from our art: yet still sex, sex: the root of roots: the life below the life! . . . It is the thing in my work which has been most misunderstood—that has excited the roundest opposition, the sharpest venom, the unintermitted slander, of the people who regard themselves as the custodians of the morals of the world. Horace, you are too young to know the fierceness, the bitterness, the vile quality of this antagonism—how it threw aside all reserves and simply tore me to pieces metaphorically without giving me half a chance to make my meanings clear. You have only heard the echoes of that uproar.

Sex Things

Traubel asks Whitman, "Do you mean that sex things will come to be more freely discussed in literature?" "It is inevitable: they will permeate all literature—didactic, poetic, fictional: they will force themselves upon the consciousness of the world, which has too long vilified the passions."

Licentiousness of Calamus

In March 1890 Traubel informed Whitman that he was going in to Philadelphia to take part in a discussion of poetry with "about a dozen men (most of them young)." Horace noticed that "the affair seemingly had a unique interest for him," epecially when he learned that the Greek licentiousness of *Calamus* was asserted. The poet granted the point of this view, adding, "But I can say further, that in the ten thousand who for many years now have stood ready to make any possible charge against me—to seize any pretext or suspicion—none have raised this objection; perhaps all the more reason for having it urged now. . . . These young men (or old) are certainly on the right road. . . ."

Note: For the full passage, see the earlier "Greek Fraternity," p. 137.

Riposte

A man was here the other day who asked me: "Don't you feel rather sorry on the whole that you wrote the sex poems?" I answered him by asking him another question: "Don't you feel rather sorry on the whole that I am Walt Whitman?"

True Indecency

How people reel when I say father-stuff and mother-stuff and onanist and bare legs and belly! O God! you might suppose I was citing some diabolical obscenity. Will the world ever get over its own indecencies and stop attributing them to God?

Prudery, the Same Old Nag

When told of someone who objected to his plain speaking about sexuality, the poet said: "There is that side to the case, too. The world is not ready to be thrown from the nag it has been astride these ten thousand years. It is a matter of slow growth, in which a man's whole patience is exercised."

Erotic Singer

In November 1890 Whitman was sent a clipping from the *Manchester Guardian* of October 20, 1890, in which he was called the "noblest of all the amatory poets" and "the most mellifluous of erotic singers."

The Sex Vortex

Early in 1891 Horace left with Walt a copy of the February 5 issue of *Twentieth Century*, a radical weekly magazine published in New York City. It contained "A Letter from Julian Hawthorne" protesting the imprisonment of Ezra Heywood in Massachusetts for seeking to reform contemporary mores concerning writing about sex. Whitman remarks: "I know him—he has been here to see me more than once. He is a bearer of the cross—a believer in *Leaves of Grass*. Heywood has cast himself into the *sex* vortex—has given all for that. . . . He . . . is a clean-cut, professional sort of fellow—looks rather ministerial—courageous, the husband of a woman, father of a family, his wife being his double—devoted, determined."

Note: Julian Hawthorne wrote in his spirited attack on Heywood's imprisonment that Heywood was "morally convinced" that "the promiscuous employment of a severely Anglo-Saxon vocabulary, and the open discussion of matters physiological and obstetrical, are conducive to the well-being and emancipation of the race." He also asserted that Heywood "ought not to be put in gaol any more than Robert Ingersoll or Walt Whitman or the editor of the great daily journal which prints in its first column applications on the part of handsome young ladies for personal and pecuniary support by congenial bachelors."

Hung

When Traubel happened to use the idiomatic phrase, "he's not built that way," Whitman recalled: "Years ago in New York there was an expression similar. . . ." He paused a moment, "but it was indelicate. The phrase was, 'He does not hang that way.' You see its import. Of course that could not find adoption, especially in literature. It was vulgar, had its brief day, is gone."

The Physiology of Leaves

Speaking of some well-meaning Philadelphians "over the river there" who would never penetrate the sexual content of *Leaves*, Whitman said that they "can hardly realize the *Leaves*—do not reach the tap-stone—face its physiological, concrete—might almost call it, its brutal, bloody—background, base. . . . There are parts, features, faculties, detached bits, beauties, perhaps—these the fellows got—but the unitariness, the uncompromising physiology, backing, upholding, all—that they do not see, do not catch the first glimpse of."

Note: For further discussion of the sexual content of *Leaves of Grass*, consult Whitman's discussion of the *Calamus* poems and of John Addington Symonds, pp. 84–86, 139–40.

The Woman Sex

In September 1888 Whitman made the remarkable comment to Traubel that Leaves of Grass was "essentially a woman's book," but Whitman's views about women were more complex and ambiguous than that statement would suggest. Though his credentials on the subject of equal rights for women are almost unblemished, a subtle vein—if not of misogyny, at least of masculinism—runs throughout his published and unpublished writings. The male body and the doings of Whitman's male friends or acquaintances were, overwhelmingly, at the core of his social life and poetizing. Still, his comments on "the woman sex" and some notable women of his day provide significant insight into his work.

Leaves: A Woman's Book

Leaves of Grass is essentially a woman's book: the women do not know it: it speaks out the necessities, its cry is the cry of the right and wrong of the woman sex—of the woman first of all, of the facts of creation first of all—of the feminine: speaks out loud: warns, encourages, persuades, points the way.

Note: For a discussion of Whitman's attitudes toward women and women's issues, see the editor's *Walt Whitman: A Gay Life* (pp. 155–67) and Sherry Ceniza, *Walt Whitman and the 19th-Century Women Reformers* (1998).

Significant

"I always say that it is significant when a woman accepts me." Whitman was speaking, in this case, about Susan Stafford, the mother of Harry Stafford.

Under His Wing

The young ladies are most faithful to me nowadays. I had one letter from New York, one from Connecticut—several others: young ladies who for some reason or other have followed me up—grown up under my wing: young ladies or about to become.

Silent Partners

Women are often the silent partners but they are quite as essential to the business of life as the men-crowd with their incessant catawauling.

Look at me—sitting here all my days now, talking, talking, talking, like a dictionary with legs on and a mouth.

Invite the Women

Whitman rankled sorely at the prospect of there being no women present for the elaborate banquet being planned to honor his seventieth birthday on May 31, 1889: "There is Mrs. Harned now—now I face it in a serious way, as I should—that here it is in a nut-shell—here in the denial to include her. It is a real hardship—entirely out of place, too, inconsistent with my best-held convictions, as expressed from the start, which would include women equally with men and on as satisfying terms."

Note: It appears, to judge from *Camden's Compliment to Walt Whitman*, a pamphlet published to mark the occasion, that in fact no women did attend the affair. Progress was later made on this front. About the attendees of the next year's birthday dinner, Horace recorded: "The full list of diners was 31—4 of them women—W. much applauding this 'tinge'—as he called it."

Heaven or Hell

I have been more than lucky in the women I have met: a woman is always heaven or hell to a man—mostly heaven: she don't spend much of her time on the border-lines.

Caught

Traubel reports Whitman's doctor calling him on a snide remark about women: "Catching him in the act of saying something petulant concerning women, Baker cried: 'I supposed from your books that you entertained quite other feelings about women.' W. at once came down. 'So I do: the books are right—I am wrong: I don't believe any man ever lived who was more fortunate in the friendship of good women. I don't mean respectable women, so-called—I mean good women.'"

Upholders

By the way, it is very curious that the girls have been my sturdiest defenders, upholders. Some would say they were girls little to my credit, but I disagree with them there.

Noble She-critters

It would seem about time something was done in the direction of the recognition of the women: for some of us to dwell upon the lives of noble big women. History teems with accounts of big men—genius, talent—of the he-critters, but the women go unmentioned. Yet how much they deserve! I know from time to time there are spasms of virtue . . . but what is that? I have no admiration for the formal elegant lives of salons. I have in mind the noble plain women I have met—*many* of them—women to whom the *word* "literature" even is unknown; mothers of families—mistresses of households—out over the country—on farms, in the villages: marvellous managers—tender, wise, pure, high—the salt of our civilization.

Woman Redeemed: Two Georges

When Walt happened to remark that George Sand "redeems woman," Horace quizzed: "Do you think woman needs redeeming?" "No indeed: no, no, no: I do not use the word in that sense: I had in mind the question, what is woman's place, function, in the complexity of our social life? Can woman create, as man creates, in the arts? rank with the master craftsmen? I mean it in that way. It has been a historic question. Well—George Eliot, George Sand, have answered it: have contradicted the denial with supreme affirmation."

On Having a Girlfriend

Horace reports this tussle on the subject of girlfriends: "He added: 'A boy can do a lot sight worse than have a girl—he may *not* have a girl—that's a lot sight worse.' I exclaimed: 'And that from a bachelor!' He snapped back half in fun and much in earnest: 'Not too much of a bachelor, either, if you knew it all!' This fling was so dead set with its teeth shut that I thought he might go on some on the subject. But he was silent and I went home."

Best Friends

"I have great friends in the women. My best friends have been women. Put that in your pipe and smoke it." Horace then asks, "What is there better than the friendship of a woman?" Whitman fervently, "Nothing at all, Horace, nothing—nothing in this whole world!"

More Like a Man

"Jeannette Gilder—Jennie—was here today, with some beautiful girls. She is large, splendid, frank, *manly*—yes, she should have been a man." Jennie was the wife of Whitman's friend Joseph Gilder; "she's a man anyway," he reiterated a few weeks later.

Man's or Woman's Body?

Traubel mentions that he was told of a debate as to whether Whitman thought "the *male* human body a superior development to the female." The poet's amused reply: "It is like asking one which he prefers—East or West." This rings a bit hollow, given his clear bias in favor of the western (see his praise of Grant and Lincoln); six months earlier Whitman, we have seen, boasted, "I am a sort of Pacific, Oceanic, Californian critter." As also noted earlier, he felt he was, at bottom, a western writer: "I always seem to expect the men and women of the West to take me . . . in one gulp! Where the East might gag over me the West should swallow me with a free throat."

Modern Abomination: Sartorial

Surely the modern woman—our modern ideals of what constitutes a pretty face—are damnable! . . . the waspish waste [and] that abomination out of hell, the modern bustle!

Good Women

She is heroic—a good woman, no doubt—and we *always* have some heart for good women.

Note: This was said of the English theosophist and writer Annie Besant (1847–1933).

Woman's Place

I consider it the glory of this age that it dares throw off restrictions—throws them right and left: demands to go free: and this freedom must be for the women as well as the men. I look to see woman take her place in literature, in art—show what are her innate potencies, powers, attributes.

A Humble Query from Australia

One day Whitman hands Traubel a letter dated August 7, 1888—a "hello from way off in a far country." It is from Jessie Taylor, who describes herself as a "school marm" at the Girls' Grammar School in Queensland, Australia, and it is charmingly flattering. Still, it asks a very interesting question (and, most unusually and perhaps also tellingly, no discussion of the letter follows Horace's reading it aloud): "I have only had the pleasure so far of reading two of your books," Taylor says, "*Leaves of Grass* and *Specimen Days*. They are both moral tonics in their joyous healthiness and seem to me just the antidote that is needed to all the morbid self-analysis and sickly sentimentality of the present age. I never read them without feeling more strongly than ever what a beautiful sane thing human life is. I wish, as I am a woman, you had told us more of your views about us. I wonder what your ideal of woman is. I should not have ventured to write you only I see you are 'alone' and that is a word which always touches me, specially now, when as an English teacher in a new land I am without one friend near me."

Memories of Washington
and the Secession War

One Saturday evening Whitman draws Traubel's attention to a little note-book in his hand and explains: "This is one of my countless memorandum books—I have had hundreds of them—this is a Washington one—now 20 or 25 years old. I do not know by what combination of circumstances it has been preserved—but here it is, turned up after many days—old, grimed. Every name, every date in it, recalls a thousand scenes, multifold memories—persons, events—army incidents—those fruitful years. The written record but a drop in the bucket—I may say, a drop in the sea—to the whole story." Whitman at the same time denigrated his reminiscences about the war in Specimen Days as "most fugitive—the most slight." Read all of the Civil War poems and one can only agree that Whitman barely scratched the surface of the full horror of "the whole story." Still, many of his comments to Horace about the war clarify its "watershed" significance for his career. One early fall day in 1888 Walt asked Horace to read aloud an old 1864 letter from William O'Connor. In it O'Connor told of reading a Whitman letter in the New York Times about his hospital days, then added wistfully, "Only it filled me with infinite regrets that there is not a book from you, embodying these rich and sad experiences." The following passages, surely, offer the germ of such a book.

Umbilicus

"I never once have questioned the decision that led me into the War: whatever the years have brought—whatever sickeness, what not—I have accepted the results as inevitable and right. This is the very centre, circumference, umbilicus, of my whole career." This remark was evoked by Bucke's remark that, had Whitman "stayed away from the War he would have been good for ninety years." Whitman often charged the war with his debilities. On January 27, 1890, he wrote to William Sloane Kennedy about his "old machine, the body & brain well shatter'd & gone (that secession war experience was a *whack* or series of whacks irrecoverable)."

Deeply Engaged

The War deeply engaged me: enlisted all my powers, thoughts, affec-tions: the doubts, anxieties, dubiosities: the to's and fro's, the ups and downs, the heres and theres: the sad visions—ever approaching, ever appealing—deeply, unreservedly commanded me.

Quill Pens . . . and Memories

Making a very specific request to Ed Wilkins for a new supply of his favored Esterbrook's Mammoth Falcon quill pens, Whitman fell into reminiscence: "The old army passes were written with enormous big pens. . . . They were written immense—a letter an inch high often—intended to be read at night—by light of lamp, lantern, candle, whatnot—anything. Yes, they were often forged—but not forged as much as you would suppose: the fellows grew to be very [a]cute in detecting forgeries. Oh! how the past comes back, even by such a little memory as that!"

A Leaf Unfolds

I was no spring chicken then. . . . [Going to Washington] was no youthful enthusiasm—no mere ebullition of spirits—but deliberate, radical, fundamental. . . . Deliberate? more than that: it was necessary: I went from the call of something within—something, I cannot explain what—something I could not disregard. . . . There's something in the human critter which only needs to be nudged to reveal itself: something inestimably eloquent, precious: not always observed: it is a folded leaf: not absent because we fail to see it: the right man comes—the right hour: the leaf is lifted.

Private Soldiers

It always struck me in the War, how honest and direct the private soldiers were—how superior they were, in the main, to their officers. They would freely unbosom to me—tell me of their experiences—perhaps go into minutest details—always, however, as if everything was a matter of fact, was of no value—as if nothing was of enough significance to be bragged of.

Washington Geography

Was Washington "a distinctively unhealthy city," Traubel asked when Whitman spoke of its "malarious tendencies." "I should not say so—at least, Washington itself is not. But beyond Washington, around it, are boggy, swampy immensities—flats . . . great exposures at the out-tide. Probably no city in the world can beat Washington in respect to this malarial curse. Yet the town direct might be considered a fortunate place—fortunate in its soil. . . . I should say that Washington, if it continues to be for 50 years (and I am not sure that it will), might loom up a great town." Would it continue as the capital, Horace inquires. "Not at all—I have not the slightest notion that it will . . . by and by the capital will go west—somewhere along the Mississippi."

Capital Ethos

Oh Horace, they were great, great years—tumultuous years!... At that day Washington was the hotbed of intrigue: we were borne on and on— we would often ask, to *what?* wondering over the probabilities—what would finally come: full of dubious moods, upset by fears: the Government itself rocking with treason—honeycombed with villainy: the departments full of Secession: a sort of snickering venom on the one hand: infidelity, I may call it, on the other hand: the atmosphere saturated with distrust: it radiated Confederatism. The expert clerks in the departments, the fellows along in the higher grades, the heads, the more necessary men, were most of them Southerners, or with proclivities that way ... then Lincoln was keen, circumspect, realized the dangers, pursued a conservative policy: temporized, as we would call it today: never did anything to aggravate feeling—to add to the already great enough acrimony.

No Pedestals

I never had any desire to hunt up, even to see, the great men—indeed, avoided the magnates. I was quite contented to be with plain people— to keep close to the ground. I didn't do much with pedestals.

Hard Day at the Office

After a week on the job as a copyist in the Office of Indian Affairs in the Department of the Interior, Whitman wrote to his favorite brother, Jeff, and explained his daily routine with tongue in cheek (Traubel includes the letter, dated January 30, 1865, in full): "I take things very easy—the rule is to come at 9 and go at 4—but I don't come at 9, and only stay till 4 when I want, as at present, to finish a letter for the mail—I am treated with great courtesy, as evidence of which I have to inform you that since I began this letter I have been sent for the Cashier to receive my *pay* for the arduous and invaluable services I have already rendered to the government." Five months later Whitman would be fired, not for lassitude but for shocking verse.

Fired by Secretary Harlan ...

Secretary Harlan ... abstracted the book [*Leaves of Grass*] from my desk drawer at night after I had gone, put it back again, and discharged me next day. ... The more or less anonymous young writers and journalists of Washington were greatly incensed—made my cause their own— wrote almost violently about it: but the papers generally as well as literary people either ignored the incident altogether or made light of it. This was the hour for O'Connor: O'Connor was the man for this hour: and from that time on the "good gray," William's other name for me, has stuck.

Note: Whitman's dismissal took place on June 30, 1865; the offending book was the 1860 edition. O'Connor, then a minor government clerk, published his rousing pamphlet defending Whitman, *The Good Gray Poet*, in New York in 1866. Just after making the preceding remarks, Whitman added, "Long after Harlan acknowledged to one of the newspapers in St. Louis: 'The removal of Whitman was the mistake of my life.'"

. . . but No Big Grudge

Don't ever assail Harlan as if he was a scoundrel: he wasn't: he was only a fool: there was only a dim light in his noddle: he had to steer by that light: what else could he do? Then, Horace, remember this too—that he was afterwards sorry for it: I have been told so by newspaper men . . . he told them he thought it was a mistake: he was a bigot—that was all: yet he had the courage of his conviction . . . his heart said "throw Walt Whitman out": so out I went: I have always had a latent sneaking admiration for his cowardly despicable act. After all, the meanest feature of it all was not his dismissal of me but his rooting in my desk in the dead of the night looking for evidence against me. What instinct ever drove him to my desk? He must have had some intimation from some one that I was what I was.

Attorney General's Office

I was at the Attorney General's office there and did a good deal of writing. He seemed to like my opinions, judgment. So a good part of my work was to spare *him* work—to go over the correspondence—give him the juice, substance of affairs—avoiding all else.

A Nurse's Wares

One day Whitman gave Traubel a "document" from his "war records"— a manuscript draft of a letter he sent to Massachusetts, dated October 1, 1863, acknowledging a $20 gift in aid of wounded soldiers. The long letter describes his hospital routine in moving terms and elaborately notes what kinds of items the donation will provide: "I distribute nice large biscuit, sweet crackers, sometimes cut up a lot of peaches with sugar, give preserves of all kinds, jellies, &c. tea, oysters, butter, condensed milk, plugs of tobacco (I am the only one that doles out this last, and the men have grown to look to me)—wine, brandy, sugar, pickles, letter-stamps, envelopes and note paper, the morning papers, common handkerchiefs, and napkins, undershirts, socks, dressing gowns, and fifty other things—I have lots of special requests." He adds, "I have been here and in front nine months doing this thing and have learned much—the soldiers are from fifteen to twenty-five or six years of age—lads of fifteen or sixteen more frequent than you have any idea." After Horace read it, Walt confessed, "Sometimes I am myself almost afraid of myself—afraid to read such a letter over again: it carries me too painfully back into old days—into fearful scenes of war. I don't think the war seemed so horrible to me at the time, when I was busy in the midst of its barbarism, as it does now, in retrospect."

A Condolence from Terrible, Beautiful Days

Whitman gave Traubel the manuscript draft of a lengthy letter he had written on August 10, 1863, to the parents of a New Yorker who had died in Washington's Armory Square Hospital—along with these memories: "they died all about us there just about in the same way—noble, sturdy, loyal boys. I always kept an outward calm in going among them—I had to, it was necessary, I would have been useless if I hadn't—but no one could tell what I felt underneath it all—how hard it was for me to keep down the fierce flood that always seemed threatening to break loose." Did he often return in thought to these days, Traubel asks. "I do not need to. I have never left them. They are here, now, while we are talking together—real, terrible, beautiful days!"

Note: In this letter, surely one of the essential documents of the poet's life, Whitman writes to Mr. and Mrs. Haskell of their son Erastus (he was a fifer), addressing him toward the end in the first person: "Farewell, dear boy—it was my opportunity to be with you in your last days—I had no chance to do much for you, nothing could be done—only you did not lay there among strangers without having one near who loved you dearly, and to whom you gave your dying kiss."

Emotional Stirrings

After re-reading a "huge" hospital letter Whitman had written to one of his New York friends in 1863, the poet reminisced: "My relations with the boys there in Washington had fatherly, motherly, brotherly intimations—touched life on many sides: sympathetically, spiritually, dynamically: took me away from surfaces to roots. I don't seem to be able to review that experience, that period, without extreme emotional stirrings—almost depressions. . . . I don't want to wipe out the memory: it is dear, sacred, infinitely so, to me: but I would rather not have it recur too frequently or too vividly: I don't seem to be able to stand it in the present condition of my body."

Writing Blind, in Tears

One day Whitman flourishes several little notebooks from the war. From one, marked "September & October, 1863," he reads some passages and then elaborates: "I carried sometimes half a dozen such books in my pocket at one time—never was without one of them: I took notes as I went along—often as I sat—talking, maybe, as with you here now—I was writing while the other fellow told his story. I would take the best paper (you can see, the best I could find) and make it up into these books, tying them with string or tape or getting someone (often it was Nellie O'Connor) to stitch them for me. My little books were beginnings—they were the ground into which I dropped the seed. See, here is a little poem itself. Probably it is included in the *Leaves* somewhere. I would work in this way when I was out in the crowds, then put the stuff together at home. *Drum-Taps* was all written in that manner—all of it—all put together by fits and starts, on the field, in the hospitals, as I worked with the soldier boys. Some days were more emotional than others, then I would suffer all the extra horrors of my experience—I would try to write, blind, blind, with my own tears."

Lies for the Dying

Any Doctor will tell you how necessary it is—a species of mind cure. I could not count the times I did it—not deliberately—for its own sake— not because I would not have preferred to tell the truth. I did not seek to have to say anything—but said what I felt to say to fit the gravity of the cases. Oh! You've no idea how the poor fellows would cling to the last— crave hope, cheer, sunlight; and all I could free—all that could flow out of me—was theirs, theirs.

Down with Diarrhœa

How much I knew of diarrhœa in the hospitals—the army: diarrhœa was of all troubles the most prevalent . . . it meant death, death: I nursed many and many a man down with diarrhœa.

Dr. Walt

The young surgeons of the army—such a power!—and so philosophic, too!—with minds so open and free—with hands fit for any emergency! They would not resent advice, even from me. They would be apt to say—well, that is new, and it will not hurt to try. I think of one case . . . a young fellow down with a bad case of diphtheria—we all liked him— his case was very serious, critical too. I suggested one day a copious mixture of chloroform and sweet oil—to form a plaster, and this to be set close on the swollen neck. I remember the young surgeon who had him in charge (I can see the surgeon's face now—remember it well— though his name is forgotten), he looked at me, seemed to think it over—finally said, "I never heard of that before—but it can do no harm, if it does no good—and has the *sound* of being radical, to say the least," and so it was tried—and saved the fellow's life. It has its danger to the skin—will create severe blisters—but is drastic, the necessity of critical decision.

No Leaves

Horace asks whether his poems aided Walt's hospital work: "No: I don't think so: I can't recall a single case in which I gave away *Leaves of Grass*."

The Telegraph Boys

There were three classes who served nobly during the War to whom justice has never been done—the telegraph boys, the cadet physicians, the nurses in the hospitals. . . . The telegraph boys were a remarkable body: picked up here and there—often waifs, mechanics, sometimes boys of well-to-do families: they were wonderfully sharp-witted—distinguished so, as a body: alert, active, noble, industrious, temperate . . .

every general with some, every high officer with many: they did most valiant service.

An Average Soldier (A Poem in Itself)

It was the average soldier, after all—the average soldier, north and south—who was the golden swordblade of our war. . . .There was one man among these who had known Lincoln in his early days—in the Springfield days—had worked in the principal store at Springfield, as clerk, helper, assistant, laborer, I don't know what. It was from him I learned many of my best things about Lincoln. Already at that time Lincoln was a man of some note. . . . He would come down to this store to buy. Oh! many's the little items of description this man imparted, how Lincoln appeared then—appeared in his purchasings, his buying this, his not buying that, why he felt he needed one thing, why not another: items, insignificant details, which the man soon understood were of an intense interest to me. This man, occupying a place as a teamster, was very subordinate. . . . I said to him one day, "Don't you know that Abe Lincoln is big Injun now—that he could do almost anything for you—put you in almost any convenient position?" He answered at once, "Yes, I do!" Then I urged, "Well—why don't you go to see him then—why don't you call? Don't you think he would remember you?" "Oh yes, he would." "Well, why don't you call, then?" I shall never forget the man's emphasis in replying—the tone of his voice—his look—it was a poem in itself. "What—me call on him? Add to his burdens?—on a man worried from morning to night not only by his great cares but by applicants for this, applicants for that, applicants for the other thing? No indeed: I could never do it!" It was a flash out of heaven: the man was a hero to me at once: I was enthusiastic over my discovery. Did I never tell you of this before? It was typical of the common soldier—not uncommon in any sense: my experience has been full of just such noble consideration, tact, [a]cute human feeling as this.

Real Work

I did a lot of work in the hospitals: it was in a sense the most nearly real work of my life. Books are all very well but this sort of thing is so much better—as life is always better than books—as life in life is always superior to life in a book.

A Southern Boy

Some of my best friends in the hospitals were probably Southern boys. I remember one in particular, right off—a Kentucky youngster (a mere youngster), illiterate, extremely: I wrote several letters for him to his parents, friends: fine, honest, ardent, chivalrous. I found myself loving him like a son: he used to kiss me good night—kiss me. He got well, he passed out with the crowd, went home, the war was over. We never met again. Oh! I could tell you a hundred such tales . . . there's a lot of that stuff I never put down anywhere—some of the best of it.

A Generous Offer

Traubel records: "A hospital talk with W. led him to speak of a letter he had just received from a western man, now prosperous, who had as a soldier been nursed by W. and was offering to send money, 'with love and out of my great surplus.' W. was visibly touched."

Emotional in the Wards

If I had any rule at all that I observed it was just this: satisfy the boys themselves, at whatever sacrifice: always: except in rare cases humoring them. There were cases in which good reasons obliged me to run counter to them: I hated to do it: I did it with some pain. The doctors would most times leave the boys absolutely in my hands. . . . I know the work I did was commonly considered more fit for preachers, cadets, women: that was the average notion of it: but the boys themselves didn't look at it that way: they saw it in other aspects: related it to other emotionalistic backgrounds.

A Reassuring Letter Cuts to the Marrow

Whitman gave Traubel an almost illegible letter dated September 7, 1863, from a colleague in one of the Washington hospitals named Gregg. She had heard Walt make a remark ("partly in fun") that the wounded soldiers were undemonstrative and wrote to assure him: "I have heard the ward A patients speak of you with gratitude, sometimes with enthusiasm. . . . I thought it would be sweet to your tender and womanly heart to know what I have so often heard from the soldiers about you as I sat by their sick cots." Whitman said of the letter, "It cuts to the marrow—at least to my marrow: is a sort of confession of faith on my part," adding this summary: "The hospitals put our feet right on the ground—put us into immediate association with the bottom facts of virtue."

Grave Times

Traubel says of a Civil War–period letter found among Whitman's papers, "That's not so serious as you led me to believe." Walt smiles and says, "The undertone is serious: they were grave times: I was not feeling gay and festive in those years: never could get away from the terrible experiences."

Unforgivable Rebel Hyenas

There seems to be this hyena disposition, some exceptional (thank God, rare) venom, in some men which is never satisfied except it is engaged in some work of vandalism. I can forgive anything but that. I feel the same way about the Secession fellows: the Southerners—Rebels: I forgive, condone, overlook, everything except that last, that greatest, that almost incredible fact, that they starved our soldiers—starved them in insufferable prison-pens: the average helpless prisoners: that, I never, never, never can forget.

Diarrhea and Glory

O God! that whole damned war business is about nine hundred ninety nine parts diarrhea to one part glory: the people who like the wars should be compelled to fight the wars. . . . God damn the wars—all wars: God damn every war: God damn 'em! God damn 'em! . . . I shouldn't let myself go—no, I shouldn't—but I say God damn 'em anyway!

"I Got the Boys"

"I was always between two loves at that time: I wanted to be in New York, I had to be in Washington: I was never in the one place but I was restless for the other: my heart was distracted: yet it never occurred to me for a minute that there were two things to do—that I had any right or call to abandon my work: it was a religion with me. A religion? Well—every man has a religion: has something in heaven or earth which he will give up everything else for—something which absorbs him, possesses itself of him, makes me over into its image: something: it may be something regarded by others as very paltry, inadequate, useless: yet it is his dream, it is his lodestar, it is his master. That, whatever it is, seized upon me, made me its servant, slave: induced me to set aside the other ambitions: a trail of glory in the heavens, which I followed, followed, with a full heart. When once I am convinced I never let go. . . . I had to give up health for it—my body—the vitality of my physical self. . . . I never weighed what I gave for what I got but I am satisfied with what I got. What did I get? Well—I got the boys, for one thing: the boys: thousands of them: they were, they are, they will be mine. I gave myself for them: myself: I got the boys: then I got *Leaves of Grass*: but for this I would never have had *Leaves of Grass*—the consummated book (the last confirming word): I got that: the boys, the *Leaves*: I got them." Traubel records that Whitman had "fired up" and "looked almost defiant" in uttering these words. He asks Walt why he didn't look after his own health, and Walt replies, "My body? Yes—it had to be given—it had to be sacrificed: who knows better than I what that means?" Then he picked up a "soiled, stained sheet of blue paper on which was some of his writing" and asked Horace to read it aloud because it "falls in with what we have been talking about." What was on the sheet appears in the "Credos" section as "Perfect Health." Traubel chose this day's poignant ebullition to end the third volume of *With Walt Whitman in Camden*, perhaps sensing that it would be the last he would see into print.

The Lesson of America

There were years in my life—years there in New York—when I wondered if all was not going to the bad with America—the tendency downwards—but the war saved me: what I saw in the war set up my hope for all time—the days in the hospitals . . . not chiefly the facts of battles, marches, what-not—but the social being-ness of the soldiers—the revelation of an exquisite courtesy—man to man—rubbing up there together: I could say in the highest sense, *propriety*—*propriety*, as in the doing of necessary unnamable things, always done with exquisite delicacy. And in the hospitals, illustrated in extreme considerate-ness, generosity—as in this case: one man will have a dozen oranges sent him; he will not hoard them—he will keep one—give eleven to eleven others.

Turned to a Generous Key: Abraham Lincoln

If Ralph Waldo Emerson sat supreme in Walt Whitman's literary pantheon and William O'Connor sat supreme in his personal pantheon, Abraham Lincoln was by far the American public figure he loved most deeply and praised most unreservedly. It perhaps goes without saying that many of the characteristics he found so charismatic in the sixteenth president were characteristics he also took pride in possessing.

His Radical Element

The radical element in Lincoln was sadness bordering on melancholy, touched by a philosophy, and that philosophy touched again by humor, which saved him from the logical wreck of his powers.

Western

Lincoln was more Western [than George Washington]—his habits so— his dress—speech, but in the things which really establish the hero, the majestic genius, he was Roman, Greek, Biblical. . . .

And Grant

Out of all the hubbub of the war, Lincoln and Grant emerge, the towering majestic figures.

Cheery

Lincoln the man was not basically serious—at least, not to the point of seriosity: he was rather cheery—cheery is just the word.

Equal to All

When General John C. Frémont died, Walt's reminiscences led back to Lincoln: "I often saw him, have talked with him. He was a romantic figure. . . . Lincoln had to tell him, *I* am running this machine—those were his very words. Ah, yes! Frémont was like many of the fellows— most of them, at that time—it was not till late, late, late, *very* late, that they sized Lincoln for what he was: saw the eminent fitness of the man to cope with all the circumstances of the time: Lincoln equal to all situations."

Uncaptured

I think I must at one time have collected fully fifty pictures of Lincoln: there were lots of them; they were countless: most of them very cheap and hideous—ugly as the devil. . . . Lincoln has for the most part been slanderously portrayed.

I know of no satisfactory picture of Lincoln. All sorts of pictures exist—many of them good in themselves, good as pictures—yet all of them wanting in the last essential touch.

Lincoln's wonderful reserve, restraint of expression—fine nobility staring at you out of all that ruggedness [has never been] stated pictorially.

Near

After my dear, dear mother, I guess Lincoln gets almost nearer me than anybody else.

A Street View Remembered

I vividly remember a street view I once had of Lincoln: he was on a balcony speaking to a big crowd—a mixed popular assemblage—a usual American audience—not too still, not too noisy: it affected me powerfully: Lincoln stood just as we see him here [in a photograph in the *North American Review*]—he had one hand behind him, he was in spite of his speechifying calm and in a way reposed: his face—its fine rugged lines—was lighted up: it seemed removed, beyond, disembodied: I see it all over again now.

Gigantic

It is wonderful—it has come so soon—the unanimity of the world in regard to Lincoln: the universal acknowledgment of his gigantic significance.

Lincoln Visits Dangerous New York

All Lincoln's life was turned to a generous key. When he went to New York, as I have described it, at a time when men's hip-pockets abounded in knives and revolvers—the men only looking for a chance, a pretext, to whip them out, to set the town ablaze, to murder Lincoln, others: at this time, at all later times, Lincoln's policy was not to offer this opportunity—not to strike this spark. Who can measure the value of such a personality—in its way all-seeing—to America at that time?

Patience Grandest of All

Think of the Lincoln of those days!—his inexhaustible patience—patience passing all the power of ordinary men to believe possible. Indeed, it seems to me, now I look back—now I survey the old road—years elapsed, and calm in age—it seems to me grand among all Lincoln's grand qualities—grandest of all, topping all the rest—noble in all the ages—was his patience, his longwaitingness, his suffering the last pang to be drawn, before he resented, spoke.

Radiantly Kind

A question about Lincoln's laugh sparks glowing memories: "I do not remember that as remarkable, but I remember his cheer, his storytelling—always the good story well told. His ways were beautiful and simple—how well I knew them, watched them! He delighted in simplicity, ruggedness, naturalness, straightforward nativity—in plain habits, clear thinking, doing. And he was the same man in all relationships— for instance, to the boys—the messenger boys—who came often, he would put his hands on their shoulders—say, 'My son, is there an answer?' or 'Sit down there, my son,' something in that way, with a radiant kindliness, humanity—in a natural tone, as if out of a great heart. Though not slangy—not slangy at all—Lincoln was in current with our average life—a great, great presence in our age, our land."

A Last Performance for the Man

When Traubel quizzed Whitman in April 1890 about his being well enough to give his Lincoln lecture one more time on the anniversary of the assassination—he had been delivering it since 1879—the poet explained emphatically: "I doubt if even you or Doctor Bucke know just the egotism that backs me in such an undertaking as this. It is in part the explanation of my work—of *Leaves of Grass*. There is a chance I cannot come, but on the whole I shall fight it out: if I can get there I shall. I feel pledged to it—not to you but to myself. It will probably be its last deliverance. I hope to be identified with the man Lincoln, with his crowded, eventful years—with America as shadowed forth into those abysms of circumstance. It is a great welling up of my emotional sense: I am commanded by it: only a severe chastisement could hold me from my contract."

The appearance at the Philadelphia Art Club proved (in Traubel's view) a triumph: "His tone strong, melodic—at times rising to great eloquence—as when treating of the battle fields—then of Lincolnian meanings. His figure—background: all grand. It was an extraordinary gathering—from 3 to 4 hundred. A victory his, after 3 decades of scorn and slander—brought into the very citadel of literary fashion and bequeathed the hour's (and future's) triumph. He was applauded several times—once responding with a wave of the hand. At times he would throw his body back in order the more sharply to define his emphases. After he had finished the address, he read 'O Captain!'—with greatest effect—power and pathos."

. . . and Abe's View of Walt

Whitman rejoiced greatly when one particular letter, long lost among his papers, finally appeared. It was a letter written from New York by

A. Van Rensellaer and dated July 30, 1865. It seemed to verify a story that had long circulated about Lincoln making an approving remark about the poet on a day in the winter of 1864 when the president looked out a window and saw Whitman walking by the White House. Rensellaer, who was present, relates in his letter: "Mr. Lincoln asked who you were, or something like that. I spoke up and said, mentioning your name, that you had written *Leaves of Grass*, etc. Mr. Lincoln didn't say anything but took a good long look till you were quite gone by. Then he says (I can't give you his way of saying it, but it was quite emphatic, and odd), 'Well,' he says, '*he* looks like a *man*.' He said it pretty loud but in a sort of absent way and with the emphasis on the words I have underscored." Horace looked up after reading this letter aloud and saw that Whitman "looked extra pleased." Whitman then preened a bit: "I have sometimes thought you had an idea we were romancing a bit in telling that story about Lincoln: now you can see for yourself that we've kept strictly, literally prosaically to the figures—have added nothing to them."

Race

Whitman's greatest spiritual bond with Lincoln was the shared conviction that the supreme political priority in "These United States" was preservation of the union. Very early in the conversations, Whitman told Traubel, "Not the negro, not the negro. The negro was not the chief thing: the chief thing was to stick together. The South was technically right but humanly wrong." But in the crucial period of the late 1840s and early 1850s, Whitman was a busy and highly vocal antislavery partisan. Indeed, he lost the editorship of the Brooklyn Daily Eagle in 1848 because of his antislavery, Barnburner Democrat sentiments (the paper's owner favored the proslavery Hunker wing of the party). In an editorial he had insisted that Democrats must be "true to the memory of the Revolutionary Fathers who fought for freedom, and not for slavery." His repulsion at slavery is notably captured in two early poems: "Resurgemus" (the only poem allowed in the first edition of Leaves of Grass that had been previously published) and "A Boston Ballad" (untitled when it first appeared in 1855), Whitman's acerbic response to the 1854 arrest, trial, and return from Boston of the slave Anthony Burns under the federal Fugitive Slave Law. Whitman's allegiance shifted when the Republicans nominated John C. Frémont on an antislavery platform in 1856 (James Buchanan, despised by Whitman, won the election), and the Dred Scott decision of 1857 galvanized his fears that slavery might doom the union. By 1860, in the third Leaves edition, he could prophesy grimly, "I say where liberty draws not the blood out of slavery, there slavery draws the blood out of liberty." Following here, distanced by several decades from some of Whitman's most heated rhetorical excursions, are a number of his illuminating—and, to our ears now, sometimes troubling—afterthoughts and summations on race in America. His private remarks reveal a more conflicted stance than his published views would lead us to suppose.

Toleration

America means above all toleration, catholicity, welcome, freedom—a concern for Europe, for Asia, for Africa, along with its concern for America. It is a fact everywhere preciously present.

First Breath of American Genius

The idea of slavery—of the holding of one man by another, in personal subjection—under dictatorial investments—was palpably bad—

damnable—not only condemned by civilization, by development—but condemned in the first breath of our American genius—of that force and faith at the base of American institutions. We all believe every man born should have a fair chance, move about as he chooses, possess and retain what justly belongs to him: it is the entrance step to all the rest.

Note: Whitman, attempting to describe the weight of all his illnesses, had earlier summoned up the memory of seeing slaves in iron collars during his trip to New Orleans in 1848. See "The Body's Slave," p. 272.

A Crying Sin

All my friends are more ardent in some respects than I am: for instance, I was never as much of an abolitionist as [Frederick] Marvin, O'Connor, and some of the others. [Wendell] Phillips—all of them—all of them—thought slavery the one crying sin of the universe. I didn't—though I, too, thought it a crying sin. Phillips was true blue—I looked at him with a sort of awe: I never could quite lose the sense of other evils in this evil—I saw other evils that cried to me in perhaps even a louder voice. . . . Some of the fellows were almost as hot with me as with slavery just because I wouldn't go into tantrums on the subject: they said I might just as well be on the other side—which was, of course, not true: I never lost any opportunity to make it plain where I stood but I did not concentrate all my moral fire on the same spot.

Anti-slavery Always

I may have been tainted a bit, just a little bit, with the New York feeling with regard to anti-slavery: yet I have been anti-slavery always—was then and am now: and to all and any other slaveries, too, black or white, mental or physical.

Exaggerating Abolitionists

The abolitionists have always exaggerated the importance of that movement: it was not by any means the beginning or end of things. It was a pimple, a boil—yes, a carbuncle—that's it—out of the nation's bad blood: out of a corpus spoiled, maltreated, bruised, poisoned. The Southerners, by acts of folly—acts like that of beating down Sumner—added to the fuel. . . . And although at one time four-fifths of the country was for slavery, yet slavery seemed doomed. A great something, uncaught yet by writers, explainers, expositors of our history, worked out the great end. [It was] a case of bad blood: it had to come out—and out it came: a great flood, leading upwards!

Laggard Southern Chivalry

In the South they have what they call a chivalry: a toplofticality: it is not a real chivalry—not by a damn sight: what men may call the moral toplofticality, that belongs to the North: here is a distinct difference: they are behind the North, anyone can see it—behind it at least a generation. They will evolve—but will they ever catch up?

Amalgamation

Talk of "the quadroons and octoroons in the South" causes Traubel to ask if Whitman believes in an ultimate "amalgamation" of the races: "I don't believe in it—it is not possible. The nigger, like the Injun, will be eliminated: it is the law of races, history, what-not: always so far inexorable—always to be. Someone proves that a superior grade of rat comes and then all the minor rats are cleared out." Horace observes that this view "sounds like Darwin," and Walt—after reminiscing about the octaroons "with splendid bodies . . . fascinating, magnetic, sexual, ignorant" he observed during his stay in New Orleans in 1848—elaborates: "Do you tell me that amalgamation is likely? I do not see it. The American white and the Southern black will *mix* but not *ally*. I have considered the problem from all sides. It is wonderful the readiness with which French and Negro, or Spanish and Negro, will marry—interlock—and the results are always good. It is the same with the Injun and Nigger—they too will ask no questions: they, too, achieve equally fine reproductivities. . . . Now, the Southern white does not encourage such intermixtures: there are psychological, physiological, reasons for it—back of all psychologies, physiologies, some deeper fact. They are a study, too—the poor white South: lank, sallow, coughing, spitting, with no bellies (and bellies seem a sine qua non). . . . For all that is said to discountenance them they maintain their independence, stand aloof, are not familiar, run affairs, govern, domineer."

"Black" or "Colored"

In my abolition days, some of my friends were furious at my allusions to the *blacks*: as if *colored people* were nearly so definite—*colored*, which might mean red or green as well as black. It is a violence we do the use of words.

"Darkeys"

Mention being made of the "calamus and the darkeys who bring it into town" for commercial preparation, Whitman reminisced about the "darkey population" he had known in New Jersey and Washington: "There are queer interesting old figures in South Jersey—I have met many—but the queerest, interestingest in Washington, in the markets there, with their odd ramshackle rigs—the gearing of the barges, old arms, metal, anything—a curious spectacle." Horace adds, "To W. the darkeys were 'a superstitious, ignorant, thievish race,' yet 'full of good nature, good heart,' too." Traubel then records Whitman recalling "negro experiences worth noting" when he visited the family of his close friend Harry Stafford in rural New Jersey south of Camden: "laughed that the darkey settlement nearby should be called Snow Hill. Described the darkeys: walking great distances to save their few cents, a darkey returning from town with a couple of quarters or a half, the magnate of his neighborhood."

Propping Don't Civilize

I never went full on the nigger question—the nigger would not turn—would not do anything for himself—he would only act when prompted to act. No! no! I should not like to see the nigger in the saddle—it seems unnatural; for he is only there when propped there, and propping don't civilize. I have always had a latent sympathy for the Southerner—and even for those in Europe—the Cavalier-folk—hateful as they are to me abstractly—un-democratic—from putting myself in a way in their shoes. Till the nigger can do something for himself, little can be done *for* him.

A Negro Visitor with Praise

"A Negro came in the other day," Whitman tells Traubel, "an educated man: very simple: very black skin: he was a reader of *Leaves of Grass*: said: 'You will be of great use to our race.'"

The Vote: Siding with the Whites

Responding to the view that black males would not be granted the vote until they could be counted on to vote for both parties, Whitman confessed, "I know enough of Southern affairs, have associated enough with Southern people to feel convinced that if I lived South I should side with the Southern whites." Traubel, puzzled, asks how does "that consist with [Whitman's] democracy," and the nonanswer is: "I should be forced not to explain that: I would have to evade the issue."

Whites Going to the Devil

The "hearty laugh of a negro out on the street" causes Walt's nurse Warrie to remark, "I do believe the niggers are the happiest people on the earth." Walt quickly replies, "That's because they're so damned vacant." Horace laughingly retorts, "That would be a bad thing to tell an anti-slavery man." Whitman comes down a bit and explains, "It would—it was a bad thing. But I used to say it, though it always raised a storm. That was one of the points on which [William] O'Connor and I always agreed. . . . That the horror of slavery was not in what it did for the nigger but in what it produced of the whites. For we quite clearly saw that the white South, if the thing continued, would go to the devil—could not save themselves. What slaveholding people can? Not, of course, because I could be cruel to the nigger or to any of the animals—to a horse, dog, cat, anything—especially *me*—for my dear daddy was remarkable everywhere he went for his kindness to the dumb beasts."

The Jewish Question

Traubel raises the subject of Jews in Russia, noting that, considering "Russian ideas of national destiny," the "Jews (aloof, not sharing) were not unnaturally subjected to persecution." Whitman erupts: "Damnable, horrible doctrine! It is, every word of it, low, mean, inhuman, cruel, poisonous, viperous! I hate it—yes, hate it! Expatriation is never a solution—never was, never can be—neither for Jew nor Negro. . . . It is a poor thing for a people when it has no destiny but must be carved out of wrong—written in blood. I, too, know, acknowledge the difficulties. I see man, his beastliness hanging to him—see the murderer, why people will steal, the onanist, the weary sorrowful whore—but I do not feel that this explains all. There is yet more to be said—not to condemn persons yet to condemn an event. Poor Russia, poor America, if either must travel the principle (they would call it that) of expatriation."

It is a damn bad custom. The exclusion of the Chinese, the tariff, prohibition, all that is of one piece, and I for one not only despise it but always denounce it—lose no occasion. . . . If the Jews are unpatriotic, who can wonder? How could they be otherwise, treating with such a government?

Educating Indians

When I was a young man, these men were interested with others in educating Indians. They reasoned: we will select samples out of the tribes, put them in the schools, colleges—inform them—use them to our ways—then send them forth among their people, to enlighten, to reform them. And so they persevered—sent out many men in this way—with the usual result: one out of a dozen would come to a little something, the others almost totally relapse.

The Irish and Indian Question

The "labor" question arises in conversation, and Whitman likens it to two notable ethnic problems percolating on opposite sides of the Atlantic: "This question is like the Irish question—there are two interests conflicting—strings pulling two ways—the one all Ireland, all for Irishman, who know nothing but Ireland—the other for the British Empire—that compact of vaster interests touching all parts of the globe. Indeed, it is our Indian question repeated—which has interests purely for the Indian, interests then of the whole body of states, leading to the largest results. In the meantime the poor aboriginals, so to call them, suffer, go down, are wiped out."

Funny Land Grab

Traubel notes that Whitman "Thought 'the Oklahoma land grab' a 'funny affair altogether'—but took no minute interest in it."

Note: The comment was made on April 27, 1889. President Benjamin Harrison had earlier proclaimed that a huge tract of Oklahoma land "purchased" from Creeks and Seminoles would be opened to homestead settlement at noon, April 22, 1889.

Famous Authors

In public, Whitman's manners as a literary celebrity were impeccable. Reporters who came to Mickle Street spoiling for a fight, eager for titillating gossip, or ravenous for colorful obiter dicta invariably went away empty-handed. However, in private with Traubel or someone else in his inner circle, Whitman was considerably more willing to express in unminced, often vivid terms his likes, dislikes, and lukewarmnesses. It quickly becomes clear that Walt was much taken by those who exhibited Whitmanesque traits and was very likely to despise those who did not.

The Big Fellows . . .

In all imaginative work, all pure poetic work, there must especially come in a primal quality, not to be mentioned, named, described, but always felt when present: the direct off-throwing of nature, parting the ways between formal, conventional, borrowed expression and the fervor of genuine spirit. [Heinrich] Heine had it—so do all the big fellows have it.

. . . versus the Little Ones

It's the generosity that makes the big fellow. It will do for the little crowd to have all the bickerings, the mean jealousies, the quarreling ambitions, the mean policies. And you know that's the way to distinguish the little from the big. The thing we call smart, clean, skillful—that thing is not big. Those who regard literature as an exercise, a plaything, a joke, a display, are not big—they are small of the small. There's nothing so riles me as this exhibition of professional acquirement. Literature is big only in one way—when used as an aid in the growth of the humanities—a furthering of the cause of the masses—a means whereby men may be revealed to each other as brothers.

Lasting Old Crony: Epictetus

Epictetus is the one of all my old cronies who has lasted to this day without cutting a diminished figure in my perspective. He belongs with the best—the best of the great teachers—is a universe in himself. He sets me free in a flood of light—of life, of vista.

This book [*Encheiridion*] has become in a sense sacred, precious to me. I have had it about me so long—lived with it in terms of such familiarity.

Traubel observes that Epictetus (born about A.D. 60) "appeals profoundly to W. Is always quoting the *Encheiridion*—quoting rather to the spirit than the letter." Whitman later says it was to him "a dear, strong, aromatic volume." Traubel also notes his copy "has been all underscored with purple pencillings."

Over-stately Milton

I could never go Milton: he is turgid, heavy, over-stately. . . . It seems to me that Milton [in *Paradise Lost*] is a copy of a copy—not only Homer but the *Æneid*: a sort of modern repetition of the same old story: legions of angels, devils: war is declared, waged: moreover, even as a story it enlists little of my attention: he seems to me like a bird—soaring yet overweighted: dragged down, as if burdened—too greatly burdened. . . . Milton soars, but with dull, unwieldy motion.

Note: Six months earlier Whitman brushed off Milton—and another celebrated European poet—more abruptly. After Traubel remarked, "I will be honest. I don't care much for Milton or Dante," Walt replied, "I will be honest, too. I don't care for them either. I like the moderns better."

Voltaire's Mighty Anger

Now there was a great man, too: an emancipator—a shining spiritual light: a miraculous man whose ridicule did more for justice than the battles of armies. Voltaire never was of a mind to condone Shakespeare: Shakespeare's crudities were offensive to him: there was something crude, powerful, drastic, in the Shakespeare plays: Voltaire could not reconcile his nerves to their brutal might. But you cannot shift such luminaries from their orbit by a sneer—by an adjective. Do you think *Leaves of Grass* was ever really hurt by the people who went at it with a club?

Voltaire, after the intellectual sinuosities, deep down down, to bottom truths, was triumphantly on our side. A wonderful force—his anger persistent, mighty—as when after some priesthood, how he clutched, swore, persisted, indignation deepening in him down to the very joints of his toes.

Rousseau (Heine and Burns)

It [Rousseau's *Confessions*] is a singular mixture—plenty of the petty, the minor, the mean, the dirty—then surprising streaks of genius— often and often. . . . The best autobiography is not built but grows. [Traubel suggests Heine.] Yes, Heine—preeminently, above all others— and Burns: take Burns—the heart of him: drops of his blood on every page: if I may say it (is there such a word?) the ear-marks of the one human fact in every line.

Alexandrine Device

Pope was of course a machine—he wrote like a see-saw.

Note: The reference, of course, being to the regular rhymed iambic pentameter couplets employed by Alexander Pope.

Ponderous Johnson

Johnson does not impress me. . . . I don't admire the old man's ponderous arrogance: he talked for effect—seemed rather inclined to bark men down, like the biggest dog—indeed a spice of dishonesty palpably possessed him. Johnson tried rather to impress than to be true. . . . Johnson fills me with a great heaviness. He gives me no lifts—never takes me up anywhere; always fastens me to the earth.

Dr. Johnson, it is plain, is not our man: he belongs to a past age: comes to us with the odor, the sound, the taste, the appearance, of great libraries, musty books, old manuscripts. . . . He is a type of the smart man—a ponderous type . . . who does anything to score a point—who is not concerned for truth but to make an impression.

Roaring Johnson, Braying Boswell

Just after finishing *The Life of Samuel Johnson*, Whitman summed up bluntly: "I read it through, looked it through, rather—persisted in spite of fifty temptations to throw it down. I don't know who tried me most—Johnson or Boswell."

"The more I see of the book [*The Life*] the more I realize what a roaring bull the Doctor was and what a braying ass Boswell was." He drove the nail in further a few days later: "He's the champion brayer in literature. I swear I'll never try to read him again."

Goethe's High Place

While I am willing to accord Goethe a very high place, I could not accord him the highest: the highest place would seem to demand first of all passion, warmth—not artistic power, deftness of technique, primarily, but human passion.

Flamboyant Byron

Byron has enough fire to burn forever.

Byron deserves one great point to be made for him—this point, namely—that his alleged wickedness, queernesses are no more than the doctor's enumeration of diseases. The whole spirit of the persecution of Byron is the spirit of the town police—just as the spirit of the obscenity hunter anywhere (in mails and whatnot)—the spirit that will ignore all the gigantic evils—steal a way down to the shore—lay low—pull in a lot of little naked boys, there to take a bath—snake 'em in! It well pictures for me what is too commonly called the greatness and majesty of the law.

Ethereally Opposed: Shelley

I have a warm place even for Shelley. He seems so opposite—so ethereal—all ethereal—always living in the presence of a great ideal, as I do not. He was not sensual—he was not even sensuous.

Whitman receives a letter from England conveying a question from members of a Shelley society: what did the poet think of their man? "That's what Walt Whitman would like to know himself. . . . I am not a reader of Shelley—I don't come so near him, or he to me, as some others. . . . I know nothing about Shelley—at least not enough to go on record formally about him."

Superbly Fused: Heine

I always stand up for Heine—am hotly inclined his way: resent all the puritan criticism of his character as a man and his significance as a writer, am eager (more than willing) to recognize his high estate. . . . I find Heine everyway interesting.

I look on him as a genuinely great soul—not yet justly measured: hot, turbulent, but gifted highly—perhaps as highly as any modern man. . . . I find in Heine a superb fusion of culture and native elemental genius.

Woman Redeemed: Sand

Asked whom he preferred, George Eliot or George Sand, Whitman hedged at first and then let fly: "Both women were formidable: they had, each one had, their own perfections: I am not inclined to decide between them: I consider them essentially akin in their exceptional eminent exalted genius. Yet my heart turns to Sand: I regard her as the brightest woman ever born. . . . Why, read *Consuelo* . . . it displays the most marvelous verity and temperance: no false color—not a bit: no superfluous flesh—not an ounce: suggests an athlete, a soldier, stripped of all ornament, prepared for the fight—absolutely no flummery about her. She was Dantesque in her rigid fidelity to nature—her imagery: she led a peculiar life—obeyed the law of her personal temperament: she redeems woman."

One day Traubel found Whitman repairing the loose covers on one of the three volumes of Sand's novel *Consuelo*, in its 1840s English translation: "I have always treasured it: read, read, read—never tiring. The book is a masterpiece: truly a masterpiece: the noblest work left by George Sand—the noblest in many respects, on its own field, in all literature." When an article by Molly Seawell in the *Critic*, "On the Absence of the Creative Faculty in Women," was brought to Whitman's attention, he demurred: "Damn the woman! But stick to George Sand!" The next day Whitman dwelt further on Sand's "palpable genius." Whitman also called Sand "a wonderful woman, [a]cute before her time."

Sweet Keats

I have of course read Keats—his works: may be said to have read all: he is sweet—oh! very sweet—all sweetness: almost lush, lush, polish, or-nateness, elegancy.

Tonic Nature—but with a Growl: Cooper

Cooper was a master-man in many very significant ways. Cooper had a growl—the cynicism of [Thomas] Carlyle, without the toplofticalness with which Carlyle carried it off: and there was a healthy vigor in every-thing Cooper did. . . . I have always regarded Cooper as essentially fresh, robust, noble: one of the original characters—the tonic natures.

Natty [Bumppo in *Deerslayer* is] peculiarly a *Leaves of Grass* man. . . . I look upon Cooper as new rather than old—as belonging to our era, cultivating our graces.

Cooper was a curious paradox—very hard to deal with—possessing great shining qualities—some harsh ones, too—perhaps in the direc-tion of a too severe individualism if that can be; but breathing the open airs—never, never the odor of the libraries. . . . Cooper was one of the first-raters—had a vein of asperity which sort of cut him loose from the literary classes—perhaps preserved him.

I consider Cooper greater, greater—much greater—than Hawthorne, just as I consider Bryant—though the world will not have it so—in-comparably greater than Longfellow. But such comparisons, I suppose, are not good, wherever made.

Cooper at his best is always the best: very inspiring, vitalizing. In some of his later works he is more prosaic, dull, flat. *The Deerslayer*, for in-stance. It is inexpressibly dry to me; full of dialogue, full of long impos-sible speeches—at the end leaving you nowhere.

Note: Whitman and Mark Twain were of one mind here, at least. In the latter's hilari-ous essay "Fenimore Cooper's Literary Offenses," he writes: "Cooper's art has some defects. In one place in *Deerslayer*, and in the restricted space of two-thirds of a page, Cooper has scored 114 offenses against literary art out of a possible 115. It breaks the record."

Perennial Sir Walter . . .

Scott is my chief pleasure nowadays—the novels: I read them every day, some: read them because they are not to so frivolous as to be useless and vulgar, and not so weighty as to set my brains into a snarl.

Perennial . . . I can always go back to him and find him fresh.

. . . but Not All of Him

Take *Robert of Paris*, where the scene is laid in Constantinople—flat, flat, flat—flatulent, flatulent, flatulent—dull, dull, dull—tedious past all a fellow's patience.

Tolstoy's Dull Questionings

Anna Karenina, or some such name—I have downstairs still: wrestled with it at the time: never had such a task. . . . I persisted—went through with it—feeling that along somewhere the truth would out—I would get my reward: but nothing eventuated: the book was big in bulk alone—it seemed to me there must have been at least three volumes in that one: all my plodding failed to relieve it of its dullness.

Having gotten through only a third of Tolstoy's *My Confession*, Whitman explained to Traubel: "I find little pleasure in it: it's poor reading for me: I was never there. Tolstoy's questionings—how shall we save men? sin, worry, self-examination—all that: I have never had them. I never, never was troubled to know whether I would be saved or lost: what was that to me? Especially now do I need other fodder: my mind is in such a state I need food which will frivol it. I know a bright girl: she expressed this for me: she would sometimes say 'We went out for a drive, came home, had our supper, then *frivolled* the evening away.' I want to *frivol* my evening away. . . . There are undeniable and undoubted marks of the great man in all that Tolstoy writes, but the introspective, sin-seeking nature makes no appeal to my constitutional peculiarities."

Note: But see, in the earlier Expurgation section, Whitman's extravagant praise for Tolstoy's *Kreutzer Sonata*, p. 114.

Giant-man Carlyle

Carlyle always stirs me to the deeps. He was a giant-man, none more so, in our time.

Thackeray's Shallow Sinker

Thackeray as a whole did not cast his sinker very deep, though he's none the worse for that.

Languid Spectrality: Poe

Traubel asks Whitman if he likes Edgar Allan Poe: "At the start, for many years, not: but three or four years ago I got to reading him again, reading and liking, until at last—yes, now—I feel almost convinced that he is a star of considerable magnitude, if not a sun, in the literary firmament. Poe was morbid, shadowy, lugubrious—seemed to suggest dark nights, horrors, spectralities—I could not originally stomach him at all. . . . I was a young man of about thirty, living in New York, when

'The Raven' appeared—created its stir: everybody was excited about it—every reading body: somehow it did not enthuse me."

Poor Poe! Poor Poe! who shall not say he did not have failings, defects, weaknesses: serious weaknesses—grave, oh! so grave!—from which he suffered?

Note: On November 17, 1875, Whitman was the only literary figure present for the reburial of Poe and dedication of a Poe memorial in Baltimore.

I have seen Poe—met him: he impressed me very favorably: was dark, quiet, handsome—Southern from top to toe: languid, tired out, it is true, but altogether ingratiating.

William [O'Connor]'s sweep . . . was tremendous—astounding: he found a place for all—even for poor Poe in the days when I myself would question and doubt.

No Dickens Enthuser

When it was reported in *Current Literature* that Whitman's "greatest pleasure" was in perusing Dickens's novels, he responded: "That's news to me! I was a reader of Dickens from the first—liked his books—*Nicholas Nickleby, Oliver Twist,* others: but a dweller-upon, an enthuser, a make-mucher-of, I never was—never—am not today. And you know, today I don't read him at all."

Some time later, Whitman was more blunt: "Dickens one queer fellow, Hawthorne another, a queerer."

Farthest-influencing Darwin

"Darwin—the sweet, the gracious, the sovereign, Darwin: Darwin, whose life after all was the most significant, the farthest-influencing, life of the age." Two weeks later Traubel records that Whitman "spoke tenderly of Darwin. Darwin is one of his loves that will last. So of Clifford, so of George Eliot: 'Darwin, simplest, greatest, however, of all.'"

Note: Darwin's *Origin of Species* was published in 1859, but did not arrive in the United States until after the Civil War; Whitman was much taken by his theories.

Cooper versus Hawthorne

Whitman spoke of Cooper's *Deerslayer* as being "inexpressibly dry to me" but felt his influence on American letters healthier than Hawthorne's because Cooper's was "always an outdoor influence; he is perennial fresh air, pure seas; a living accuser of our civilization."

Mellifluous Tennyson

Tennyson rather expresses elegance—and such elegance as at least our age has nowhere else displayed—workedness, sublime care. And so it is, I think, while Tennyson does a good deal of good—oh! incalculable good!—he does harm too—often much harm: his mellifluosity—one may call it: it is great, overwhelming, everything in his imitators is sacrificed to accomplish that.

Whole Hog or Nothing: Swinburne

He is always the extremist—always all pro or all con: always hates altogether or loves altogether: as the boys say, he goes the whole hog or nothing: he knows no medium line.

Able but Unrooted: Oscar Wilde

I never completely make Wilde out—for good or bad. He writes exquisitely—is as lucid as a star on a clear night—but there seems to be a little substance lacking at the root—something—what is it? I have no sympathy with the crowd of scorners who want to crowd him off the earth.

Wilde may have been some of him fraud at the time but was not all fraud. My letter from him [see next entry] seems wholly sincere. He has extraordinary brilliancy of genius with perhaps rather too little root in eternal soils.

Shortly after his visit to Mickle Street in 1882, Wilde wrote Whitman an effusive letter from New York that ends, "there is no one in this wide great world of America whom I love and honor so much." Before giving this letter up to Traubel, Whitman commented, "There is no parade in this note: it wears the simplest clothes—has no sunflower in its button hole—has in fact a cast of virgin simplicity, sincerity." After Traubel read the letter, Whitman added, "It all rings sound and true to me there. Everybody's been so in the habit of looking at Wilde cross-eyed, sort of, that they have charged a defect of their vision up against Wilde as a weakness in his character."

Wilde was very friendly to me—was and is, I think—both Oscar and his mother—Lady Wilde—and thanks be most to the mother, that greater, more important individual. Oscar was here—came to see me—and he impressed me as a strong, able fellow, too.

Note: Several months earlier Oscar Wilde's one published review of Whitman appeared in the *Pall Mall Gazette* (January 25, 1889); it seems that a copy made its way to Mickle Street, but since it was unsigned Whitman does not acknowledge Wilde as its author. In the review, Wilde writes that Whitman "is the herald to a new era. As a man he is the precursor of a fresh type. He is a factor in the heroic and spiritual evolution of the human being."

Really Fat Howells

I think well enough of [William Dean] Howells, too. He is very much like our friend Dr. [John] Johnston . . . looks like him, though *fatter*: Howells is really *fat*. He is inclined to be suave, kind, courteous—has his parts and holds them well.

No Thanatopsisian: Bryant

Bryant was trained in the classics—made no departures. He was a healthy influence—he was not a closet man: belonged out of doors: but he was afraid of my work: he was interested, but afraid: I remember that he always expressed wonder that, with what he called my power and gifts and essential underlying respect for beauty, I refused to accept and use the only medium which would give me complete expression. I have often tried to think of myself as writing *Leaves of Grass* in Thanatopsisian verse. Of course I do not intend this as a criticism of Bryant—only as a demurrer to his objection to me: "Thanatopsis" is all right in Thanatopsisian verse: I suppose Bryant would fare as badly in *Leaves of Grass* verse as I would fare in "Thanatopsis" verse. Bryant said to me: "I will admit that you have power—sometimes great power." But he would never admit that I had chosen the right vehicle for expression.

Note: After Whitman elaborated further on Bryant, Traubel observed this about the poet's still formidable powers of articulation: "I wonder often over W.'s long sentences—if they are to come out right at last (as they mostly do) after devious windings. He was serenely glowing to-night. He stirred me." Later Whitman summarized more bluntly, "take Bryant, for example—cold, exteriorly, in a way—marbeline—to coin a word—yet superbly true on all sides." Bryant's most famous poem, composed in 1810 when he was sixteen, is in blank verse.

Mixed Views of Hawthorne

I think he is monotonous, he wears me out: I do not read him with pleasure.

What a devil of a Copperhead he was! I always more or less despise the Copperheads, irrespective of who they are, their fame—what-not: but aside from that, all my tendencies about Hawthorne are towards him—even affectionate, I may say—for his work, what he represented.

Feathered James

James is only feathers to me.

Note: Sour grapes perhaps, for Henry James had in 1865 reviewed *Drum-Taps* for the New York *Nation* and began: "It has been a melancholy task to read this book; and it is a still more melancholy one to write about it." James also opined: "We find art, measure, grace, sense sneered at on every page." James's review is reprinted in full in *Walt Whitman: Selected Poems 1855–1892*, pp. 469–71.

Undrastic Longfellow

[He] never traveled new paths: of course never broke new paths: in fact was a man who shrank from unusual things—from what was highly colored, dynamic, drastic.

Well-booked Bret Harte

He is a star—though not of any first magnitude, and not lustrous in our heavens. He is very critical—makes several good points—and he writes well, very well. He is sharp, raspy. . . . He is well-booked—has knowledge of many things of the bookiest order, but he fails to know, understand, that last fruit of philosophy, of poetry, as I call it, which controls, or shows, the large reserves of nature.

Bruising Browning

It would be a hard tussle for anyone to take Browning up in the bulk. . . . I don't believe I could do it. I don't find Browning's technique easy—it beats me sore, bruises me—though I don't make much of that: the fault is mainly my own.

No black crepe was draped at Mickle Street when Robert Browning died: "So Browning is dead," he wrote to Bucke, "as it happen'd I never read him much—(Does he not exercise & rather worry the intellect—something like a sum in arithmetic?)."

Porcelain Arnold

I have tried to be just with [Matthew] Arnold: have taken up his books over and over again, hoping I would at last get at the heart of him—have given him every sort of chance to convince me. . . . The result was always the same: I was not interested: I was wearied: I laid the book down again.

I can never realize Arnold—like him: we are constitutionally antipathetic: Arnold is porcelain, chinaware, hangings.

The worst I could say of him—the severest . . . [is] that Arnold brings coal to Newcastle—that he brings to the world what the world already has a surfeit of: is rich, hefted, lousy, reeking with delicacy, refinement, prettiness, propriety, criticism, analysis: all of them things which threaten to overwhelm us.

There seems to be a temperamental reason why I can't know Matthew, why he can't know me. . . . Arnold is as inveterately one thing as I am another: we can't be remade: no doubt we both belong in the world: there's no use trying to make oil and water mix. . . . Arnold was weak on the democratic side: he had some intellectual perception of democracy but he didn't have the feel of the thing.

Two Errand Boys: Howells and Aldrich

They run a few temporary errands but they are not out for immortal service.

Note: The reference was to pillars of the American literary establishment: William Dean Howells and Thomas Bailey Aldrich, both novelists and editors (notably of the *Atlantic Monthly*).

Expensive Morris

Horace: "Do you like the William Morris books?" Walt: "I may say yes: I may also say no: they are wonderful books, I'm told: but they are not books for the people: they are books for collectors. I want a beautiful book, too, but I want that beautiful book cheap: that is, I want it to be within the reach of the average buyer."

Unfitting Ruskin

I don't quote him—I don't care for him, don't read him—don't find he appeals to me. I've tried Ruskin on every way but he don't fit.

Missing Fire: The Sober Twain

I think he mainly misses fire: I think his life misses fire: he might have been something: he comes near to being something: but he never arrives.

I have always regarded him as friendly, but not warm: not exactly against me: not for me either.

I have met Clemens, met him many years ago, before he was rich and famous. Like all humorists he was very sober: inclined to talk of the latest things in politics, men, books, a man after old-fashioned models, slow to move, liking to stop and chat—the sort of fellow one is quietly drawn to. Yes, my experience with humorists is that they are all of the more serious color.

Whittier's Limited Range

Whittier has very few strings—very few—to his harp—only three or four—though, to be sure, these are pure and strong.

Whittier is but a snivel: not a line he ever wrote or writes but is propped—leans up against something.

In a letter to William Sloane Kennedy dated October 10, 1889, Whitman lectured with some edge: "Whittier's poetry stands for *morality* (not its *ensemble* or in any true philosophic or Hegelian sense but)—as filter'd through the positive Puritanical & Quaker filters. . . . Whittier is rather a grand figure—pretty lean & ascetic—no Greek—also not composite & universal enough (don't wish to be, don't try to be) for ideal Americanism."

Mansioner Lowell

I think I could easily state the difference myself: Lowell an elegant mansion, equipped with all that is luxurious, rich—not to be despised, after its own kind and degree; Walt Whitman, emulous of the seashore, the forest, even the prairie—or the surging manifold streets of the cities. . . . Note: At this moment, Traubel told Whitman to hold up while he found an old envelope on which to continue recording this gem for later quotation. To which Whitman responded, not willing to let such a cut go public from his lips: "I have no objection . . . but I don't want to be quoted as the author." Traubel wrote an essay comparing Lowell and Whitman, and Burroughs wrote this in a letter complimenting the piece: "W. is so hard to grasp, to put in a statement. One cannot get to the bottom of him; he has so many bottoms, he is bottomed in nature, in democracy, in science, in personality— but you did well in getting your lever under him as far as you did."

Horace Greeley, Idiocrat

He was often in Washington—came to see me: would try to debate, raise questions, involve me. . . . Greeley was a contribution—a curious idiocratic fellow—a considerable contribution, but he was not a great man . . . pale—had not color in his hair. Greeley's great consuming trait—seizing and subordinating all other traits—was his smartness— his ability to occupy the smart side of things, every time. It is the New England gift—almost all of them have it.

I ought to like him—and *do*—for he was very sweet and kind to me. . . . I always felt drawn. He was a tremendously stubborn man—had what some thought a damnable perversity—especially, he would dress as he chose, caring nothing whatever for others' opinion of his appearance. His obstinacy was a great hurt, but he was a great power, too: it would not do to lose sight of that.

Deft Garland

Hamlin is deft—is a college man: has a hand in everything. . . . He is a well-dressed man: has a manner which my word "deft" describes: a manner which in the odious sense of that word would be oily, slippery: but there's none of that poison in Garland: he is very frank, outspoken— has the courage of his convictions: is never afraid to avow, assert himself—stand his ground . . . is much better mettle than his polished exterior would indicate.

Formal Holmes

An Oliver Wendell Holmes essay on Emerson and Whitman in the *Atlantic Monthly* was much discussed at Mickle Street. Whitman expressed very grudging acknowledgment of his critical eminence but finally found Holmes an impossibly stuffed shirt (Holmes did say of Whitman that he "*goes* at her [poetry] like a great hirsute man"). "I am to him 'Walter,' not 'Walt,' because he does not recognize the primary color of character. Holmes knows me—would know me—as little as he would an old woman making her tea, a big Injun, a brawny stalwart nigger— say, one of those magnificent niggers I have seen on Mississippi steamboats." The next day he says of the essay, "As a nigger would say in the

South, it ain't worth shucks!" Yet he read it again a few days later and found it "very dull, unsatisfactory. . . . It sticks in his craw to have anyone Billed, Jacked, Walted: I am Mr. Whitman throughout. I was interested in it as I am always interested in what is said by the opposition. I have always craved to hear the damndest that could be said of me, and the damndest has been said, I do believe."

Walt and the Bard

What play of Shakespeare, represented in America," Whitman asked in one of his early unsigned rave reviews of Leaves of Grass, *"is not an insult to America, to the marrow in its bones?" Especially early in his life, Whitman was deeply antipathetic to all European—cultural and political. "What perfect cataracts of trash come to us at present from abroad," he editorialized in the* Brooklyn Eagle *in July 1846. Inevitably, Shakespeare epitomized the cultural hegemony of the Old World, at least for English speakers, and the Bard suffered accordingly in Whitman's estimation. Still, in unguarded moments he granted the achievement of the man from Stratford—or whoever it was who wrote the plays in the First Folio (the debate about authorship ignited often in Mickle Street). And Whitman left no doubt that Shakespearean performances were among the most exhilarating memories of his theater-going heyday in the 1840s and 1850s. "As a boy or young man I had seen (reading them carefully beforehand) quite all Shakspere's acting dramas, play'd wonderfully well," he recalls in* Specimen Days. *Memorable Shakespearean actors are also prominent in his glowing memoir, "The Bowery: A Reminiscence of New York Plays and Acting Fifty Years Ago," in* November Boughs *of 1888.*

Low Shelf

Traubel remarks on a critic who asserted that Shakespeare "lacked the religious as distinguished from the poetic faculty," and this sets Walt off: "That seems to me to be profoundly true. The highest poetic expression demands a certain element of the religious—indeed, should be transfused with it. Frothingham has hit upon the truth: scholars will not, dare not, admit it, but it is the truth. The time will come when Shakespeare will be given his right place—will be put on a low shelf . . . a master, sure enough: yes, a master: but subject to severe deductions. People don't dare face the fact Shakespeare. They are all tied to a fiction that is called Shakespeare—a Shakespearean illusion. . . . It is very difficult to talk about Shakespeare in a frank vein: there's always somebody about with a terrific prejudice to howl you down."

Gloomy

Shakespeare . . . is gloomy, looks upon the people with something like despair: does so especially in his maturer plays: seemed to say: after all the human critter is a devil of a poor fellow—full of frailties, evils, poisons.

Greeks versus Shakespeare

The Shakespeare plays are essentially the plays of an aristocracy: they are in fact not as nearly in touch with the spirit of our modern democracy as the plays of the Greeks—as the Homeric stories in particular. Look at the Homeric disregard for power, place: notice the freedom of the Greeks—their frank criticism of the nabobs, rulers, the elect. You find the Greeks . . . had some recognition of the dignity of the common people—of the dignity of labor—of the honor that resides in the average life of the race. Do you find such things in the Shakespeare plays? I do not—no, nothing of the kind: on the contrary everything possible is done in the Shakespeare plays to make the common people seem common—very common indeed.

Offensive

There is much in the plays that is offensive to me, anyhow: yes, in all the plays of that period: a grandiose sweep of expression: forced, false phrasing: much of it, much of it: indeed, I find myself often laughing over its sophistications.

Note: Whitman phrased this view somewhat more diplomatically in a short essay, "A Thought on Shakspere," that he first published in the *Critic* magazine in 1886: "The inward and outward characteristics of Shakspere are his vast and rich variety of persons and themes, with his wondrous delineation of each and all—not only limitless funds of verbal and pictorial resource, but great excess, superfœtation—mannerism, like a fine, aristocratic perfume, holding a touch of musk (Euphues, his mark)—with boundless sumptuousness and adornment, real velvet and gems, not shoddy nor paste—but a good deal of bombast and fustian—(certainly some terrific mouthing in Shakspere!)." Toward essay's end, while bowing to the "dazzle" of the playwright's "sun-like beams," Whitman pronounces, "The comedies are altogether non-acceptable to America and Democracy."

Prolix, but Not Ignorantly

Shakespeare shows undoubted defects: he often uses a hundred words where a dozen would do: it is true that there are many pithy terse sentences everywhere: but there are countless prolixities: though as for the overabundances of words more might be said: as, for instance, that he was not ignorantly prolific: that he was like nature itself: nature, with her trees, the oceans: nature, saying "there's lots of this, infinitiudes of it—therefore, why spare it? If you ask for ten I give you a hundred. . . ."

Splashy Plays versus Lush Sonnets

Try to think of the Shakespeare plays: think of their movement: their intensity of life, action: everything hell-bent to get along: on: on: energy—the splendid play of force: across fields, mire, creeks: never mind who is splashed—spare nothing. . . . The Sonnets are all that is opposite—perfect of their kind—exquisite, sweet: lush: eleganted: refined and refined then again refined—again: refinement multiplied by refinement. . . . [V]igor was not called for: they are personal: more or less of small affairs: they do their own work in their own way: that's all we could ask and more than most of us do, I suppose.

His Humor among the Leaves

The humor in the Shakespearean comedies is very broad, obvious, often brutal, coarse: but in some of the tragedies—take *Lear* for instance—you will find another kind of humor, a humor more remote (subtle, illusive, not present)—the sort of humor William [O'Connor] declares he finds in the *Leaves* and in me.

Overdone Sonnets

They are often over-done—over-ornate—their elaboration is extreme, at times utterly obscuring the idea, which might be presumed to be of the first importance.

Richard's Vehement Juices

One Sunday Traubel observes, lying at Whitman's feet, a pamphlet "home-bound in brown wrapping paper." It proves to be the text of *Richard II* that Whitman had long ago excised from a large Shakespeare volume for "practical use" in his theater-going. Walt exults nostalgically: "What a flood of memories it lets loose. It is my old play-book, used many and many times in my itinerant theatre days: Richard: Shakespeare's Richard: one of the best of the plays, I always say—one of the best—in its vehemence, power, even in its grace." Whitman finds the larger volume and returns the sheets to their original place, then continues: "that is Richard—this same Richard. How often I spouted this—these first pages—on the Broadway stagecoaches, in the awful din of the street. In that seething mass—that noise, chaos, bedlam—what is one voice more or less: one single voice added, thrown in, joyously mingled in the amazing chorus?" A few days later Whitman elaborated: "I felt it necessary to have books about me: not cumbersome—light: carried them in my pocket: Shakespeare, for instance—one of his Plays: I think it was *Richard II*, in some respects the most characteristic—I carried it most."

Collegiate Idol

Do you suppose I accept the almost loony worship of Shakespeare—the cult worship, the college-chair worship? Not a bit of it.

His Women

I think anyhow, if Shakespeare had any weakness, it was in his women. All his women are fashioned so: in *King John*, in *Richard*—everywhere—the product of feudalism—daintily, delicately fashioned.

Sine Quibus Non

The qualities I always insist upon as requisites for the Shakespearean: abandon: the subtle southern passion: fire, glow, the absence of calculation.

Note: Whitman made this remark apropos the acting of the Italian actor Tomasso Salvini.

Taste for Glitter

[The plays indicate] a great taste for glitter: a desire to surpass, overawe: a resolve to overdo: to create the fiercest emphases: to succeed by the very force of the flood—a literal inundation of power.

Good Enough for Walt, but . . .

"Shakespeare, whoever he was, whoever they were: he had his place: I have never doubted his vastness, space: in fact, Homer and Shakespeare are good enough for me. . . . [Traubel asks about the playwright's "defects."] It is not well for us to forget what Shakespeare stands for: we are overawed, overfed: it may seem extreme, ungracious, to say so, but Shakespeare appears to me to do much towards effeminacy: towards taking the fiber, the blood, out of our civilization: his gospel was of the medieval—the gospel of the grand, the luxurious: great lords, ladies: plate, hangings, glitter, ostentation, hypocritical chivalry, dress, trimmings . . . of social and caste humbuggery. I can say I am one of the few—unfortunately, of the few—who care nothing for all that, who spit all that out, who reject all that miserable paraphernalia of arrogance, unrighteousness, oppression. . . . As for the Plays, they do not seem to me spontaneous: they seem laboredly built up: I have always felt their feudal bias: they are rich to satiety: overdone with words." Traubel remarks on this end to a lengthy broadside, "I never saw W. more vigorous." No wonder, given such views, that Whitman was susceptible to the much-debated theory of Oxfordian or Baconian authorship of the plays: "the emphasis that the author of the Plays places upon these fripperies points an unmistakable finger towards Bacon. Bacon himself loved all this show, this fustian: dressed handsomely: tunic: fine high boots: brooches: liked a purse well filled with gold." The authorship debate at Mickle Street focused in particular on Ignatius Donnelly's *The Great Cryptogram: Francis Bacon's Cipher in the So-called Shakespeare Plays* (1888).

The Authorship Question: A Last Word

In the Shakespeare matter, my sympathies are with the fellows who are disturbed, chaotic, off rudderless at sea—who question, don't see enough to believe—the men who riot with accepted notions. . . . I go with the sinners who are not so damned sure.

Note: A few days later Whitman received a letter from Bucke, who doted on the controversy: "Am deep into Bacon-Shakespeare studies every available minute. Bacon wrote the plays you may put that down as certain and in a few more years it will be proved." The irony of Bucke's writing from the grounds of a Canadian mental asylum might be noted.

Directness

Traubel reports Whitman "grew humorous" over how to spell the playwright's name: "Miss Porter wrote asking if I had any objection to spelling Shakespeare their way, that is, the orthodox way, with all the *e*'s and *a*'s. I answered . . . that I did not stickle for it. Nevertheless 'Shakspere' is the latest authoritative way, with all the advantages of directness." Earlier Whitman told Traubel, "I am glad to see you spell Shakspere the short way . . . it is always my way—has something in the look of it I like."

Mystery

It is remarkable how little is known of Shaksper the actor as a person and how much less is known of the person Shakespeare of the plays. The record is almost blank—it has no substance whatsoever: scarcely anything that is said of him is authorized.

Mystic Cipher

The notion that the identity of the true author of the plays was ciphered in their texts often arises in the conversations. Facing page 180 of the first *With Walt Whitman* volume, Traubel reproduced in facsimile the proof slip of the following short poem, typeset for private distribution, containing Whitman's view of the matter.

Shakspere-Bacon's Cipher
(*A Hint to Scientists*)
I doubt it not—then more, far more;
In each old song bequeath'd—in every noble page of text
(Different—something unreck'd before—some unsuspected author),
In every object, mountain, tree, and star—in every birth and life,
As part of each—finality of each—meaning, behind the ostent,
The mystic cipher waits infolded.
WALT WHITMAN

Sweet Magnetic Man: Ralph Waldo Emerson

If Abraham Lincoln was the American political celebrity who most pro-foundly engaged Whitman's sensibilities, Ralph Waldo Emerson was un-doubtedly the American literary figure who appealed to him most deeply. In Lincoln the poet found a perfect soul mate; about the president he scarcely ever said a discouraging word. But with Emerson there was a fascinating element of conflict. In the privacy of Mickle Street, Whitman allowed him-self the latitude to express some of the most movingly affirmative salutes . . . but also some of his most revealing reservations about the sage of Concord.

The First Visit

I shall never forget the first visit he paid me—the call, the first call: it was in Brooklyn: no, I can never forget it. I can hear his gentle knock still— the soft knock—so [indicating it on the chair-arm]—and the slow sweet voice, as my mother stood there by the door . . . the simple unaffected greetings on both sides—"How are you, Mr. Whitman," "How are you, Waldo"—the hour's talk or so—the taste of lovableness he left behind.

Redeemer

As I have been more and more confirmed in believing, Emerson, by his striking personality, suffices to redeem the whole literary class. This is his greatest fruit—his best result—showing after all the infinite literary possibilities.

Effulgent Being

Emerson's smile was not common—it was rare indeed. But his usual manner carried with it something penetrating and sweet beyond mere description. There is in some men an indefinable something which flows out and over you like a flood of light—as if they possessed it il-limitably—their whole being suffused with it. Being—in fact that is precisely the word. Emerson's whole attitude shed forth such an impression.

Magnetic

He was one of those affable, sweet, magnetic men, whose atmosphere— which was his greatest gift—utterly charmed, captured, compassed anyone . . . who came near. He was not a man to waste himself on desert beholders, on empty witnesses. He had his reserves—as who has not who has *anything* that is worth while.

No Sex Please

Emerson so far forgot who I was and who he was as to suggest that I should expurgate, cut out, eliminate: which is as if I was to hide some of myself away: was to win success by false pretences: which God forbid: I'd rather go to eternal ruin than climb to glory by such humbug. [Traubel probes: "Emerson didn't call it humbug when he gave you that counsel, did he?"] Oh no: it wasn't humbug to him: he was anxious to have people read me: he thought it was better to have the people read some of me, even the worst of me, than not to read me at all: that's the way he put it himself.

"Your Nonchalance with Men"

On Christmas Day 1888 Whitman asked Traubel to read aloud a very affectionate letter from his Civil War days in Washington to a young friend from his New York circle. This took the poet back again in memory to conversations thirty years past: "Emerson said when we were out together in New York and Boston—said it more than once: 'I envy you your capacity for being at home with anybody in any crowd.' Then he asked me on another occasion: 'Don't you fear now and then that your freedom, your ease, your nonchalance, with men may be misunderstood?' I asked him: 'Do you misunderstand it?' He put his hand on my arm and said: 'No: I see it for what it is: it is beautiful.' Then I said to him: 'Misunderstood? Yes: it will be misunderstood. But what is there I do that is not misunderstood?' He smiled in his sweet gentle way and murmured: 'True! true!' "

Two Quakers Together

I loved Emerson for his personality and I always felt that he loved me for something I brought him from the rush of the big cities and the mass of men. We used to walk together, dine together, argue, even, in a sort of a way, though neither of one of us was much of an arguer. We were not much for repartee or sallies or what people ordinarily call humor, but we got along together beautifully—the atmosphere was always sweet, I don't mind saying it, both on Emerson's side and mine: we had no friction—there was no kind of fight in us for each other—we were like two Quakers together.

Never an Egotist . . . Almost

Curiously, too, Emerson enjoyed most repeating those stories which told against himself—took off his edge—his own edge: he had a great dread of being egotistic—had a horror of it, if I may say so: a horror—a shrinking from the suspicious of a show of it: indeed, he had a fear of egotism that was almost—who knows, quite?—an egotism itself.

Phenomenal Font of Sweetness

As a man, a companion, an intimate, he was impeccable—a character of essences, elements—no man ever lived more so: a certain stateliness, dignity, reserve—of course he had it—but none too much—not more than was required. Who more, who ever so much as, Emerson, demanded, was entitled to, a reserve? *Every* man needs it. . . . He was not hail-fellow in the sense of the good general, the old sailor—the sailor put in earliest years before the mast—roughing it in that line a life through—but he was a man, every inch of him—as I may say it again, using my old story—he was a font of type—a genuine letter—only set into a new text. The wonder is, considering all, that he maintained his phenomenal sweetness.

Liquid

Emerson was not inclined to talk to strangers—not that he was without grace—indeed, he had irresistible grace—but that he would not unbosom himself easily. That was his characteristic: I noted it in him in his intercourse with others. With me he was always quite free, easy, liquid—his own free self, it appeared to me at all times.

Unbrawny

There were times when the good Emerson shrunk back from brawn, from the brutes, from realistic fellows.

A Clean Face

One day Traubel finds a photograph of Emerson on the floor: "I picked it up a dozen times and put it on the table here but it always seems to get back to the floor. It is a noble little bit of portraiture—shows Emerson at his best: radiant, clean, with that far-in-the-future look which seemed to possess him in the best hours. Emerson's face always seemed to me so clean—as if God had just washed it off. When you looked at Emerson it never occurred to you that there could be any villainies in the world."

Not Priggified

[Emerson was] not what you would call a funny man: he was something better than that: he would not cut up—make a great noise: but for cheer, quiet sweet cheer—good humor, a habit of pouring oil on waters—I have never known his equal. Emerson was in no sense priggified—solemnfied.

Bookish

I did think Thoreau and Emerson, both of them, years ago, in the Brooklyn days, were a little bookish in their expression of love.

Always for Poise

Emerson was always for poise, poise . . . it's the sort of thing which in a little man would damn his soul but which in a man of Emerson's sufficient great size is only a foible smiled over and easily forgotten.

Peculiarly Tremendous

Emerson lived according to his lights—not according to libraries, books, literature, the traditions: he was unostentatiously loyal: no collegian, overdone with culture: so gifted, so peculiarly tremendous, that, if I may say so, knowing too much did not, as it so often does with the scholar, hurt him.

Ideal

Emerson's personality was the most nearly perfect I ever came in contact with—perhaps the most nearly ideal the world has ever known.

Don't-care-a-damn-ness

I think almost all of the fellows—literary fellows (poets, writers)—except Emerson—are led off, astray, into the field of despair—led off by a tendency of the moment. Emerson is exceptional—I think Emerson inevitably begets a healthy don't-care-a-damn-ness.

Thin Blood

But take Emerson, now—Emerson: some ways rather of thin blood. . . . But I hate to allow anything that qualifies Emerson.

A few months later, this point was reiterated: "I love Emerson—I do not need to say that—but he was somewhat thin on the physiological side."

"Was it your impression that Emerson was less physical than yourself?" Traubel asks. Whitman was quiet for a minute, then said, "Yes, he was less physical: but he did not hesitate to say he regretted that as a defect in himself."

Couldn't Say Damn

Traubel goaded Whitman about there being "no Rabelaisian passages" in his dealings with Emerson, and the poet had to agree: "Emerson couldn't say damn." Did Walt mean that literally? "Yes—literally: it amounts to that: it was a defect in his education. . . . In general I used to wish his perfect circle had a dent somewhere: but he was wonderful with all his excellence: he put on no sanctified airs."

Passive

The essential Emerson was there to the last, but his faculty was passive—it no longer asserted itself.

Beware the -Ism

I always insist that Emersonism, legitimately followed out, always ends in weakness—takes all color out of life. Not that this could be said of Emerson himself, because, as I point out—as is plain to me—Emerson supplies his own antidote—teaches his own destruction—if seen at his best. Besides, it is more to know the actual Emerson—the corporeal, physiological Emerson—to come in contact with him, his voice, face, manner—for I believe Emerson was greater by far than his books.

On Thoreau and Whitman

[Emerson] said to me (speaking of Thoreau) that, "strange as it may seem, Henry being an outdoor man (he called him Henry)—he shrinks from some formidable things in you—in your book, in your personality—over which I rejoice!" And he said this too: "I don't say it by way of flattery at all—I would as readily say it to any man like you who had not written a book—but I say that meeting you is a peculiar refreshment to me—puts something needed into my tissue which I do not seem to get in my own established environment." Questioned by Traubel, Whitman said he thought some of these sentiments were conveyed on the famous walk on Boston's Common, some during a talk at Astor House in New York.

Not Honeyfugled

I except Emerson from the catalogue of honeyfugled old men . . . that is, men lionized and deferred to in their old age.

But Not the Missus (and Daughter)

I, of course knew nothing of Emerson's first wife, but the second I knew—met—and to me she was a hideous unlikely woman. How Emerson could ever have got spliced to her beats my explanation.

When Walt called Emerson's daughter, Ellen, "the old hag," Horace demurred. Walt reiterated: "She is a nasty old hag—a Puritan gone to seed." When Horace remarks on her reputation as Emerson's "right hand helper," Walt shook his head, "Not so: interferer."

"Ellen hates me like the devil—always did." The next day Whitman elaborated on the reason for such uncharacteristic ferocity: "Ellen? Oh! that hag! She is a hag! That guardian, watcher—afraid the great old man would make a mistake, commit some error! She is repulsive to me beyond utterance. . . . [N]either of them—neither mother nor daughter—was our woman at all."

Think of Emerson—the great, the free, the pure—united in marriage to a conventional woman: yes, a conventional woman and worse, a fanatically conventional woman.

The Damned Shirtsleeve Lie

In the summer of 1890 a book called *Talks with Emerson* was published by Charles Woodbury; its recounting of the story of Whitman being invited to dine with Emerson at the Astor House in New York and appearing without his coat caused a sustained tizzy at Mickle Street: "It is all a lie—an entire lie—and it is not the first edition of the same lie, either. I have got the character, and this only repeats and repeats. He gives it as though it was from Emerson himself, but if Emerson remembered, he would not have said it. The worst lies, as I have said, are those with just a shred of truth—enough truth simply to get the ear. . . . They must rub it in, or they would not be happy. You see—the story of the shirt is quite circumstantial—it has been told before—it is long put upon me and will stick—but they are all lies—all stories of the kind. It is like Lincoln and the smutty stories—time was, when a fellow got a particularly dirty story, he would say, I've heard a good one on Lincoln—listen—and all would crop up ears and Lincoln would be pilloried again." Whitman *did* give plenty of "circumstance" for such a story, having made his 1855 debut with an engraving of himself facing the (nameless) title page of *Leaves* that showed him in shockingly coatless dishabille.

Acutest Brain

Emerson had the [a]cutest, justest, brain of all our world: saw everything, literally everything, in right perspective—things personal, things general.

Something Awry

In 1863 Emerson wrote Whitman a letter of recommendation for employment in the office of Secretary of State William Seward. Whitman never made use of the letter; Traubel asked why: "For a number of reasons, probably—for one, I did not altogether like it . . . there seemed something awry, not just as I felt for the best." Traubel reproduces the letter in full, and one can guess which parts did not sit well with the poet: "he is known to me as a man of strong original genius, combining, with marked eccentricities, great powers & valuable traits of character . . ." and "his writings are in certain points open to criticism. . . ." A newly discovered letter, published in the *Walt Whitman Quarterly Review* (summer–fall 2000), reveals Whitman's hope to receive a cushy government sinecure through an Emerson recommendation, the better to focus on his own writing. On January 16, 1863, he wrote to his brother Jeff, "my general idea was (and is) to make application to Chase and Seward for some berth on literary grounds, not political ones."

Oxygenated Men and Women: Walt's Pantheon

In his speech at Whitman's interment, Tom Harned said, "A predominant trait of his character was gratitude" and then recalled the poet saying, "Don't forget to say thanks, thanks, thanks." In Mickle Street, Whitman often broke into eloquent hurrahs praising those who aided him in his daily life and, most specially, those who performed acts of partisanship on behalf of Leaves of Grass. He also had strong personal opinions about the likeable traits of character in his fellow humans—and in public figures of the day. Here are some of his more striking effusions. Between their lines, not surprisingly, emerges a portrait of the man and poet Whitman thought himself to be.

Salient Fellers

I like salient men—the men of elements—oxygenated men: the fellers who come and go like storms come and go: who grow up out of honest roots: not the titillated gentlemen of boudoir amours and parlor fripperies.

Note: Whitman had William O'Connor particularly in mind when he said this.

Backbone Men

We can't get on with a world of masters: we want men—a world of men: backbone men—the workers, the doers, the humbles.

Originals

I have had wonderful good luck anyhow in my life to have met a number of . . . originals—not men of usual build, of usual ways, but men inherently set apart, a world each for himself.

Radical Preference

Although my philosophy includes conservatives, everything else being equal I prefer the radicals as men and companions.

Grand Soul: Frances Wright

"She was more than beautiful: she was grand! It was not feature simply but soul—soul. There was a majesty about her. . . . There were people who objected to Fanny Wright as radical and all that. She was

sweeter, nobler, grander—multiplied by twenty—than all who tra-
duced her. . . . I have never felt so glowingly towards any other woman
. . . she possessed herself of my body and soul." Whitman counted
the militant and eloquent social activist Frances Wright (1795–1852)
among the great "unpopulars," like Tom Paine and Elias Hicks.

Eloquentest Woman: Delia Bacon

The sweetest, eloquentest, grandest woman, I think, that America has
so far produced—a woman rare among women, rare among the rare.
Romanesque, beautiful, not after the ideals of the fashion plates, but after Greek ideals. A nature sweet, noble, sure, attracting when encountered in the right way. No, I never met her, but somehow feel that I have
known her, nevertheless, known her better, perhaps, than if meeting
her—coming upon her, as it is understood—that breaker of charms too
often—personally. . . . Of all women in America so far she stands alone,
in advance. Greater than Margaret Fuller—a larger type.

Note: Delia Salter Bacon (1811–59), Ohio-born but well traveled, became a fervent
Emersonian, a novelist, and, most important, a spellbinding public speaker on
women's rights and antislavery. She also authored a book arguing Sir Francis Bacon's
authorship of the Shakespeare plays.

A Real Critter: Joaquin Miller

Big, wholesome, does things his own way, has lived in the open, stands
alone—is a real critter: I rate him way up.

Note: Joaquin Miller (a pseudonym: his real name was Cincinnatus Hiner Miller
[1837–1913]) was a minor poet with whom Whitman struck a happy acquaintance,
though their poetic styles were utterly distinct; most of Miller's verse was composed in
tetrameter.

Brave Woman: Julia Ward Howe

When Traubel told Whitman he was going to hear Julia Ward Howe
speak, Whitman made this request: "If you come within her radius, tell
her, for me, I wish her well of all her years. I do not know much about
her, but she has been a brave woman—I honor her. Don't go out of your
road—but if a place occurs for the right word, put it in—put it in. Everything consists in the use of the right word."

Direct Genius: General Phil Sheridan

He was in essentials a genius: he had almost phenomenal directness,
and genius is almost a hundred per cent directness—nothing more. He
was characterized by a rough candor which always meant what it appeared to mean. Of all the major men developed by the War he was closest to the top.

Noble Containing Eye: Ernestine Rose

Talk of the November 1890 election leads Whitman to a derisive comment about politicians that reminds him of a favorite feminist orator:

"Did these fellows think the people were all blocks of wood or boulders of stone? That was an expression of Ernestine Rose. You have heard of her? Oh! She was a splendid woman: big, richly gifted, brave, expansive—in body a poor sickly thing, a strong breath would blow her away—but with a head full of brains—the amplitude of a Webster. . . . I can see the flash of her eye now—the noble containing eye!"

Note: Polish born and of Jewish ancestry, Rose was closely associated with Susan B. Anthony and lectured across the country for two decades.

Reborn by War: Edwin Stanton

Stanton was another vehement figure there [in Civil War Washington, when Edwin Stanton was secretary of war]: he had a temper—was touchy, testy, yet also wonderfully patriotic, courageous, far-seeing: was the best sort of a man at bottom: had been a Democrat—saw trouble coming: was alert, simple-minded: when the shock came was reborn, kindled, into higher, highest interpretations, resolutions: dropped his old partial self away wholly and entirely without a murmur.

Living the Virtues: Edward Carpenter

He is a man who shares the view of Jesus, of Bacon—who says don't let us talk of faith any longer—let us *do* something. Any man can jabber, tell a story—any fluent-tonguey man can do that. But the man who can live the virtues, needs no courier, announcers—*is* the fact that other men only dream of—he is the man we want—the man to *absorb* morality.

Note: Edward Carpenter (1844–1929), who lived openly with his working-class male lover, published widely on a variety of reforming topics. He came to the United States twice, in 1877 and 1884, mainly to visit his idol, Whitman. In 1906 he published his reminiscences of these visits as *Days with Walt Whitman*. Among his titles are *Towards Democracy* (1905) and an exploration of homosexuality, *The Intermediate Sex* (1908).

Giuseppe Mazzini

Mazzini was the greatest of them all down there in Italy: infinitely the greatest: went deepest—was biggest around.

Note: Giuseppe Mazzini (1805–72) was an eminent Italian revolutionary patriot.

Frans Hals

Art now is all made with reference to social conventions—the notions, instincts, of parlors, gentlemen, ladies. It does not come direct from nature, but through *media*: receptions, carpets, elegant, showy outsideness. And Hals, none of these old fellas (broad as breadth) could have worked, done, what they did, from such inspirations, background. . . . What careless power! How this breathes! How the blood pulses in this fellow: I can see the man, see him walk, sit, joke, drink, live his natural daily life.

Note: Whitman was responding to Hals's *Portrait of a Young Man* in *Harper's Bazaar*.

Ulysses S. Grant
HOMELY GENIUS

The real military figure of the war ... was Grant, whose homely manners, dislike for military frippery—for every form of ostentation, in war and peace—amounted to genius.

HIS WAY

There was Grant—see how he went about his work, defied the rules, played the game his own way—did all the things the best generals told him he should not do—and won out!

SEVERE SIMPLICITY

Grant was the typical Western man: the plainest, the most efficient: was the least imposed upon by appearances, was most impressive in the severe simplicity of his flannel shirt and utter disregard for formal military etiquette.

NO SHOW

Grant hated show—liked to leave things unsaid, undone—liked to defy convention by going a simple way, his own.

AMERICAN

We have had no one from the keel up so American as Grant.

Henry David Thoreau
ELUSIVE BUT LAWLESS . . .

My prejudices, if I may call them that, are all with Emerson: but Thoreau was a surprising fellow—he is not easily grasped—is elusive: yet he is one of the native forces—stands for a fact, a movement, an upheaval: Thoreau belongs to America, to the transcendental, to the protesters: then he is an outdoor man: all outdoor men everything else being equal appeal to me. . . . One thing about Thoreau keeps him very near to me: I refer to his lawlessness—his dissent—his going his own absolute road let hell blaze all it chooses.

. . . ALSO SUPERCILIOUS

Months earlier Whitman delivered this devastating précis: "Thoreau's great fault was disdain—disdain for men (for Tom, Dick and Harry): inability to appreciate the average life—even the exceptional life: it seemed to me a want of imagination. He couldn't put his life into any other life—realize why one man was so and another man was not so: was impatient with other people on the street and so forth. We had a hot discussion about it—it was a bitter difference: it was rather a surprise to me to meet in Thoreau such a very aggravated case of superciliousness."

NOT ACCOMMODATED

Henry was not all for me—he had his reservations: he held back some: he accepted me—my book—as on the whole something to be reckoned with: he allowed that I was formidable: said so to me much in that way: over in Brooklyn: why, that very first visit: "Whitman, do you have any idea that you are rather bigger and outside the average—may perhaps have immense significance?" That's what he said: I did not answer. He also said: "There is much in you to which I cannot accommodate myself: the defect may be mine: but the objections are there."

DISDAINFUL

Later, on Horace's expressing an interest in the writer, Whitman tried to give away a Thoreau volume—permanently: "I suppose you would be seized by it: it is a seizable book. Keep it as long as you choose— forever if you choose. I don't believe *I* shall ever be moved to read it again. . . . I liked Thoreau very much: yet there was something in him, as in his books—a superciliousness, a disdain, of civilization—which was extremely offensive to me."

John Boyle O'Reilly
ALIVE WITH INDIGNATION

If ever a fighter lived, Boyle O'Reilly is that fighter: he writes me fiery letters, he tells me fiery stories. . . . I shall never forget the first time he spoke to me about his prison life. He was all alive with the most vivid indignation—he was a great storm out somewhere, a great sea pushing up against the shore.

Note: The famed Irish writer (1844–90) had been transported to Australia, escaped, and eventually made his way to Boston.

FIERY

Boyle's charm came out of his tremendous fiery personality: he had lived through tremendous experiences. . . . I had wonderful talks with him there in Boston when I was doing the *Leaves*: he came every day. Oh! he was not the typical Irishman: rather, Spanish: poetic, ardent.

SPONTANEITY INNATE

"What we need in art, in literature, are more fellows like O'Reilly— spontaneity innate—the absolute frank contact with life on all its sides." This was one of several eulogies pronounced by Walt shortly after O'Reilly died in 1890 after taking an overdose of his ailing wife's chloral to cure a fit of insomnia.

Anne Gilchrist
OPEN-EYED DREAMER

She was not a blind dreamer—a chaser of fancies: she was concrete— spiritually concrete.

Note: There is a rich irony in this comment on the gallant Englishwoman, for she had become enamored of Whitman through his poetry and a personal correspondence and eventually arrived in Philadelphia for a several-year siege that finally proved unsuccessful, though a very close friendship was forged. Gilchrist (1828–85) returned to England and maintained a cordial correspondence with Whitman until she died. Her son Herbert, a painter, became one of the poet's friends.

HIGH ENTHUSIAST

She was strangely different from the average: entirely herself: as simple as nature: true, honest: beautiful as a tree is tall, leafy, rich, full, free— *is* a tree. Yet, free as she was by nature, bound by no conventionalisms, she was the most courageous of women; more than queenly: of high aspect in the best sense. . . . She had the largest charity, the sweetest, fondest optimism. But however able to resent she was not able to be discourteous: she could resent but she resented nobly. . . . She was a radical of radicals: enjoyed all sorts of high enthusiasms: was exquisitely sensitized: belonged to the times yet to come: her vision went on and on.

MIRACLE ON A LARGE PLAN

She was a wonderful woman—a sort of human miracle to me: built on a large plan—delicate, too: oh! so profoundly considerate, intuitional, knowing: I guess I should not talk about her: not even to you, maybe: my emotion gets the better of me. . . . Her taking off—Mrs. Gilchrist's death—was a great shock to me: I have never quite got over it: she was near to me: she was subtle: her grasp on my work was tremendous.

WOMAN JUSTIFIED

Mrs. Gilchrist was a great woman—a greater woman than she is generally known to be—a woman who, I am fond of saying, goes the whole distance of justifying woman.

DON'T-CARE-A-DAMN-ATIVENESS

Mrs. Gilchrist, with her supreme cultivation, was gifted in a rare degree with a necessary don't-care-a-damn-ativeness. In fact, this was so marked in her that it was often thought she was inviting destruction.

ACUTEST OF ALL

In most respects [Gilchrist was] the finest, [a]cutest most womanly woman I have ever known.

Scoundrel Time

As we have seen, Whitman was proud of having been "in the old times" capable of "saying something very snubbing to a fellow I thought impudent." The reader of his conversations with Traubel finds that even in his last years Whitman still had the knack for the squelch and the put-down when impertinents and fools crossed the public stage—or appeared on his doorstep.

Embrace the Scamps, Too

Besides, we must recollect, man is such a scamp, such a wickedee—so essentially an ignoram that it is hard often to stand him—yet it is but right that the scamp should be represented. We must conclude that as long as there are Presbyterians, Presbyterians ought to be.

Journalistic Conceit

A typical arrogant conceited journalist is one of the hardest scoundrels of all to deal with.

A Presidential Shit-ass

Of all documents ever issued from the Presidential office I consider that inaugural address the other day the most gassy, diffused: if I were called on to give [Benjamin] Harrison a name I should call him the gas President: it seems to me the whole affair is nothing but gas—gas ever more gassy . . . it's just such a temperance pissy thing. . . .

"It is the bitterest sarcasm possible on the Harrison administration—Harrison the scalawag who was and is. . . . But it is of a piece with Harrison—the shit-ass! God damn 'im!—and no more than need have been expected." Whitman also called Harrison "a great phu-phu," whatever that might be. The abrupt dismissal of the postmaster of New York, a political appointee, is what set Whitman off here.

I think Harrison is the smallest potato in the heap—that he will go down in history so regarded. I think him mainly a gas bag.

To me, the most insignificant—perhaps the only really insignificant man—in the long line of our Presidents. Let me predict this—that as long as Harrison remains in office, the aura of the Presidency will give him prominence—be his savior—but after that—oh! what will be his oblivion—utter!

When Harrison defeated Grover Cleveland in 1888, Tom Harned boasted that he was "good for eight years now." Whitman demurred: "Let us not be too quick to dismiss Cleveland: he will be heard from again." And, indeed, four years later, just after Whitman died, Cleveland was reelected. Whitman had kind words for few presidents (other than Lincoln); see his withering short poem "To a President," written when James Buchanan was the incumbent. Harrison, president throughout most of the *With Walt Whitman* years, was a regular punching bag at Mickle Street. Here is one small suggestion why Walt might have sided with Cleveland: "I am told he has read *Leaves of Grass*—read it to some purpose."

Bed-buggiest Man

That whelp Charlie Heyde [husband of Whitman's favorite sister, Hannah] . . . is a skunk—a bug. . . . He has led my sister hell's own life: he has done nothing for her—never: has not only not supported her but is the main cause of her nervous breakdowns. He is a leech: is always getting at us: himself gets most of the money my sister has from us—squanders it on himself: still leaves her sick, poor, uncared for. . . . he is the bed-buggiest man on the earth: he is almost the only man alive who can make me mad: a mere thought of him, an allusion, the least word, riles me.

He is not an ordinary *sponge*—I could figure that—he is a sneaking canting scoundrel, making a trade of my weakness—knowing the spot where I am sore—my love for my sister—ramming his knife in *there*! Note: Still, Whitman wrote his sister regularly until the end (his last letter was to her), always including one or two dollars. Both Hannah and her husband had mental problems; in 1892, the year of Whitman's death, he was committed to Vermont State Hospital.

Rottenest Secretary in High Place

I think [Salmon P.] Chase was the rottenest man in high place at that time [during the Civil War]—doing a vast deal of good, too, but capable of damnable meannesses, past the ability of most even mean men. The timber in him was rotten, or gone. He was easily, early, stung with that respectability bee. . . . A man like Chase could not be expected to penetrate Lincoln—to know the first letter of the alphabet. Chase always constituted himself schoolmaster—as [James] Harlan did— yes, as many men do, in official as in other history. He was fair to look at, serene, but in the deeper moral intentions, in the fundamentals, in bottom principles—he was vacant—did not grasp the situation— America.

Note: This uncharacteristically elaborate ad hominem attack can be explained: Chase was Lincoln's secretary of the treasury from 1861 to 1864 (and had declined to hire Whitman, who came with a letter of recommendation from Emerson); from 1864 to 1873 he was Chief Justice of the Supreme Court. Harlan, secretary of the interior, dismissed Whitman from his office in 1865 (Whitman was hired the next day by the attorney general). Earlier, Whitman called Chase "a trivial, damnable man—a dangerous, handsome man."

Temperance Bigots

Those temperance fellows who thought rum was accountable for all the woes of man—who even dignified this by thinking it a *principle*. . . . A temperance man, so-called—that is, a bigot.

Vacuous Agnes Repplier

Take that Repplier woman, for instance: she's one of them ["dull critics"]: she, with her shining emptiness—with her smart vacuums.

Note: Agnes Repplier (1855-1950) was a prolific essayist for magazines, notably the *Atlantic Monthly* beginning in 1886, and the author of nearly two dozen books. She was everything Walt was inclined to dislike: sophisticated, witty, and comfortable in high-toned literary circles.

Brazen Reporters

It is well enough known to us, so to say it, on the inside that the average reporter (of course there are exceptions) . . . has no notion—no more intention—towards veracity than if veracity was never called for. The lyingness of the news is most astonishing—brazen.

So Many Monkeys: Reviewers

Most of these book reviews so-called are echoes of echoes: the fellows don't seem to have a bit of originality: they run after each other like sheep: one says a thing: then the other says a thing: then they chorus together—the whole kit and crew: they say one, two, three "damn so and so": they say four, five, six "save so and so": that's the way they proceed: like so many monkeys on the limb of a tree chattering in concert. . . . Emerson was quite vigorous in talking about the critics—talking with me: he said: "I seem to mystify them—rather mystify than antagonize them": which I guess was true. I seem to make them mad—rile them: I mystify them, too, but they don't know it: they only know I am vile, indecent, perverted, adulterous.

Toploftical Officers

He [General George Corse] was an army officer with a lot of toploftical ideas—ideas such as military men are apt to get: glory, spreadeagle, show, gilt, bluster—a splurgey sort of fellow.

The Snarling Press

"It seems to me that in the whole range of journals pretending to anything, the [*Philadelphia*] *Press* is the greatest mess—gives most evidence of being shovelled together. It is made up as if the head man at the eleventh [hour?] (or 50th minute) had come in and said: 'Here boys, all get your shovels, set to work, shovel in and shovel out—now we must get the paper up!'" But Whitman had to confess, "And yet somehow I read the *Press*—read it straight along—probably because there is nothing else to do while it is here." A few days later he referred to the *Press's* "utterly indescribably witless way."

Take the *Press* . . . its frightful sourness—its disposition to snarl like a small dog, to make complaint, to be small whatever the occasion.

Scholar Swells

His letter is friendly but he has the excessive caution of the university man. The scholar swells rarely—I may say never—let themselves go.

I must seem like a comical, a sort of circus, genius to men of the severe scholarly type. I am too different to be included in their perspective.

When Traubel tells Whitman he worked for four years in a printer's shop, Whitman naturally applauds, this being his own employment history: "Good! good! that's better than so many years at the university: there is an indispensable something gathered from such an experience: it lasts out life. After all the best things escape, skip, the universities."

A Damn Fool Drama Critic

William Winter . . . what an arrant damned fool he is—a little fellow in all ways: must measure everything with a tape: knows nothing beyond traditions, customs, habits, stage inventions. If he had lived at the time of Garrick—Garrick was the first to break through the old bonds—he would have insisted that Garrick should play Hamlet wearing small clothes and a periwig, as it had once to be played. That was the tradition: a tradition is everything. Winter always calls for the rules.

That Titivated Man Olmsted

In N.Y. and Brooklyn [Frederick Law] Olmsted was the famous man . . . but I don't think much of him—don't think he knows much. With him titivation was the word: titivate things. I can give you an instance: it will mark the man. You know Prospect Park in Brooklyn: it is a grand hill—a gradual hill, taking three or four miles to complete the ascent. This man Olmsted had been commissioned to spend two hundred thousand dollars to start with: and what do you think he did? of all things the most absurd, ridiculous, fantastic: he build an artificial hill there! My brother [Jeff] was a young engineer: was very much worked up about it: indignant: and so was I: though I took that thing, as I take most things, more calmly.

Note: Among the landscape architect's most significant legacies were Central Park, Riverside Park, and Prospect Park. The word "titivate" means "to add decorations to, spruce up" (possibly from "tidy" and "cultivate"—two concepts abhorrent to Whitman).

Ecclesiastic

Traubel remarks in one day's entry that "W. has a rather general objection to the clergy." That is putting it very mildly. Peter Doyle recalled a bit more vividly of his years with Walt in Washington, D.C., that he "never went to church—didn't like form, ceremonies—didn't seem to favor preachers at all." As one might gather, for instance, from Whitman's withering late poem "The Rounded Catalogue Divine Complete," bourgeois religious piety and moralizing were anathema to the poet. Then there are some famous lines from the early Leaves *editions: "logic and sermons never convince" and "Let the physician and priest go home" and "Allons . . . O bat-eyed and materialistic priests," for example. The "prayer and Jesus business," Whitman said, was "overdone," and whenever the topic arose in the privacy of Mickle Street, ecclesiastical fur was guaranteed to fly in words he would never have dared to utter in public.*

Walt or Jesus?

Traubel found Whitman "much amused" one day by a sixteen-page pamphlet of verse titled "To Walt Whitman (America's Great Poet)" he had just received. It was, he said, "by a woman who evidently thinks I am in danger and wants to save me from hell fire. There are eleven poems in the book preceded by a Prologue, all directed to show that the religion of Jesus is superior to the religion of Walt Whitman. I always thought they came to about the same thing, but this woman evidently thinks they do not. I ought to be saved in the end. I should say fifty or a hundred people are busy all the time trying to convert Walt Whitman from *Leaves of Grass*."

Fair Deal

The church has not bothered me—I do not bother the church: that is a clean cut bargain.

Priests and Ministers

Traubel tells Whitman that "some had wondered why he had not called in the priests when he was so sick." "Oh hell!" Whitman exclaimed.

233

I never object to a man—any kind of man—but I object to a priest—any kind of a priest. The instant a priest becomes a man I am on his side—no longer oppose him.

I often get mad at the ministers—they are almost the only people I do get mad at—yet they, too have their reasons for being. If a man will once consent to be a minister he must expect ruin.

Scientists are different from the damned Methodistic snifflers, who know *everything.*

What an infernal cabbage-head that man [the Reverend Thomas] Talmage is! I look over his sermons in the papers. They are the vilest nonsense, as stupid rags, dishwater, as any man would dare to get off. . . . I heard he had spoken of George Eliot as an adulteress. It is horrible, horrible—and I say, to hell with his lies, filth, arrogance! What was George Eliot if not *clean?* And this man, *unclean*—yes, full of poison, venom, hate.

Horace notes that William Dean Howells addresses Walt as "Doctor," then notes it is "better than being addressed as I have been, as 'Reverend.' " Walt cried out, "A *thousand* times better. How horrible, horrible!"

Preachery

One day a friend named Tom brought a preacher with him: "A clever fellow but preachery all over, like a man in a lather. It did my eyes good to look away from him towards Tom—Tom, who is a normal man, gruff, honest, direct, simple, strong."

Damn the preachers! . . . the smooth-faced, self-satisfied preachers.

I am not willing to admit that we have further serious use for the old style authoritative preacher.

The damnable psalming, praying, deaconizing of our day is made too much the liberal cover of all sorts of sins, iniquities.

Unitarian

Tom Harned drags Walt to a Unitarian service, and Horace asks afterward how he liked the sermon: "Not a bit: all preaching is a weariness to me—[the Rev.] Corning's as much as any other's. . . . Corning is all right—the man Corning: I can like him, I do like him: but the Corning in the pulpit last night tried my corns. I am always impatient of the churches—they are not God's own—they rather fly in the face of the real providences."

Christian Persecutors

Commenting on the Y.M.C.A., a few years earlier, refusing him the use of a hall for a lecture on Elias Hicks because Hicks did not believe in atonement, Whitman noted, "On the face of it that seems like bigotry: it may be bigotry, but it is also consistency. I do not blame them. Such stuff as now passes for Christianity is liable to lead a man into any extreme of persecution—honestly lead him. I am against the whole business. I really think the Y.M.C.A. objection was not to Hicks but to me."

Sermon on Empty Pews

Whitman, amused to learn of a conference of preachers on why so many pews were empty, put his oar in on the subject: "The simple truth is: from time immemorial theology has built itself upon mythology—and now the time has come when that mythology can no longer be believed—believed by any one of any account. We need a reconstruction—*are having* a reconstruction in fact—of theology. . . . I have heard it said that the church and genius are divorced—the church and the masses, too—and when we ask why, the preacher will say from pride in the genius, stupidity in the others—that contrarity is at fault whatever. Damn the preachers! what do they know or care to know? The churches have constructed a god of moral goodness—wholly, solely moral goodness—and that is its weakness. . . . According to such a standard of moral goodness—the standard of the churches—probably nine-tenths of the universe is depraved—probably nine-tenths denied a right in the scheme of things—which is ridiculous, outright. . . . What can science have to do with such a spectre as the present church? All their methods are opposed—must be opposed—utterly opposed: for one means restriction, the other freedom: the church—ill-adjustment, science—harmony."

Saints

I believe in saints if they're far enough off.

Leaves: *Crammed Full of Faith*

One day Whitman received a postcard from Paris with the advice to pray to Saints Peter and Paul for cure, study up on Lourdes, and arrange for votive masses. He tells Traubel he does not "make light of such messages—indeed, they have a profound place in my consideration. Of course I haven't a particle of faith in Lourdes—in faith cures—bones of saints, such things—not a shred of it." Then he adds, "People often speak of the *Leaves* as wanting in religion, but that is not my view of the book—and I ought to know. I think the *Leaves* the most religious book among books: crammed full of faith. What would the *Leaves* be without faith? An empty vessel: faith is its very substance, balance—its one article of assent—its one item of assurance."

Ex Cathedral

The wisdom of America—its spinal thought, deed—says *no* to Catholicism, the priests—casts them back, back, back into the past, into dead history—not willing longer to have their stupid superstitions, slavery.

Note: Traubel records this comment by Bucke: "Did you ever notice how Catholics look with holy horror on LG—look on it as a visitor from the pit."

Sermonizing

The world is through with sermonizing—with the necessity for it: the distinctly preacher ages are nearly gone. I am not sorry.

We might as well think of curing people of the measles, the smallpox, what not, by mere sermonizings, yawpings, as of saving their souls by such tactics. . . . No amount of formal, salaried petitioning of God will serve to work out the result aimed for.

No Church

I see no use for the church: it lags superfluous on the stage.

For the church as an institution I have the profoundest contempt.

Whitman recalled of his own churchgoing that he "went oftenest in my earlier life—gradually dropped off altogether: today a church is a sort of offense to me."

Religious Copulation

I think [Emanuel] Swedenborg was right when he said there was a close connection—a very close connection—between the state we call religious ecstacy and the desire to copulate. I find Swedenborg confirmed in all my experience. It is a peculiar discovery.

Damnable

. . . the damnable Methodistic Presbyterianistic god . . .

The Earth Struggle

It is best we should not know too definitely what is to come: the important thing to us now is the life here—the people here: yes, that's the important immediate thing: the earth struggle—our effort, out task here, to build up the human social body into finer results. . . . the beyond: we are not called upon to bother about it . . . our responsibilities are on the earth.

The Miracle Dogma Business

The whole miracle dogma business has been swung as a club over the head of the world: it has been a weapon flourished by the tyrannical dynasties of the old world—dynasties murderous, reeking, unscrupulous, barbarous: they have always tried to justify their crimes by an assumed divine grant of some sort.

$2 + 2 = 5$

I anticipate the day when some wise man will start out to argue that two and two are not four but five or something else: history proving that two and two couldn't be four: and probability, too: yes, more than that, the wise man will prove it out of his own consciousness—prove it for somebody—for a few: they will believe in him—a body of disciples will believe: then, presto! you have a new religion!

.

Music, Opera, and Marietta

Whitman's whereabouts and activities during the several years immediately preceding the astonishing appearance of the first Leaves of Grass *in 1855 are unknown, though he did say in a thumbnail autobiography penned in 1888 that he was involved in "building houses and selling them." But Whitman makes it abundantly clear, as seen previously among his comments on* Leaves, *that at this time he was deeply and actively devoted to opera—and to one fabulous singer in particular, the Italian contralto Marietta Alboni.* Leaves, *Whitman insisted, was impregnated with his love of opera, as its vocabulary of more than two hundred musical terms and numerous "Songs" suggest. For Bucke's 1883 biography of Whitman, the poet penned this line for inclusion in the text, referring to himself in the third person: "It has already been told how, during the gestation of the poems, the author was saturated for years with the rendering, by the best vocalists and performers, of the best operas and oratorios." See, in particular, the passage in the twenty-sixth section of "Song of Myself" that begins, "I hear the chorus, it is the grand opera, / Ah this indeed is music—this suits me." Emerson wrote of music that it "takes us out of the actual and whispers to us dim secrets that startle our wonder as to who we are and for what, whence and whereto." Music had precisely this effect on Whitman, and his late reminiscences and remarks on music throw further light on America's preeminent poet-singer.*

Susceptible

I am particularly susceptible to voices: voices of range, magnetism: mellow, persuading voices.

Bass

Oh! the true bass is the most precious of all voices because the rarest of all. I have known so many yet so few—so few with the full equipment—one or two (not more than two) in all my experience.

Wagner

So many of my friends say Wagner is *Leaves of Grass* done into music that I begin to suspect there must be something to it. . . . I was never wholly convinced—there was always a remaining question. I have got rather off the field—the Wagner opera has had its vogue only in these later years since I got out of the way of going to the theater.

It's one of my regrets that the Wagner operas have never come my way—that I for my own part have not found it possible to indulge in them. I am quite well aware that they are my operas—belong to *Leaves of Grass*, to me, as we belong to them: they are an unmistakable entity in our treasure-box.

Traubel observes to Whitman that Wagner "has done for music what you have done for poetry: freed it, disclosed its unity with life, set aside the harassing traditions," and Walt responds: "no doubt Wagner is our man—the man for us. . . . Yes, I can conceive why you should see it so— why you should say that."

Late Bloomers

Traubel remarked to Whitman, "The women who sing often mellow up at 50, losing brilliancy, but gaining in power to pierce men and hold them." Whitman agreed: "That is so, that is truly so—I could quote cases to fit it."

Great Voice—but a Cod-fish

One day a friend, Ben Starr, visited and happened to recall the evening long ago when he and Walt heard the tenor Pasquale Brignoli sing for the first time: "the opera was *Martha*: Brignoli sang an aria which carried you away: you listened to it with your neck craned forward, drinking it in—dead, buried, and resurrected till the last: then you sank back in your seat exclaiming: 'Lord! the voice of an angel and the manners of a cod-fish!'" When Traubel asked if this reminiscence was accurate, Whitman laughed and said, "It does sound plausible." But a few minutes later he drew back: "But the fish part is very fish: I am not inclined to accept it. . . . I was a great lover of Brignoli: knew him, too, personally: I always stood up for him. These things, like that of the fish, were often said of him by others. I doubt if a singer ever lived, a tenor, with a sweeter voice than Brignoli had then. . . . I never thought of his manners when I heard him: they were not present: they were easy to forget." When Brignoli died in 1884 Whitman wrote a poignant homage to him, "The Dead Tenor." Its first lines: "So firm—so liquid-soft—again that tremulous, manly timbre! / The perfect singing voice—deepest of all to me the lesson . . ."

Hungry for Gossip

Traubel includes the full draft of Whitman's letter from Washington to Hugo Fritsch dated October 8, 1863. In it Walt writes, "O Hugo I wish I could hear with you the current opera—I saw [Donizetti's *Roberto*] *Devereux* in the NY papers of Monday announced for that night, & I knew in all probability you would be there—tell me how it goes, &

about the principal singers—only don't run away with that theme, & occupy too much of your letter with it—but tell me mainly about all my dear friends, & every little personal item. . . ."

Vocal Gossip at the Window

Traubel records: "After going out, as I passed the window, W. leaned forward—called me—'Horace—I should like you to take Ed [Wilkins] here to the opera. It is to be my treat. I should like him to see *Fra Diavolo* and *The Bohemian Girl*—especially the latter—the latter first. I see Castle is there with that troupe—still singing.' Asked me if Castle was 'any good' any more—and upon my negative, 'Well I supposed not, as a singer—but 15 or 20 years ago, when he was in his prime he was prime indeed. They were his halcyon days—I saw him often. In the rollicky characters, his abandon was great—a thing to be studied and pleased with.' So I promised to go with Ed and he was satisfied."

Note: William Castle possessed a fine sweet tenor and probably honed his comic skills during his years as a minstrel singer.

Vocal Powers

Whitman reports to Traubel of a jaunt in his wheelchair during which he met Ed Lindell, a fiddle-playing ferryman on the Delaware River. Lindell, Walt recalls, "impeached the importance of the human voice, its musical quality." He then tells Horace, "I doubt if he has ever heard a voice that justifies what we call the vocal powers: the great, overwhelming, touching, human voice—its throbbing, flowing, pulsing qualities. Alboni—or that strange, awkward, obesely ridiculous figure, the Italian who recently died—oh yes! [Pasquale] Brignoli. Such voices—do they not justify all—explain all?"

Boning Up

"In my opera days, I always took care to get a libretto the day before, then took care to leave it at home on the day itself!" This advice was given to Ed Wilkins, whom Walt was eager to introduce to opera.

Remembering Lucia Di Lammermoor

Traubel records: "We spoke of impressive hours at the theater and opera. W. saying 'You know *Lucia* well—I am sure you do. You remember Edgardo (isn't it Edgardo?)—how, when he has the scene with her over the letter, the promise of marriage—and he grasps her by the wrist, holds her at arm's length—asks her if she wrote the letter. It is thrilling. And she is so frightened by his display of passion, she hesitates—and he then the more stirred, continuing his hold with one hand and exhibiting the letter in the other.' Here W. leaned way out of his chair—his gray hair shaken, his eye bright with fire, his voice deep and full of music. 'And then he says to her several times—only the one word: "Respondez! Respondez!" And she thereupon admits, "I wrote it! Yes! I wrote it!" Then the bag bursts—he turns about and sings the very devil's rage, sorrow.' W. ending in a laugh, resuming thus, 'But it is so, in a word often, that the whole act is vibrant!' I had been saying that Italian was music even where a word was not understood and W. asseverated, 'It is! It is! And no one with more memory and conviction of it than Walt Whitman!' "

Greatest Pleasure: Opera

Traubel includes in full a long, newsy letter written by Whitman from Brooklyn to Lewis Brown, a soldier hospitalized in Washington in 1863 (he expected the letter to be circulated). In it he decides to describe his attendance at an opera at Manhattan's Academy of Music; this concludes: "Comrades, recollect all this is in singing and music, and lots of it too, on a big scale, in the band, every instrument you can think of, and the best players in the world, and sometimes the whole band and the whole men's chorus and the women's chorus all putting on the steam together—and all in a vast house, light as day, and with a crowded audience of ladies and men. Such singing and strong rich music always give me the greatest pleasure—and so opera is the only amusement I have gone to, for my own satisfaction, for last ten years."

Note: See also "At the Opera," p. 75.

Alfresco Concerts

"I looked upon these concerts in the open air—the nights so beautiful, calm—as bright gleams athwart the sad history of that harrowing city and time. Yet my enjoyment was altogether untechnical: I knew nothing about music: simply took it in, enjoyed it, from the human side: had a good ear—did not trouble myself to explain or analyze." Whitman is reminiscing here about concerts he heard "in the Washington days."

Marietta Alboni

FINEST VOICE

I never think of Alboni but I think of the finest voice, organ, that ever was. Her contralto—what a purity! what a range! And whatever her change of pitch, there was no loss of power, of integrity.

ABOUNDING PRESENCE

When Traubel remarked that he had read "A Song of the Rolling Earth" aloud in his room, Whitman discoursed on the sound of the voice: "There is a mysterious, wonderful quality in the human voice which no plummet has yet sounded—to which literature has not done any sort of justice—as it could not, I suppose. . . . I often say to the elocution fellows that, in spite of all their study, the deepest deep of all they have not yet sounded. There is the consciousness of abounding presence in a fine organ—a superb voice—I have known some—Alboni's 40 years ago—the magnificent contralto." Earlier, speaking of certain performers "of magnetic presence" who seem "instantly to take down all bars," Whitman referred again to Alboni: "Alboni's voice! What a joy, a grandeur, an illimitable inspiration."

SUBTLER, DEEPER ART

Just before going off to a concert featuring the tenor Italo Campanini (America's first Don José in *Carmen*), Traubel speaks of preferring male voices, and Whitman remonstrates: "You never heard Alboni: you would not say that if you had heard her." This led to a short argument about voices. Traubel: "But I had heard [the coloratura songbird Adelina] Patti a number of times and did not like her: she was cold perfection." Whitman: "I see what you mean—another Jenny Lind," who was Alboni's rival in New York in the 1850s. Traubel demurs: "I imagined Jenny Lind had magnetism." Whitman: "She was not all intellect—but was much intellect, too. The perfection of a singer to the average is in trills, flutes, pirouettings, intellect, perfect poise—utter, invariable. But no—no—no!—*that's* not it, I am sure: it's something subtler, deeper, not so perfect!"

Note: Whitman's devotion to opera and to Alboni is treated at length in *Walt Whitman: A Gay Life*, pp. 1–68.

HAIL AND FAREWELL

Suffering from a headache several months before his death, Whitman made his last extant recorded reference to Alboni. Traubel records: "[Whitman] spoke of Alboni—the Italian opera—no being more than Alboni had moved and possessed him. 'She roused whirlwinds of feeling within me.'" Whitman then questioned "whether Italian opera possessed the greatness of which he was conscious when she sung it, 'she, at least, must have had it—bestowed it. If [greatness] was not in the opera then it was in her. She shed tears, real tears. I have been near— often within a seat or two—and seen her.'" Traubel says Whitman, in this vein, created "an atmosphere thrown out, crimsoned with good blood and sympathy."

Bottoms Up

While several speakers were honoring him at Camden's Morgan's Hall on his seventieth birthday, Traubel reported in Camden's Compliment to Walt Whitman, *Whitman "dealt affectionately by a special bottle of champagne that was brought him." A week later Walt was at Tom Harned's for one of his frequent Sunday dinners, and Traubel observed that "he drank joyantly—with his accustomed good humor." This, as Whitman cheekily noted, in spite of Dr. Bucke's instructions to the contrary: "I have a spice of wickedness in me—a vein that makes me rejoice to tell Bucke of my exploits with the wine now and then!" Though the somewhat embarrassed author, very early in life, of a temperance novel (albeit written, he asserted more than once, while under the influence), Whitman was a lifelong taker of drink and ridiculer of temperance activists. Though not a friend of swilling, he clearly took considerable, if apparently always moderate, pleasure in alcohol, as the following passages show, sometimes with a happy Falstaffian flair.*

How to Write a Temperance Novel

Whitman considered *Franklin Evans, or The Inebriate*—the lurid temperance novel he published in 1842 in the *New World*—one of the nastier skeletons in his literary closet. One day he reminisced about how he composed it. The publisher's "offer of cash payment was so tempting—I was so hard up at the time—that I set to work at once ardently on it (with the help of a bottle of port or what not). In three days constant work I finished the book. Finished the book? Finished myself. It was damned rot—rot of the worst sort. . . . I never cut a chip off that kind of timber again."

Years of Genuine Drinkingness

Conversation about the greatly admired actor Junius Brutus Booth turned to his weakness for liquor ("he would get drunk—get as drunk as the devil"), and this in turn led Whitman to recall how liquor flowed in the New York of the 1840s and 1850s: "It is very hard for the present generation anyhow to understand the drinkingness of those years—how the 'gentlemen' of the old school used liquor. . . . At the time such things as prohibition, pledges, abstinences, could hardly be said to have been known: a good deal of the difference consisted, I suppose, in the fact that the whiskey, rum, gin, of those days was genuine—thoroughly genuine: not adulterated, as it nearly all is in our time."

Confessional

Bucke knows I drink—at least that I used to whenever I got the chance—was in the mood.

A Debate Resolved

Traubel arrives one evening in January 1889: "Found W. and Harned animatedly talking: questions of diet, drink, &c. Harned vehemently opposed Bucke's notion of abstinence in W.'s case. W. very mild regarding it: very humorous over it, too: 'Whether right or wrong, one of the main considerations with me is that I have it, I want it, I get it. Besides, it is very little I take: I am living on a very low plane: everything is shaved down: way down: eating, drinking.'"

Two Kinds of Whiskey

You know there are two kinds of whiskey. One that burns your throat as it goes down. Some like that—I do not—I call it vulgar. Then the other has a milder, more serene taste—does not offend—only elevates—only possesses good manners.

Thespian Whiskey

"That whiskey, that is the whiskey sent over by Francis Wilson, the actor. I think it is the best I have ever tasted. Though I am not a great judge, I think I can detect the true article." A few days later, Traubel observed, "I notice Wilson's whiskey is little by little disappearing."

Tom Harned's Whiskey. . .

"I intended asking you to bring me more whiskey. I am quite out of whiskey and Tom's is the bestest ever was! Oh! It is genuine stuff. I know nothing near so good anywhere else." The Philadelphia lawyer became, it would appear, an "enabler" of the poet's desire for spirits. In a letter of January 8, 1889, Whitman wrote to Harned: "Tom, if you have it and you can, I wish you w'd fill my bottle again with that Sherry." Several months later Whitman's beloved William O'Connor died. Walt wrote several one-sentence letters to members of his circle telling the news. But to Harned he wrote: "If you will, fill the brown bottle with sherry for me, and the small white bottle with Cognac. My dear friend O'Connor is dead." At one Sunday dinner Whitman praised a "mixed toddy" served him thus: "If the law ever goes back on you, Tom, you can hire out for a barkeeper!"

. . . and His Champagne

The champagne up there at Tom's is the finest in the world . . . whenever I come there is a bottle: sometimes two bottles are put out: and luckily for me no one else who comes there seems particularly to care for champagne!

I think champagne and oysters were made for me: that they are *prima facie* in my domain.

In a September 1890 letter Whitman told of a Sunday visit to the Harneds, who "treated me to a splendid meal of oysters and champagne—to wh' *abstemious me* did fullest justice (I think the best ch. I ever drank)."

Gossip

Traubel referred to "someone who prints W. 'a guzzling whiskey-drinker.'" Whitman laughed and replied, "that is mild, compared with other things, words, I have met."

Tremenjuous Spirit

The great thing with me is the *spirit*: as the old man said, my *spirit* is *tremenjuous—tremenjuous*, thanks to myself in part, thanks in part to an occasional sip of sherry!

Prohibition

Take whiskey from a man as he is constituted now, and he will take absinthe, hasheesh.

I do not enter at all into what I call the "quabble" of prohibition, but believe firmly that no man no more now than at any time is eligible to be made good by law.

If drink, why not clothing, what we eat?

Prandial

A dinner with no drink whatever seems strange to me.

Pfaff's

Having fine champagne at a dinner, Whitman reminisces about his favorite New York hangout: "It took me back to Pfaff's. What a judge of wines that fellow was! He made no misses." Later, speaking of a favored supplier of brandy, Walt is reminded again of the café: "When I would go to see Pfaff after an interval from absence he would say, 'First of all, before anything else, let us have a drink of something,' and would go down in his cellar and bring out from his cobwebs a bottle of choice champagne—the best. Cobwebs are no discount for champagne! . . . And Pfaff never made a mistake—he instinctively apprehended liquors—having his talent, and that talent in curious prolixity, almost. Often I would wonder—*can* he go *wrong?*"

Tiny Bubbles

One day a letter arrived asking whether the poet liked champagne. Walt smiled and said, "Does a duck swim?" and laughed. "Yes—let him send a sip or two—it has a wonderful lift for a man!" Later we learn that Robert Ingersoll kept Walt in champagne ("the dryest"), sending it from his Wall Street law office. Walt's nickname for New Jersey moonshine was "lunar champagne." "Drank a little champagne," Davis noted a few weeks before his death.

If I had the means of doing so here I should break a bottle of champagne every day. It does me no harm.

Of champagne he was served a few days earlier at a festive birthday banquet in 1889: "It was an extra good brand, sure—and I never shared it with a soul—drank perhaps four-fifths of it before I left."

After the next year's birthday dinner, Whitman had special praise for the quality, if not the quantity, of the champagne: "It was the finest I ever tasted—but I feel short of my measure of it—some one of the waiters must have confiscated it, or a part of it. Some rare brand, stowed away somewhere for select ends!"

Seventy-first Birthday Party Menu

Plain food and plenty to drink . . .

No "Late" for Whiskey

When Horace says, "I was at Tom's last night but it was too late to bring the whiskey," Walt responds, "there's no late for whiskey!"

Touch of Stimulant

I am glad you drink nothing, Horace—that will hold finely for a young fellow, even in middle life. I am inclined to think that, when a man gets old and his fires slow down some, some touch of (never much) stimulant may be necessary.

Worldly Brandy

Walt says this liquor "has done me a heap of good." When Horace arrives with a fresh supply, the poet says, "That is good news. There's a whole world in that bottle." Once into it: "Oh! That is good—it freshens me, if anything can!" It was noted as a clear bad sign, ten days before he died: "For the present asks no more for brandy."

Walt's Way with Words

Unsurprisingly, for one who was eager all his life to associate with what he called the "lower orders" of society, Whitman delighted in slang. Discussing the subject one day with Traubel, he praised the "naturalness" and "fittingness" of it, adding, "The boys in the army were first rate slangists— invented lots of words—'switching-off'—'skedaddle'—lots of others. And genuine creations, too—words that will last." Of his earlier years in New York he also recalled: "In the old days . . . down in the Bowery there was much slang. It was all sorts: derived from all tongues and no tongue: the French call it argot, patois—we call it slang. There were many fine examples of it current, particularly among the theatrical people."

The Mickle Street conversations show the poet a brilliant slangist himself, as well as an inveterate twister-up of familiar words and a neologist. A librarian can become a "bookophite," and "publisherial" manners can become the object of scorn. The usual raft of autograph requests, he will say, "infuriates me," but then with a laugh: "though the infuriation is not very violent." He could look about his cluttered bedroom and find "a devil-may-care-ness everywhere." Horace, in argumentative mood, becomes an "argyfier." He ridiculed the "flummeriness, the tinsel" of the South. Narrating a colorful Emerson anecdote, by combining "flustered" and "frustrated," he creates a word that deserves frequent use: "flustrated." All humans experience "dyspepticisms," and the typical lawyer is "buried deep in red-taperies." He sees some paintings by Bucke's daughter, and she becomes a "dabster." His discomfort with gushing "Whitmaniacs" is thus phrased: "I am afraid of the 'enthusiastikers.'" "Dupishness" was for Whitman the ability to be crafty. Being no great fan of Shakespeare, he said he felt the "staggering-ness" of all the evidence Robert Ingersoll brought to bear for the claim that Francis Bacon really wrote the plays. And the "remarkablest note" about him in January 1892 was simply "that I live still."

Following is a sampling of the results of Walt's playful grasp of idiomatic American English. Most of his invented words did not last, but some of the most piquant surely deserve resurrection.

Mannahatta

For the word "Mannahatta" I believe I have the best authority ever was, Judge Furman, in Brooklyn—and Jeremiah Mason. I doubt if better

247

philologists—knowers of the Indian tongues—ever existed than these men. . . . You know I very fondly use Mannahatta—I doubt if anybody ever used it as advisedly as I have done. Do you know what Mannahatta means? The Indians use the word to indicate a plot of ground, an island, about which the waters flow—keep up a devil of a swirl, whirl, ebullition—have a hell of a time. To me it is all meaning and music!

Note: Several weeks later Whitman referred to his two informants again: "I am sure, now, of these men—authorities: they came much in contact with chiefs of the Six Nations. . . . 'Mannahatta' meant to these a point of land surrounded by rushing, tempestuous, demonic waters: it is so I have used it—and shall continue."

Queerities

[Bronson] Alcott had a lot of queerities—freakishnesses: not vegetarianism—I do not count that—but transcendental mummeries.

Presidentiad

My word "Presidentiad." Oh! that is eminently a word to be cherished—adopted. Its allusion, the four years of the Presidency: its origin that of the Olympiad—but as I flatter myself, bravely appropriate, where not another one word, signifying the same thing, exists!

Note: Whitman wanted this neologism included in the forthcoming *Century Dictionary*.

Printerially

It [a copy of Charles DeKay's *Nimrod*] is quite a handsome book printerially speaking.

Likeacality

Traubel arrives and Whitman at first mistakes him for his doctor, Walsh. When he discovers his mistake: "Well—you are not unlike him—don't even look unlike him: your manner is much similar: as it is said, there is great likeacality."

Nifty

Traubel asks Whitman how he feels: "Not a bit nifty—not a bit nifty." The word puzzles him. "Did you never hear that colloquialism?—nifty—n-i-f-t-y—[meaning] sassy, on edge."

Consentaneous

As plans for his 1890 birthday became firm, Whitman told Traubel: "If you can get a light carriage—an easy one—do that: with that I can go almost anywhere. I am in your hands. Whatever you do, you will find me consentaneous—willing to connive. All I would urge is—no hifalutin!"

Dive

When Horace happened to refer to "an oyster dive," Whitman approved the locution: "I like the word, like it a great deal. How much better it is than 'parlor' or 'saloon'—of all, 'saloon' is the worst. The word 'saloon' came into use first to my knowledge in this country fifty years or so ago through a novel, by some one celebrated in that day—probably now forgotten—a novel treating of the Salons of Paris. It was a novel of the gentleman class—the Disraeli stamp. Some critic or other said of one of Disraeli's novels that there was not a character in it with an income of less than five thousand pounds a year."

Dubiosity

In April 1890 Whitman said he "had considerable of dubiosity" about being able to attend his seventy-first birthday party.

Sorification

Whitman's brief summaries of his physical condition whenever Traubel came in the door are sprinkled with fanciful locutions. One day he will profess "nothing but utter giving-out-ness"; on another he will note "the exquisite sorification" on one side of his body.

Virile

There was one of the department heads at Washington who conceived a great dislike for the word *virile*—gave out orders that it should not be used in any of the documents issuing from that department. I was very curious about it, and asked him once how his antipathy (and it was a *virile* antipathy!) arose. He said that he hated the word—that it called up in him images of everything filthy, nasty, vile. It was very amusing. I remarked to him: "Did it never occur to you that the fault is in you and not in the word? *I* use the word—like it—am never once brought by it in touch with the images you speak of." But he was obdurate. . . .

Peeves

Most un-Quakerly, Whitman could on occasion express himself pejoratively with considerable sharpness and heat when his tastes were crossed.

A Typical Literary Critic

[Edmund] Gosse is a type of the modern man of letters—much-knowing, sharp witted, critical, cold—bitten with the notion that to be smart is to be deep—able to assume wit. Shakespeare was beginner in that field—but Shakespeare was more—this was in him but a tint, a spice, a subordinate phase entirely.

He is to me the perfect example of what *culture* may do for a man. In the technical sense he is without a flaw; yet in vital quality empty to the very bottom. But these men are used for their emptiness, if nothing else. They are part of the scheme. Gosse utterly lacks oil, blood, pulse.

Commas

I hate commas in wrong places.

Newspaper Men

You know, Horace, you must not predicate a man's judgment by anything you see in the papers about him. We ought to know, of all men! For you have often heard me say it is with a newspaperman not "What is the truth? What can I tell here that is true?" but "What is interesting, spicy? What can I tell here that will interest, sparkle, attract?"

Lemonade

While planning the menu for his seventieth birthday banquet, Whitman remarked: "It's a damnable drink, I wouldn't have it."

Pretty

I know of nothing I think so little of as pretty words, pretty thoughts, pretty china, pretty arrangements.

High Hats

The fad now is to wear the high hat with the nearest to no rim at all: a damnable practice at the best.

Comedians

Asked his opinion of a currently popular comedian, William Nye, Whitman said: "I have very little liking for deliberate wits—for men who start out, with malice prepense, to be funny—just as I should distrust deliberate pathos—the fellow who sets out to be serious, to shed tears, or make others.

Showered with Lies

On hearing that it was being gossiped that a young poet had come to his door and been treated badly, Whitman opined morosely but philosophically: "Probably the story is a lie—our planet seems now in the orbit of lies. And they say of the meteoric showers, sometimes we fall within their orbit and they are copious, so with these liars, who copiously shower us from day to day."

Camden Pols

It is typical of the Camden politician to be the dirtiest of his species—I mean that from the Mayor down.

Note: *Plus ça change*: in the spring of 2000, Milton Milan became the third Camden mayor in twenty years to be indicted for racketeering and corruption.

Camden Newspaper

When the *Camden County Courier* "blackguarded" Tom Harned in his campaign for the state senate as an independent, Walt's temper blew: "It is throwing all the muddy mud it can. Oh! It is a vile sheet—full of distortion, of smut—a nasty, back-biting, slanderous, back-house, sewery sheet. The lowest, I think, I have known anywhere, which is to say a good deal."

Camden Post Office

"I think there is no office in America where everything is so ordered for the convenience of the men who work it—or pretend to. . . . The policy of the men is to profess ignorance—to know nothing." Walt a week later exempted his own letter carrier, Brown, who lived a few doors away, from this blanket opprobrium: "He is very frank, truthful, obliging—knows more than all the rest of the force"; "He is the best yet: a jewel of a man."

New England Culture

There was a time when New England culture made me sick, mad, rebellious, though now it does not seem to matter—I have become hardened to it.

That Damnable Yankee Accessory

[Senator Charles] Sumner had that damnable Yankee accessory—the shudder for a word misspelled, misused, a false intonation. Even Emerson had it.

That speech matter is the peculiarity—I may say the inevitability—with New England people: it is almost universal with them; even the wise Emerson had it, in some measure. . . . It is a sort of extreme grammaticism. Yet I confess that when it is made too prominent—when it is indeed insisted upon—when it is too much poked in one's face—I turn my back on it, it offends me.

New England Self-regard

The typical New Englander is always discussing his own affairs—the latest trouble, sickness, complaint—all that—lugging it forward at all times, into any company.

Musical Corpses

Horace is puzzled when Walt laughingly says, "Music is my worst punishment," so he explains: "Oh! the bands out in the street—the drum and fife corpses that go rattling and banging past: they beat my miserable head like hammers."

Wrong Number

Traubel reports that Walt's "neighbor, Button, is notified by city authorities that the number of his house has been changed to 332. This would make W. 330 [instead of 328], which he does not like. It makes him indignant."

Autograph Mail

I have had no mail today except an autograph mail. . . . They all write me—hundreds write—strangers—they all beg autographs—tell funny tales about it, give funny reasons (some of them are pitiful—some of them are almost piteous)—I practically never answer them any more. It takes about all the strength I have nowadays to keep the flies off. I make what use I can of the return stamps and let the rest of the matter go.

Not a day but the autograph hunter is on my trail—chases me, dogs me! sometimes two or three appear in the very same mail. Their subterfuges, deceptions, hypocrisies are curious, nasty, yes damnable. I will get a letter from a young child—a young reader—this is her first book—she has got fond of me—she should be encouraged in her fine ambitions—would I not &c &c—and I would *not*, of course—why should I? I can see the grin of an old deceiver in such letters.

I am not to be taken in: I am too old a bird at that: I have experienced all sizes and styles of the autograph monster.

One daily entry ends thus: "While I was with Walt he opened a letter Ed brought him, which proved to be an elegant request for an autograph, immediately (except for return stamp) consigned to the woodbox."

Whitman found one autograph hound irresistible: "One of the autograph fellows intimated that I might die soon, which made his request a very urgent one. I was so tickled with his cheek and honesty that I signed and sent him the card."

Matinees

I don't like afternoon performances—never did—they seem very unpropitious.

" _____ "

Quoting is a thing that gets to be a disease.

Pleasures

Whitman was not inclined to stint when he was delighted.

Stick Candy

Traubel records, "Mrs. Davis handed him a bag of mint-candy and he at once gave me a stick. 'You favor it?' he asked, and then dilated like a child on his own fancy for it."

Good Cooking

"Her cooking is in itself a treat—everything gets appetizing in her hands: she has a decided genius that way. A good cook is born, not made. Your sister never makes the right thing the wrong thing by bad treatment. She is one who could make the desert vegetate." Whitman is speaking of Augusta Harned, Traubel's sister and Tom Harned's wife, at whose table he regularly dined on Sunday afternoons, usually after a jaunt in his horse-drawn buggy. A few weeks later he reiterated, "She is a genius.... She never fails in knowing just when to stop—just what to do to make the mark: her cooking is inevitable."

Spacious Pens

Whitman explains his preference for Mammoth Falcon quill pens: "I find I get to like the vast pens: they give me something to take real hold of: they encourage me to write spacious things. There's a spiritual side of the simplest physical phenomena: not only a spiritual side: more than that: a spiritual outcome." A few days later: "it makes a great difference what sort of a pen. . . . I am sensitive—I especially hate the little bits of pens—the dwarf ladylike pens: I don't seem to be able to do anything fullsized with them: they interfere with my ideas—break my spirit."

Confectionary

Traubel notes: "On the bed a plate of candies. He has a sweet tooth, 'but not for the *made* candies'—plain molasses candy in all ways 'satisfying' him, he said. 'This much of the child,' with 'this much of the old simplicity,' he said, persisted."

Long Island Hydrography

The Brooklyn water . . . is the best in the world. What feeds the springs nobody knows. It is some body of water far off—perhaps in the Canadas or our great West. They gush out not by ones or hundreds even, but by thousands! Few people appreciate the marvelous hydrography of Long Island. At these springs much peat has accumulated—the pack of many years. But if it is removed, it reveals the most beautiful gravel bottom you know. I have seen nothing like it for color, purity—it has delighted me to look at it for hours.

Note: Croton water he could not abide, however: "it is reputed good, but I can't take it, which people say is my fault and not the fault of the water."

Cheap Paperbacks

There is a great satisfaction getting a cheap book—a soft book you can mush in your hands, so—a book you are not afraid to injure.

Walt on Various and Sundry

There was no regular ebb and flow in the conversations at Mickle Street. Events reported in the papers, contents of the day's mail, and the serendipitous array of callers guided the daily confabulations. Following is an appropriately serendipitous potpourri of views Whitman uttered on a variety of topics.

The Human Critter

There is a strain of slipperiness in the human critter: we all pray to be delivered from it: it is perhaps in some measure in all of us.

What a poor miserable critter man is! A joke—a great joker for his little time: then nature comes along, buffets him once or twice, gives him two or three knocks: nature, the strong, the irresistible, the great bear: then what is man? where is the joker?

I have seen in the later years of my life exemplifications of devilishness, venom, in the human critter which I could not have believed possible in my more exuberant youth—a great lump of bad with the good.

The Beaten Track

There seems to be the spice of the gambler in all of us: we'd do anything to get out of the beaten track—even commit crimes!

Wisdom of Brooklyn

I was bred in Brooklyn: initiated to all the mysteries of city life—populations, perturbations: knew the rough elements—what they stood for: what might be apprehended from them.

New York: No Heroics

New York is ahead in engraving, in printing, in certain of the fine arts—in enterprise, business—in venture, hazarding for trifles: but in all big things, in the heroics, it is left without a sign. I can see no future for literature in New York. All seems so hedged in—closed, closed.

Editorials

I suppose the news in newspapers gets better every year. But as the news gets better the rest of the paper gets worse. I read editorials from force of habit, now and then: what else could excuse such a waste of time?

Fourth of July Fireworks

They call this noise "patriotism"—a queer patriotism it is, to my mind!

A Philosophy of Letters

A letter from Symonds, read aloud, ignites discussion of why Symonds's published essays and private letters displayed such a "difference of temperature." Whitman remarks on letters from two English admirers, John Johnston and J. W. Wallace: "The letters from the fellows there—from Johnston, Wallace—are mainly made up of thankfulness to me, to my work. Yet Wallace, too, now and then tells me what he *sees*, leaving the *thought* of what he sees unsaid. This shows power—too latent, too little exercised, perhaps." Traubel responds with the view that "letters, journals, should be free: float along word by word, as it comes, like the toss, the rhythm, of a song." Whitman replies affirmatively, then elaborates his ideas about correspondence: "Beautiful! I like that. I guess it is so! I live it—our fellows—say, a hundred years ago—they have a certain stateliness, measure—preparedness—yet a charm, too. . . . But every one to his kind. And we must see to it, every fellow is acknowledged for what he brings, not what we think he *should* bring. A letter is very subtle! Oh! The destiny of a letter should be well-marked from the first. We should know, make, every letter to fit its purpose—to go to the doctor, to the intimate friend, to the admirer, and so on and on, each having a quality its own, and for a specific end. It may seem queer for me to have a philosophy of correspondence, but I have. And of course, *freedom* is the charm of a letter—it before all other qualities. And a letter without freedom certainly has nothing left to it."

The Scribblers' Deluge

When a few volumes of poetry from unknown parties arrived in the mail, Whitman steamed: "Everybody is writing, writing, writing—worst of all, writing poetry. It'd be better if the whole tribe of the scribblers—every damned one of us—were sent off somewhere with toolchests to do some honest work." A month later: "I believe if I met a man who had not written a book I should hug him—he would be a monumental exception—an honorable exception."

Quaker Essence

The Quaker nativity [of Whittier] seems to tell, somehow—the absence of too great artificiality—a certain sort of almost impossibility to make-believe. I think the Quaker—the typical Quaker—is a certain sort of materialist—they like the world, and all that: but a certain spirituality remains—a purity, aspiration.

Buddhism versus Whitmanism

Traubel asks what Whitman has in common with Buddhism: "I can see union, agreement at some points, perhaps many, but one point of differentiation seems to be here: that whereas the Buddhist puts stress—primary stress—upon absorptive, final loss of individuality, I put the contrary emphasis upon, if so to say it, an extreme individuality, identity—that the individual is the crown, master, god of all."

Secret Societies

I never believed in them: their damnable nomenclature if nothing else would have been enough to scare me off. As [Dickens's character] Mrs. Gamp would say, I *despige* secret societies—nomenclature and all—particularly the nomenclature. Sir Knight this, Sir Knight that—imported sounds, with no significance except to excite contempt.

Celebrities

The world goes daffy after phantom great men—the noisy epaulette sort: a man has got to set up a howl if he wants people to take him right off: if you have the real stuff in you, you've got to wait for it to be recognized: and you are far more likely to die than to live in waiting.

The Theatre in Perspective

I don't think this matter of acting absorbingly important. I don't feel as if civilization, progress, life (American or other) hangs in any way upon the existence of theatres, actors. There was a time when the stage held a rarer place in human life, but now other factors enter in—share the feast, the gifts.

The Taint of Books

The best man in the world is the man who has absorbed books—great books—made the most of them—yet remains unspoiled—remains a man. It is marvellous what capacity books have for destroying as well as making a man.

Literati

Literary men learn so little from life—borrow so much from the borrowers.

Literary Dazzle

"That is what they are all doing, all society, all professionalism, in books, poems, sermons—a strain to make an impression—everything loved that will dazzle the beholder, everything hated that will not." Whitman was thinking in particular of the prolific writer Agnes Repplier: "She is a woman who tries for smartness at all hazards—that is her caliber."

Sensation-seeking Editors

"You remember what I said the other night about Bret Harte—men of that stamp: how they take up a single phase of our life—lay such stress on it that it would be supposed all was concentrated there—there was no other life—when in reality this is but a drop in the sea." A few weeks earlier Whitman had complained that magazine editors of the day, like Harte and John Hay, were too "fond of the Western types—the delirium tremens type" at the expense of the common individual: "how much that is disregarded because it is commonplace, yet is greatest because it is commonplace, too!"

Higher Unlearning

I consider it the bane of the universities, colleges, that they withhold, withdraw, men from direct, drastic contact with life.

Of Cities and Some Great Rivers

One day Traubel told of a journey north up into the Pocono Mountains and of achieving a view of the Delaware River below. This sets off the inmate of Mickle Street "as if his whole heart was in every word": "It is always painful to come back into the cities—the streets—the stinking reeking streets—Mickle Street—sluttish gutters—women with hair a-flying—dust-brooms clouding the streets—confinement—the air shut off. Oh! I know with the most knowing what you have described. And I know best of all the rivers—the grand, sweeping, curving, gently undulating rivers. Oh! the memories of rivers—the Hudson—the Ohio—the Mississippi! It would be hard to put into a word the charms of the Mississippi: they are distinctive, undoubted—do not consist in what is called beauty—which, for instance, would be picked out as essentially the wonders of the Hudson—consist rather in amplitude, power, force—a lazy muddy water-course, immense in sweep—in its various wanderings. The Hudson is quite another critter—the neatest, sweetest, most delicate, clearest, cleanest river in the world. Not sluttish—not a trace of it and I think I am pretty familiar with it—at least as it was—for the matter of 200 miles or so, which is about the whole story. The beginnings of the Delaware are scattered all through southern New York—delicate threads finally making way to union and power. Rivers! Oh the rivers! When you described the Delaware as you saw it from that mountain-top—the fields and hills about it—the placid flowingness—I was there—I saw it all—I felt the odor of it steal about me, envelope me!"

Phenomenal Denver

Denver is bound to be one of the most wonderful of our city-growths. . . . The land about there is remarkable for its natural parks—there are numbers of them, fine, satisfying, Paradisaic, bits of reserve—the noblest the earth affords. . . . Denver is phenomenal for its background—

its ample background: not much of a river there, but a river that does. Denver has its own excuse for being—it is a center—a natural center—a rallying point: it is one of the great towns that had to be.

Denver's Brawny Men

I never forget the plenty of big-backed men there at Denver: it seemed to me, wherever I went, it was to see one after another of these remarkable fellows—stature almost giant-like: looked at from the rear, the broadest, brawniest backs under the sun. We see no such grand men—at least, in any frequency—here: and yet at Denver they seemed commonplace.

Inartistic but Ordained New Orleans

New Orleans, not at all attractive in itself—not what would be called beautiful by an artistic eye—is yet a pure necessity: America, traffic—traffic even before the railroad; none the less since—ordained that a city was needed at just that precise point—a distributing center—a depot—and so this city grew, and so is likely to last for some time yet—last while the need lasts.

Walt's Favorite Couplet

Did I ever quote you my favorite couplet? I've no doubt I have ["but he had not" Traubel inserts]. It reads something like this—

> Over the past not God himself has power,
> For what has been has been, and I have had my hour!

It has a Drydenish sound—yet is very noble and grand.... I have no distinct idea at all where my couplet is from.

Smoking

Whitman's response when asked if he regretted not being a smoker: "I would as lief regret that I had not murdered my mother."

Asked the same question a few months later, Whitman elaborated: "Not one regret: only satisfaction: sometime there will be a change: now most men smoke—then most men will not smoke: the tobacco habit may have its joys but it also has other integers that are neither glad nor beautiful: it's one of the avenues through which people today get rid of some of their nerve surplus: it goes with things as they are: but it is so filthy a practice taken for all in all that I can't see but people must inevitably grow away from it."

When Whitman submitted a short prose piece to *Cope's Tobacco Plant* (London) in 1878, his P.S. sang a different tune! "I am *not* an antitobacconist—On the contrary have seen how important & valuable the sedative was in the extensive military hospitals of our Secession war—Still I do not smoke or chew myself—Sometimes wish I did smoke now in my old age & invalidism—but it is too late to learn—But my brothers

& all my near friends are smokers, & I am accustomed to it—live among smokers, & always carry cigars in my pocket to give special friends who prize them."

Sunday Unplugged

When talk at Mickle Street turned to baseball and "agitation" for Sunday as a secular holiday, Walt exulted: "I believe in all that—in baseball, in picnics, in freedom: I believe in the jolly all-round time—with the parsons and the police eliminated."

"I, too, more and more . . . am persuaded towards the confirmation of the Sunday to liberty. I believe in unplugging the day—in inviting freedom—in having the boys play their ball, people go to the seaside, boating, fishing, frolicking, visiting, the whole air one in fact of a grand spontaneity." Traubel quizzes further: "Then the preachers would denounce you for espousing a Continental Sabbath: that is their great bugbear." Whitman says with a laugh, "Yes, that—I do favor a Continental Sabbath." Later, after a gloomy Sunday wheelchair ride when "neither boy nor ball [was] to be seen," he reiterated, "how much better the play, the open air, the beautiful sky, the active movement, than restriction, Sabbathism."

Sports for a Dyspeptic Race

I like your interest in sports—ball, chiefest of all—base-ball particularly: base-ball is our game: the American game: I connect it with our national character. Sports take people out of doors, get them filled with oxygen—generate some of the brutal customs (so-called brutal customs) which, after all, tend to habituate people to a necessary physical stoicism. We are some ways a dyspeptic, nervous set: anything which will repair such losses may be regarded as a blessing to the race. We want to go out and howl, swear, run, jump, wrestle, even fight, if only by doing so we may improve the guts of the people: the guts, vile as guts are, divine as guts are!

America's Game: Baseball

Traubel happens to refer to baseball as "the hurrah game of the republic," evoking Whitman's enthusiastic agreement: "That's beautiful: the hurrah game! well—it's our game: that's the chief fact in connection with it: America's game: has the snap, go, fling, of the American atmosphere—belongs as much to our institutions, fits into them as significantly, as our constitutions, laws: is just as important in the sum total of our historic life." Later Traubel remarks on a regular destination of Whitman and the new wheelchair when Walt announces "It was baseball today": "He takes a great interest in the boys out on the common. Sits watching them for long stretches."

An Ideal Raconteur

[Thomas] Donaldson [is] a rare raconteur: among the very best: perhaps the very best. Burroughs tells some Greek story of two armies, one of them nearly conquered yet not despairing. A moonlight night comes on: the weaker combatants are under arms, not knowing what to do. All at once, on a new angle of the moon, the position of the enemy was revealed by the glint of their spears. Then assault—a victory—the tide turned! When it comes to a story Donaldson can give you that glint . . . he can give you that glint: he has the genius of that glint.

Doctors . . .

Ah! these doctors! after all, Horace, do they know much? . . . I love doctors and hate their medicine.

From the medical point of view they tell me I'm getting on all right, but from the point of view of my own comfort I'm in a pretty boggy condition indeed. But so the doctor feels all right about it I don't suppose it matters what I feel. I like to see the doctors comfortable, anyway.

. . . and Patients

The trouble is not with the doctors alone, but the patients: the patients, too, are responsible for the tomfoolery. The patient wants the worth of his money, so he must have a powder or two—some medicine—whatnot. Then the whole medicine business is a sort of "now you see it now you don't" affair, sifted down, don't you think?

The Scientific Spirit

I like the scientific spirit—the holding off, the being sure but not too sure, the willingness to surrender ideas when the evidence is against them: this is ultimately fine—it always keeps the way beyond open—always gives life, thought, affection, the whole man a chance to try over again after a mistake—after a wrong guess.

Bigots

We seem to require all kinds of bigots to complete the chapter of our sorrows—Methodist bigots, Presbyterian bigots, bigots for the Bible, bigots against the Bible, Quaker bigots stiffer than their hats: all sorts, all sorts: we need them all to finish off the ornament of our hari-kari world.

Republican Party

When Tom Harned returned from being a delegate at the Republican Party convention that nominated Benjamin Harrison, Whitman calls it "A rather dubious compliment for Tom" and lets fly about the party: "I hardly seem in line with the Republican party any more—in fact, the Republican party is hardly in line with itself." Has he lost faith in it? "I never had entire faith—now I hardly have any faith at all. It is not impossible they will rise to the occasion—it's not improbable they'll sink to the bottom and go to the devil!"

A Modestly Talented Literary Critic
I don't think he fishes with a very deep sinker. [Edmund] Stedman don't seem to have vision, soul—depth of nativity—sufficient to make him capable of the highest interpretations.

Elections: Hollow Triumph
A party may win elections and be defeated anyway. The Republican party as it is constituted now might win twenty elections without a single moral victory: the moral victories are the only victories that count.

Tariffs and Free Trade
The spirit of the tariff is malevolent: it flies in the face of all American ideals: I hate it root and branch: it helps a few rich men to get rich, it helps the great mass of poor men to get poorer.

I am for free trade because I am for anything which will break down the barriers between peoples: I want to see the countries all wide open.

We are indebted to our friend Tom Donaldson in good part for the imposition of this tax [a tariff on art]: he mainly lobbied it, I think. Though how a fellow can be a *Leaves of Grass*–man and fall into such a ditch defeats all my explanations! No, no: there is an inevitable, implacable antagonism!

Protectionism
I shall take the ground that it is a false ideal from the start—that it is never good. Infant industry? Why, it is to take the infant, put it in a warm room, curtain it, carpet it, sickly it—and then you have— and then you have—what do you have? Everything but virility, self-dependence, the show of men and women. And that is protection—that only; and wrong from the start. I had a friend, who had a sickly son: a poor, pale, frail, useless creature, who even threatened not to live at all; coddled, having every wish gratified, cared for wherever he went, whatever he did. That is protection. But then along came another, a wiser, who said, "If that boy is to live, he must be set free: must be sent into the fresh fields." Before, they had hardly dared let him breathe the air of heaven. And the good advice was taken. They bought him an ass—a donkey—the queerest, shabbiest, dirtiest devil of a creature you ever saw, and set the boy free with him—and straightaway the youngster prospered; got strong, robust, almost lived with the animal. That was free trade, and free trade in the natural state.

Noble Interstates

Fifty years or so ago—or forty—there was a great scheme to connect all America by noble roads—the west to the east—the north to the south—and some of them were even commenced. There are said to be several great roads—roads that will compare with the Roman, the best so far known in history—out around Pittsburgh. But the scheme came to nothing—for soon we had the [rail]cars—the great railroads—and then such a thing as a turnpike became vulgar—no one would hear to it. And yet a great road is a great moral agent. Oh! a great road is not the stone merely, or the what-not, that goes to make it—but something more—far more!

Voting

Whitman to Traubel: "While out in the [wheel]chair I remembered it was election day—still did not vote. Did you? I always refrain—yet advise everybody else not to forget."

Lotteries, Baseball . . . Hellfire

As for me, I am in favor of lotteries, Sunday baseball, boats, cars, gin-mills even: not that I am friendly to gin-swilling, but for liberty's sake. As the lady would say and say: let them go on thinking there is no hell! It is gaping for them all the while!

Most Poems

The trouble with most poems is that they are nothing but poems—all poetry, all literary, not in any way human.

Bostonees

Boston is damp and raw—and the Bostonee by no means takes commensurate care of himself. The great features of the typical Bostonee are intellectuality, consumption, dyspepsia.

I have been told that in the Boston Public Library they have a copy of *Leaves of Grass*, but keep it under lock and key, afraid that it may get out and be read!

Sinners

What would we do without sinners? Take them out of literature and it would be barren.

Divorce

Tom Harned speaks of divorce as signifying "chaos" for a man, and Whitman interrupts, "Say, rather, Tom, *freedom*."

The Pianner

When some one spoke of a "pee-a-nist" in Walt's presence, he laughed and asked: "Do you mean a pianner player?" Traubel notes that Whitman objected to the piano, saying that it "seems so unequal to the big things." When Horace later tried to raise interest in an article on the Polish virtuoso Ignace Jan Paderewski, Walt brushed it off; Horace records, "I find he has no enthusiasm over the best piano playing."

English Reticence

One day Traubel noticed a photo of "a young military man" on a table. It was of an English soldier who showed Walt around the Citadel in Quebec during his 1880 trip to Canada: "He showed me every kindness, all those sweet graceful generosities of youth." The memory evokes these ethnic generalizations: "I often think what a vast fund of English reticence is packed up there in Canada. The English character has its reserves—the Irish and French are more possessed of the genial human traits—can have a good time, whatever the nation or individual it treats with. The Englishman broods, muses, reserves himself for a group, a few friends, his family. The French and Irish certainly have the advantage here. And no one can overvalue the importance inhering to this eligibility to comradeship."

Letter-carriers

Letter-carriers always seem a picked class—always seem of the best sort—only the best seem to gravitate to that business.

Southerners' Complexion

Cadavers—complexion of a most remarkable stripe—yet lasting and lasting into 70 years as often as the rest of us.

Sleighing Orgies

Doctor [Bucke] takes to sleighing like some men take to rum: he gets drunk with it—he goes on sleighing orgies.

The Age of Reason

I have heard it said that reason comes with the forties. I should say as to most men, that reason does not come even then—does not come at all—for I am impressed with the general lack of it.

An Abolitionist—with a Screw Loose

There's something in public life—in the life of the stage—the addresser of public life—flare, blare, blaze—which turns the head. Look at poor Anna Dickinson just now!—mad as a hare—and vicious too—barking, biting, right and left—everybody—scolding, screaming, swearing. . . . I remember years ago, meeting her in New York—talking with her—and I can recall coming away then, saying to myself, there was a screw loose—very loose. And you heard, saw, her Hamlet? What another force that must have been—another argument. Nor was she the only one turned by public attention.

Note: Dickinson (1842–1932), born to a Philadelphia Quaker family, became an ardent abolitionist voice in her teens and was greeted by large audiences as the Joan of Arc of the movement. Her later career as an actress and playwright was, as Whitman suggests, troubled.

Genius

Genius is almost a hundred per cent directness—nothing more.

Historians

My experience with life makes me afraid of the historian: the historian, if not a liar himself, is largely at the mercy of liars.

Medieval Illuminated Books

They are pathetic to me: they stand for some one's life—the labor of a whole life, all in one little book which you can hold in your hand . . . they are exclusive: they are made by slaves for masters: I find myself always looking for something different: for simple things made by simple people for simple people.

The Cosmic Color

"Do you know what the wise men call the prevailing cosmic color?" Whitman asks Traubel. When he says it is yellow, Walt replies, "Yes—yellow . . . a yellow with a tinge of brown."

Art for Art's Sake

Think of it—art for art's sake. Let a man really accept that—let that really be his ruling thought—and he is lost.

After Oscar Wilde visited Whitman at Mickle Street in 1882, Walt told a reporter for the *Press* of Philadelphia that he permitted himself but one criticism of the visiting apostle of art for art's sake: "Why, Oscar, it always seems to me that the fellow who makes a dead set at beauty by itself is in a bad way."

Part Five

Whitman in his room in Camden, 1891.

"A Frightful Gone-ness"
—The Physical Decline

Covering as it does the last precarious years of Whitman's life, With Walt Whitman in Camden *is often obliged to report melancholy thumbnail assessments of the poet's physical condition. Almost every daily entry begins with a brief summary of his current status. These are typical: "W in bad shape all day—sleepy, confused, somnolent"; "Improvement in W.'s condition today. He seems to alternate bad with good days. But on the whole he mends"; "Looked ill, tired, worn, almost haggard"; "rather cranky tonight"; "not appearing bright"; "the depression hangs heavy." Frequently, Whitman's own assessments of his status are cast with a certain colorful wit: "I am a lame though not yet quite dead duck," he tells Horace one day, or "my flag is no more at half mast: I feel the touch of life again." Other examples of his bittersweet phrasemaking: "I am old, weak, toppling, full of defections"; "I have substantially gone out of business"; "miseble, as the darkies say." One day he speaks of having experienced "two days way down in the valley" and another of "a frightful gone-ness." Fretful that he might not see* November Boughs *(1888) through the press, Whitman tells Traubel, "No one knows better than I do that I may go to pot any minute—vamoose, as they say out West." And death itself is sometimes charmingly phrased, as when he speaks of the time coming "for me to slip cable" and of being "near eclipsed" and seeming to "go forth with the tide—the never-returning tide."*

Happily, some days brought cheer: "In good feather, 'feeling rather pert,' as he said"; "had rather a fresh, good look"; "was in a bright, cheery humor—color good"; "W. vigorously like his full self again all the evening"; "W said he felt 'almost quarrelsomely well' today"; "in great good trim"; "W. in very good humor."

The following excerpts are arranged in chronological order.

Wine or Doctor's Orders?

One day Walt receives a bottle of old California wine, and Horace asks, "What about that wine? Bucke puts his ban on it." "The way I have felt the last two or three days I owe myself a glass now and then: Maurice is all right: the wine is all right, too: sometimes even Maurice must be adjourned!"

Deceptive

A great big lubber like me (my burly body—red, full face)—gets very little credit for being sick—for being an invalid.

The Ideal Nurse

For one thing: be sure you get a large man—no slim, slight fellow.

Note: The notion of hiring a nurse was first suggested to Whitman by his caregivers on June 9, 1888, and, though constitutionally averse, he fairly quickly consented to the idea. This was his first specification of what form a nurse should take.

Two and a half years later and Whitman had refined his view: "The true nurse must be a male: that is the upshot of my experience. A male, at least, for men. There are a few women, girls, who take it up *intellectually*: but how far does *that* take us? . . . What I need is a man to control me— to suggest, initiate, to save me the trouble even to mention his duties. A man to nurse me, not one I must nurse. Oh, that is very essential."

The First Scare

On June 4, 1888, the day after Whitman had taken his horse and buggy down to Pea Shore on the Delaware River and watched the sunset for blissful fifteen minutes, he suffered some kind of stroke or strokes that left him "not irrational—only not consecutive" and his speech slurred. In his wanderings, Traubel noted, he even began addressing his long-gone boyfriend: "Where are you Pete? Oh! I'm feeling rather kinky— not at all pert." Bucke, who happened to be in town, examined him and said, "It looks to me as if the old man was dying." Concern was aroused when it was learned the poet had no will. His first nurse, a young doctor named Nathan Baker, was summoned, and the scene of his first tussle with his client is both funny and sad: "Bucke and Baker had already on my return decisively set about undressing W., who was kicking like a steer. He also objected to having the nurse sleep there in the room with him. 'I am all right—good for the night: let him come back in the morning. I would rather be alone. I hate to have anybody around, right in my room, watching me. Maurice, do I need to be watched?' He was finally persuaded, 'browbeaten,' he said. He was still clear about the courtesies, for he said to me: 'Of course the nurse knows that my objection is not personal to him.' " A few days later Traubel summarizes, "A long day full of unspeakable anxieties."

After several days had passed, Whitman quizzed Traubel on his recent departures from the *compos mentis*: "Was I a little daffy? Did I talk nonsense? That was only a mood: Horace, I do not think my mind will ever go: I think I will go before my mind goes. The throne may occasionally reel but it never gives way." By June 18 Traubel was able to record, "W.'s mind very clear," and Whitman himself declared, "I am decidedly mended."

Funeral Philosophy

On June 11, 1888, the first discussion of Whitman's funeral occurred, and it was agreed "no minister should officiate." The only speaker mentioned (by Bucke) was Robert Ingersoll "in one of his affirmative moods," and, nearly four years later, he was easily the most controversial speaker at Whitman's funeral. No one who was not a Whitman friend would be allowed to say anything. Horace clearly intended to follow the spirit of an earlier Whitman comment on funerals, which he quotes in this day's entry: "Most formal funerals are insults: they belittle the dead. If anything should be honest a funeral should be honest."

Note: On June 12, Whitman announced his intention (later carried out) to appoint Bucke, Harned, and Traubel his literary executors.

The First Last Will

The matter of a will "hung fire between Harned and W." until June 29, when it was signed, Mary Davis and Nathan Baker being the witnesses. Notable among its provisions: $1,000 for each of his two sisters, with the remainder held in trust by Whitman's brother George and wife, Louisa, for his brother Eddy's benefit; $250 for Davis and Susan Stafford (mother of his friend Harry Stafford); his gold watch to Harry and his silver one to Peter Doyle; and the appointment of his three literary executors.

Solicitous Piety

Whitman made a sour face when he learned that the editor of the *Long Islander*, the paper he had founded half a century before, had published the hope that "a heavenly father would smooth" Walt's way to the grave. He explained, "I don't know why it is—I approve of piety and all that, but somehow piety turns sour." Traubel adds, "W. always shies at conventionally pious condolences."

Grip Is Gone

In the aftermath of his apparent minor strokes of the spring of 1888, Whitman several times expressed his awareness of mental slippage, as on June 19: "[My] grip is gone—irretrievably lost: I seem to have lost the power of consecutive thought, work—mental volition, I might say: as if the ground had been swept from under my feet—as if I had nothing whereon to stand. My brain will not solidify."

Inclination to Flop

It's funny how unambitious my body is. I am possessed of an incredible inclination to flop. I am like a wet rag—I seem to be eligible to do anything except stand erect.

Whitman's letters contain several colorful expressions of infirmity: "Hawser'd here by a pretty short rope"; "*the grip* swoops down on me yet from time to time like a hawk"; "what a wretched physical shack (a western word) I really am—What was that of Epictetus ab't 'a spark of soul dragging a poor corpse shell around'?"; "the horrible lassitude & caved-in feeling is upon me to-day."

Good News
I don't want Bucke to know the worst until the worst is hopeless: he worries over bad news: write him in a cheerful vein—lie to him, buoy him up.

Misunderstanding
It is hard for a perfectly well man to thoroughly understand a perfectly sick man, and vice versa.

But Sleeps Well . . .
I have belly aches and head aches and leg aches and all other kinds of damned aches but I hain't got no acheless insomnia: thank God for that!

Last Resort
Traubel reports of his arrival on September 25, 1888: "Bad day today. The folks were in a state of quiet anxiety about him. Trouble with his stomach. Must have felt rotten, for he expressed a wish to have Dr. Osler come over. This was the first time that he has asked for a doctor himself."

. . . and Imperfect
Osler made light of my condition. I don't like his pooh-poohs: the professional air of the doctor grates on me.

Monologist
"I am getting to be a sort of monologuer: it is a disease that grows on a man who has no legs to walk on." A few months earlier Whitman had caught himself in this self-regarding mode: "See—I am off again—talking about my health—as if there was nothing in the world but my pains and aches to be considered."

The Body's Slave
I have seen the iron collars on the slaves in the South—bits on the wrist here, a chain—back of the collar a spike: the effect of all not pain, not anguish but a dull weight—making its wearer incapable of effort—bearing him down. It is such a collar I wear day by day: a burden impossible to shake off—vitiating all my attempts to get on my feet again.

Dangerous Stairs
On October 31, 1888, after Traubel left in the evening, Whitman made a trip downstairs alone, explaining the next day, "I went silently, so as not to disturb Mary, but I realized my exhaustion." Traubel chides him:

"Why don't you listen to our warnings? Why don't you warn yourself?" and then records: "He made no kick. I thought he would. He said: 'I'll never again attempt to make the trip alone—never: I promise.'"

Cheerful

It is wearisome, almost sad, to be confined in this way, imprisoned for days, months, years. Yet I have made up my mind to be cheerful.

Like Lear

On December 12, 1888, Traubel found Whitman's behavior reminiscent of the scene in the fourth act of *King Lear* when Lear awakens from his madness ("I fear I am not in my perfect mind . . ." 4.7.58–69): "How much like Lear—the waking Lear—W. seemed: shaken, on the boundary of reason, to-night: his gray hair long and confused: W. opening his eyes wide trying to see Harned—the pillow as a background— the splendid strong hand lying out on the coverlet—the light of the room half down: W.'s voice."

"Up" Is Down

A few days later, Traubel records, "W. unchanged. He had got up— been what Ed calls 'up' all day—(that is, he got dressed—laid on instead of under the cover)—Ed's 'up' to the reporter yesterday not covering the exact truth." A morning newspaper on this day, December 12, 1888, reported that Whitman had "sat up the greater part of the previous day" on information given at the door late at night. Traubel notes Ed Wilkins's annoyance at these journalistic intrusions: "Ed is disturbed by the reporters every night. They come at unconscionable hours. One came at 2 A.M. Rang lustily. Ed did not answer. He went away."

No Hospital Person

I don't seem to be a hospital person: I rebel against the idea of being nursed, cared for: but it's of no avail: here I am, tied up to the wharf, rotting in the sun.

Jesuitical

Most doctors—though it may seem harsh to adopt the word, it stands to me as a fact—most doctors appear to reason that it belongs to the necessary ethics of their business to be more or less jesuitical—to obscure facts, the why of medicines, the wherefores of applications. Bucke has nothing of that in his composition: not an atom of it: he'll tell anybody anything: he has no reserves, mysteries.

Whitman was always restive about the obliqueness of doctors. Just before his last Christmas, when his doctors propose to leave him and consult, he puts his foot down: "Yes, go out, and tell the result to Warrie or

Mary Davis and let them tell me—but *tell them the result.* I want to know it—no doctorial hidings and seekings."

Familiar Bucket

Traubel records, "He spoke calmly of 'kicking the bucket'—a most frequent phrase. He discusses his death without despair. 'Death is like being invited out to a good dinner.'"

Grim Jokers

Horace happens to remark, using a common slang expression, "have your own way: it's your funeral." Whitman, thinking of printing plans that could be upset by such an event, says, "That's what I was just saying: it's my funeral that's in the way!" Horace responds: "Walt you're a grim joker." Walt: "We can't cut out our fun even at the edge of the grave." Horace: "You mean that a joke says to the grave: where is thy victory?" Walt: "You're joking yourself now! Just the same I think fun is entitled to its innings even with death." Horace: "If we live again then the joke's on death anyway!" Walt: "So it is: we must, will, can't help, living again: death can't have the last word."

Dangerous Renaissance

Whitman's morale perked up markedly with the "jaunts" out-of-doors that were made possible by the purchase of a wheelchair in May 1889. But Traubel observes a down side: "He tries in every way to test his strength. Often, he will come downstairs alone—seizing a moment when nobody is about, so as to avoid their offers of assistance. A dangerous procedure. All this has come about since the arrival of the chair. It seems like renaissance."

On the Minus Side with Drugs

So I took quinine—and what did it do but set my head spinning like a wheel. And I took it—kept on taking it—for 2 or 3 days—and the more I took it the more I wheeled. And then I stopped. And it has almost always been so—I may say, always so, without the 'almost.' Drugs, for me, always defeat the best purposes: always, always. . . . I find that the drugs always excessively affect me—almost violently—that my nature seems set against them. It is true, that the drugs may effect the end for which they are applied, but I find they effect more, too—so much more, that the balance of good is on the wrong side—that I come out minus.

Near-death Experience

On May 27, 1890, the *Philadelphia Record* published a story on the poet "Succumbing to Old Age" and "Preparing for the Final Scene." Whitman's reaction: "According to the *Record* I am dying. I suppose I am, in a sense, dying: but I have been pretty sick these past six years, and the past two badly sick: so I do not see that it needs to be remarked upon now."

Rock, Endlessly Dawdling

I suppose I do nothing practically but *dawdle*—wait—let things happen. But that is as much as the rock does to fulfill its part—growing best in keeping to its place! I sit here, let the elements play about me—see what they will bring about.

Tantalizing Memory

My memory is very bad and becoming worse! The most tantalizing habit it has is of remembering just enough of a thing to remind me of how much is forgotten. . . . I don't suppose I can repeat one of them [his own poems]. They go utterly, utterly—in fact, do not even do that, for I never have them in the sense we are speaking of.

Perfect Bedside Manner

He [Dr. Daniel Longaker] has the happy faculty by which to perceive without probing for facts. Some doctors get at conclusions by intellectual, almost mathematical means. But others—masters and their kind—catch the truth as by an inspiration, by a trick of nature which we can't describe.

Note: Longaker was Whitman's physician until Whitman's death. Special contributions by the poet's friends paid his fees. On April 1, 1891, Bucke wrote, along with his $9 payment: "My idea is that the 'Fund' should pay Dr Longaker and I increase my subscription to meet this, I calculate that Dr L. should have $30.00 or $40.00 a mth. f'm now on."

Bedridden

I have been on the bed here, more or less, all day—seem to love the bed more and more—which is a bad sign.

Thinking to the Woods, Streams

In the midst of a June 1891 heat wave, Whitman reports: "I have just been enjoying the first whisper of the wind! Surely this has been the hottest day ever was. . . . Yet I seem to weather it well, too—except for the sweat, feel comfortable enough . . . [have] sat here enjoying myself—thinking myself to the woods, streams." On this same day Whitman wrote to Bucke about the heat, enclosing a letter "f'm an old Broadway omnibus driver, N Y chum." This reminds him of feats of lost strength: "F'm 25 to 45 I c'd hop on & get up front a stage while going a good trot—also put my hand on a six barr'd fence & leap over at once—(terrible reminiscence now)."

"A Voice from Death"
—The Last Months

October 12, 1891

It is a beginning of the end—disabilities multiplying—life becoming every way more difficult.

October 19

You cannot know how these days of my waiting, this night-coming time of my life, are confident, happy, secure, in you, in your right arm, in these friends you seem to have clustered, sworn. Good to me—necessary to me. Oh! the pathetic pathos of it! the deep of feeling below the deep!

November 1

"The New York papers have me dead—or substantially so. They have been driving hot and fast in each other with dark stories: the worst of which is, that the prospects ahead are *not* cheery." Traubel then says, "I am already preparing for your next birthday." "I would not do so. By next birthday I shall occupy the house out there." Horace says Walt throws "his hand east, as if to welcome Harleigh and its asylum. Still we laughed down his fears and said we would go on."

Note: Harleigh Cemetery was Whitman's chosen burial site.

December 8

I am fuddled and oppressed: these days are, some ways, the worst I have ever known. O this confinement! It is horrible!

December 13

"For about three years past I have been little by little deleted—robbed of one thing after another—till now I am in a low tide indeed." Traubel records that, at this moment, "He looked very bad—strangely and ominously feeble. . . . Brinton remarked a greater deafness, after, to me, and added, 'I can see how enfeebled he is. I should say he would not weather the winter.'" The day before, Whitman recalled, in a letter to Bucke, a disconcerting "saying of my dear old father": "Keep good heart—*the worst is to come.*"

December 15

On this day Traubel finds Whitman "in great conviction about his precarious tenure": "With no eating of account, and no exercise, no out-of-doors, what can we have ahead of us? Only wreck—only wreck!"

December 19

Traubel, just before visiting his mother and receiving from her tender hand "an old cherished copy of Tasso" as a thirty-third birthday present, visits Whitman, who is experiencing a serious worsening: "Somnolent—asks for sleep, rest. Endeavors today to use the catheter unavailing, Warrie having to operate it for him. Darkness thickens—my heart trembles on its throne—the end not unprobably near." He also notes, "The Press men getting ready for W.'s death." The next day, having heard about the newspapers from Warrie, Walt asked Horace, "Have they got me dead?"

December 20

This day, Walt admits, "I am a little confused about the days, Doctor. I had to ask Warrie this morning what day it was." He also speaks of taking some whiskey and of Warrie not thinking he should drink much water: "Warrie is a very faithful nurse, Doctor. He is very insistent. He quotes against me the old Scotchman, 'Ye ken have yer whack, Johnny, but nae ma! nae ma!'" Later this day, Dr. Alexander McAlister gives Whitman's caregivers grim news: "He is a dangerously sick man." Fatally? "Yes, I think fatally." How long can he live? "I should say, about four days." The doctor gives up, then? "Not absolutely, but the chances are only one in a million."

December 21

The next day ("providentially!") Traubel received a letter from J. W. Wallace in England that contained a "Telegraphic Cypher" list of twenty words that would allow instant and secret conveyance of news of the poet's condition. Among the resonant words and their signification were these:

Very ill, no alarm at present	Paumanok
Ditto, no hope, have sent for Dr. Bucke	Osceola
A little better	Pioneers
Much better	Joys
Worse, likely to be fatal	Starry
Worse, expect death in a day or two	Sunset
Sinking	Finale
Dead	Triumph
Funeral day after tomorrow	Lilacs

Horace's cable to Wallace this day included the words "Sunset" and "Osceola."

Note: It is most ironic that Whitman's English friends had chosen the word "Triumph" to convey news of his death.

December 28

Bucke, visiting from Canada, pays his last visit to Whitman. Traubel records it in full, wrenching detail: "Then [Bucke] broke forth, 'Well, good-bye Walt! I must go!' 'I suppose! I suppose!' 'Well, I *ought* to go, Walt. I don't *want* to go! But you know I am not my own master—that I have duties.' 'Yes, Maurice, I know.' 'But if I go now, I can no doubt get back soon to see you again.' 'No, Maurice, you will never see me again!' And after a pause, 'I ought to be gone now—it were best all over now—I would be more than satisfied.' The voice—the desire! Bucke could hardly speak—the tears sprang to my eyes. 'This is the end of all, Maurice. This is the end—you will never see me again!' 'Well, Walt, these things are not in our own hands. We have to submit to them. I hate to go.' 'Yes, it tears me up to have you leave.' Bucke stooped over and kissed him—kissed him again—withdrew from the bed a minute, 'Oh! so loth to depart!' then back and took W.'s hand again, and stopped over and once more kissed him . . . then back for another look (oh! the pain—the solemn sad secret thought and heart-throb!). . . ."

January 2, 1892

An old, well-knit, strong-timbered keel takes a long time to break up. . . . It is no triumph to get where I am now from where I was a week ago—no triumph—no victory—I do not glory in it. You ought to wish—all our friends ought to wish—as I wish—that this was all over now—all. What does the ship come to, Horace—the old hulk—the useless, clinging old hulk—its last voyage over—its tasks all done?

January 23

Had Walt any words for Moncure Conway? "Yes, my best respects! Tell him I am here, very low, very low—but holding the fort, after a way—not yet surrendered. Yet very near surrender-point."

February 3

No strength—not the least: lassitude, lassitude, lassitude—inability, inability, inability!

February 4

"Haven't you now a hint of a suspicion of health?" Traubel asks. "Not even that, Horace, nothing but what you see—nothing but utter giving-out-ness—failure. I feel almost as if emptied of the last fill of life."

February 8

Bad—bad—bad—bad—bad! Horace, it is wearing me out. I am slipping away—slipping, slipping—the tide is falling. I feel the last turn. [Traubel tries to console him.] You all try to buoy me up—you are brave—you have fought like lions, hyenas—doctors, all: but, dear boy, we must not deceive ourselves—no, there is no gain in that—we are at the last twist of the road, the very last.

February 12

In the last months even satisfying the desires of the "damned autographites" became a struggle: "Warrie put his strong arm back of W. and lifted him up. I was at hand with light, pen and ink. W. breathed hard from the effort—wrote 'Walt Whitman' first—stopping at 'm' as if to resume strength—and then followed with 'Sculptor's photo: Feb. 11, '92'—stopping again at 'Feb.,' closing his eyes—then finally making a desperate lunge for the rest and getting it. I took the card and he sank back exhausted."

March 3

Traubel observes: "Evinces little interest in anything. Lies there with his eyes closed, often, and submits without word or sign of life to the operations of attendants. The hastening signs of decrepitude worry us and he perceives them. Was detected the other day feeling his own pulse."

March 7

"I have had as bad a day as ever was prepared. I have gone down and down—as if resistlessly, hopelessly, inexorably, pressed. Oh! Horace, it is the *feeling of death.*" Horace says this was "Uttered calmly and sweetly, with no tone of complaint. The voice very weak, however."

March 12

Traubel records: "He has been spending a very bad day—a day of incuriosity, silence—without appetite, relish, strength. The west window still unopened, the papers untouched, the mail unasked for. . . . He instantly recognized me, dark as it was, and attempted to say my name—choking on the 'O! Hor—' "

March 18

In reply to Traubel's question how he felt, Whitman said, " 'Like fifty thousand devils'—his manner making me laugh and my laugh exciting him to laughter and with the laughter coming a cough and choke (constant rattling of the mucus in the throat)."

March 21

Traubel asks, "How have you passed today?" "It has been a dreadful day: I suffer all the time. I have no relief, no escape—it is monotony, monotony, monotony—in pain!" Traubel notes this was "not uttered complainingly at all. Coughed violently, choking a good deal, and the constant rattling of mucus in the throat. His words throughout our talk uttered feebly—brokenly—but the sentences and thought coherent and clear as 20 years gone. Hand cold—forehead warm. He pressed my hand again and again while I stayed."

March 23

Traubel records: "Once today Mrs. Davis forgot to return W. the urinal when she shifted him. He called out, 'Urinal, Mary,' and she laughingly returned. 'You've got so many attachments I'm sure to forget some.' He laughed heartily himself at this—twice repeating his laughter."

March 24

On this day, in the midst of painfully moving the poet in order to install a new waterbed, Traubel said to Davis, "He could not look worse if he was dead." When Walt begged to be put back in bed, Traubel comments, "Oh! the music and pathos of that tone! I looked up. He was as if on the brink—about to break. My heart stood almost still. Stretched along the lounge, death itself might have come then and there. We had great difficulty getting him in a comfortable position."

March 25

Warrie gets a laugh from Walt when he likens the splashing of the waterbed to the "splashing up the side of a ship." Traubel comes and finds him "weak to dullness. . . . No words, no messages, no interest in anything or anybody." Traubel visits again after midnight, and Whitman says, "I don't rest any way I am put, but a change now and then relieves the terrible pressure." Traubel notes that he asks for no food "but pulls again at the brandy punches."

March 26

About 5 P.M. Davis sends for Dr. McAlister; when he arrives he examines Whitman and says, "This is the last—he is dying."

"The Last Mile Driven"
—The End

Whitman's life and his Leaves of Grass *were intertwined, like a double helix, for the last four decades of his life. Fortunately, the poignantly climactic end of each was powerfully captured by Traubel in his final transcriptions. Whitman announced a kind of* requiescat in pace *for his life's work on January 26, precisely two months before he himself "slipped cable." Though Traubel found the poet "quite as feeble as yesterday" when he arrived for his evening visit, Whitman later "spoke majestically of his work, of 'its now near close' and of the 'doors soon to be shut.' Then suddenly—I standing at the foot of the bed, he almost raised from his pillow—spoke these solemn words, as if with the air of a charge and farewell." The rousing finale of these words follows here.*

After it comes Horace's emotional farewell as Walt (in the words of his short poem "Life and Death") solves at once "The two old, simple problems ever intertwined, / Close home, elusive, present, baffled, grappled. . . ." Just after Dr. McAlister announced "This is the last—he is dying," Traubel arrived at Mickle Street ("at 6:07"); Tom Harned appeared at the top of the stairs and told him, "Walt is dying . . . it is nearly over." Traubel's narrative begins at this moment.

"The Only Path Possible"

"All writings heretofore have been done on other suppositions—even Shakespeare's, Virgil's—yes, after a big, big drop, Lowell's. But my own departure has been quite definite and conclusive: and here, today, at the end, with the book closed or closing, I glory in the surrender—have no regrets, have nothing to recall. It is by such unhesitating lines I have aimed to draw, or remain, near the mysteries of nature: near them, to feel their breath, even when I knew nothing of what they meant, and could but wonder and listen, as if to vague music. I had all this clear from the start—I had all these determinations—I never erred—never strayed. And now, whether to be charged as a fool, or as reckoned victor, I am sure of my choice, at least for me, was well-taken—was, finally, the only path possible for me to foot." Traubel records the little coda to this final flourish: "This was all uttered as readily as his physical condition would allow, with tones almost of vigor, and with eyes wide open, and several times even the lifting of his hands. I could have wept and laughed, with the conflict of my feelings. I exclaimed, 'Yes, yes, Walt—I hear it all—I love it all.' And he, 'Love it? Yes! And I loved it—oh! so much!—and now an end! But the book, Horace: there are things resting on you, too, to fulfill—many things—many—many. Keep a firm hand—stand on your own feet. Long have I kept my road—made my road: long, long! Now I am at bay—the last mile is driven: but the book—the book is safe!'"

"Last Touch of Life"

It struck my heart, yet it was the hourly fear at last fulfilled [Horace records]. I hastened into the room and up to the bed. His face was looking towards the windows and his eyes were closed. Dr. McAlister sat at the head of the bed—Warrie and Mrs. Davis were on the other side—Tom strolled in at the foot. McAlister accosted me in quite positive tones, which seemed for an instant to arrest W., whose eyes fluttered open as he struggled to get his right hand out from under the bedclothing, as if to grasp my own (as so often in days gone)—but the effort died of its own weight and the eyes closed wearily. Once he moaned. McAlister remarked, "This will not last long, unless he rallies—and he can hardly do that." I took W.'s right hand and from this moment to the end held it, as if it was my last touch of his life. (I write this now, 10:30, in the back room, after another look at him as he lay front there, stretched out and still. Over my head the little bell. No more its pull—no more the summons—for another summoner hath summoned him!) He breathed on, more lightly, more quickly—the mouth open, now and then twitching—his color all gone and death's white upon him. Again the Doctor said, "See, it grows fainter." And Warrie leaning forward, ears and eyes intent (as ours, too), exclaimed, "Did you see—he skipped a breath or two," as indeed was the case. This phenomenon growing more marked and the breath very irregular—the mouth working again and several times the brows contracting as if from the difficulty of breathing. "What we expected in December is happening now?" "Yes." I asked, "And still there's no hope?" "None—he will go." "And rapidly?" "Very soon." At 6:25 he emitted a marked "Oh!" and seemed to stop breathing. Harned exclaiming, "It is all over." McAlister announced, "No, his heart still beats." After a struggle again there was a flutter of life. At 6:28 came a long gasp—we all took it to be the last. The Doctor cried, "A candle—let me have a candle." And by its light peered at W. For a minute breath was suspended. At 6:29 another slight heave of the chest, a twist of the mouth and a labored breath. Here his eyes opened but gave no sign of recognition and languorously closed again. These were the final flickerings of life—a breath again at 6:30, 6:31 (three here overlapping each other), at 6:32 and at 6:34—and this was the last. Harned turned his head away—I heard a choked sob from Mrs. Davis—and nearby was Warrie, still eagerly observant, but with a mixed sigh and cry in his throat. "Is he gone" I looked at McAlister, who had his head low over

W.'s breast. "The heart still beats." But there seemed no pulse. "Put your fingers here," he counselled; and I did so, and caught the feathery beat, as a gentle breeze on silk. (When I first took W.'s hand the palm was warm and its back cold—and I touched his head, which was cold.) And so Warrie felt—and so Harned—and still the life seemed to stay. "He is dead!" said McAlister, "practically dead—see," and he lifted the fallen eyelid and touched the ball of the eye, which was fixed and showed no sense of impact. But at 6:43 came the last. The heart was still! No contortion, no struggle, no physical regret—and the eyes closed of themselves and the body made none of the usual motions towards stiffening out—towards rigidity. By and by McAlister and I together laid him decently and reverently straight. I laid his hand quietly down—something in my heart seemed to snap and that moment commenced my new life—a luminous conviction lifting me with him into the eternal. Harned murmured, "It is done," and I could not but exclaim, "It is triumph and escape." The life had gone out at sunset—the light of day not yet utterly gone—the last rays floating with timid salutation into the gloom . . . all was peaceful, beautiful, calm, fitting. The day clouded—a light drip of rain now descending. I leaned down and kissed him, hand and head—and then I went out, shadowed, into the penetrating night.

Whitman's bedroom in the Mickle Street house,
shown after a scrupulous restoration in 1998.
© *Jeanne Bening, photographer.*

The End 283

"The Touch of Peace"
—Mortuary

Traubel leaves to speak "the dark word" at the post office, stops by to tell his parents the news, and then goes home to tell his wife, Anne, and have supper. Only then "the flooding tears at last!" But a few hours later in the evening he returns to begin supervising mortuary arrangements, among them the taking of a plaster deathbed cast by Thomas Eakins. An autopsy was also planned. George Whitman objected strenuously to it, but it was made clear to him that Walt had consented to the postmortem the previous December. It took place in the early evening of the 27th in the rear parlor at Mickle Street and lasted four hours. Present were four doctors, an undertaker, Traubel, and, briefly at intervals, some others (even a newspaper reporter— "we had some trouble dismissing him").

Repose and Majesty—the 26th

The face already assumes a repose and majesty. The emaciation very evident but not painful and growing less so. The body was already getting rigid. Eyes beautifully sweet and lips closed. Hand not nearly so fallen away as other members. He lay there in the light, his splendid head seen at its noblest and all the history of his tumultuous years wiped away by the touch of peace. The strange quiet smote me. I leaned over and kissed his forehead (oh! that kiss! and the afternoon's kiss, the life just gone!)

Bulletin—the 26th

The bulletin at door effective. I escape reporters entirely. The end so uneventful—so simple, quiet—so without dressings and puerilities—a simple few words will tell all.

The bulletin, composed by Harned, McAlister, and Traubel and signed by the doctor, was indeed simple: "Whitman began sinking at 4:30 P.M. He continued to grow worse and died at 6:43 P.M. The end came peacefully. He was conscious until the last. There were present at the bedside when he died Mrs. Davis, Warren Fritzinger, Thomas B. Harned, Horace L. Traubel, and myself."

Death Mask—the 27th

Walt's face serene and sweet and composed. The head never seemed so marked. Eakins threw back the shirt from the shoulders. How like one of the grand classic pictures of gods, with the hands calmly folded and that strange yellow-white, and peace everyhow lined however the eye looked! They worked and worked—I watched and watched. In from the north the gray light—outside the beating rain—the room, so long dedicated to his sacred work, still redolent of his nature. I could catch the faint odor of his hair. I touched his hand. Though cold it was yet somewhat pliable.

The death mask has been wholly successful, though it had taken three rather than two hours. . . . No slips—no stumbles. And the hand also was done. The head tonight seemed no way the worse. The wavy float of the beard rather damaged, and a red line burns the bridge of the nose, as if the plaster had at that point been stubborn. I carry that scene upstairs: the busy workers—Eakins directing and laboring both—and W.'s serene face and folded hands and bared shoulders, as a good stretched out on god's own altar, dead.

The Autopsy—the 27th

The wonder of the doctors as the operations proceeded seemed to grow. Once [Dr.] Cattell said, "This man must have lived weeks and weeks simply by force of will power." I put in, "And serenity," and he then, "Yes, that too." . . . When the brain was extracted Cattell put it into his gupsack. The work kept us up till towards ten. . . . To hear the claw and dip of the instruments—to see the skull broken and opened and the body given the ravening prey of the investigator had its horrors—then its compensations. I looked beyond and saw science, man, with benediction sweet. I stood all without hurt and wrote Cattell's notes in his book as he called them out. Somehow I could not have gone home, leaving them at this work, or avoiding. I seemed to hear an injunction out of space, "Keep then close to the temple till the final toll is paid." And so I braved and threw that inner protest which so closely attended me throughout. To these men, body and brain yielded unexpected fruits.

Note: The contents of Dr. Cattell's gupsack came to rest in Philadelphia's American Anthropometric Society. Later it was transferred to the Wistar Institute of Anatomy and Biology for examination of signs of genius; afterward, it was accidentally destroyed.

Gathering of the Forces—the 28th

March 28 Traubel devoted mostly to informing Whitman's circle and thinking about travel plans for mourners. He greeted Bucke on his delayed arrival from Canada ("Looked well . . . approved of autopsy heartily"), wired "Lilacs" as per the cipher to England, denoting "funeral day after tomorrow," and fielded a note written in high dudgeon by Talcott Williams of the *Philadelphia Press* objecting to the thought of the unbashful Robert Ingersoll speaking at the funeral service: "Mr. Ingersoll's presence will lead to grave misconception and do serious injury now and in the future." Ingersoll ultimately did speak, though with his fiery agnostic views somewhat doused. A note from John Johnston in New York included his memory of a remarkable parallel to the recent death scene: "Fifteen years ago yesterday Walt was with us when my wife was taken sick and died. He was in the room until the last." Traubel also had to draw up a list of pallbearers and confirm their willingness to serve. And all this on a day when Traubel had to work: "Spent today at the Bank. Feeling all broken up." Still, at day's end he was able to note, "Saw the body several times today. The face is getting more and more composed." The day's last entry: "The world oppresses me. I cannot rest."

A Near Ecclesiastic Catastrophe—the 28th

But the real crisis of March 28 was caused by the machinations of George Whitman's wife, Louisa: "Mrs. Whitman has done an extraordinary thing, going to Dr. McConnell in Philadelphia and asking him to conduct the services at the grave. Bucke says, 'My God! It was like to wreck us all! I wouldn't go to the funeral—no, I wouldn't: I couldn't—dear old Walt would be outraged! But as luck would have it Mrs. Whitman came in this morning and in about half an hour I had everything amicably fixed, so that McConnell will not be present!' A narrow escape from catastrophe."

A Publisher's Feeler—the 29th

Wishing to get in on the ground floor of a publishing venture that would, in the end, take nine decades, Jeannette Gilder, a woman much admired by Whitman, wrote to Traubel: "John Burroughs has just told me of the interesting ms. you have of Whitman's conversations. If you have not arranged for the publication of the work I feel quite sure that the Cassell Publishing of New York & London, of which I am literary advisor, would be glad to undertake this publication."

Perhaps with this feeler in mind, Traubel records that he "spent several hours, to 1:30 [A.M.], working on W.'s literary effects. Warrie secured barrels and we filled them. Many manuscripts and letters on the floor. . . . Four or five old scrapbooks (containing manuscript beginnings from notebooks, etc.). We packed things together, pell-mell, intending to send them to my house for me to sort."

The Public Viewing—the 30th

Finally to 328 Mickle Street, arriving at 10:40. They had admitted a group of people who passed the coffin (set in the back parlor), thinking soon to have the curious throng over with. But somehow this was merely the taking down of the bars, as it proved: for this group was followed by another, and these by others, as if risen by instinct from all quarters of the wind, till a magic stream was in fully play, and no break was at all thenceforth possible. The line grew longer and longer—it was silent, sympathetic, curious, expressive. It stretched out and up the street and then north through Fourth to the railroad—and it continued its reach and play for three hours till, at 1:50, we were compelled to stem and refuse it, in order to prepare for the cortege. . . . I caught glimpses of tradesmen and familiar faces in all walks—men whom W. had known well and seen often. . . . Said a ferryman out of the line to me, as I stood there, "I have a picture—a portrait—at home, just in the frame he gave it me in." . . . Overhead the clear blue—the day mild. The throng sedate, serious.

Many Camerados, but One (Almost) Missing

Whole row of reporters in hallway, ranged up the stairs. People curious to see Walt's room, but we soon cleared them all out and locked the doors. . . . Someone was sure Peter Doyle was seen somewhere in the crowd, but I saw nothing of him till we had got to Harleigh, when he was pointed out to me (by Burroughs) up the hill, twirling a switch in his hand, his tall figure and big soft hat impressively set against the white-blue sky. (Returning, we stopped our carriage, seeing him on the road, leisurely walking, and Burroughs called him, he running up, shaking hands all around and calmly talking some to us, as to himself and Walt. Is on a Providence line of railroad. . . . Seemed immobile, not greatly moved by the occasion, yet was sincere and simple and expressed in his demeanor the powers by which he must have attracted Walt.)

Maurice Traubel Absents Himself

My father would not come here, though he went to Harleigh. "I want to paint a picture of him—one that is worthy of his best days, in the flush of his life—and so I must keep the old image, without this pallor and show of death." (My father a man of exquisite organization, vibrant to all enthusiasms and impulses of beauty.)

Last Communion

Then the final view of W. . . . I pressed my lips to the calm brow, now unresponsive, but memoried over with the traceries of joy and care. The beard combed and not quite freely flowing and playing as of old, but the lips very sweet, not set—and the fine nose and line of cheek and brow and arched eyes past description. Burroughs wept—and I?—yes, I wept, too—for somehow even this dead form reached up to me, as if for a last embrace, and I held it in my arms long and long and pressed it with a passion of love. And Burroughs there, alone. I took his hand, and together we stood, gazing, thinking, remembering, loving—consoling, he me and I him: and then a gaze backward and the calm face there, undisturbed, warning as to content and visioning us in the future. . . . And as we stood there together, I heard the lid drop, the door closed, the face forever shut out, the new life begun.

The Cortege

The day bright and cloudless. Burroughs quiet—Bucke profoundly moved by the popular aspect the day had assumed, and Burroughs responding, "Yes, it would have been Walt's own wish." We passed the many familiar spots—passed the tollgate (the curious man to whom Walt had given some books hurrying to the door to say, "It is Mr. Whitman's funeral! Good old man!").

The Funeral Service

Horace gave a full report of the ceremonies at Harleigh in an essay, "At the Graveside of Walt Whitman," which appeared at the end of *In Re Walt Whitman* (1893), a large volume of essays on the poet that was edited by his three literary executors, Traubel, Harned, and Bucke, and printed by his old associate David McKay. Here is a brief summary of the highlights from Traubel's narrative.

> The funeral was attended with no form and little ceremony. . . . The services at Harleigh were in the open air. The platform and a little area fronting it were covered with a tent. . . . The bearers of the coffin were preceded by a few of Whitman's friends and followed by others. The procession into the tent, past the thousand eager, serious, on-pressing faces, and under the folds of the tent, was touched with the ardent color of a new faith. No words were said. . . . When all [the speakers] were seated, quiet fell upon the gathering as by its own free feeling. The sides of the tent were all out. Far on every hand, up the incline of the hill, down towards the lake, was a stretching, breathing arena of faces. . . . It had been the purpose to have nothing done that could not be done by Whitman's nearer lovers and friends in his own spirit, without the insult of parade or ceremonial. And what was sought was secured.

First, Francis Howard Williams, a Quaker poet and dramatist who was one of Whitman's oldest and closest Philadelphia friends, read the hermit thrush's song from "When Lilacs Last in the Door-Yard Bloom'd." Then Tom Harned spoke, asserting justly (to anyone who has read all of *With Walt Whitman in Camden*) that "no one could detect any intellectual sluggishness or the timidity of age. His keen insight and clear vision never failed him."

Williams then recited three short passages from Confucius, Gautama, and "Jesus the Christ" (Matthew 5:3–8, "Blessed are the poor in spirit"). The next speaker was Daniel Brinton, a professor of anthropology at the University of Pennsylvania and one of Whitman's inner circle. He spoke of Whitman's "contending spirit" having "reached the end of the untried roads he loved to follow." And: "No idler was he, no dallier with the golden hours: but arduous, contentious, undissuadable and infinitely loving. He came bearing the burden of a Gospel, the Gospel of the Individual Man; he came teaching that the soul is not more than the body, and that the body is not more than the soul; and that nothing, not God himself, is greater to one than one's self is."

A passage from the Koran and verses from the Bible (Isaiah 12:1–2 and John 11:25–6) was then read by Williams. Bucke spoke next of Whitman's "trust in the essential friendliness to man of the infinite universe; his calm and contented acceptance of all that is or that happens; his absolute assurance that he and all of us came well and shall go well . . . in fine, his faith, intense, glowing, vital beyond the limits of any I have elsewhere known or read of." These, Bucke said, "have been to me the great solace of my life."

Williams then read short passages from the *Zend Avesta* and this sentence from Plato: "Considering the soul to be immortal and able to bear all evil and good, we shall always persevere in the road which leads upward."

Speaking at somewhat greater length (perhaps for ten minutes), Robert Ingersoll delivered—as no doubt was hoped for—a climactic oratorical hurrah. "A great man, a great American, the most eminent citizen of this republic, lies dead before us," he began. Calling Whitman "a free, untrammelled spirit" and identifying as "one of the greatest lines in our literature" his "Not till the sun excludes you do I exclude you," Ingersoll praised him for "caring nothing for the little maps and charts with which timid pilots hug the shore" and for walking "among verbal varnishers and veneerers, among literary milliners and tailors with the unconscious majesty of an antique god." The "famous atheist" also praised Whitman as one who "wrote a liturgy for mankind; he wrote a great and splendid psalm of life, and he gave to us the gospel of humanity—the greatest gospel that can be preached."

After Ingersoll's resounding peroration, Traubel reports, "the great hush that had fallen was broken by the faint sobs of men and women overcome by the strain of emotion. Again the coffin was lifted—again the procession trailed its burden on. And at the tomb nothing was said; only at every point the faces: up the hill, along the road—some so distant they could not share in the direct scene and yet were loth to go until it was known that all was done. Birds sang, the fresh leafage rustled in a gentle breeze, the smell of the new year filled the senses. A great man stood near me. He said: 'We seem to leave a greater part of the best that is in us here with him'—adding, however: 'And yet curiously we will go out afresh into life, double-armed by what he has given in return.'"

Traubel adds as his own finale: "We thought we had buried him. But he eluded the darkness and the pall. He reappeared in us. We turned from death and took up 'the burden and the lesson' eternal of life."

The Burial House
at Harleigh Cemetery

*A much-vexed topic of discussion at Mickle Street through the later volumes
of* With Walt Whitman in Camden *was the design, planning, and payment
for the construction of a rather elaborate burial vault in the grand Harleigh
Cemetery that had been laid out in 1885 in the new "forest lawn" style on
the outskirts of Camden. The notion of Whitman's being buried there appears
to have been planted in December 1889. The poet reports to Traubel, "I have
had a visitor from Harleigh Cemetery. We had quite a talk. He wishes to give
me a lot in the Cemetery, I to write a poem on it." Though Traubel thought
the idea "curious," Whitman said he would entertain the idea. On December
18 Whitman wrote to Bucke: "The Harleigh Cemetery Supt. has just been
here—they propose to give me a lot, & I wish to have one in a small side hill
in a wood—& am going out soon to locate it." He visited Harleigh in May
1890 "to look again at my burial lot—(it suits me)." Eventually, in October
1890 he contracted with Reinhalter & Co. for a $4,000 structure (this was
more than twice the price of 328 Mickle Street). The simple design was
based on William Blake's etching,* Death's Door. *Construction began on
October 1, 1890, and was pronounced complete a year later. The final bill
was greater than anticipated, and a long squabble ensued over payment.
"How happy I am!" he said, just a month before he died, when the matter
was finally settled. (He was not told that Tom Harned paid $1,000 of his
own to resolve the dispute.) All of Walt's inner circle considered the expendi-
ture outrageous, and Walt's own conscience was tender about the project
jeopardizing future care for his brother Eddy.*

Beautiful Lot

Did I tell you I went out to the Cemetery yesterday [Christmas Day
1889]? I selected a beautiful lot—to me the most beautiful in the
place—the land slopes down to Cooper's Creek. I think there must be
fifty or more buried there already.

Alas, Poor Yorick

On an April day in 1890 when Whitman went out and found the air "a
little pungent—champagney: but strong, pleasant," he announced
that he now possessed a deed to his cemetery lot: "So you see I am now

sure of a place to be buried in—if that has any importance. Wasn't it Hamlet who said it had *not?*"

Into the Woods

On May 14, 1890, Whitman visited Harleigh and elaborated to Traubel on a highly characteristic choice of terrain for his tomb: "I went down to the Cemetery—Harleigh: I want you to go there, too—see my lot. Ask for Moore, the superintendent. He will treat you well: he is an Irishman of the better kind: I like him. And curiously, he is the first man of the kind, in such a position, whose views coincide with my own. He is eager to keep the trees—to keep nature out there in her own character—not to have her spoiled, deflected. I think they wanted me to go in the open, in some prominent place, conspicuous—but I went deep in the woods. Moore is not bitten with the art-side of life: not sacrificed to that bane of all literary, artistic ambition: elegance, system, convention, rule, canons. In that respect he is our man."

Death's Ponderous Door

On June 4, 1891, Whitman wrote to Bucke of difficulties with the heavy granite door planned for the tomb: "the ponderous door is *not* yet hung, baffles even the machinist & stone-cutters—when done &c. Will probably be the rudest most undress'd structure (with an idea)—since Egypt, perhaps the cave dwellers."

Irrational

Traubel records that "W. says to Harned that he promised his mother on her dying bed to care for Eddy, that the tomb contract is irrational in face of that, as I have known and contended all along." In a letter to Traubel dated January 25, 1892, Bucke refers to the "tomb matter" as "this (foolishness or freak—if you like to call it so) this false step of his old age," but he urges going along with the business. In a letter the next day he writes: "Yes, he has a little money—he has also a crippled brother to whom he is leaving it. Yes, he spent money on a tomb—was it foolish? Well which of us has not spent money foolishly?"

Prospective Residents

In November 1891, we have seen, Whitman told Tom Harned that "he had two dead children whom he wished to put into the tomb." Some time later, Whitman said merely to Traubel, "I have no particular wish, except that father and mother be put there, I between them."

Note: In the event, no Whitman progeny arrived, and the later wish was fulfilled. There are eight crypts in the tomb, arranged in two rows of four. On the top row, from left to right: Louisa Whitman (wife of George) and her eight-month-old, son Walter; brother George Whitman; brother Edward Whitman; sister Hannah Heyde (but *not* her despised "viper husband"). Bottom row: mother, Louisa; the poet; father, Walter; and a vacant crypt.

Walt on a Memorial

Horace reads to Walt an extract from the *New York Herald* in which money is solicited for flowers for the poet's "sick chamber" and, should a surplus remain at his death, for "some memorial as a souvenir of departed worth." The response: "I am not in favor of either—not in favor of the flowers or the memorial."

The Last Hurrah:
May 1919

Horace Traubel's extraordinary labors on Walt Whitman's behalf by no means ceased with the interment at Harleigh. Not only did he see into print the first three volumes of his transcribed conversations and several other Whitman-related volumes, but, as the introduction describes, he also kept the poet's flame alight in the pages of the Conservator, *a liberal monthly he founded in March 1890 and edited for thirty years. Scarcely an issue appeared that did not have a Whitman article or item.*

Each issue of the Conservator *began with a wide-ranging editorial called (borrowing a word from Whitman) a "Collect" by "H.L.T." In the end, Traubel's weak heart held out just long enough for him to be able to celebrate the centennial of Whitman's birth in the next-to-last Collect he composed. In the May 1919 issue it was devoted entirely to Whitman. Following here, somewhat abbreviated, is this final word on the poet's career and fundamental meanings. Full of characteristic plain speaking, acerbity, and verve, it makes an eloquent and fitting conclusion to this book.*

On the first page of the next Conservator, *Traubel informed his readers that, due to his "serious physical disabilities," he had asked for and gained post office permission to combine the following four issues. But the June* Conservator *was indeed the last. Traubel died September 8 while on an excursion to Bon Echo, Ontario, near Montreal.*

I know you can tell me how old Walt Whitman is this year. But how old are you? That's more important. How many years old or young are you? How many years sensible or senseless? How many years merciful or malignant? How many years illuminated or blind? It don't matter so much whether he served or not. Have you served? Are you serving? Can you really tell your own age? You think you've done enough when you've told about him. But you haven't. Not till you've told about yourself. You speak of honoring him with celebrations. You don't, you can't, honor him. You honor yourselves. His account is closed. Yours is still open. Tell your own story. Not mostly of what you've done. Chiefly of what you are. How old were you on your first birthday? Are you any older now? I hear the sayers say they've lived through so many noble years. How many noble years have the sayers lived through? He wasn't perfect. Nor are you or we. We'd be afraid of each other if we were. We don't have to romance about him or ourselves. The truth's good enough. Light enough and shadow enough. It's too late to pace him. Now we must pace ourselves. It's all right to indicate his loyalties. But what of our own? I've said at Whitman meetings: "We'll never have a real Whitman day till we come together to celebrate ourselves not him." I hear wonderful things said about him today by people who when he was alive greeted him with derision and deliberate venom. I don't say it's too late for them to see. It's never too late, of course. But it's some late, quite some. He toed the mark fairly well. Do we? . . . Well, I'm sixty. And you: what are you? They're just as significant in all cases if we've made them so. What have you made of your years? What have I made of mine? I've won my way to sixty years by an untraveled route and I've not had a free pass, either. You've made your years also suggestive. Suggestive of what? That's the test of all. Not what Whitman was but what you are and what I am. One of us may precede the others for a while but all arrive just the same. Jesuses and Judases. We're always tempted to glorify big men when they reach to big names. But when they're just as big with little names we refuse to speak, except, perhaps, in scorn or skepticism. We say: "God, the father." And yet we rob the man next door. We say: "Whitman the universal comrade." And yet we hate the alien. One of our most eloquent orators at the Brevoort Whitman meetings used to be continually talking of "the God damned Jews." Is your sense of fraternity parochial or international? Is it white or yellow or black or all three or none of them? Everything we say of Walt comes back to us. Good and bad. Wise and foolish. To paraphrase Walt himself: "Idolatry's to the idolater and comes back most to him." The initiatory lesson from Walt is to be stuck on yourself. Then there's another to go with it. That is, to let every other fellow be stuck on himself. Just as though all the stars were made for him, whoever he is. As though everybody was just for him and he was for everybody. The preacher-priest class as a class (there were always exceptions) reprobated the theory of evolution till all culture and science as a class accepted it. Then they claimed it as their own. And when the time comes for the succeeding hypothesis they'll stand by evolution with their usual vehement anathema till the next step is safe. Then they'll take the next step. And say they always knew it was in order. And claim the new ground as they did the old. The literary class as a class (there were always exceptions) derided Whitman till Whitman became inevitable. There are a few feeble echoes of that derision yet. Now they're acclaiming him and possessing him. It's the same old story. When we pass to the next man they'll caustically and brutally defend Whitman against our new adventure. Walt said: "Greater than me will follow." . . .

Walt was ushered into heaven with the ribald noise of brass bands. Yes. Especially brass. As long as he could be denied he remained an outlaw. Schools, customs, rejected him. Scholarship, fashion, professionalism and professorialism, church and state, in the dubious measures of their silences and laughters, treated him as a negligible claimant. But he stayed round till they melted. He wasn't scared off by bad weather. He wore out the patience of thousands of hells. They gave in. He didn't. Of course he had only the usual steering chart to go by. Every man, derelict or divine, has this and no more. He took his medicine as they take theirs. With mingled emotions of gladness and sorrow. He was capable of being way down as being way up. He didn't like being cursed and denounced any more than you or I do. You see, Jesus needed his Judas. Whitman needed his persecutors. We all need something. Our poverty. Our misfortunes. Even our ignominy. Malignity plays its part with mercy. I never complain for Whitman. I rather complain for his traducers. He didn't lose. They lost. They paid for all postponements and delays. Just as in our average life the system pays for all the sufferings of its victims. Who paid the cost of hanging John Brown? Tradition says Brown did. But we know that America, civilization, did. The shadow of affliction gives the proper accent to every portrait. I never resent the interrogation. . . . There seems to be no end to the historic questionings. You cant be so little as to be missed. Nor can you be big enough to be feared. There's a no for every yes. A black for every white. A discord for every harmony. Walt was called out in the usual way. He told us who he was. Where he came from. Where he was going. The world questioned all. It permitted no angle to go unexamined. Dagger thrusts. Thwartings of will. Confession of dereliction. Erratic crimes of intention. Nothing avoided its vigilant eyes. That was the proof of the pudding. Natural, inevitable and welcome. He emerged from the great darkness. The tests are universal. They compass the range of all benevolence and malevolence. They subject us to all the petticisms of intrigue and pettifoggery. Things are flung in the road to trip us up at every step. Friends go back on us. Promises are broken. Notes defaulted. Death, even with murder, complicates the issue. Fifty hold back for one who rushes on. Chaos. Bedlam. Hoots and howls. Warnings. Threatenings. There are no two ways. There's truly only one way. For bootblack and bard. . . . That's the reason Walt to his very last day was concerned lest he hadn't made, as he said, his fellowship for the criminals, outcasts, unpopulars, unmentionables, sufficiently unmistakable. He craved no isolated eminence. He in fact craved no eminence. He was a real crowd man though he didn't call himself such in my terms. He recognized his intimacy with those social classes who are not qualified on the lists. With the forgotten. With those who if they're ever named at all are only included apologetically. The and-so-forths. The oh-yeses that we never invite unless someone shames us into hospitality. . . . He much preferred to be the nearest of men than to be the only man. "It's deadly black today," he said to me once, "but I guess the shadow's proper for my light." So you see the brass bands wont hurt his feelings now. Not even the brass. The most tragic of the experiences he was subjected to were the vital accompaniments of his exaltation. As they also are of yours and mine. With the after brass and all.

Well, boys, girls, everybody, we can tell each other how old old Walt was when he died and how old he'd be if he was still with us in the flesh. We all know all about that. But let's take a more immediate account. How old or dear are you to me and us? How many years to the good or how many years to the bad? Walt did his stunt. And on the whole did it handsomely. Have you done your stunt? Have I done mine? Let's see. I don't ask you to limit yourselves in talking of Walt or to withdraw anything you've said. But what of yourselves? Where have you stood? . . . This is a good time for Whitmanites to confess. Not to the authority of a priest. Not even to the authority of Walt. But to the impressive authority of the self. Every one of us. Have we gone to jail with the innocent? Or have we backed water at the jail door? Whittier once wrote to a young man: "Ally yourself with some unpopular cause." Have we done that? Hugo said: "Fear the popular high roads. Take to the wilderness." Have we taken to the wilderness? Zola warned authors: "The way of the academy is the way of death." Have we avoided the way of the academy? When we play with the game the game plays us. Walt one day said to me when his enemies were particularly active: "Let them howl: we'll outdo them with silence." Have we proved capable of meeting public clamor in that spirit? . . . Have we put Walt into a cabinet for observation or into the flesh and blood of our virile living activity? Is he an oil painting on a wall? Or is he the outcast of some slandered password of revolution? Is he a volume of poem words or the flaming tissue of a challenging reform? Has he become a book of reference or a way of life? He has said to himself that he don't teach a lesson but rather takes down the bars to a lesson. He takes down the bars. We are the lesson. He says again that he's best understood in the lesson by which he's himself destroyed. He don't take us as a possession. He leaves us to our own ownerships. We're to find out how many years worth while we are not how many years illustrious he is. He used to say that when you got his meaning *Leaves of Grass* was no longer "I, Walt Whitman, of Manhattan the son," but just as much "I, Horace Traubel, of Camden the son," or I, anybody, man or woman, of anywhere, the son or daughter.

Citations

Passages are identified by their initial phrase. Unless otherwise indicated, all citations are from With Walt Whitman in Camden, giving first the volume, then the page number. Quotations from Whitman's Correspondence in The Collected Writings are cited C, volume number, page number.

INTRODUCTION

I am disposed 3:279 Nothing new C4:159 Never miss 9:352 greeted me 6:145 called out 7:389 Four times 9:304 the fourth time 9:334 Eight o'clock 3:194 I did not prolong 5:79 Wrote a dozen 1:326 I suppose 9:372 Wrote 12 or 20 9:383 Up home 9:419 My letter-writing 9:476 Striking change 9:473 I shall need 1:186 Running about 2:193 W. had returned 1:362 This looks like 2:449 At home I 3:363 our affairs 9:309 you are our 9:460 I can die 9:387 with a whimsical eye 1:5 I took a look 6:2 W. sometimes 1:27 You always come 1:390 You can throw 4:33 As I was leaving 2:57 Under the stove 7:55 the Horace corner 3:56 a lot of merriment 3:65 No day passes 3:424 the odds 8:375–76 Some day you 1:398 I am laying aside 2:279 I'm doing all 4:43 I see more value 7:44 In your conception C5:72n My life C5:72 It seems to me C5:73n Suddenly his face 7:67 I have only one 1:viii W. is wonderfully 5:26 I just get going 1:56 My method and Other times 2:70 Horace, you are 2:200 You, who are 9:33–36 The bearer 1:171 You seem to have 2:207 You bother me? 2:244 The instant you 2:351 W. rarely gives 2:261 Walt do I come 2:375 I want to be 4:88 Well—you are 6:85 That is just the way 4:5 to many people 4:199 W. was very 1:207 You are doing 1:332 I wonder 4:186 Johnston has some 2:302 all up and down 2:23 You don't mean 3:550 Some day I'll 8:209 This will undoubtedly 6:433 strongly impulsive 4:8 Walt, don't you 4:61 showed himself 4:154 You have a few 4:293 A boy can do 2:328 I am not sure 7:328 I think it clumsy 2:333 greeted me 7:208 never know how 3:358 That's all 4:142 W. lay on 3:370 He was serenely 3:515 Happy this night's 7:358 Spent a half hour 7:454 Seeing me 7:234 He slept 9:261 Ever since 5:99 I was well 5:182 He keeps 5:105 W. kissed me 1:171 W. said 2:82 I reached 9:270 And as I leaned 9:328 In leaving 9:339 Every word 9:544 specially notable C4:318 Am feeling pretty C4:307 3½ p m C4:274 do not eat C5:55 night-rest C5:25 fair bodily C5:70 Horace is most C4:207 H remains C4:231 Should not get C5:189 rarely brought himself C5:108n Glad to see you C4:273 Ed gives me C4:329 The compliments C4:343 W.'s mind

5:123 I guess C4:332 Tom Harned C4:231 My earliest memory 9:xiv radical violence 1:223 dishwatery imitations *Conservator*, Aug. 1911, p. 87 lacking in nothing *Conservator*, June 1910, p. 55 often is defective *Conservator*, Nov. 1917, p. 137 the greatest *Conservator*, Sept. 1908, p. 104 Whitman is a crescent and One volume *Conservator*, June 1908, p. 57 To say that *Conservator*, July 1914, p. 73 It is easy *Conservator*, Sept. 1915, p. 102 unfortunately it continues *Conservator*, Apr. 1915, pp. 23–25 If somebody *Conservator*, July 1915, p. 71 highly emotional *Conservator*, June 1908, pp. 54–55 What does matter *Conservator*, Sept. 1913, p. 108 I've been allowed *Conservator*, June 1918, pp. 60–61 Perry's book and Carpenter is *Conservator*, Feb. 1909, p. 188 I have no *Conservator*, June 1907, p. 57 Life was reviving 3:407 I can't forget 4:223 People in Camden *Conservator*, Feb. 1908, p. 189 I did not read 2:141 I spoke of 7:278 Talked with W. 8:241 How strange 8:259 heated correspondence 9:xx He held no *Conservator*, Sept. 1907, p. 103 If all the theologies *Conservator*, June 1919, p. 61 an indescribably lovely *Walt Whitman Quarterly Review* 14 (1996–97), pp. 102ff A friend of mine *Conservator*, Feb. 1913, pp. 188–89 shift 9:598 Laugh, for God's sake David Karsner, *Horace Traubel: His Life and Work* (1919), p. 37

THE MICKLE STREET MÉNAGE

I was making money 1:291 little Camden shanty C4:162 It was an unpretentious Elizabeth Keller, *Walt Whitman in Mickle Street* (1921), pp. 18–21 His method 1:448 let me introduce C5:219 has my cordial 5:381 People often criticize 1:280 Now that the room 1:337 that definite something C4:274 plenty for my meals C5:85 Mary thinks 1:420 Always good 1:292 Nowadays Mary 6:401 She hit the 7:410 Mrs. Davis yesterday 1:393 There's a certain 1:401 W. stood 1:419 Depressed 2:3 resents the attentions 2:51 the gentleman 2:65 Mr. Musgrove will 2:214 Mr. Musgrove was 2:383 I do not hear 2:536 W. is eager 2:558 Musgrove is curt 1:3 He is put out 1:34 He was tall 3:29 Ed is very 3:52 a clean strong C4:233 I am coming 3:53 I don't know 3:98 Ed has a violin 3:135 W. told Ed 3:155 Ed seems to be 3:385 Ed is well fit 3:451 told me of his 6:8 has spoken 6:52 Well—I have 6:69 W. is so well 3:496 we are all sorry C4:385 less than a quarter 6:82 I like him 1:282 I felt quite C5:86 One of my two C5:87 Warrie and I 6:82 Warrie rubs me 6:139 Warrie is a noble 8:9 generally just before C5:53 have had a good C4:407 Bill Duckett came 5:329 think of it 4:64 amused . . . into great 6:79 *lie* in big, big type 6:167 He was rather 9:278 You will find 9:283 I don't think 9:321 The dog made 6:137 Well, if there's 6:114 There are good dogs 6:166 a big setter 9:211 W. had remarked 9:166 The dog had barked 9:178

SERENDIPITY: VIGNETTES AND VISITORS

I make every 7:64 There is all sorts 1:155 He sat much 2:110 took out the little 4:514 How many saw 5:250 He had a couple 4:8 I attribute 7:422 Some neighbor 1:25 I rescued it 3:421 There is no 7:366 Who knows but 5:491 a few words 4:241 Dave did not 9:58 The original is 7:419 No, but I 7:426 It will turn 7:427 W. expressed 7:439 Kicking about 9:44 I found

W. 6:8 A story 5:360 You have not 6:290 Oh! What mites 5:199 took this very 7:254 My sister Agnes 1:82 Mrs. Davis came 5:106 I want to 1:255 I have seen 4:474 W. was inquisitive 3:344 W. is always 1:288 There's a whistling 7:76 Goddamn your soul 7:22 What a quiet 7:371 I had a visitor 3:209 We ought to 9:301 He got up 5:297 a curious character and I am still 1:11–13 Tom was here 6:40 Walt Whitman, America 9:10 A woman broke in 4:429 some questions he 4:501 it won't pass 2:157 W. received 6:2 Since I am 1:5 I wonder 7:370 There was some 1:166 was immensely 5:224 they spoil me 1:176 I remember 6:367 (Nearly a fire 8:255

WALT ON WALT

I used to be 1:120 Some of my friends 2:183 It was to 5:298 The "Walt" 6:58 In spite of 7:95 I like best 8:525 Your invariable answer 2:30 In fibre 3:204 conviction that 2:143 The Quakers 1:78 "Hurry" was never 1:348 I seem to be 2:38 I'm no hurrier 4:194 At the near 5:482 I can see 2:39 Some people 1:152 I am not 9:128 I am not much 1:137 I never was 1:316 There's one thing 7:65 If there's anything 7:91 My leanings 1:193 I interest 1:397 I am not surprised 6:187 "damnable" 7:380 It was a young 7:87 This stars 9:414 He was almost 5:103 The idea 4:9 I pride myself 4:49 I told him 7:25 That after all 7:266 I have always 2:338 The best biographical 6:53 I am always 1:47 He is 1:185 For thirty years 1:204 W. is a slow 2:369 God Almighty 4:19 He hates 4:141 It is good 6:221 talkers bores C5:55 They are 7:130 I was a great 5:463 It plays 1:48 I am inclined 5:384 I never knew 1:141 It seems as though 3:422 The abolitionists 5:287 I always 2:21 Some day you 1:398 I do not 1:325 I used to thrust 4:503 I am more famous 1:149 My infernal 2:36 not very strong 2:360 I am what 1:385 You always seem 4:31 Oh! I use 5:164 huge and sprawling G. T. Atkinson, *Cornhill Magazine* (May 1929), p. 560 That sounds 2:181 it's mainly 3:438 I had a way 6:249 I am no longer 1:456 I am an open air 1:105

WALT ON THE WHITMAN FAMILY

A man's family 3:525 No one of my 1:227 I asked 4:473 Do you think 4:387 You will drag 7:381 My father was 3:109 She married 7:381 His visit was 4:192 Was aware of 7:304 Gloomy & depressed C5:123 Dear brother Jeff 7:377 George and I 3:541 George once said 4:267 George Whitman in 4:473 You get more 4:192 George could never 4:473 I think George 5:538 The first manuscript 2:56 The meeting 2:66 is well, & seems C4:282 It is pretty sad C5:123 Your brother Jesse 1:294 Too much is often 1:78 All Republicans 4:473 Would you say 3:526 I say again 3:529

WALT ON IMAGES OF HIMSELF

I suppose 5:297 I give painters 1:284 I thought 9:526 I hear 9:526 No man 2:45 They have photographed 2:446 I suppose 5:297 I have been 1:367 I am persuaded 5:225 Nothing can be 5:339 There are difficulties 3:553 I am always 1:131 How does that strike 2:412 his picture is 1:154 Eakins' picture 1:39 Of all portraits 1:131 Eakins! How nobly 6:301 W.'s friends 3:526 So it has 1:335 what hits me 4:398 begets a healthy 6:258 gifted in 5:150 a pic-

ture from 3:542 The art is growing 3:23 The human expression 5:479 The
photograph 4:125 I have wavered 1:192 So much of Sidney 1:158 Does it
look 3:378

Memories of Long Island, Brooklyn, and Manhattan

The best way 7:108 It must have been 7:373 My own favorite 2:71 Camden
was 2:29 New York's the place 4:100 Many, many 1:44 My own greatest
1:417 Would you not 2:379 We talked 3:116 I found 7:438 I spent 1:455
It arouses 5:321 I first discovered 2:72 New York is a dampener 7:111 It is
life 1:62 New York is ahead 7:187 I have just 7:434 The main matter 7:443
this whole crowd 7:446 Let a man go 8:384 He is one 8:903 I always went
7:24 It was the reaction 7:442

Credos

Why shouldn't we 1:78 All my sympathies 5:277 Walt, you seem 4:321
Yes—I suppose 5:403 Arnold always gives 1:232 Respectability has 4:504
Canadian preacher 6:287 I am a great 5:317 considerable quiet 5:203 the
preparatory C5:204 You mustn't 2:72 Oh! I hope 5:298 There is a perfect
C5:286 Bucke is no crank 5:265 I think the world 7:145 It's a profound
4:37 I more 5:473 I always mistrust 1:256 Life is like 7:407 I always
designate 1:267 Why everybody 5:308 The great thing 5:449 Oh! that's so
3:141 I must see 2:104 Hawthorne's method 6:88 But isn't it 1:255 It is
rare 7:281 but then a fellow 5:224 I have always 6:386 If that is so 3:47
Walt Whitman is 2:535-36 Well, that depends 7:430 Time was 2:227 It has
always 6:457 To be spontaneous 7:27 Beecher said 8:400 My old daddy
2:41 You annex 2:363 Literature is big 1:283 This whole crowd 7:446 A
certain amount 8:146 I am in favor 5:14 Beware of 2:167 Myself am 5:109
It is best for 1:436 I think things 5:29 Perfect health 3:582 I do not lack
1:383 It is well 3:96-97 Whether it is 2:430 The common heroisms 1:51
I don't want 3:14 Protection rubs 3:366 she insisted 5:440 I am a great
5:276

Walt on the Literary Life

seem to be disturbed 3:328 All genius defies 8:12 Now and then 1:433
Bucke urges 8:10 If a fellow 2:346 And the secret 2:25-26 Who more
6:334 One's life 6:140 Some of my 2:136 I have never 3:132 I hope he has
6:232 Walt, some people 3:459-60 Yes—sometimes 3:326 In most of us
1:350 What lying things 4:452 Poor Jesus 7:38 I hesitated 7:1 He asked
me 7:46-47 I don't know 2:287 I avoid 1:65 I am not 1:140 I don't recite
9:124 W. rarely reads 2:287 I like any 4:220 When you talk 1:104 I
should think 6:231 My friends could 4:145 That has mainly 3:149 There
are consciences 5:398 the John Burroughs 5:465 It is the very 1:440 I in
the main 2:286 O pshaw! 3:433 I always object 5:110 laughed much 7:386
I can see 7:43-44 I know how 7:139 What do they want 2:379 I get
humors 4:13

Before *Leaves of Grass*

In these older 1:69 Yes—I guess 6:379 days when I 8:410 Dr. Bucke
8:551 I was at 1:467

About *Leaves of Grass*

I am well satisfied 1:186 as so often 5:61 What a fight 6:197 I should say
6:475 old suggestion 7:266 I was once 2:107 I have found 3:577 He did
not see 1:51 For a long time 3:467 I wouldn't know 2:154 If I have any
3:545 It is a book 1:375 *Leaves of Grass* is not 2:373 If *Leaves of Grass* 4:43
Leaves of Grass may be 1:436 Oh! I expect 7:42 How William 8:351 It *is*
cold 7:414 important in the things 8:54 LG is less 8:71 Did I tell 6:95 I suppose 8:423 The reality 2:113 My younger life 2:174 certain actors "Plays
and Operas Too," *Complete Poetry and Collected Prose* (Library of America,
1982), p. 703 Suppose the whole 3:327 I pride myself 4:49 I am aware
2:252 the very centre 3:95 What did I get 3:582 had I *Leaves of Grass*
4:389 I see— 2:178 *Leaves of Grass* takes 5:208 In my philosophy 5:227
Leaves of Grass . . . is based 7:72 *Leaves of Grass* has its own 7:238 Catholicity— 7:355 *Leaves of Grass* has its patriotism 7:72 Damn the Professor
8:178 Commenced putting *Camden's Compliment to Walt Whitman*, ed. Horace
Traubel (1889), p. 4 Here is the kernel 8:179 The *Leaves* are 1:7 Millet is my
1:63 Millet excites 2:32 Millet's color 3:89 Not convincing 3:93 Two Americans 5:133 There is one 5:369 I do not teach 5:310 I have no axe 6:340
The idea 6:27 I almost pity 6:33 I put it aside 2:19 *Leaves of Grass* is an
iconoclasm 6:343 I should say 6:475 Often it is by 6:440 Beecher declared
once 7:441 it can never 7:156 to leave men healthy 9:19 there is no delicatesse 9:61 I am not astonished 9:395 College men 1:286 It is an old 9:538
If these fellows 2:142 It should not 8:102 My *Leaves* mean 8:208 the idea of
human 7:381 Solidarity— 9:27 the heroic animality 9:61 Doctor seems
3:343 yes it is mainly C4:250 *Leaves of Grass* is a mystery 8:321 One of the
valuable 7:287 This indirect mode *Notes and Unpublished Manuscripts* (1:233),
The Collected Writings

Individual Poems and Sequences

objections often 5:46 I shall ever and *Children of Adam* stumps 1:2 She, too
1:381 It has always been 4:119 "Calamus" is a Latin word 6:342 Leaves of
Grass 8:360 a royal good fellow 1:73–77 kind of mental *The Memoirs of John
Addington Symonds*, ed. Phyllis Grosskurth (1984), p. 189 He harps 1:202
I exchanged 8:57 Morris had asked 8:117 Well, that is 9:37 I want you
3:385–86 I'm honest 2:304 I ought to have 2:317 The thing that 2:333 In
some cases 7:268 It was very 5:28 There's more 1:156 I made that 2:98
Tell her 5:63 About *that* 7:370 roared when I 8:116 Yes, it was 1:390 It is
part 7:294 It is a wonderful 7:329

Printing *Leaves of Grass*

He is stubborn 1:358 It is tragic 1:92 The first *Leaves* C6:30 I don't think
2:472 I had a funny 3:359 They say— 6:289 I wish I had 6:385 I do not

think 8:82 I like to 1:194 I am sensitive 2:237 Having been 5:390 I sometimes 4:233 I often think 7:97 If I had been 1:357 Does it seem 1:359 It is
wonderful 5:337 What a tribe 4:490 Very few people 6:267 He is an 8:82
I have great respect 8:142 This man in a great 8:7 I have great emotional
3:12 It is a saying 2:324 Authors always 1:168 I am familiar 2:132 What a
cute 2:176 There is no appeal 1:180 This time 3:168 So they wonder 1:248
Why in the world 5:468 It seems to be 4:170 *Leaves of Grass* looks 7:402
That book has 4:282 Everybody interferes 3:359 What a sweat 3:561 You,
too 1:280 Drifted into 8:421 Some of the 1:207 any volume 1:283 a suggestion if 9:537 *L. of G. Junior* 9:584 I do not know 2:107 That may give
4:468 resented margins 4:75 All my own tastes 1:462 I have long teased
2:175 Books are like 1:176 They were trying 3:54 George Chainey C5:317
Walt Whitman is 7:288 Laughingly told 6:368 This, of course 9:379 This is
now 9:382 The point is 9:388

LEAVES OF GRASS AND THE CRITICS

He is very 1:337 I would have to 2:154 I seem to make 3:425 A man can't
3:437 It's astonishing 4:312 I expected 3:515 I get many 4:6 Every whipper-
snapper 2:324 Horace, there are 3:513 *Leaves of Grass* has had 6:340 I
think everything 1:184 Some of my 1:112 Henry Clapp 1:236 If there are
5:368 Sour, dissatisfied 3:411, 413 It seems to be 5:96 I liked one 7:396
And although 7:404 That is a slap 1:337 We have enemies 5:392 I got a letter 3:461 You know 2:372 Oh! I take no note 6:95 Oh! damn Higginson
6:362 Higginson has always 7:253 No matter 2:149 There are a 2:229 The
fact is 1:185 It is a good 5:105 We are always 6:210 The world now 3:126
Leaves of Grass is made 6:340 I have the 7:98 isn't that 5:375 The world
5:467 I am sure 7:43 I don't mind 2:81 It amounts 8:4 I suppose 2:226 a
rowdy Emerson 9:401 I do not value 1:58 They are mainly 1:55 Literary
men 1:63 Arthur Stedman 7:86 They do not 7:391 He is a good 8:251 College men 1:286 Harvard never 4:48 that dreadful press 7:251 These New
England 8:154 He was first 8:352 The real 8:453–54 I have asked 4:41 It
has been 2:113 a young man 2:161–63 I answered 4:338 They do the best
1:217 We are not 1:251 Thayer is 6:312 I never wish 1:64 The store is full
1:98 had a good deal 4:321 You seem to 3:267 I wouldn't know 2:154 The
main wonder C4:384 Stedman is 1:70 I meet new 1:108 It is a new 7:11 It
is one of my 9:3 What I quarrel 8:524 I admire 2:142 the respectable army
6:473 I am not 6:132 You have a great 3:318 Every time I criticize 1:66 My
dismissal 4:59 I had a paper 6:78 It does a man 3:327 I have suffered 2:558

ADVICE

Take my word 1:152 And you, Horace 1:174 To vary 1:150 It is one 4:135 I
have another 1:187 Be cocky 2:136 Be individualistic 3:122 Be bold 4:469
and 5:381 The conventionals 2:135 laughed a bit 1:87 I do not object 2:126
What a shame 2:40 Take the last edition 3:133 Don't you think 3:440
When you write 1:48

man 2:277 is the quintessence 7:457 Symonds, of the literati 6:51 concrete
passionate faith and contentment in love *The Memoirs of John Addington
Symonds*, ed. Phyllis Grosskurth (1984), pp. 246, 176 more intimate 6:211 I
might have been 9:534–36 Democratic Art C5:64 deep, heavy C5:69

A Flaminger Soul: William Douglas O'Connor

How much I owe 6:135 There is hilarity 1:162 William will die 2:176
William says 3:352 William is in 2:11 I wonder 3:55 William is one 3:562
William would talk 4:70 he had an ideal 5:166 His was the most 6:7 I need
not 7:298 He undoubtedly 7:303

Magnificent Potencies: Robert Green Ingersoll

Damn if I don't 3:54 Ingersoll is the man 6:106 He has a 7:42 one of *the
very few* C5:92 Bob is very 7:303 the Ing affair C5:107 I have known 7:223
Oh! that is a great 7:128 Ingersoll is a free 7:141 He has that 7:281 Horace,
I consider 7:457 Bob has humor 7:387 If ever we had 7:418

Walt and His Boys

noble, slim 3:117 William gets 3:352 *Dear son* 2:380–82 Lew I wish 3:102
What comes before 2:369–71 Well, it was 9:34 Then he went 1:298 Pete
Doyle was over C4:174 I have been reading 1:376 Pete Doyle was in 1:349
This cane was 1:415 It was at 2:511–12 Oh! that's so 3:141 I found every-
body 3:543 I was quite 6:371 What do you think 7:265 He has not been
8:348 Poor old fellow 7:264 Harry Stafford in 9:162 Do you remember
C5:30 he is poorly C5:32 After Stafford 9:163 Harry Stafford's wife 9:211
Never mind 9:266 on January 1, 1891 9:292 He was one 8:210 Give my
love 1:426 W. knows 3:362 hopelessly of 5:10 lassitude and 8:195 Tell him
it'll 8:543 chewing on 9:47 There was 5:121 We struck up 5:133

Walt's "Big Secret"

charming, winning 1:389 I came today 2:86 Said again 2:146 W. said to me
2:316 You'll hear that 2:306 that big story 2:415 Walt, are you 2:511 W.
referred to 2:543 Just before 3:80 W. still refusing 3:119 I mentioned 3:140
I nudged him 3:253 He said to-night 3:364 As I was about 4:71 very specific
9:146 Harned has not 9:199 He has grandchildren 9:220 I brought up
9:263

Views of America

America means 3:277 To know me 6:376 The point with us 4:32 I should
make 6:203 Certainly, in our 5:423 I may concede 2:307 The best politics
1:15 I do not seem 1:406 It's coming 2:519 No man can 3:21 The whole
gang 1:359 I see the real 1:14 I did not bite 8:140 Restrict nothing 1:113
America is for 2:34 the drunken pedagogue 5:358 Execrable names 6:415
The prairies 6:10 Since the war 6:314 The great country 2:84 a stained
piece 1:25 They are beautiful 3:123 In Canada 5:379 that damnable idea
7:26 The American people 1:59 Perhaps I took 7:82 Have this week 7:85
But that is 7:418 Our best work 6:120 I never knew 1:81 If they had 3:30

We are too 3:30 A little 9:385 Washington is 1:148 this is a stupid 4:270
Yet no city 6:323 There was a 3:157 It has always 6:457 The ornamental
4:491 I have seen 7:148 I am convinced 2:282 I am even 7:75 According
to 1:331 It seems to be 5:137 I wonder 5:350 The people 1:372 God help
2:24 The trouble 2:187 We are growing 1:215–16 I like the Scotch 7:448
The Greeks 3:81 What I am afraid C5:53 suddenly roused 8:465 It comes
6:126

AFFECTION, LOVE, AND SEX

Someone has 1:128 The world is 3:385 We have got 3:452 Do you mean
4:376 about a dozen 6:342 A man was 1:381 How people reel 3:321 There
is that 5:507 noblest of all 7:274 I know him 7:454 Years ago 5:143 can
hardly realize 9:84

THE WOMAN SEX

Leaves of Grass is 2:331 I always say 2:20 The young ladies 3:384 Women
are often 2:63 There is Mrs. Harned 5:218 The full list 6:437 I have been
2:140 Catching him 1:322 By the way 3:117 It would seem 7:440 Do you
think 3:35 He added 2:328 I have great 9:46 Jeannette Gilder 9:78 she's
a man 9:145 the *male* human body 7:8 I am a sort 6:187 I always seem
2:163 Surely the modern 5:293 She is heroic 9:202 I consider it 3:510
hello from way off 2:451

MEMORIES OF WASHINGTON AND THE SECESSION WAR

This is one of 6:227 Only it filled 2:402 I never once 3:95 old machine
C5:23 The War deeply 3:560 The old army 5:391 I was no 3:204 It always
struck me 2:138 I should not 5:89 Oh Horace 4:472 I never had 1:99–100
I take things 3:540 Secretary Harlan 1:3 Don't ever assail 3:476–77 I
was at 6:147 I distribute nice 1:196–98 they died and Farewell, dear boy
1:115–18 My relations with 3:110–11 I carried 2:137 Any Doctor 7:356
How much I 3:250 The young surgeons 7:56 No: I don't 4:63 There were
three 4:97 It was the average 5:362 I did a lot 1:434 Some of my best 1:147
A hospital talk 1:26 If I had any 4:63 I have heard 1:232 That's not so
3:370 There seems 4:24 O God 3:293 I was always 3:581–82 There were
years 6:194

TURNED TO A GENEROUS KEY: ABRAHAM LINCOLN

The radical element 1:4 Lincoln was more 8:11 Out of all 8:6 Lincoln the
man 5:480 I often saw 7:9 I think I must 3:22 I know of no 5:225 Lincoln's
wonderful 3:554 After my dear 1:38 I vividly 3:23 It is wonderful 7:385 All
Lincoln's life 6:386 Think of the 5:288 I do not 5:481 I doubt if even 6:353
His tone strong 6:365 Mr. Lincoln asked 3:179–80

RACE

Not the negro 1:13 true to the memory *The Gathering of the Forces*, ed. Cleveland Rodgers and John Black (1920), vol. 1, p. 222 I say where "Says," *Leaves
of Grass* (1860 ed.), p. 418 The idea of slavery 5:276 All my friends 1:363 I

may have 3:76 The abolitionists 6:353 In the South 4:331 the quadroons
2:283–84 In my abolition 6:151 calamus and 9:48–49 I never went 6:323
A Negro came 4:429 I know enough 7:158 hearty laugh 8:439 Russian
ideas 9:122–23 It is a damn 9:228–29 When I was 6:56 This question is
6:423 Thought 'the Oklahoma 5:91 America means 3:277

Famous Authors

In all imaginative 2:562 It's the generosity 1:283 Epictetus is 2:71 This
book 3:253 appeals profoundly 1:337 a dear, strong 2:175 has been all
underscored 2:72 I could never 3:185 I will be 1:105 Now there was 2:16
Voltaire, after 7:379 It is a singular 3:355 Pope was 1:126 Johnson does
not 145–48 Dr. Johnson 1:272 I read it 1:146 The more I see 4:211 He's
the champion 4:218 While I am 4:350 Byron has 1:41 Byron deserves
5:351–52 I have a warm 1:41 That's what Walt 2:345 I always stand 2:553
I look on him 2:560–62 Both women 3:35 I have always 3:423 Damn the
woman 9:203 a wonderful woman 9:125 I have of course 3:85 Cooper was
a master-man 2:531 Natty peculiarly 4:62 Cooper was a curious 5:302 I
consider Cooper 6:36 Cooper at his best 7:5 Cooper's art *The Portable Mark
Twain*, ed. Bernard De Voto (1946), p. 541 Scott is 2:251 Perennial . . . I 4:100
Take *Robert of Paris* 7:5 *Anna Karenina* 3:272 I find little 3:494 Carlyle always 9:11 Thackeray as 2:552 At the start 1:138 Poor Poe 3:413 I have
seen Poe 4:23 William's sweep 5:180 That's news 5:395 Dickens one 6:94
Darwin— 3:70 spoke tenderly 3:166 inexpressibly dry 7:4 Tennyson rather
5:5 He is always 1:166 I never completely 2:192 Wilde may have 2:279
there is no one and There is no parade 2:287–89 Wilde was very 5:284 I
think well 7:39 Bryant was trained 3:515 take Bryant 6:335 I think he
1:111 What a devil 6:123 James is only 1:78 never traveled new 3:24 He is
a star 9:389 It would be 2:93 So Browning C4:405 I have tried 1:105 I can
never 2:391 The worst 3:400 There seems to be 4:37 They run a few 1:111
Do you like 4:20 I don't quote 1:92 I think he 4:208 I have always 4:391 I
have met 7:98 Whittier has very 6:294 Whittier is but 9:223 Whittier's poetry C4:381 I think I could 9:157 W. is so hard 9:401 He was often 5:295 I
ought to 7:27 Hamlin is deft 4:298 I am to him 7:87 As a nigger 7:93 very
dull 7:112

Walt and the Bard

What play of Shakespeare unsigned review in the *American Phrenological Journal* (1856), in *Walt Whitman: The Critical Heritage*, ed. Milton Hindus (1971),
p. 42 As a boy *Prose Works 1892*, ed. Floyd Stovall (1964), vol. 1, p. 21 lacked
the religious 1:163–64 Shakespeare . . . is gloomy 3:443 The Shakespeare
plays 1:240–41 There is much 1:234 The inward *Prose Works 1892*, ed.
Floyd Stovall, vol. 2, pp. 557–58 Shakespeare shows 3:35–36 Try to think
3:83–84 The humor in 2:252 They are often 1:248 What a flood 2:245–6
I felt it 2:265 Do you suppose 1:135 I think anyhow 6:175 The qualities
3:431 a great taste 4:54 Shakespeare, whoever 4:54–56 the emphasis that
4:55 In the Shakespeare 9:148 Am deep into 9:156 Miss Porter wrote 7:121
I am glad 5:445 It is remarkable 1:136

Sweet Magnetic Man: Ralph Waldo Emerson

I shall never 2:130 As I have been 6:203 Emerson's smile 5:119 He was one
7:120 Emerson so far 4:30 Emerson said when 3:388 I loved Emerson 1:61
Curiously, too 1:46 As a man 6:334–35 Emerson was not 7:107 There were
times 9:165 I picked it 2:105 not what you 4:9 I did think 2:52 Emerson
was always 3:266 Emerson lived 3:353 Emerson's personality 4:167 I think
almost 6:258 But take Emerson 1:23 I love Emerson 1:461 Was it your
3:453 no Rabelaisian 4:309 The essential Emerson 1:70 I always insist 6:23
He said to me 3:354 I except Emerson 1:226 I, of course 5:178 the old hag
2:298 Ellen hates me and Ellen? Oh 5:176–79 Think of Emerson 5:238 It is
all 7:50–51 Emerson had 2:505 For a number 9:68 he is known 9:64

Oxygenated Men and Women: Walt's Pantheon

I like salient 2:177 We can't get 3:491 I have had 5:76 Although my 2:429
She was more 2:499 The sweetest 5:336 Big, wholesome 3:225 If you come
7:342 He was in 2:103 Did these fellows 7:258–59 Stanton was 3:58 He is
a man 6:317 Mazzini was 3:146 Art now is 9:149 The real military 1:257
There was Grant 1:446 Grant was the 2:139 Grant hated show 8:7 We
have had 8:10 My prejudices 3:374 Thoreau's great fault 1:212 Henry was
not 3:403 I suppose you 6:413 If ever a fighter 1:8 Boyle's charm 1:17
What we need 7:62 She was not 2:268 She was strangely 3:97 She was a
wonderful 3:377 Mrs. Gilchrist was 5:12 Mrs. Gilchrist, with 5:151 In most
respects 6:22

Scoundrel Time

Besides, we must 5:227 A typical arrogant 8:154 Of all documents 4:293
It is the bitterest 5:65 a great phu-phu 4:493 I think Harrison 5:117 To me
5:450 good for eight years 5:202 That whelp 3:498 He is not 8:279 I think
9:193 a trivial, damnable 6:38 Those temperance fellows 9:53, 55 Take that
Replier 4:42 It is well 6:312 Most of these 3:424 He was an army 9:78
It seems to me 5:3 utterly indescribably 5:15 Take the Press 5:119 His letter
is 1:286 I must seem like 1:104 Good! good 1:166 William Winter 3:430
In N.Y. 3:528

Ecclesiastic

W. has a 1:142 never went to church Calamus: A Series of Letters Written
During the Years 1868–1880, ed. Richard Maurice Bucke (1897), p. 128 prayer
and Jesus business 5:17 by a woman who 1:121 The church has 1:11 some
had wondered 9:438 I never object 1:144 I often get 1:139 Scientists are
9:24 What an infernal 9:25 better than being 9:438 A clever fellow 1:62
Damn the preachers 6:298 I am not willing 1:108 The damnable psalming
5:17 Not a bit 1:182 On the face 1:173 The simple truth 6:298 I believe
1:107 make light of 1:371–72 The wisdom of 8:328 Did you ever 8:468
The world is 1:106 We might as 1:109 I see no 1:110 For the church 4:85
went oftenest 2:51 I think 5:376 the damnable Methodistic 8:477 It is best
3:317 The whole miracle 4:352 I anticipate 2:323

Music, Opera, and Marietta

building houses *Notebooks and Unpublished Prose*, ed. Edward Grier (1984), p. 37
It has already Richard Bucke, *Walt Whitman* (1883), p. 56 **takes us out** *The Journals and Miscellaneous Notebooks of Ralph Waldo Emerson* (1969), vol. 7, p. 137 **I am particularly** 1:102 **Oh! the true bass** 2:123 **So many of** 2:116 **It's one of** 4:445 **has done for music** 4:506 **The women** 9:412 **the opera was** 4:249 **O Hugo** 3:579–80 **After going out** 5:406 **impeached the** 5:174 **In my opera** 5:419 **We spoke of** 9:89 **Comrades, recollect** 3:104 **I looked upon** 3:510 **I never think** 6:303 **There is a mysterious** 5:454 **of magnetic presence** 5:152 **You never heard** 7:368 **spoke of Alboni** 9:49

Bottoms Up

dealt affectionately *Camden's Compliment*, ed. Horace Traubel (1889), p. 13
I have a spice 5:298 **offer of cash** 5:224 **It is very hard** 4:485 **Bucke knows** 2:197 **Found W.** 3:534 **You know there** 8:543 **That whiskey** 8:25 **I notice Wilson's** 8:48 **I intended** 6:304 **Tom, if you have** C4:264 **If you will** C4:335 **If the law** 7:155 **The champagne** 3:45 **I think champagne** 7:156 **treated me to** C5:89 **someone who prints** 8:26 **The great thing** 5:192 **Take whiskey** 5:23 **I do not enter** 5:137 **If drink** 5:210 **A dinner** 5:210 **It took me** 9:225 **When I would go** 9:370–71 **Does a duck** 6:337 **the dryest** 9:311 **lunar champagne** 1:256 **Drank a little** 9:524 **If I had the** 5:219 **It was an extra** 5:260 **It was the finest** 6:445 **Plain food** 8:227 **I was at Tom's** 9:75 **I am glad** 1:393 **has done me a heap** 9:412 **That is good news** 9:468 **Oh! That is good** 9:520 **For the present** 9:552

Walt's Way with Words

The boys in the army 5:194 **In the old days** 4:96 **For the word** 5:470 **I am sure** 6:56 **Alcott had** 1:130 **My word** 5:194 **It is quite** 1:171 **Well—you are** 3:322 **Not a bit** 2:244 **If you can** 6:311 **I like the word** 6:148 **had considerable** 6:381 **nothing but utter** 9:420 **the exquisite sorification** 9:426 **There was one** 8:186

Peeves

Gosse is a type 5:494 **He is to me** 7:5 **I hate** 4:8 **You know, Horace** 6:15 **It's a damnable** 5:219 **I know** 2:188 **The fad** 7:297 **I have very little** 5:456 **Probably the story** 7:65 **It is typical** 7:36 **It is throwing** 7:240 **I think there is** 7:355 **He is very frank** 7:380 **He is the best** 7:408 **There was a time** 1:392 **Sumner had** 7:41 **That speech** 5:45 **The typical** 5:494 **Music is my** 1:361 **neighbor, Button** 7:243 **I have had** 1:366 **Not a day** 2:83 **One of the autograph** 1:401 **I am not** 3:496 **While I was** 5:9 **I don't like** 5:419 **Quoting is** 3:115

Pleasures

Mrs. Davis handed 5:385 **Her cooking** 1:355 **She is a genius** 1:460 **I find I get** 4:24 **it makes a great** 4:51 **On the bed** 7:373 **The Brooklyn water and it is reputed** 7:409–10 **There is a** 6:264

Walt on Various and Sundry

There is a strain 4:402 What a poor 3:309 I have seen 1:449 There seems to 4:118 I was bred 3:205 New York is ahead 7:187 I suppose 1:100 They call this 5:344 The letters from 9:2–3 Everybody is writing 1:205 The Quaker nativity 6:259 I can see 7:131 I never believed 6:53 The world goes 3:562 I don't think this 6:306 The best man 1:275 Literary men 1:63 That is what 2:77 You remember 6:128 fond of the Western 6:89 I consider it 2:562 as if his whole 5:402 Denver is 5:357 I never forget 5:272 New Orleans 5:358 Did I ever 5:386 I would as 3:345 Not one regret 4:45 I am *not* C5:305 I believe in 1:267 I, too, more 5:64 neither boy nor ball 6:129 I like your interest 2:330 the hurrah game 4:508 He takes a great 5:282 Donaldson a rare 2:357 Ah! these doctors 1:433 From the medical 1:400 The trouble is 3:534 I like the 1:101 We seem to 2:95 rather a dubious 1:340–41 I don't think he 3:500 A party may 1:341 The spirit of 1:99 I am for 1:149 We are indebted 6:356 I shall take 7:266 Fifty years or so 6:295–96 While out in 6:113–14 As for me 7:34 The trouble with 2:144 Boston is damp 6:144 I have been told 6:103 What would we 6:293 Say, rather 7:156 Do you mean 1:223 I find he has 9:500 He showed me 7:74 Letter-carriers always 5:385 Cadavers—complexion 5:486 Doctor takes 4:89 I have heard 2:230 There's something in 8:173 Genius is 2:103 My experience with 2:543 They are pathetic 4:20 Do you know 6:453 Think of it 4:121 Why, Oscar, it always The full *Press* story is reprinted by Rollo Silver in *The Colophon* (1935), n.p.

"A Frightful Gone-ness"—The Physical Decline

What about that 1:37 A great big 1:267 For one thing 1:291 The true nurse 7:400 not irrational 1:294 A long day 1:299 Was I a little daffy 1:309 W.'s mind 1:347 no minister should 1:305 hung fire between 1:310 a heavenly father 1:342 grip is gone 1:354 It's funny how 2:36 Hawser'd here C5:26 *the grip* swoops C5:51 what a wretched C5:136 the horrible lassitude C5:214 I don't want 2:115 It is hard 2:235 I have belly aches 2:356 Bad day today 2:376 Osler made light 2:383 I am getting 2:455 See—I am off 1:427 I have seen 2:544 I went silently 3:1 It is wearisome 3:92 How much like Lear 3:287 W. unchanged 3:309 Ed is disturbed 3:311 I don't seem 4:71 Most doctors 4:84 Yes, go out 9:248 He spoke calmly 4:89 have your own way 4:219 He tries 5:182 So I took 5:373 According to 6:426 I suppose I 7:55 My memory 7:132 He has the happy 8:86 My idea is C5:177n I have been 8:174 I have just been 8:268 f'm an old Broadway C5:215

"A Voice from Death"—The Last Months

It is a beginning 9:22 You cannot know 9:52 The New York papers 9:106 I am fuddled 9:213 For about three 9:226 saying of my dear C5:272 in great conviction 9:233 Somnolent 9:243 Have they got 9:246 I am a little 9:246–49 "Telegraphic Cypher" 9:252 Then broke forth 9:280 An old 9:296 Yes, my best 9:379 No strength— 9:419 Haven't you 9:420 Bad—bad 9:433 Warrie put his 9:451 Evinces little 9:501 I have had 9:518 He

has been 9:533 In reply to 9:562 How have you 9:575 Once today 9:582
He could not 9:592 splashing up 9:595 This is the last 9:598

"THE LAST MILE DRIVEN"—THE END

All writings heretofore 9:388 It struck my heart 9:598–600

"THE TOUCH OF PEACE"—MORTUARY

The face already 9:601 The bulletin 9:602 Walt's face serene 9:601 The
death mask 9:605 The wonder 9:605 Looked well 9:606–11 Mrs. Whitman
has 9:609 John Burroughs has 9:612 Finally to 328 Mickle 9:616 Whole
row of reporters 9:619 My father would 9:620 Then the final view 9:621
The day bright 9:622 The funeral was attended *In Re Walt Whitman*, ed.
Horace Traubel, Richard Bucke, Thomas Harned (1893), pp. 437–52

THE BURIAL HOUSE AT HARLEIGH CEMETERY

I have had a visitor 6:175 The Harleigh Cemetery C4:407 to look again
C5:47 Did I tell you 6:212 a little pungent 6:381 I went down 6:405 the
ponderous door C5:206 W. says to Harned 9:147 this (foolishness 9:397
Yes, he has 9:399 he had two dead 9:146 I have no particular 9:313 viper
husband 2:493 I am not in favor 9:466

Bibliographical Note

Views on the Traubel-Whitman collaboration figure briefly in most biographies of the poet and in many monographs. See, in particular, the appropriate entries in J. R. LeMaster and Donald Kummings, *Walt Whitman Encyclopedia* (New York: Garland, 1998), and the chapter "Walt and Horace" in the present editor's *Walt Whitman: A Gay Life* (New York: Plume, 1997). The introduction by Ed Folsom for the ninth and last volume of *With Walt Whitman in Camden* should also be consulted. A somewhat jaundiced view of Whitman's home life is offered in Elizabeth Keller, *Walt Whitman in Mickle Street* (New York: Mitchell Kennerley, 1921). Keller, a nurse for Whitman briefly just before he died, wrote this short book at about the age of eighty, mainly in spirited defense of the housekeeper, Mary Davis, against whom some aspersions had been cast. Still, its homely details offer a flavor of life at 328 Mickle Street.

Three highly affectionate biographical studies of Traubel were written during his life but none since, with the exception of one Russian study published in Moscow in 1980: Mildred Bain, *Horace Traubel* (New York: Boni, 1913), William English Walling, *Whitman and Traubel* (New York: Boni, 1916; rpt. Brooklyn: MSG Haskell House, 1969), and David Karsner, *Horace Traubel: His Life and Work* (New York: Arens, 1919). All make much of Traubel's vigorous socialism. Karsner, a longtime member of the Walt Whitman Fellowship who even named a daughter Walta Whitman, was intimate with the Traubel family and hosted them in Beekman Place when they visited New York. The vast archive of Whitman and Traubel manuscripts, memorabilia, and related ephemera amassed by Traubel eventually came to reside in the Library of Congress.

The publication history of *With Walt Whitman in Camden* can be briefly summarized. Traubel supervised the publication of the first three volumes (Boston: Small, Maynard, 1906; New York: D. Appleton, 1908; New York: Mitchell Kennerley, 1914). After a hiatus of nearly four decades, his wife, Anne, and daughter, Gertrude, assisted in publishing the fourth volume, which was edited by Sculley Bradley (Philadelphia: University of Pennsylvania Press, 1953). After Anne's death in 1954, Gertrude produced volume five (Carbondale: Southern Illinois University Press, 1964); volume six appeared from the same press in 1982, a year before Gertrude's death; volume seven was also published by

Southern Illinois University Press in 1992, edited by Jeanne Chapman and Robert MacIsaac. The same editors produced the final volumes, eight and nine, which were published in 1996 (Oregon House, Calif.: William Bentley). The period covered by each volume is as follows:

Volume 1: March 28 to July 14, 1888
Volume 2: July 16 to October 31, 1888
Volume 3: November 1, 1888, to January 20, 1889
Volume 4: January 21 to April 7, 1889
Volume 5: April 8 to September 14, 1889
Volume 6: September 15, 1889, to July 6, 1890
Volume 7: July 7, 1890, to February 10, 1891
Volume 8: February 11 to September 30, 1891
Volume 9: October 1, 1891, to April 3, 1892

Index

Main entries are shown in boldface.

Trowbridge, John Townsend, 117
Twain, Mark (Samuel Clemens), 202, 208

Upward, Allen, 128

Virgil, 199, 281
Voltaire, François Marie Arouet, 199

Wagner, Richard, xxiv, 108, 238–39
Wallace, J. W., xvi, xxix–xxx, 86, 138, 139, 153, 257, 277–78
Walt Whitman Fellowship, xxx, xxxi, 311
Watch (dog), 9–10
Whitman, Andrew Jackson, 33
Whitman, Edward "Eddy", 33, 36–37, 290, 291
Whitman, George Washington, xxvii, 33, 34, 35–36, 38, 76, 271, 284, 286, 291n
Whitman, Hannah, 18, 229, 291n
Whitman, Jesse, 33, 37
Whitman, Louisa Orr, xxvii, 271, 286, 291n
Whitman, Louisa Van Velsor, xxviii, 12, 33, 34, 36, 37, 75, 190, 291
Whitman, Mary Elizabeth, 33, 34–35
Whitman, Thomas Jefferson "Jeff", 33, 35, 181, 231
Whitman, Walt
His views about himself, works: 23–32, agitator, 59; ailments (*see* physical decline *below*); bad temper, 25; "big secret," 154–57; cautiousness, 31; circumspection, 63; Civil War, influence of, 76; correspondent 25; criticism (favorable), 97, 98, 105, 106, 123–31; criticism (negative), 19–20, 51, 55, 73, 81, 96, 97–109, 111–12, 199, 230, 233–34; early career, 69–70; egotism, 56, 59, 60, 109; haste (*see also* slowness *below*), 72; iconoclasm, 73, 74, 77–78, 80, 222, 256,

264; idiosyncrasy, 53, 58, 62, 77; images of himself, xii, 39–43; improviser, 75; individualism, 26, 27, 53, 56, 58, 62, 109; language skills, 29; *Leaves of Grass* (*see main entry*); Long Island founder, 44; memory, 29, 65; minority voice, 51, 53, 73; monologist, 272; name, 23, 209–10; nobody, 30; opera-goer, 75, 78, 238–42; optimist, 60; oratorial delights, 57; outdoorsman, 32, 54–55, 74–75, 95, 141–42, 150–51, 204, 209, 259, 275; physical decline, 269–75, 276–80; political views, 51, 53, 73; procrastinator, 30–31; Quaker affinity, 24, 37–38, 52, 80, 217; Rabelaisian, 25; reader, 30, 46; reciter, 29, 65; reviser, 63–64, 65, 74; revolutionist, 26; sartorial tastes, 26, 221; self-promoter, 64; self-questioner, 64; sense of humor, xvii, 20, 27, 76, 213; slowness (*see also* haste *above*), 24, 31; Socratic traits, 25; spontaneity, 55, 57, 63, 66, 75, 79; spouter, 29; swimmer, 30; theater-goer, 32, 45–46, 47, 78; timidity, 13; toleration, 26; unexplosiveness, 31; waning powers/old age, 116–19; Western affinities, 26
His views on (*see main entries for views of individuals*): abolition, 30, 193–95, 265–66; actors, 135; advice, 16, 110–12; alcohol, 16, 55, 243–46, 269; American life, 161–70; authors, 67; autobiography, 62; autograph-seekers, 123, 252–53, 279; babies, 19; baseball, xxviii, 261, 264; blue laws, 261; biography, 65, 68; books, 52, 56, 91, 95, 185, 208, 255, 258, 266; Boston, 264; brother-in-law, 18, 229;

Whitman, Walt (*continued*)
brotherhood, 55, 58, 74, 77–
78, 81–82, 198; Camden, New
Jersey, 3, 44, 251; Catholicism,
235–36; censorship, 114–15;
Civil War, **179–88**; clutter, xi–
xiii, 14; college/collegians, 20,
52, 81, 104, 106–107, 214, 231,
259; correspondence, 105, **123–
31**, 133, 136, 257; dedications,
95; Denver, 259–60; doctors, 4,
54, 262, 269, 273–74, 275; European culture, 77–78, 211; expurgation, 112, **113–15**; fame,
67; free trade/tariffs/protection-
ism, 55, 61, 263; friends/friend-
ship, **132–40**; genius, 62, 266;
Greek culture, 137, 212, 223;
historians, 266; human nature,
256; humor, 165; ideal men/
women, **222–27**; journalism/
journalists, 26, 228, 230, 231,
250, 257, 259; late bloomers, 31;
law/lawyers, 170, 200, 247;
Leaves of Grass (*see main entry*);
literary analysis/criticism, 67,
68, 99, 107, 108; literary celebrities (*see also main entries for individuals*), 75, **198–210**, 258; literary life, 46, 56, 58, 59, **62–68**,
74; love, 171, 218; marriage, 16;
morals/moralists, 53–54, 76;
nature, 54; New York City, 44,
45–48, 75, 78, 104, 135, 136,
138, 247–48, 256; New Orleans,
44, 260; opera, 75, 78; oratory,
57; painting, 39–42, 78–79;
perfect health, 60; photography,
19, 39–43; poetizing, 63, 83,
264; politics, 29, 38, 222, 258,
262–63, 264, 265; postal service, 19, 251, 265; prime of life,
24; prohibition, 19, 197, 245;
publishers/publishing, **89–96**,
208; punctuation, 65, 250; purpose of life, 61, 76; Quakers, 18,
24, 37–38, 52, 80, 217, 257;

questioners, xv, 28, 63, 84–85;
race, **193–97**; religion/religion-
ists, 76, 77, 79, 92, 211, **233–37**,
262, 264, 271, 286; respectability, 52, 66; reviews/critics, 98,
230, 231, 250, 263; rivers, 44,
259; sex/sexuality, 76, 82, **83–
86**, 101, 105–106, 126, 130,
171–74; slavery (*see also* abolition *above*), 193–94; smoking,
260–261; socialism, 29; Southerners, 194, 265; spirituality, 56;
style, 66, 81; temperance movement, 230; tolerance/wide embrace, 26, 61, 77, 79, 143, 144,
163, 193, 228; Walt Whitman
societies, 68, 105; Washington,
D.C., 135, 167, 180, 181; Whitman family, **33–38**; women,
175–78, 201, 214, 223–24,
226–27
Works: "As a Strong Bird on Pin-
ions Free," 87; "As I Watched the
Ploughman Ploughing," xxxi;
"Autobiographic Note," xii, 78;
"Boston Ballad, A," 193; "Bowery: A Reminiscence, The," 211;
Calamus, xiii–xiv, xxx, **84–86**,
128, 137, 139–40, 149n, 157,
172; "Child Went Forth, A," 88;
Children of Adam (*see L'Enfants
d'Adam below*); *Complete Poems
and Prose*, ix, 13, 89, 133; *Complete Writings*, xxix; "Crossing
Brooklyn Bridge," 83; "Dead
Tenor, The," 239; *Democratic
Vistas*, 63, 161; "Dismantled
Ship, A," 88; *Drum-Taps*, xxii,
183, 206; "Elemental Drifts,"
131; *Franklin Evans*, 69–70,
243; *Good-Bye my Fancy*, 116;
Leaves of Grass (*see main entry*);
L'Enfants d'Adam (*Children of
Adam*), 19, 36, **83–84**, 125, 129;
"Life and Death," 28; "Long I
thought that knowledge alone
would suffice," 85; *November*